Policy Capacity, Design and the Sustainable Development Goals

Policy Capacity, Design and the Sustainable Development Goals: Wicked Problems in Uncertain Environments

EDITED BY

ANDREA LIPPI

University of Florence, Italy

AND

THEODORE N. TSEKOS

University of the Peloponnese, Greece

emerald
PUBLISHING

United Kingdom – North America – Japan – India – Malaysia – China

Emerald Publishing Limited
Emerald Publishing, Floor 5, Northspring, 21-23 Wellington Street, Leeds LS1 4DL

First edition 2024

British Library Cataloguing in Publication Data
A catalogue record for this book is available from the British Library

ISBN: 978-1-80455-687-0 (Print)
ISBN: 978-1-80455-686-3 (Online)
ISBN: 978-1-80455-688-7 (Epub)

Contents

List of Contributors

Inese Abolina	University of Latvia, Latvia
Edoardo Amato	University of Milan, Italy
Ilze Auliciema	University of Latvia, Latvia
Daniela Bernaschi	University of Florence, Italy
Paul Cisneros	Instituto de Altos Estudios Nacioanles, Ecuador
Giulio Citroni	University of Calabria, Italy
María Alejandra Costa	University of Montreal, Canada
Alberto de la Peña Varona	University of the Basque Country, Spain
Giovanni Esposito	Université Libre de Bruxelles, Belgium
Maria Camilla Fraudatario	IRPPS-CNR, Italy
Solange Hernandez	Aix-Marseille Université, France
Aapo Hiilamo	ITLA Children's Foundation, Finland
Michael Howlett	Simon Fraser University, Canada
Javad Keypour	Tallinn University of Technology, Estonia
Andrea Lippi	University of Florence, Italy
Kate Macdonald	University of Melbourne, Australia
Jaione Mondragón	University of the Basque Country, Spain
Éric Montpetit	University of Montreal, Canada
Cristhian Parrado	Ecuador
Magdalena Potz	Aix-Marseille Université, France
Iveta Reinholde	University of Latvia, Latvia
Tiina Ristikari	ITLA Children's Foundation, Finland
Kidjie Saguin	University of Amsterdam, Netherlands
Ileana Daniela Serban	Comillas Pontifical University, Spain

Sarah Serval	Aix-Marseille Université, France
Christopher J. Smith	Tampere University, Finland
Andrea Terlizzi	University of Florence, Italy
Theodore N. Tsekos	University of the Peloponnese, Greece
Petri Virtanen	University of Canberra, Australia

Chapter 1

Introduction: Governing Sustainable Development From Theory to Practice: Wicked Problems, Expected Capacities, and Design in Uncertain Environments

Andrea Lippi[a] *and Theodore N. Tsekos*[b]

[a]University of Florence, Italy
[b]University of the Peloponnese, Greece

Abstract

The introduction of the book is aimed at providing the reader with a comprehensive analytical framework on the purpose and content of sustainable development analysis as a wicked problem in policymaking. The UN's 2030 Agenda is an ambitious and far-reaching initiative that encompasses 17 broad goals and 169 targets, which may be too general and potentially conflicting. Translating this agenda into practice is a challenging and possibly frustrating task that requires a pragmatic and methodologically structured approach. Accordingly, the introduction is organized around five key concepts that favor a translation into practice: the definition of problems and solutions, the policymaking of Sustainable Development Goals (SDGs), the wicked nature of policy problems in a sustainable development perspective, the specific kinds of capacity the policymakers must get to accomplish any task in the field of sustainable development, and, lastly, the type of policy design allocating ends and means for solving the problems. In particular, the theoretical framework supports the reader in understanding the wicked nature of sustainable development policies and the additional capacities policymakers must have in order to be able to design effective and coherent strategies. After a detailed presentation of each of the 12 chapters divided into two parts (six chapters in a section dedicated to the analysis of wicked sustainable development policies and six chapters dedicated to the analysis of the capacity of institutional instruments in resolving wickedness), the introduction anticipates the reader the rationale of the book.

Policy Capacity, Design and the Sustainable Development Goals, 1–23

doi:10.1108/978-1-80455-686-320241002

Keywords: Wickedness; Newtonian logic; conflict; administrative capacity; policy capacity; UN 2030 Agenda

1. Introduction

Alleviating poverty and hunger, enhancing good health and well-being, ensuring gender equality, producing affordable and clean energy, ensuring decent work and economic growth, facilitating industrial innovation, reducing inequality, building sustainable cities and communities, adopting responsible consumption and production practices, fighting climate change, guaranteeing peace and justice, strengthening institutions are all goals whose solution faces potential social conflict and trade-offs in formulating, deciding, and implementing them (OECD, 2019).

In a virtual world, the achievement of those goals may be conceived as feasible thanks to the strength of the related ideals: good values may be presumed to be good premises for leading to effective change. According to this assumption, the UN 2030 Sustainable Development Goal (SDG) Agenda was designed as a "blueprint for global development" with a transformative potential concerning five crucial areas for human beings: people, planet, peace, prosperity, and partnership (UN, 2015, 2016).

This approach took on and relaunched values and aims that had already emerged in previous documents, such as the Millennium Development Goals and the Brundtland Report on Our Common Future (1987) which established the link between development that meets the needs of the present without compromising the ability of future generations to meet their own needs.

All those ideals are embraceable and fully convincing, on paper, since they trace a milestone of human emancipation. The universalist ambition of a balance between generations by matching the limits and needs of people around the world is almost a moral duty in a changing and turbulent world. As such, the pursuit of the 17 goals and the annexed 169 targets of the 2030 Agenda may be interpreted as a political aim of all the governments that undersigned the international memorandum.

In the real world, the implementation of such ideals is instead very problematic because of the interdependent nature of the relations among the goals and the intrinsic complexity strictly deriving from any attempt to translate them from theory to practice. Such complexity is not theoretical but empirically rooted in the potential tensions that arise from governing public action between divergent streams of interests, cultures, priorities, or actors who have in mind different expectations and roads to gain the results.

2. The Problem: How to Make Sustainable Development Real and Feasible Beyond Good Intentions

In other words, the implementation of the 17 goals is not a consequence of a stated claim, but an open problem to be solved thanks to the political mediation by the policymakers. Seen from this point of view, the governance of the SDGs can be understood as a challenge. This complexity does not concern the ambition of the expected change, as one might think, or the selection of appropriate tools, nor does it concern the culture required to tackle such a project, but the process of implementation and the related interaction.

More concretely, the complexity concerns the number of interconnections between objectives and problem, effects, actors, and resources, on the one hand, and, on the other, the definition of the problem itself: what is meant by sustainable development in every specific decisional setting and how to understand its implementation in a dynamic and turbulent environment where even just touching on interests, visions, values, and actors is enough to trigger conflicts that can hinder any attempt to achieve it.

Indeed, the implementation of UN Agenda 2023 is not a foregone conclusion, nor is it mechanical, nor can careful planning ensure the expected impact, as the complexity of its implementation is equal to the magnitude of the expected change.

Implementation is a complex matter because it depends on several factors that any policymaker must consider, beyond goodwill and good intentions, but also beyond the remit of a rational government, which normally aims to achieve ends through means.

This book addresses the issue of SDGs implementation as an open problem and a process to be managed through the intelligence of policymaking that has to take into account a number of complexity factors.

These factors can be summarized in five: the definition of problems and solutions, the policymaking of SDGs, the wicked nature of policy problems in a sustainable development perspective, the specific kinds of capacity the policymakers must get to accomplish any task in the field of sustainable development, and, lastly, the type of policy design allocating ends and means for solving the problems.

The first point is the issue of defining what "sustainable development" really is and what we should mean and, consequently, what might be appropriate and acceptable solutions and strategies to solve the problems of sustainability.

Regarding the concept of sustainability, the Achilles heel of "sustainable development" concerns its polysemic nature and multifaceted literature. For the sake of brevity, it is possible to identify five main theoretical frameworks that bring out the leading keywords related to sustainable development and addressed with the acronym "HEEEL," namely: Human-Environmental-Economic-Ethics-Local.

The five keywords Human-Environmental-Economic-Ethics-Local (HEEEL) show how, over time, the one environmental concept of sustainable development that we find in the UN Stockholm Conference of 1972 has been enriched and broadened, as reflected by the dominant perspectives of the UN Rio 2012 Conference, and especially, the UN 2030 Agenda (Amato et al., in this book, see chapter 10).

An understanding of sustainable development presented as three nested circles (environment, society, and economy), closely interdependent, emerges.

Goals are multidimensional and interdependent; they have a particular timescale to realize; but at the same time, they are also synergetic. Finally, they also have a latent conflictive nature as the pursuit of each potentially conflicts with the interests, values, development, or criticality of each other.

As such, in itself, the UN 2030 Agenda is not a program that can be linearly implemented following predefined patterns, but only a premise, a political direction that must be reshaped.

Consequently, any real intervention aimed at implementing one or more of the goals or targets of the UN 2030 Agenda must reckon with a definition on the ground. Specific objectives must be identified, selected, amalgamated, and made harmonious to achieve strategies that are adequate, coherent, feasible, and congruent with the aims of policymakers operating in very different institutional contexts: states, levels of government, and policy sectors.

More precisely, in order to make such an ambitious and interconnected design a reality, contingent choices are needed. These choices must be confronted with specific declinations of sustainable development consistent with each country's political climate, resources, public opinion, limitations, and challenges.

Even more, when a government begins to implement such a program, it must ask itself the question of what kind of sustainable development it really wants to pursue, with what degree of depth, and considering to what extent what potential interconnections may arise in the interaction between specific goals.

In other words, the process of defining and redefining goals and targets does not stop with the issuing of a document but proceeds as the program is implemented in each country. This opens questions about what is to be done and how the intertwining of goals can be resolved. The specific characteristic of sustainable development is that it is an excellent idea without an unambiguous political definition.

Having such a well-articulated and 169-target-specified program behind you is no guarantee of success, but neither is it a guide as to what is to be done: it is a matter of understanding, evaluating alternatives, reformulating objectives, resources, and expected impacts. In short, the definition of sustainable development does not offer solutions, but only new problems that must be redefined and solved.

More in detail, sustainable development must be translated into specific public policies. This transformation involves a political translation from a set of general objectives into specific goals. This has two implications.

The first is that the policymaking of the UN 2030 Agenda is already a new plan compared to the initial document. It is also a policy plan, but of a different kind, transferred to another level where, once general principles and universal values subscribed to by all governments through the agreement have been abandoned, we move on to specific policy arenas with actors, interests, and institutional frameworks that characterize and influence action.

The second implication is that in this shift from general to contingent, policymakers are forced to redefine the type of change expected consistent with the degree of solution they estimate they can achieve. This change is likely to be second or third order (Capano, 2020; Wison, 2000) and, therefore, makes implementation ambitious and risky.

This kind of implication means that change resulting from sustainable development policies is challenging, open-ended, and problematic. The problem concerns the definition of goals and contingent solutions, actors and resources, ends and means, etc. It is important to note that there are no ready-made solutions for our problems or any successful models to copy or shared solutions to adopt.

Furthermore, there is no generalized agreement on what the exact problem is, except for the fact that we are all faced with a challenge that is closely linked to the UN 2030 Agenda, which represents a set of values that drive us toward progress and growth, but we are yet to find a way to actualize these values.

This is the kind of policy problem that the policymaking literature labels as wicked or super wicked, and which we will deal with in the next section, since this book assumes that the implementation of the SDGs is a wicked problem.

3. The Framework of Wickedness in Public Policy

3.1 From Rittel and Webber Toward a Hyper-comprehensive Concept

The concept of "wicked" problems in the theory of public policy first appeared in the seminal article by Rittel and Weber published in 1972 and titled "Dilemmas in a General Theory of Planning." In their paper, the authors, approaching the issue from the point of view of spatial planning and, broadly, social planning, argue that confronting social policy problems is bound to fail, because of their nature. While science is prepared to deal with "tame" problems and seems unable to do the same with policy problems that cannot be definitively described as far as in a pluralistic society there is no incontestable public good, there is no objective definition of equity, and hence, policies dealing with social problems cannot be meaningfully correct or false, so it makes no sense to talk about "optimal solutions" (Rittel & Webber, 1973, p. 155).

Consequently, social problems become "wicked" problems for which efficiency is being challenged by a preoccupation for equity; thus the apparent "consensus around distributional problems is being eroded by social pluralism and the differentiation of values that comes with differentiation of publics." As a result, policy styles based on "Newtonian mechanistic physics" do not adapt to contemporary interacting open systems, while wickedness is produced at the "juncture of goal-formulation, problem-definition and equity" (Rittel & Webber, 1973, p. 156). A multitude of competing objectives generated by pluralities of interests and values makes it "impossible to pursue unitary aims" and produces "tenacious difficulties" regarding rationality. This is why the classical paradigm of "engineering" scientific rationality is not applicable to the "wicked" problems of open societal systems (Rittel & Webber, 1973, p. 160).

It becomes clear that Rittel and Webber directly connect wicked problems, firstly with social problems and secondly with the pursuit not of universal technically correct solutions but with competing definitions of the socially fair and desirable solution to a given problem. What explicitly differentiates the problems that we can consider as wicked from the others that, on the contrary, can be considered as tame is that the solution of the former requires a different rationality that escapes from the "classical paradigm of science and engineering" (Rittel & Webber, 1973).

However, the concept evolved to be extremely comprehensive and generic, ending up including a very wide range of problems and, almost, losing its specificity (Head, 2022, p. 21; Peters, 2017, p. 386). Attempts to classify individual subcategories of wicked problems increase the complexity. An example is the article by Alford and Head (2017) where the authors attempt a classification based on two variables: technical complexity and (value-based or interest-based) disagreement in the perception and definition of a given problem (p. 402). In the first dimension of a bidimensional matrix, they record three alternatives. (A) In the first, both the nature of the problem and the solution may be clear to the decision-makers. (B) In the second, the nature and causes of the problem may be known, but the solution is not, due to analytical or political complexities. (C) In the third, neither the problem itself nor the possible effective solutions are clearly known to the decision-makers. In the second dimension of the matrix, they also list three alternatives. (A) Neither knowledge nor interests are fragmented. (B) Knowledge is fragmented among various parties, but the stakeholders are broadly in consensus about the nature of the problem and the possible solutions. (C) Knowledge about the problem is divided across multiple actors, each with a different part of that knowledge, but also, with conflicting interests that make them reluctant to share understandings with others, perceived as rivals.

The combination of these two variables produces nine different types of wickedness, with tame problems at one end and "very wicked" problems at the other end, and with seven other types in between, five of them based on complexity (analytical, communicative, cognitive, political complexity) and two based on the divergence and antagonism between actors (politically turbulent and conceptually contentious problems). A main characteristic of this classification is that it incorporates both technical complexity and political or value opposition without differentiating them.

The fact that within the framework of wickedness some scholars consider it necessary to define a more specific subset of unquestionably wicked problems, that of "very wicked" or even "super wicked," (Auld et al., 2021; Gruetzemacher, 2018; Lazarus, 2009; Levin et al., 2012) confirms that the term has become excessively inclusive and has lost its specificity (Peters, 2017, pp. 386–387).

3.2 Technicalities, Interests, and Values

One of the main reasons that the concept of wickedness acquires such complexity and becomes unable to analytically capture and classify an already complex reality is that it includes two distinct forms of complexity in the same analytical category: (a) the one resulting from poor understanding and insufficient documentation of a complex physical or technical situation and (b) that which arises from the opposition of values and/or interests, of the actors participating in the specific field.

Nevertheless, these two sources of difficulties in understanding and handling problems do not belong to the same field of causality. The first is linked to inadequacies in the construction and use of the classical tools of scientific rationality, while the second is to different value choices and different interests. So the former can be dealt with by using the rational tools in a more agile, innovative, and efficient manner, while the latter requires a completely different handling that allows the bridging of value differences and/or the convergence around common places of problem definitions and solutions. Conflictual definitions produce wickedness, while ill-defined problems and solutions due to the complexity and incomprehensibility of their technical aspects need improvement of definition and comprehension that can be achieved through the better use of classic rational scientific tools, or, in a different conceptual approach, moving outside the "satisficing" solutions framework, defined by Herbert Simon (1976, pp. 118–120).

Similarly, the 10 characteristics of wicked problems as classified by the two founding fathers of the concept, Rittel and Webber, include simultaneously elements that cause the impossibility of defining and handling the problems due to difficulties in correctly assessing the technical aspects of a policy problem and the completeness of documentation, as well as elements that influence the choice of an explanatory scheme and a relevant resolution of the problem based on divergent values, ideological priorities, and connection with opposed interests.

In relation to the above remark, Peters notes:

> To the characteristics presented explicitly by Rittel and Webber we can add the general sense from the discussion that wicked problems involve multiple actors and are socially and politically complex. The formulators of the concept did not list this as a separate dimension but much of the discussion about difficulties in reaching decisions in the emerging policy world revolved around the political difficulties of making decisions in a more participatory and politically complex environment. (Peters, 2017, p. 388)

This observation confirms that if we approach the analysis of wicked problems solely or primarily through the 10 characteristics listed by Rittel and Webber in their groundbreaking 1973 paper, then we are missing very important elements of both their approach and chiefly, the real nature of the problems in question.

3.3 Wickedness as a Characteristic of Societal Problems

On the contrary, if we get away from trying to understand wicked problems based on the 10 characteristics and focus on some other insightful observations in the same paper that are mainly related to value divergences and antithetic interests within strongly differentiated societies, then our effort changes perspective.

Rittel and Webber repeatedly emphasize the central role that value and interest differences play in the production of wickedness, locating the source of wickedness in the social context.

> Societies of the Western world are becoming increasingly heterogeneous, increasingly differentiated, comprising thousands of minority groups, each joined around common interests, common value systems, and shared stylistic preferences that differ from those of other groups[...] In a setting in which a plurality of the publics is politically pursuing a diversity of goals, how is the larger society to deal with its wicked problems in a planful way? How are goals to be set, when the valuative bases are so diverse? Surely a unitary conception of "public welfare" is an anachronistic one. We do not even have a theory that tells us how to find out what might be considered a societally best state. We have no theory that tells us what distribution of the social product is best- Social science has simply been unable to uncover a social welfare function that would suggest which decisions would contribute to a societally best state. As the population becomes increasingly pluralistic, inter-group differences are likely to be reflected as inter-group rivalries of the zero-sum sorts. If they do, the prospects for inventing positive non-zero-sum development strategies would become increasingly difficult. What was once a clear-cut win-win strategy, that had the status of a near-truism, has now become a source of contentious differences among sub-publics [...] Our point, rather, is that diverse values are held by different groups of individuals- that what satisfies one may be abhorrent to another, that what comprises problem solution for one is problem-generation for another. Under such circumstances, and in the absence of an overriding social theory or an overriding social ethic, there is no gainsaying which group is right and which should have its ends served. Whichever the tactic, though, it should be clear that the expert is also the player in a political game, seeking to promote his private vision of goodness over others' [...] Planning is a component of politics. There is no escaping that truism [...].
>
> We are also suggesting that none of these tactics will answer the difficult questions attached to the sorts of wicked problems planners must deal with. We have neither a theory that can locate societal goodness, nor one that might dispel wickedness, nor one that might resolve the problems of equity that rising pluralism is provoking. We are inclined to think that these theoretic dilemmas may be the most wicked conditions that confront us. (Rittel & Webber, 1973, pp. 167–169)

As all public policy problems are societal problems, by applying the main criterion used by Rittel and Webber, they must be considered potentially wicked, even if, as usual, they comprise technical dimensions. Technical dimensions should be considered in principle as "tame" subproblems as far as classic rational approaches are sufficient for resolving them – even if they are very complicated ones. Complexity increases the difficulty and requires additional efforts and innovative solutions but remains within the area of standard scientific rationality. Technical dimensions of policy problems can become "wicked" only if their definition and the potential array of solutions are positively or negatively affected by the interests and values of concerned social actors. That means only if contrasting problem definitions leading to different technical solutions become part of their collective strategies.

Experts and policymakers may dispute on facts due to insufficient evidence, which can be rectified with more and better evidence. This involves applying the rational scientific approach more deeply and agilely. On the contrary, if the disagreement over facts stems from differing value judgments and/or alignment on various group interests, a different approach is required.

3.4 The Political Nature of Wickedness

Considering the above, we will argue here that wickedness must be used as a tool for analysis not for classification. That means that the "wicked" approach does not refer to a specific category of policy problems but to a different perspective on policymaking and a different rationale on dealing with social problems. It is some other way of understanding public policy as a whole (Peters & Tarpey, 2019). All major policy issues, namely all topics that could produce extended or intense effects on social systems, are characterized by

- internal (=multidimensional topics) and/or external (=interactions with multiple other policy areas, issues that are subsets of wider sets) complexity,
- diversified approaches by collective actors due to divergent interests or values but also by,
- technical uncertainty, largely due to the effects of the previous variables.

Head (2022, pp. 4–5) argues that wicked problems are political. In fact, all public problems are political. All are dealt with politically. The political framing of public problems does not aim, nor does it lead to, their universal and comprehensive understanding and solution. After all, in most cases, a comprehensive and universal problem-solving process is impossible within stratified societies. The various issues that arise concern the particular interests and aspirations of different social groups and affect them to various degrees and in a disparate manner. At the bottom, the fact that these issues "emerge" or do not "emerge" as public problems, are or are not registered on public agendas, depends on the social groups that will attempt to put in the foreground and frame them and relies on their power and their capacity to do so. Among these groups, the political-administrative elites play a key role due to the central function they ensure in structuring the respective political-administrative agenda and making public decisions.

Especially for problems whose understanding escapes from narrower circles of interested parties or experts and comes to concern wider social groups, the policy actors – those interested in influencing relevant decisions – are required to convince larger or smaller parts of public opinion in order to gain the political support necessary to legitimize their positions and proposals and to increase the chances of their adoption and implementation. In these cases, the elites offer simplified and persuasive narratives about problems and solutions, to attract wide support for their preferred approach (Head, 2022 p. 7). Such kind of simplified descriptions usually do not facilitate but, on the contrary, may hinder the understanding of the problem and reinforce its wicked character.

The technicalities of dealing with a social problem – which can also be economic, technical, or environmental but becomes social when it affects the everyday life and the perspectives of larger or smaller social groups – are not without importance nor are they socially neutral. How a problem is defined [structured or framed] depends on how this problem is related to individual interests that may be more or less, positively or negatively, affected (or even not affected at all) by it. These interests can be material (financial gains or losses, social or environmental consequences) or nonmaterial (values or ethical issues). Potential positive or negative effects are what determine the technical dimensions that will be proposed and the technical solutions that will be selected by each of the involved groups.

Finally, in several cases, path dependence, i.e., the attachment to acquired ideas and perceptions and established practices (Bacchi, 2009), is what determines the general orientation regarding both the understanding and structuring of the problem and the solutions that are prioritized.

In addition, in modern societies, the fragmentation of media framings may generate "preference-based reinforcement" (or groupthink) (Head, 2022, p. 10) with the result that the communication strategy of the policymakers focuses distinctly on separate arguments and documentation on different social subgroups. Such a diversified approach to the policy framing intensifies the wickedness of the issue at stake.

Furthermore, it is often the proposed solution – that favors specific interests or, more rarely, is dictated by a value system – that determines the reception of the problem and leads to a specific structuring and framing of it. Let us recall here how Cohen et al. (1972) describe organized anarchy as "a collection of choices looking for problems, issues and feelings looking for decision situations in which they might be aired, solutions looking for issues to which they might be the answer, and decision makers looking for work."

Therefore, within a given political-administrative system, whether and how any issue will become the subject of public discussion and action is a result not of some one-dimensional technical parameters but of complex social, political, and administrative processes and correlations (Wedel et al., 2005).

Whether the political-administrative system will take up an issue, contributing to – or accepting – its transformation into a public problem is a function of many factors. It depends in principle on whether any social group is interested in dealing with it.

There may be, alternatively or simultaneously, an internal concern of the political-administrative elites per se or of their political clienteles, or the decision-makers could become the recipient of strong external pressures, for example, from influential epistemic communities that invoke crises or major events (environmental, social, etc.) or even by mass mobilizations that request and have the power to force the introduction of the issue on the political agenda.

Other factors that influence – facilitate or hinder – the transformation of an issue into a public problem are the availability of adequate and accessible ("satisficing" according to Herbert Simon) methods of handling it, with the simultaneous absence of factors that oppose or make it difficult to use these solutions, such as reactions of powerful groups, high costs, technical uncertainty or incompatibility with prevailing perceptions within the political-administrative or economic system – or superordinate systems such as the EU in the case of member states. All these contingencies make any question subject to them wicked.

Depending on which mix of the above variables applies in each specific case, a given political-administrative system can choose a corresponding mix of responses ranging from refusal or avoidance of engagement to symbolic or purely "communicative" responses to placing the issue high on the priority scale that may lead, depending on the dominant political-administrative culture and the policy style of the specific government, either to technocratic/centralized or democratic/participatory responses.

The outbreak of crises provides evidence of the wicked nature of the problems associated with them. In such cases, the wicked character of the topic becomes indisputable, and for this reason, the concept of wickedness is sometimes identified with issues that lead to – or emerge through – crises. Intense political disagreement and political polarization are other situations that lead to the characterization of its stakes as wicked.

Sometimes, however, it can be the political disagreement that causes the crisis either directly or indirectly, i.e., either the political conflict constitutes the crisis or the political disagreement prevents the taking of measures that burden the (social, economic, or environmental) problem that is left to develop and cause a crisis. All SDGs mostly fall into the above two, intertwining, categories: issues that are involved in – or linked to – crises and are the subject of intense political polarization.

4. Capacity and Design of Sustainability Policies

The fourth and fifth factors of this book concern two sides of the same coin, both of which relate to the characteristics of policymakers and their contribution: the presumed capacity that we consider necessary to define problems and solve them through coordinated and coherent actions that prevent or manage conflict, on the one hand, and the resulting policy designs, on the other.

4.1 Sustainability Is a Matter of Capacity by the Decisionmakers

Assuming that "the government, or more vaguely 'the policymakers', addresses a 'problem' which demands attention" (Colebatch, 2018, p. 369), we can ascertain that it is called at "'inventing', developing and fine-tuning a course of action with the amelioration of some problems or the achievement of some targets in mind" (Dryzek, 1983, p. 346).

Such behavior relates to the real core of the "governing abilities" needed to cope with challenges in charge to the public authorities and that can't be solved without their intervention. It deals with all those features concerning the "assembly work" and the elaboration of ideas, actors, rules, and resources oriented to improve the capacity to solve the problems that in that contingency are perceived as urgent and interconnected.

Wicked problems are the case in point. While, as mentioned above, tame problems theoretically don't request special attention or superior kinds of attributes, since the available set of rules, resources, knowledge, and procedures could provide what's needed for a 'deductive' policymaking, wicked problems imply all those attributes that are urged to be effectively against them.

In other words, wicked problems, more and more urgently in comparison with the tame ones, call for a matter of "capacity," or better "additional capacity," to solve them.

The capacity is consequently presumed to enhance the policymaker to become well performer and effective. At the same time, capacity is an essential source of legitimation for those who are called to make decisions. As such, according to this reasoning, when coping with wicked problems, the policymakers must be (and must show to be) "capable" (Peters, 2015).

4.2 Types of Capacity

The idea of a specific capacity as an intrinsic skill of the government is inborn in the history of the public policies and institutions. Capacity can be intended, in general terms, as the ability that the policymaker or the public bodies in general do or should possess (Addison, 2009). It refers to a set of expected skills "ranging from the ability to anticipate and influence change; make informed, intelligent decisions about policy; develop programs to implement policy; attract and absorb resources; manage resources; and evaluate current activities to guide future action" (Honadle 1981, pp. 577–578).

Additionally, capacity can be argued as "capacity to govern" in terms of rational structures, authority, and leadership (Graham, 1960) or as the political responsiveness and learning capacity, namely the ability to restructure ideas and organizations.

More generically, capacity is also a catchword broadly considered an unavoidable trait of the political system to respond to or "absorb" new demands arising from its social environment (Eisenstadt, 1963). Similarly, it also concerns the functions taken on by the political system over time to react to a new range of problems.

According to the literature, we can also acknowledge the nuanced nature of the concept by distinguishing different meanings, such as the *institutional capacity* (Coremans and Meissner, 2018; Farazmand, 2009), the *policy capacity* (Brenton et al., 2022; Newmann et al., 2017; Wu et al., 2018), the *administrative capacity* (Caiden, 1973; Verheijen, 2000), and some subsets of notions partially included in these, like the *governance capacity* (Kattel et al., 2016; Nelissen, 2002), the *implementation capacity* (Incaltarau et al., 2020; Polverari, 2020; Polverari et al., 2022), the *institutional development capacity* (El-Taliawi & Van Der Wal, 2019; Haque & Puppim de Oliveira, 2021), the *performance capacity* (Honadle, 1981), the *innovation capacity* (Caiden, 1973), etc.

Among the many meanings and the different streams of studies, that of policy capacity better fits the features of wicked problems, but other meanings, like those of administrative capacity and governance capacity, are not excluded from this target and are strictly related to the same goals.

4.3 Policy Capacity for Solving Wicked Problems in Sustainability Development Policies

A general definition of policy capacity has been provided by Howlett and Ramesh (2015) to grasp the intrinsic nature of the rational property the policymaker must achieve. It deals with

> …the capacity of government leaders to achieve long-term improvement in a policy field [that] depends on the quality of leadership, the capacity for stakeholder collaboration, the capacity to identify effective options and policy strategies, the availability of core skills and resources and the overall governance capacities of the system. (Howlett & Ramesh, 2015)

In other words, policy capacity is a multifactorial attribute that evolves over time and varies through different contexts. It is contingent and can't be generalized into a delimited set of categories. The policy capacity can be verified only when in use.

Indeed, policy capacity is the "set of skills and resources – or competences and capabilities – necessary to perform policy functions" (Wu et al., 2018). All those skills and resources are usually observed along three dimensions: (i) the analytical capacity, (ii) the operational one, and (iii) the political one. These dimensions matter since they depict complementary abilities to be enacted to solve problems and deliver policy responses.

The analytical capacity relates to knowledge generation and mobilization and refers to "the cognitive dimension of policymaking where actors accumulate data and evidence" (Denis et al., 2022, p. 2). Here, the ideational and knowledge set of resources are involved. The operational capacity is related to resources and know-how to act upon policy intentions and achieve policy goals. Finally, the political capacity mobilizes stakeholders to increase the acceptability of policy measures (Denis et al., 2022).

This is not only a matter of competence or resources, but it deals also with the different environments where the ability is requested and operates. Looking at this aspect, policy capacity can be observed in different institutional arenas.

For Brenton et al. (2022), four realms for observing capacity can be detected: (i) the program level, (ii) the policy sector level, (iii) the cross-sectoral level, and (iv) the governance system level. Similarly, Wu et al. (2018) distinguish among three levels, according to the institutional level of government and ranging from the micro to the macro: (i) the individual level concerning the setting of service delivery, (ii) the organizational one concerning the specific governmental institution implementation, and (iii) the systemic one affecting the wider arena where the policymaking takes place.

Policy capacity is not only a matter of institutions but also the ability to combine different institutional levels of government when facing policy problems. For instance, Denis et al. (2022) mention that all three types of policy capacities can operate within governments at national, regional, or municipal level. In this respect, policy capacity matters precisely because of the multilevel arrangement that characterizes wicked problems, especially concerning multilevel systems (Agranoff, 1990).

Differently, Lodge and Weigrich (2014, pp. 16–18) pointed out that the capacity is not only a specific ability to solve a problem but, above all, the skill of coordinating the different dimensions and levels in a common strategy, such as a presumed "coordination capacity" or "governance readiness."

They conceive the policy capacity as the mix of the ideational (including rules and know-how), political, and organizational expertise that allows the policymaker to react to external shocks and to be prepared to activate governance networks of public and private stakeholder when he or she is called to face challenging decisions or implementations. Lodge and Weigrich highlight that "governance readiness involves preparedness and the ability to solve problems" (Lodge and Weigrich, 2014, p. 18).

Similarly, but concerning the wider concept of administrative capacity, Nelissen (2002, p. 13) shed light on the dimension of coordination: capacity is not an attribute but the ability to coordinate the attributes in succeeding combinations that allow to solve problems. Formerly Caiden stated capacity is intrinsically related to change (1973): it must be intended as the power to change the existing arrangement toward another one able to cope with the emerging problem.

As in the words of Caiden, it deals with the capacity of triggering positive evolution of the administrative system including ideational, organizational, and political properties toward new arrangements suitable to face the policy challenges. As argued also by Schoen and Rein (1994), capacity is a matter of innovation by the policymaker, such as the "intelligence" for restructuring the variables of a problem, that's exactly what's urged by wicked problems.

As such, we can gather all the mentioned definitions into an instrumental classification that concerns alternative behaviors: (i) capacity as performance, (ii) capacity as a stock of resources (ideas, technologies, money, organizations, personnel, etc.), and (iii) capacity as readiness in restructuring the existing governance into an innovative and more suitable one.

The performance capacity (Honadle, 1981) is one of the oldest and widest perspectives on the concept of policy capacity and in general refers to the ends of whatever policy a public organization must achieve through a set of means. The capacity to perform in general entails the ability to manage policy processes from the beginning to the generation of output and outcomes, including an anticipation of potential feedback, but when managing wicked problems, it assumes a specific relevance.

The performance capacity of a government can intuitively belong to the wicked policymaking since it relates to the skill to produce expected outputs and outcomes according to a fragmented and disputable environment.

Specifically, performance capacity refers to the ability to carry out the decision and implementation in spite of obstacles and to render treatable what is (apparently or substantially) incurable. Performance capacity consists of many dimensions at the same time. It certainly includes a cognitive background but is not properly only a cognitive skill, even if managing policy processes also includes an unescapable background of knowledge and information, but it consistently concerns political and organizational virtues, namely all the needed abilities to adopt suitable strategies and that can allow solving wicked problems.

In such a way, the performance capacity assumes that some alleged "good ideas" have already been invented or present in the minds of policymakers somewhere (Peters, 2018), but that at the same time, they were not directly feasible due to the difficulties of the policy arena.

Of course, the capacity of performance doesn't imply that the design adopted to solve problem should be necessarily good or attractive but affects the challenge to bring those ideas to the end of the policy process, also including the availability for restructuring or substituting them when the process takes a break or the expected outcomes are not (also partially) achieved. The skill to mobilize organizational elements and to get support through coalition and the consensus of policymaker is essential, from this perspective, to understand the complexity and to mediate inside that arena.

Performance capacity affects all the strategies allow the policymaker to mediate conflicts, including the use of participatory democracy strategies, and to anticipate opposition, as well as the organizational solutions that allow to avoid stalemates in the implementation. All these strategies relate to the capacity to perform the policy in some way.

Differently from performance capacity that explicitly concerns the policy process, the stock capacity affects the structures. Stock capacity is a concept that originated in the literature of administrative capacity and has traditionally focused on the properties a capable bureaucracy must hold; the concept of stock capacity concerns the idea of a potential. This way, the meaning of capacity is related to the idea of a receptacle, a container of a range of virtues and attributes (fairness, efficiency, accountability, etc.) that qualify the potential of the public administration and of policy making as well.

Consequently, stock capacity is the number of attributes and resources the policymaker has got before launching a policy: they can include a wide variety of resources at the same time, ranging from financial resources to human ones, rules, ideas, and technologies. The capacity also concerns space (such as buildings or territories) and time (the possibility to accomplish a task in a different span of time).

It also encompasses reforms for modernizing the public administration, tracks for recruiting young top civil servants, strategies to simplify red tape and reduce the number of rules, as well as, the reorganization of Ministries, agencies, the intergovernmental relations.

According to this definition, the relevance of resources, including institutional arrangements, allocation of tasks and duties, quality and clarity of rules, soundness of financial statements, matter when trying to manage untreatable policy problems. Policymakers who afford to rely on solid or efficient and indisputable institutions as structures, rules, or budgets can consequently be acknowledged to face wicked problems with more chances to succeed. A cumulation of resources concerning public bureaucracies is consequently estimated to be a decisive and powerful role in enhancing policymakers to disentangle wicked policies. The stock concerns many things at the same time, but traditionally involves the procurement of ideas, advisors, instruments to achieve knowledge about participants and their views on the problem. Well-informed policymakers are reputed likely more capable, although it is impossible to get all the needed available information. Likewise, organizational equipment, financial resources, and political consensus result as essential to manage challenging decisions. Financial resources can allow distributive games, strong coalitions can support difficult decisions, and organizational resources can allow the policymaker to manage implementation in a successful way.

Of course, all these attributes can't automatically assure a success but play a significant role as premises. But this is the reason why governments have anyway a propensity to provide the policymaker and the bureaucracy with a supplementary stock of resources when coping with wicked problems. On paper, the stock allows the policymaker an additional chance in solving them through the achievement of additional (human, technological, organizational, etc.) resources, and at the same time, it legitimates the government that mobilizes them.

Lastly, readiness capacity concerns the intelligence of policymakers in restructuring ideas, organization, and consensus toward new and provisional arrangements able to face with emergency and pressures coming from the exterior when facing wicked problems (governance capacity). In this case, the idea of readiness does not refer to a previous preparation or training, but to the ability to restructure just in time the governance arrangement through effective and innovative solutions by recombining existing elements.

This fact can affect the establishing of *adhocracies*, task forces, formal and informal workgroups, the recombination of existing project and the reconversion of agencies, human resources, and technologies to face the emerging problem.

4.4 The Capacity of Designing Sustainability Development Policies

The relevance of these kinds of capacities to solve wicked problems is high, not only because they arise from external shocks or emergencies sudden emergencies, but also because they often result from endless decision-making processes or delayed choices that threaten the possibility of finding solutions. In this case, the ability to reorient the system and thinking toward other innovative strategies can be decisive. So far, if performance capacity affects the process and the stock one concerns the structure of policymaking, the governance capacity, namely the capacity of readiness, is strictly related to contingency.

Restructuring refers to situational capacity, the "smart way" in which decision-makers restructure the definition of the problem and the following set of objectives, rules, and tools. This capacity concerns as the ability to interpret the rules and information as the ability to set up a provisional coalition and coordination with private and public stakeholders to achieve ends and to create a consensus. Capability in general concerns, insights, ideas, knowledge of participants, technologies, and resources, but more than attract new resources, governance capacity relates to the readiness to recycle and combine the existing ones in order to make treatable the untreatable.

All the three mentioned capacities (performance, stock, and readiness) are intertwined, and concern different aspects of the virtues the policymaker must get when coping with wicked problems. Wicked problems may be managed and solved through the enactment of both performance and stock capacity, but also through the situational readiness to change points of view and to adjust the strategy to the times and the needs of the stakeholders. A mix of capacity probably can support the policymakers in their efforts.

In other words, wicked problems and the sustainable policies request for a "capacity of designing" policies that is more complex and more decisive than for tame problems. It means that a sustainable development design must be grounded on different types of capacity, as in terms of performance, as well as of stock. Analogously, a readiness capacity is urgently needed.

As a result, the type of design and the ability to shape it according to the complexity of the situation is a significant property that marks out the sustainable development policymaking.

Designing sustainable development calls for additional analytical skills, since the policymaker must overview more specifically the different perspectives, needs, cultures, issues definition, and the potential frictions among them.

Analogously, organizational capacity is essential in mobilizing public and private agencies, recruiting professionals and qualified actors, together with the skill to involve different kinds of stakeholders in the arena.

Finally, political capacity to mediate between promoters and opponents thanks to innovative strategies, decisional participatory approaches, and a search for consensus is equally determinant and necessary.

In other words, the design of sustainable development matters more than for sectoral policies due to the intersections, the potential frictions among the goals, and the following wicked nature that brings out the relevance of capacities in managing them.

Sustainable development designs are consequently particularly relevant and critical: framing, goals and targets, strategies and tools deployed along the different phases of the policy cycle to implement a specific goal, or some subsets of goals, may be the result of specific capacities.

5. The Core and the Structure of the Book

This book is focused on the different factors that characterize the designs of sustainable development policies looking at the capacities the policymakers adopted in a different way and with different degrees of success in translating the SDGs "from the paper to the impacts" when coping with "wickedness."

Indeed, this work is aimed at supplying the reader analyses of the factors that influenced (positively or negatively) the implementation of one or more SDGs in specific policy sectors at the intersection of more than one. Looking at this perspective, both successful and unsuccessful strategies matter, and the reasons for failures as well as the factors that hindered the decision-making or the implementation or biased or impeded the delivery output and the production of outcomes are taken into consideration.

A collection of case studies based on national examples and some comparative approaches have been selected and assembled to demonstrate the wicked nature of sustainability problems and the following pathways the policymakers adopt to overtake the obstacles of wickedness. The reading of those 11 case studies refers on how wicked problems related to SDGs are managed by policymakers in terms of formulation, decision-making, implementation, and evaluation by looking at successful and unsuccessful relevant strategies. So doing, this work is at enhancing the potential inside the 2030 Agenda: the capacity of designing policies and the following knowledge of the key factors in decision-making and implementation that can favor successful outcomes.

The core of the book is also to depict how and why policy-makers adopted certain designs in place of others and combined goals and target to solve common problems and to overpass potential conflicts.

Similarly, a specific scientific interest is devoted to the abilities of policymakers, the type of capacity they used, and the shape of the resulting design they adopted: the definition of aims, strategies, the selection of tools, and the creation of coalitions and modes of governance they adopted. At the same time, the book aims at identifying the factors that make a public problem evade efforts to address it and make it unsurmountable in the long run.

To achieve this goal, the work is ideally divided in two different clusters of contributions. The first cluster concerns case studies on the wicked nature of sustainable policy-making. This cluster entails six chapters where the main focus is on one or more SDGs.

The contribution by Smith, Virtanen, Hiilamo, and Ristikari is entirely concentrated on the SDG1 about poverty and supports the idea that, specifically, child poverty represents a classic "wicked problem" in the context of UN SDGs. The chapter aims at analyzing the Finnish response based on the assumption that "industrial era" welfare strategies seem incapable to produce efficient or equitable outcomes and focus on policy coherence and governance capacity.

The chapter by Citroni is focused on SDG, n.7, regarding access to affordable, reliable, sustainable, and modern energy for all. In implementing policies toward SDG7, many countries face a number of conflicting strategies and views that concern the role of nuclear power as a transition technology. Such problematic implications of the SDG7 policies are studied through the case of the storage and disposal of high-level nuclear waste (HLW).

Equally, the work by Keypour on gas flaring reduction in Iran is specifically devoted to the SDG7 and the achievement of SDG13's targets, specifically related to "adaptive capacity to climate-related hazards" and integrating "climate change measures into national policies, strategies and planning." This study explores the ways in which political-administrative relationships in the environment of oil production management in Iran, as well as factors operating at overlying levels (super systems) such as the country's position in the international relations system, military conflicts in the region, and economic sanctions, influence public policy decisions and frame the use of available technologies.

Again, the work by Costa and Montpetit deals with a couple of SDGs, the n.8 and the n.15, respectively, addressing the issues of Economic Growth and Life on Land as they describe the case of legislative agenda in Brazil coping with agricultural topic in media framing. The authors study the connection and interactions between parliamentary engagement with two opposing aspects of the specific policy – rural economic development and environmental protection – and their coverage and promotion from the media.

Again, the chapter by Esposito and Terlizzi is devoted to the study of the SDG9 that refers to building resilient infrastructures, including cross-border transport megaprojects. The chapter approaches such megaprojects as wicked policy fields characterized by a complicated web of stakeholders' interests and shaped by uncertainty, value divergence, and conflict. Finally, the work by Reinholde, Āboliņa, and Auliciema deals with two selected cases, education (SGD4) and climate change (SDG13), to outline their wickedness and the policymakers' strategies to cope with it in the decentralized bureaucratic system of Latvia, where policy capacity and coherence seem to be weak.

Beside this wide cluster of relevant policies and their problems, we also collected a number of chapters specifically concentrated on the potential of institutions and institutional tools to manage wickedness in SDGs policymaking.

It deals with six different chapters. The contribution by Cisneros, Macdonald and Parrado, focuses on the PROAmazonia Program, that is a project using the Jurisdictional Approach methodology (JA) as potential means of increasing policy capacity to tackle deforestation and improving decision making for supporting the Sustainable Development Goals. This case study is specifically related to five SDGs: SDG13 by reducing emissions from deforestation; SDG15 by protecting, restoring, and promoting the sustainable use of terrestrial ecosystems and sustainable forest management; SDG1 by supporting small producers to adopt more sustainable and economically viable models; SDG8 through the promotion of environmental certifications; and SDG12 by promoting the consumption of sustainable agricultural products.

The contribution by De La Peña and Mondragón scrutinizes the difficulties of an old institution, the inter-regional basins, in managing the challenges in management of water planning in Spain, by focusing on SDGs 6 and 7.

The chapter by Potz, Hernandez, and Serval examines the unsuccess of an innovative institutional tool (the French Citizens Convention for Climate) in favoring the SDG17 on Partnerships for the Goals.

The chapter by Amato, Bernaschi, and Fraudatario concerns the destiny of an innovative institutional arrangement (the metropolitan city) explicitly devoted to planning and policy integration at local level (SDG11).

Again, the contribution by Serban is specifically centered on Great Britain, examining the UK Integrated Review as a policy tool that attempts to help UK Government to link up policy domains that can enable the achievement of SDGs as wicked and therefore to deal with interconnected policy problems.

Lastly, before the conclusion, a specific chapter by Saguin and Howlett deals with the topic of policy integration and the UN 2030 Agenda as a whole. Here, the concept of policy nexus allows the reader to get insight into the problem of interrelations of sustainable development governance. This chapter argues that the main aim of the SDGs is to reconcile incoherent policy goals and inconsistent policy instruments and conceptualizes how better integrative strategies can be applied promoting capacity-building within conflict-ridden multi-actor and multilevel cross-sectoral policy domains.

The conclusions of the book provide a reasoning about the logic of working with designing and capacity in sustainable development policymaking, considering the alternatives to the Newtonian approach to policy versus a different logic closer to the wicked nature of problems.

6. Conclusion

The book aims at discussing the evolution of policy design and strategic planning from a simplistic focus on ends and means to a more comprehensive approach taking into account not only institutional and procedural technicalities but also the differences and conflicts – either structural and insurmountable or amenable to compromise – of values, interests, and priorities, between social, economic, political, and administrative actors in a given policy field.

Based on the policy examples and SDGs case studies presented in the individual chapters, the book also deliberates on the essential multidimensional capacities that political-administrative systems must develop to address complex and wicked problems effectively.

At the end of this reasoning in the Conclusions, the book provides the reader some limited recommendations about lessons learnt from the above collection of case studies looking forward for policymakers who are intentioned at overpassing complexity and wickedness through the improvement of capacity.

References

Addison, H. J. (2009). *Is administrative capacity a useful concept? Review of the application, meaning and observation of administrative capacity in political science literature*. LSE Papers, n.2, March.

Agranoff, R. (1990). *Frameworks for comparative analysis of intergovernmental relations* (pp. 1–22). Occasional Papers in Comparative and International Affairs, 26.

Alford, J., & Head, B. W. (2017). Wicked and less wicked problems: A typology and a contingency framework. *Policy and Society*, *36*(3), 397–413.

Auld, G., Bernstein, S., Cashore, B., & Levin, K. (2021). Managing pandemics as super wicked problems: Lessons from, and for, COVID-19 and the climate crisis. *Policy Sciences*, *54*, 707–728.

Bacchi, C. (2009). *Analysing policy*. Pearson Higher Education AU.

Brenton, S., Baekkeskov, E., & Hannah, A. (2022). Policy capacity: Evolving theory and missing link. *Policy Studies*. https://doi.org/10.1080/01442872.2022.2043266

Caiden, G. (1973). Development, administrative capacity and administrative reform. *International Review of Administrative Sciences*, *39*(4), 327–344.

Capano, G. (2020). Understanding policy change as an epistemological and theoretical problem. In I. Geva-May, B. G. Peters, & J. Muhleisen (Eds.), *Theory and methods in comparative policy analysis studies*. Routledge.

Cohen, M. D., March, J. G., & Olsen, J. P. (1972). A garbage can model of organizational choice. *Administrative Science Quarterly*, 1–25.

Colebatch, H. K. (2018). The idea of policy design: Intention, process, outcome, meaning and validity. *Public Policy and Administration*, *33*(4), 365–383.

Coremans, E., & Meissner, K. L. (2018). Putting power into practice: Administrative and political capacity building in the European Parliament's Committee for International Trade. *Public Administration*, *96*, 561–577.

Denis, J.-L., Usher, S., & Préval, J. (2022). Health reforms and policy capacity: The Canadian experience. *Policy and Society*, 1–26.

Dryzek, J. (1983). Don't toss coins in garbage cans: A prologue to policy design. *Journal of Public Policy*, *3*(4), 345–367.

Eisenstadt, S. N. (1963). *The political systems of empires: A study of bureaucratic societies*. The Free Press.

El-Taliawi, O. G., & Van Der Wal, Z. (2019). Developing administrative capacity: An agenda for research and practice. *Policy Design and Practice*, *2*(3), 243–257.

Farazmand, A. (2009). Building administrative capacity for the age of rapid globalization: A modest Prescription for the twenty-first century. *Public Administration Review*, *6*, 1007–1020.

Graham, G. A. (1960). *America's capacity to govern: Some preliminary thoughts for prospective administrators*. University of Alabama Press.

Gruetzemacher, R. (2018). Rethinking AI strategy and policy as entangled super wicked problems. In Proceedings of the 2018 AAAI/ACM Conference on AI (p. 122). Ethics, and Society.

Haque, M. S., & Puppim de Oliveira, J. A. (2021). Building administrative capacity under developmental states in Chile and Singapore: A comparative perspective. *International Review of Administrative Sciences*, *87*(2), 220–237.

Head, B. W. (2022). *Wicked problems in public policy understanding and responding to complex challenges*. Macmillan.

Honadle, B. W. (1981). A capacity-building framework: A search for concept and purpose. *Public Administration Review*, *41*(5), 575–580.

Howlett, M., & Ramesh, M. (2015). Achilles' heels of governance: Critical capacity deficits and their role in governance failures. *Regulation & Governance*, *10*(4), 301–313.

Incaltarau, C., Carmen Pascariu, G., & Surubaru, N. I. (2020). Evaluating the determinants of EU funds absorption across old and new member states – The role of administrative capacity and political governance. *Journal of Communication and Media Studies*, *58*(4), 941–961.

Kattel, R., Randma-Liiv, T., & Kalvet, T. (2016). Small states, innovation and administrative capacity. *Innovation in the Public Sector*, *1*, 61–81.

Lazarus, R. J. (2009). Super-wicked problems and climate change: Restraining the present to liberate the future. *Cornell Law Review*, *94*, 1153–1233.

Levin, K. B., Cashore, S. B., & Auld, G. (2012). Overcoming the tragedy of super wicked problems: Constraining our future selves to ameliorate global climate change. *Policy Sciences*, *45*, 121–152.

Lodge, M., & Weigrich, K. (Eds.). (2014). *The problem-solving capacity of the modern state: Governance challenges and administrative capacities*. Oxford University Press.

Nelissen, N. (2002). The administrative capacity of new types of governance. *Public Organization Review: A Global Journal*, *2*, 5–22.

Newmann, J., Cherney, A., & Head, B. W. (2017). Policy capacity and evidence based policy in the public service. *Public Management Review*, *19*(2), 157–174.

OECD. (2019). *Policy coherence for sustainable development*. https://www.oecd.org/gov/pcsd/

Peters, B. G. (2015). Policy capacity in public administration. *Policy and Society*, *34*, 219–228.

Peters, B. G. (2017). What is so wicked about wicked problems? A conceptual analysis and a research program. *Policy and Society*, *36*(3), 385–396.

Peters, B. G. (2018). *Policy problems and policy design*. Palgrave.

Peters, B. G., & Tarpey, M. (2019). Are wicked problems really so wicked? *Perceptions of policy problems, Policy and Society*, *38*(2), 218–236.

Polverari, L. (2020). La capacità amministrativa: letteratura, criticità e un'agenda di ricerca a servizio del policymaking. *Rivista giuridica del Mezzogiorno*, *34*(3–4), 743–762.

Polverari, L., Domorenok, E., & Graziano, P. (2022). Empowerment via delegation? The administrative capacity-building potential of Cohesion Policy urban development strategies. *Regional Studies*. https://doi.org/10.1080/00343404.2022.2058698

Rittel, H. W., & Webber, M. M. (1973). Dilemmas in a general theory of planning. *Policy Sciences*, *4*(2), 155–169.

Schoen, D. A., & Rein, M. (1994). *Frame reflection: Solving intractable policy disputes*. Basic Books.

Simon, H. A. (1976). *Administrative behavior: A study of decision-making processes in administrative organization* (5th ed.). Free Press.

United Nations. (2015, September 25). *The UN agenda 2030 for sustainable development*. United Nations.

UN Habitat. (2016). *Roadmap for localizing the SDGs: Implementation and monitoring at subnational level*. Global Taskforce of Local and Regional Governments.

Verheijen, A. J. G. (2000). *Administrative capacity development for EU membership: A race against time?* Working paper W107. The University of L'Aja, The Hague.

Wedel, J. R., Shore, C., Feldman, G., & Lathrop, S. (2005). Toward an anthropology of public policy. *The Annals of the American Academy of Political and Social Science*, *600*(1), 30–51.

Wison, C. A. (2000). Policy regimes and policy change. *Journal of Public Policy*, *20*(3), 247–274.

Wu, X., Howlett, M., & Ramesh, M. (2018). Policy capacity: Conceptual framework and essential components. In X. Wu, M. Howlett, & M. Ramesh (Eds.), *Policy capacity and governance. Assessing governmental competences and capabilities in theory and practice*. Palgrave-Macmillan.

A

Cases of Wickedness Among SDGs: The Wicked Nature of Sustainable Policymaking

Chapter 2

Framing Child Poverty in Finland as a "Wicked Problem"

Christopher J. Smith[a], *Petri Virtanen*[b], *Aapo Hiilamo*[c] *and Tiina Ristikari*[c]

[a]Tampere University, Finland
[b]University of Canberra, Australia
[c]ITLA Children's Foundation, Finland

Abstract

Why is Finland failing to adequately address the issue of child poverty? Approximately 150,000 children are currently "at risk of poverty." As data on at-risk-of-poverty (AROP) and financial assistance over a 30-year period illustrates, numbers, in percentage terms, remain fairly constant despite continuing "political" recognition of the problem. Child poverty thus seemingly presents as a classic "wicked problem" particularly in the emerging social space that constitutes UN Sustainable Development Goal implementation. In line with "wickedness theory," the chapter discusses the various technical and value-based possibilities for persistent policy failure around child poverty which sees increasing polarization between the majority and some increasingly marginalized social groups such as single parent and immigrant families. While definitive explanations for the persistence of child poverty in a Nordic welfare state such as Finland remain elusive, the Finnish experience suggests that interorganizational conflicts, siloed-thinking, and outdated implementation in relation to the benefits system represent key hindrances to better policymaking and thus to more equitable policy outcomes.

Keywords: Child poverty; Finland; poverty measurement; Sustainable Development Goals (SDGs); wicked problems

Policy Capacity, Design and the Sustainable Development Goals, 27–48

Published under exclusive licence by Emerald Publishing Limited
doi:10.1108/978-1-80455-686-320241003

1. Introduction

This chapter addresses child poverty in Finland in the context of Sustainable Development Goals (SDG) target 1.2 where countries shall: "By 2030, reduce at least by half the proportion of men, women and children of all ages living in poverty in all its dimensions according to national definitions." This represents an important advance over the Millennium Development Goals' (MDGs) approach for two reasons, namely, the explicit reference to "children" and that "change must happen everywhere" with the SDGs framed as a bottom-up global change project rather than as top-down development aid for the Global South. In this context, policy coherence and governance capacity to integrate the principles and targets of Sustainable Development (SD) into domestic policy become key issues complicated further by the realities of a Finnish polity enmeshed in a multilevel governance framework – upward toward the EU and downward to the municipal/county level of policy implementation and service delivery.

While Finland's overall relationship with the SDGs is generally positive, child poverty remains a problematic issue and therefore an interesting case meriting closer study in a "wickedness" context. We understand "wickedness" here not in crude classification terms but rather as a means to better understand complexity, noting that it can be decomposed into technical and value or interest-based "problematics." For their part, the SDGs are treated as a practical conceptual (and societal) frame or "societal space" within which to discuss child poverty, shedding light on the interconnected nature of the themes and topics encompassing the child poverty discussion while illustrating its inherent policy-related complexity.

To test this approach, we review government level policy platforms in respect of their child poverty-related policy outputs and associate this with the "at-risk-of-poverty" (AROP) and social assistance usage figures for the period 1995–2020. The relatively static nature of these statistics over a near 30-year period implies that there may be technical issues with the construction of these metrics, issues around governance and administrative capacity in relation to policymaking and implementation, and/or deep value-based disagreements hindering policy coherence, or a combination thereof. We note, however, that throughout the review period, Finland enjoyed a stable and highly consensual governance system while being recognized as a global leader in administrative and governance delivery and experimentation and that these "capacity-related" factors have been associated with significantly positive impacts in terms of goal attainment. This chapter concludes with a discussion on anti-child poverty outcomes in an SDG context, emerging governance capacity issues, and the multilevel service delivery approach.

2. Finland, the SDGs and Child Poverty

2.1 Overall SDG Adaptation

Finland enthusiastically supports the UN's SDGs, generating "soft power" from its participation in the process, relating, in particular, to its global ranking on goal completion. In addition, it is a global leader in governance and administrative tool implementation associated with the notion of "experimental governance," focusing on public policymaking and service delivery solutions (Leino & Åkerman, 2022). These tools resonate with the governance approach outlined in the SDG framework (specifically related to target 17.17 on multistakeholder partnerships). They are expected to strengthen the capability of the state and society, in partnership, to design and implement strategies that minimize the negative impacts of current social, economic, and environmental crises and emerging challenges through the creation of public–private partnerships and the adoption of "whole of government" thinking, including administrative practices promoting mainstreaming and implementation.

On SDG oversight and implementation, Finland has created a dense field of stakeholders and partnerships – led by the Prime Minister's Office (PMO) coordinating the actions of the Ministry of Finance and the other 12 ministries – to monitor and steer developments, maintaining a multidisciplinary approach to cooperation and focusing on the need for policy coherence through cross-sectoral coordination. The Finnish National Commission on Sustainable Development (2016) produced a plan – *The Finland we want by 2050* – which constitutes the Finnish approach to the implementation of the 2030 Agenda. This plan was aligned with both the Sipilä and Marin Government's Programme documents reflecting the political choices of each.

In 2021, Finland beat its Nordic neighbors to be ranked first in the annual international sustainable development comparison carried out by the UN in cooperation with the Bertelsmann Foundation (Finnish Ministry of Foreign Affairs, 2021) scoring 86.51% for "goal completion" – total progress toward achieving all 17 SDGs where the headline figure signifies goals achieved (Sachs et al., 2021). In only two areas, Goals 12 and 13, was it viewed as either facing major challenges or stagnating, while in terms of Goal 1 "no poverty," Finland was viewed as having already attained the goal. Despite the existence of this favorable institutional framework and global recognition of Finland's implementation success, implementation problems clearly remain.

While the PMO has a coordinating role, it remains under-resourced with line ministries taking the lead in policy terms, particularly in a multilevel governance context where domestic policy responses have to be coordinated at the EU level. This, in effect, allocates a key role to the Ministry of Foreign Affairs, essentially confirming Finland's historical approach to global governance issues through the prioritization, in an SDG context, of development aid and the environment – specifically green technology development in the private sector – while significantly underplaying social sustainability questions (Ylönen & Salmivaara, 2021).

Two problems emerge here in terms of Finnish SDG policy coherence and coordination in respect of child poverty. Firstly, the historic Finnish view of the SDGs – and the MDGs before them – has generally not included a strong focus on social policy issues in the context of social sustainability. And secondly, as social policy is weakly coordinated at the EU level, the Ministry of Health and Social Affairs is not allocated a coordinating role in the Finnish SDG response meaning that Finland's response to the child poverty issue is weakly coordinated at the international level and is reliant, primarily, on national perspectives and initiatives. In this context, interinstitutional level disputes or "turf wars" within the domestic social policy setup emerge as likely key sources of "wickedness."

2.2 SDG 1 and the Contextualization of Child Poverty in Finland

While Finland exhibits virtually no extreme poverty, the focus of SDG 1 – measured, originally, as living on less than $1.25 a day – child poverty, remains a pressing issue. Finland's national response in terms of measuring poverty – the "national definition" alluded to in SDG target 1.2 – is to use the AROP scale fixed at 60% of the national median income where the AROP rate is calculated as the share of inhabitants in poor households financially below 60% of median income, while the child poverty rate relates to the number of children, counted as 0–17-year-olds, in poor households in relation to all children.

Statistics Finland disaggregated the national poverty figures by age group and gender in their indicator 1.2.1 with figures for 2017–2018 showing a slightly higher percentage of female children in poverty than males but with both figures over 10%, while the female figure for 2017 was over 11.5%. These figures tell a story of stubborn persistence. Fig. 2.2 (see Section 4.2) maps AROP and child poverty in Finland (1995–2020). What is striking here is the persistence of both figures above the 10% mark.

While the period has seen a roughly two percentage-point drop in each headline figure, we should note that the data starting point represents the immediate aftermath of the financial crisis and thus starts from a relatively high point while the decline in the headline rates after 2019 is probably a statistical anomaly generated by a COVID-19-induced reduction in the overall rate of median income, lifting some people above the new, lower, 60% median rate. This produces the paradoxical result that in economic crises, the number of people falling below the median rate falls rather than rises, at least initially, while major policy changes – the Sipilä government's social security reforms of 2016–2017 and the Marin government's reversal of most of them in 2019 – had little impact rate-wise but proved problematic in terms of coherence. One explanation here is that these reforms did not focus on the most vulnerable groups targeting instead all families with children, e.g., in December 2022, all such families were given an extra monthly child benefit payment.

During 2022, however, the situation worsened for families with children due to energy price inflation. The Social Insurance Institution of Finland (KELA) and Itla Children's foundation estimated that approximately 30,000 children would fall into poverty during 2022, given increases in the cost of living (Hiilamo et al., 2022). Clearly, then there are technical problems with the time-trend analysis when measuring child poverty as a ratio statistic affected by factors unrelated to the specific issue of child poverty.

The conclusions of the report from the Parliamentary Committee for the National Child Strategy (Government of Finland, 2021) are also worth noting. The committee stated (Government of Finland, 2021, p. 17), that

> [...] children's wellbeing in Finland is now polarised: while most children are doing well, some are not. The polarisation of wellbeing culminates in crises and emergency conditions, and the adverse consequences of crises accumulate on those who are the most vulnerable.

The committee's report underlined that poverty erodes children's opportunities for equal and non-discriminating inclusion in society, noting (Government of Finland, 2021, p. 17) that "[...] inequality or poverty experienced in childhood can affect a person well into adulthood, and the multi-generational effects of poverty in families with children are also a cause for concern [...]."

While the report echoes the findings of poverty scholars and the views of street level practitioners more generally on child and youth poverty (Hiilamo et al., 2023), issues around its evolving nature, now increasingly confined to single parent and immigrant families in Finland – etc.

3. Child Poverty as a Wicked Problem in the SDG Context

3.1 Policymaking in a Complex World

Set against its record on child poverty, Finland's position on SDG goal attainment raises several interesting questions around "wickedness." Its strong performance in comparative global statistical terms, including that on child poverty calculated after social transfers (Leppik, 2022), needs to be weighed against the stubborn persistence of the country's child poverty headline rate and its seeming inability to reduce it below 10%.

This is particularly evident in relation to Finland's global profile on social inclusion where again, it scores comparatively highly and where reporting on progress in respect of target 1.2 is generally positive (OECD, 2022; PMO, 2020) but where the government's "no change" self-assessment in that document is effectively refuted by civil society stakeholders who view the trend in respect of 1.2 as negative.

Child poverty has then become the "forgotten stepchild" in Finland's SDG success story – an issue where, despite its comparative global ranking position, target attainment remains distant, with child poverty levels reducing only slightly in the first 5 years of the SDG period (2015–2020) and with little expectation that 1.2 will be met by 2030. Finland also failed to fulfill its commitment to "reducing the number of people at risk of poverty or social exclusion by 150,000 by 2020" as part of the Europe 2020 strategy (Järvinen & Saarela, 2021) again raising questions over policy coherence and implementation capacity.

The explanation here is clearly complex, echoing the notion of "wickedness," originally outlined by Rittel and Webber (1973). Conceived in an urban planning context, its usage has nevertheless migrated well beyond that field into the realm of public policy more generally. The descriptive literature charting this movement is already extensive (Head, 2022; Head & Alford, 2015; Newman & Head, 2017; Peters, 2017; Termeer et al., 2019; Turnbull & Hoppe, 2019) with "wickedness" understood to encompass institutional and/or organizational complexity, scientific uncertainty, and social pluralism (Head & Alford, 2015).

Organizational complexity here refers to diverging responsibilities related to the vertical division of labor related to family social security and family services (between the MSAF and KELA) and the horizontal division of labor between the, approximately, 300 municipalities responsible for the delivery of family services and the central level of governance (MSAH). Historically, health and social services including schools, libraries, and children's day care, were provided by the municipalities. On January 1, 2023, 21 "well-being service counties" formed a new regional level of governance. These elected authorities assumed responsibility for organizing all health, social care, and emergency services, thus confirming a significant administrative shift from decentralized to recentralized service provision (Tiirinki et al., 2022).

Scientific uncertainty relates to different types of poverty measurement metrics. In the Finnish context, poverty is relative. Deprivation is measured against the living standards of the population at large. Relative poverty is often defined using the AROP concept. As noted above, however, problems remain with this approach, particularly where macroeconomic changes trigger paradoxical outcomes.

Finally, *political pluralism* reflects disagreement over the causes of poverty and the best way to alleviate it. These views are illustrative of a core political philosophy divide evoking different policy responses. The historical divide between right and left was clear. For the former, poverty was caused by individual behavior such as laziness or indolence. As such, poverty was viewed in relation to individual moral decline. The policy response to this was to promote employment as the route out of poverty, if necessary, through forced labor market activation schemes and minimal social transfers. For the latter, poverty was a result of systemic factors relating to disruptions in the economic system leading to labor shedding. The response to this centered around income maintenance to enable continued societal participation. While Finnish social policy remained broadly consensus-based across our study period, with these philosophical themes recurring periodically, the political consensus that emerged was a predominantly neoliberal one around New Public Management (NPM)-inspired approaches to the work and benefits regime, driven by the need for efficiency measures and cost containment in the public sector. Only in periods of economic positivity was this fiscal policy noose loosened (see 4.3).

The child poverty issue in Finland clearly exhibits aspects of all three of these "wickedness" signifiers. Finland's social services system is multilevel with government policy (formerly) implemented at the municipal and now at the regional level. Additionally, the benefits system is highly complex, often incoherent and lacking in transparency, resulting in institutional and/or organizational disputes over competence and responsibility and their associated "benefits traps" for claimants (Verho et al., 2022).

Similarly, uncertainty surrounds the issue in regards to a range of technical questions concerning the definition and measurement of child poverty (Mikkonen,

2013) while disagreement over values and interests at the political level remained throughout the study period, although successive government coalitions employed broadly similar policy responses in respect of child poverty, suggesting a significant level of path dependence in policy terms rather than a political schism over values. This is not to say that divergent values played no part in policy choices over time or between governing coalitions, rather that such political value differences tended to be muted by the consensual nature of the political governance system.

This understanding of the Finnish polity in respect of value differences is supported by Niemelä (2008), at least for the early part of our study period covering the first half of the MDG period (2000–2008), where a fairly uniform view of the structural or system-level causes of poverty, rather than one riven by value or interest disagreement, is detected from a cross-sectional survey of the Finnish population.

3.2 Framing Wickedness

How "wickedness" is framed is then central to understanding the Finnish child poverty policy response. We need also to understand how complexity does, or does not, become "wicked," how rational-technical problems become social problems, and how we can use the notion of wickedness as an explanatory, analytical, tool.

For Head and Alford (2015), "wickedness" is manifest in terms of organizational complexity, scientific uncertainty, and social pluralism, potentially rendering a policy issue difficult if not impossible to address in the traditional rational-technical manner. This formulation can be further decomposed into a framework which understands complexity in two distinct ways. Firstly, where knowledge gaps remain in terms of stakeholder and/or policymaker understanding of a practical problem, given the likelihood that no actor has access to all the required information. And secondly, where divisions exist over interests or values between stakeholders, policymakers and, end users.

In the Finnish context, however, the centrality of social pluralism to the manifestation of wickedness in policy terms is difficult to assess, given the structured, consensual, nature of the political system based around broad coalition governments, and the existence of imbedded policy communities which tend also to function consensually (Arter, 2020).

Framing child poverty in terms of wickedness thus raises interesting questions about the basis for such claims in the Finnish context. To what extent is complexity in respect of child poverty policy generated by problems associated with its multilevel governance structure and interagency communication failures rather than by existential differences over values and culture? Or is the answer here rather more prosaic, relating instead to technical problems with measurement and implementation problems around institutional and/or governance level disputes, turf wars, knowledge gaps, and siloed thinking?

To provide a data point for our policy analysis, covering the period from the early 1990s to the present, we utilize existing official datasets on child poverty as well as data on the various government agendas since 1995 (commencing with the Lipponen I government 1995–1999 and concluding with the Marin government, 2019–2023).

4. Child Poverty as Wicked Societal Problem

4.1 Child Poverty as a Policy Continuum

The Finnish Constitution guarantees the right of those resident in Finland to adequate social and health services, basic income security, and essential subsistence and care. Finnish welfare policy focuses predominantly on rights-based universal measures covering the entire population, including low-income groups, with the reduction of child poverty viewed, rhetorically, as a crucial element of sustainable social and economic development.

The level of child poverty in Finland is among the lowest in Europe. Previous analyses have indicated that this low level is due to the role played by public transfers at the bottom of the income distribution (Bradbury et al., 2019), not the high social transfers per se in the country. The trends in child poverty, its risk factors, and its consequences are also well-established in the Finnish context. For example, the level of child poverty is substantial among single parent households and increased substantially after the 1990s economic recession (Härtull et al., 2017).

Nevertheless, child poverty patterns do shift. In a country with comparatively low immigration levels, child poverty in Finland is now increasingly combined with an immigrant background, clusters of social, educational and health difficulties, and child welfare service needs. These complex, multiple, and interlocking disadvantages present new challenges to the "one-size-fits-all" welfare state model built in the previous industrial era. Compounding this, low-income families face increasing difficulties in meeting their essential needs due to rising inflation caused by food and energy price spikes, impacting large families and families with a single adult in particular.

Below, we briefly examine the ways in which child poverty has been addressed in agreed coalition government programs and, in tandem, investigate current child poverty trends in Finland. We specifically explore the extent to which these new challenges – immigration, multiple disadvantage, and cost-of-living increases – are cited in these agreed coalition government programs. Our aim is to understand how child poverty is addressed by Finnish policymakers and, by extension, what types of measures were deployed to combat child poverty. We do not evaluate actual policy outcomes or "effectiveness" here, focusing instead on the rationales and logics behind the declaratory policy guiding the work of the government. More comprehensive assessments of social policy, in general, and family policy development, in particular, are available elsewhere (Kaarakainen et al., 2022).

Government programs are the key declaration of aims, policies, and intentions guiding policy in Finland's multiparty governance system, making them a suitable object of study. Our focus here is on the seven government programs agreed during the period 1995–2019.

4.2 Child Poverty as a Metrics Reality

We focus here on two key poverty measures – the income-based AROP threshold and social assistance payments – and use the income-based measure to assess relative deprivation. This is a measure calculated as the percentage of children aged under 18 and living in households with incomes below the AROP threshold. This threshold is set each year to 60% of the median, the Organization for Economic Cooperation and Development (OECD) equivalent measure of the disposable income of all households in Finland. Our second measure is the share of families receiving means-tested social assistance payments. Social assistance usage is an administrative measure of poverty which reflects both subjective (indicated by applying) and objective (strict means testing) aspects of economic hardship. During our review period, there were no significant changes in eligibility for these benefits. The trends in these two measures are shown in Figs. 2.1 and 2.2.

These two measures were chosen as they are widely accepted by the poverty research community, in part because they utilize the longest and most relevant time-series data available. Problems however remain in terms of measurement, particularly around indicator choice generating "wickedness" in terms of scientific uncertainty. As such, while these two measures alone are inadequate in terms of providing the full picture of multidimensional child poverty, they continue to be used as the basis for policy discussion.

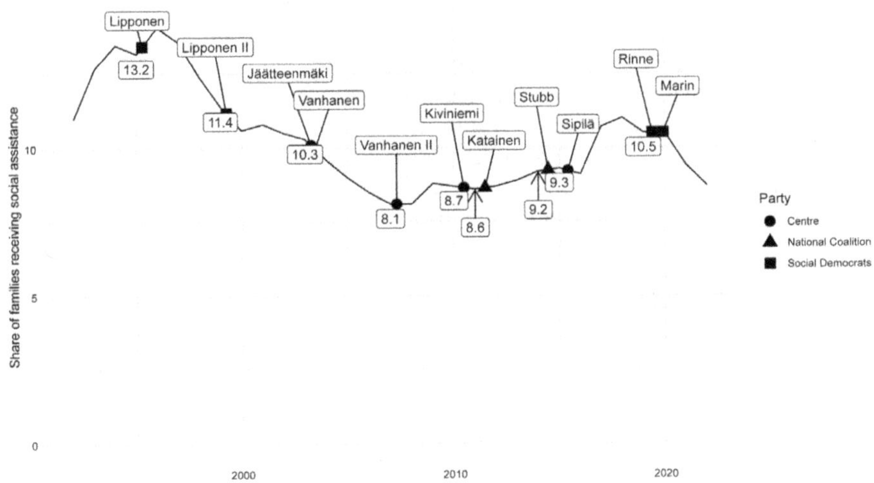

Fig. 2.1. Social Assistance Usage Among Families With Children. *Source:* Finnish institute for Health and Welfare (THL).

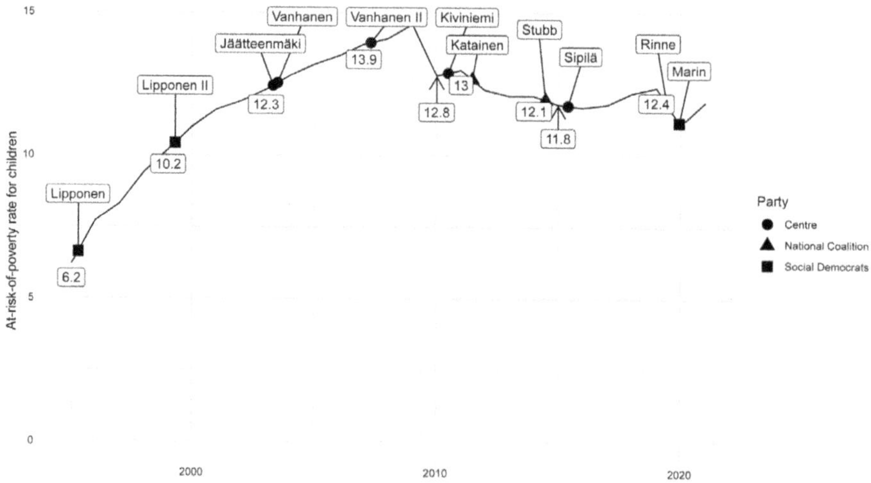

Fig. 2.2. At-Risk-of-Poverty-Rate for Children. *Source:* Statistics Finland.

4.3 Child Poverty as a Policy Narrative "Pendulum"

In this section, we reproduce, in Table 2.1, the main developments in respect of the various government programs enacted during our review period. The seven government programs outline the evolution of the Finnish national-level approach to child poverty reduction. In relation to questions over institutional complexity, the implications are threefold: (1) the lack of clear measures to monitor development, (2) the multidimensionality of the child poverty alleviation system, and (3) the decentralized nature of the *implementation* system. Moreover, from the data, we can see that the policies adopted fall into one of three approaches: increasing employment, service development, and benefit-level uplift of the universal benefit types. Innovative, administrative silo-busting measures were however rarely discussed with traditional policy approaches dominating (Virtanen et al., 2016). This likely reflects problems with "trust" between government departments and/or implementation levels.

5. Discussion: SDGs as a Learning Framework in the Context of Child Poverty?

5.1 The Essence of Child Poverty

It is tempting to conceptualize child poverty as a classic "wicked problem" echoing Head and Alford's (2015) characterization of wickedness. Questions however remain over the characterization of complexity and the explanatory power of wickedness theory. For instance, Noordegraaf et al. (2019) problematize the notion of treating societal issues as necessarily "wicked problems" and thus

Table 2.1. Content of the Government Program Documents and Child Poverty Development.

Government	Economic Context	Child Poverty Context	Child Poverty Development
Lipponen I	A five-party "rainbow" coalition took office in the wake of the early 1990s recession. The government program focused on economic policy, primarily on reducing unemployment to alleviate the country's difficult fiscal position.	Little emphasis placed on the specific needs of families with children and though public service delivery issues were addressed.	The share of families receiving social assistance declined by 2.1 percentage points, probably driven by economic recovery rather than specific anti-poverty policy interventions. The income-based child poverty rate increased by 4 percentage points. Rather than declining incomes among poor families, this increase may be partly attributed to increasing median incomes which in turn increased the poverty threshold.
Lipponen II	Another rainbow coalition took office in a much more optimistic economic environment. The level of unemployment had dropped sharply as the country recovered from recession.	The government program again focused on economic policy though more emphasis was placed on poverty reduction and social exclusion. The main poverty reduction mechanism was again employment outcomes focused.	During "Lipponen II," the children's AROP rate increased by 2.1 percentage points while social assistance usage in families declined by 1.1 percentage points.

(Continued)

Table 2.1. *(Continued)*

Government	Economic Context	Child Poverty Context	Child Poverty Development
		While poverty reduction, family policies, and services for vulnerable subgroups were emphasized, the economic well-being of families with children was not specifically addressed. Child poverty measures were taken, but they did not constitute the primary policy axis.	
Jäätteenmäki/ Vanhanen I	A center-left coalition which assumed office in buoyant economic times.	The initial program outlined an extensive list of measures to tackle social exclusion and child poverty, including the appointment of a child ombudsman and improvements in the level of child maintenance and other family benefits. The program specifically referenced poverty reduction and family economic well-being.	Progress was made. Social assistance usage was reduced by 2.2 percentage points, reaching an all-time low at 8.1% of families. However, the share of children at risk of poverty increased by 1.1 percentage points again likely reflecting increases in the AROP threshold due to increasing median incomes.

Table 2.1. *(Continued)*

Government	Economic Context	Child Poverty Context	Child Poverty Development
Vanhanen II/ Kiviniemi	A center-right coalition which assumed power just before the financial crisis.	The new program placed a smaller but still significant emphasis on child poverty. This included child benefit uplifts and service development interventions, such as combining family services in the form of "one-stop shop" family service centers. A separate policy program to improve the well-being of children, young people, and families with children was also established.	During Vanhanen II, social assistance usage increased by 0.2 percentage points, while child poverty reduced by 0.9 percentage points.
Katainen/ Stubb	A right-dominated "rainbow" coalition assumed power with the economy still experiencing difficulty.	Katainen's government prioritized employment creation as a counter to poverty and social exclusion, promoting third-sector organization's role in service provision. Cash benefit uplifts were granted, while low threshold services and a better	Child poverty, measured by the AROP measure, declined by 1.2 percentage points, while social assistance usage among families with children increased by 0.6 percentage points.

(Continued)

Table 2.1. *(Continued)*

Government	Economic Context	Child Poverty Context	Child Poverty Development
		balance between work and family life was supported.	
Sipilä	*Sipilä* inherited a more pessimistic economic outlook. Reducing public debt and improving employment opportunities were prioritized.	Child poverty was not addressed in the government program, though the intergenerational nature of social disadvantage was. Employment was the key anti-poverty focus with the introduction of the "activation model." family issues were addressed by focusing on service provision.	Social assistance usage increased by 1.2 percentage points, while children AROP increased by 0.6 percentage points.
Rinne/Marin	A left-dominated center-left coalition assumed power with an improving economy though structural problems remained.	The government program acknowledged child poverty in both its contextual and policy sections. Child poverty was addressed through increasing service provision and social benefit levels. Specific measures included a national child strategy addressing child poverty via a rights-based approach.	Around 10.5% of families received social assistance, while some 12.4% of children were deemed AROP.

the utility of wickedness theory and in particular its practical application, given the difficulty in operationalizing it as a framework for practical action by those who must, on a day-to-day basis, deal with such issues. This then raises questions around definitions of child poverty based on relative economic deprivation, the risk of lifetime social exclusion, and the need to break this cycle. How then can the child poverty issue be addressed more effectively in the context of "wickedness" and the SDGs more generally?

Michael Ungar (2018) argues that to break the cycle of intergenerational poverty or other forms of exclusion, we need to negotiate with children/youth/families about the types of recourses that they themselves deem helpful in their current life situation(s), and then navigate them through the local service/benefit system. Through this process, the complexity of the situation at the microlevel can be decomposed and the right street-level policy responses administered in a way that better supports family-level resilience. This represents a significant break from current welfare-era practice.

Given the previous analysis, three issues emerge. First, what is the link between poverty policy output and the way in which the SDGs are administered in Finland? Second, does governance capacity remain an issue, given that child poverty trends have remained static over the last 30 years, and what mechanisms and capacities are absent in the context of child poverty and in Finnish family policy more broadly? And thirdly, how successful has the impact of multilevel service implementation been on social outcomes in respect of child poverty?

5.2 Child Poverty Policy Output in the Context of the SDGs

In regards to the link between poverty policy and the SDGs, the Finnish approach to child poverty is slowly evolving though it remains unclear what, if any, impact SDG compliance has had any on this development given Finland's general approach to social sustainability and the junior position of the Ministry of Social Affairs and Health (MSAH) as regards SDG policy coordination. Compounding this is the complicated, piecemeal, nature of the social security system, lacking coherence both institutionally and in terms of its policy outputs, given the overlaps and interdependencies between different benefit types (Kangas & Simanainen, 2021, pp. 6–17).

Thus, the "wickedness" aspect of child poverty in Finland is primarily related to technical and/or institutional difficulties in the coordination of disparate policy instruments from various institutional actors at different levels. The data confirm that child poverty remains a stubborn and consistent problem, albeit one remaining at a low level by international standards. Its increasing confinement to distinct population groups, namely, immigrant and single-parent families, is however suggestive of specific policy failure and is only likely to generate further "wickedness" outcomes.

5.3 Governance Mechanisms and Capacities

The problem of persistent policy failure returns us to the issue of policy coherence. Two of the SDGs' primary messages are that "change must happen everywhere" and that "no one gets left behind." Attainment of these outcomes is however hampered by internal contradictions generated within the SDG process, some of which are visible in the Finnish context.

Policy choices are clearly limited by the political dominance of the "economic growth" paradigm (Utting & Zammit, 2009) promoting the multistakeholder framework mandating public–private "partnership." Rather than ensuring that "no one gets left behind," this mandates that everyone follows the same, pro-business trajectory with coherence generated by a series of targets and measurement metrics, themselves problematic (Hak et al., 2016), reducing issues of power and socioeconomic status to technical discourses around goal performance (Gabay & Ilcan, 2017). This is visible in the Finnish response to child poverty both in terms of political level consensus and in the interplay between the AROP and social assistance use statistics.

The sheer number of indicators, moreover, allows for "cherry picking" by governments – in the context of "change must happen everywhere" – as we see with Finland's claims on SDG 1 (PMO, 2020). More generally, the focus on individual indicator attainment can undermine coherence in policy terms as attainment in one area is not related to its potentially detrimental effects on another.

This is clearly discernible in Finland's SDG response, particularly on environmental issues where the private sector push to promote (and export) green technology involves what Berliner and Prakash (2015) term "bluewashing" – the advancement of commercial interests under the UN flag. Although this issue is mitigated to some extent in respect of child poverty, given the low priority afforded social sustainability, tough, employment-focused policies such as Sipilä's "activation model" approach do not align with the multidimensional nature of poverty, and the need to address family needs as a whole.

Mainstreaming SDG adaptation is however possible. The state budget is based on the administrative construct of ministries, government agencies, and other regional and local level public administration organizations. Better SDG integration could be generated by restructuring the state budget in line with the SDGs by introducing budget lines and program funding aligned with SDG formulations – child poverty could represent one such budget line. Realigning the state budget to the SDG goals would help consolidate the SDGs into national policymaking. This is possible, given that Finland is already experimenting with phenomenon-based budgeting, while sustainable development has been included as a cross-sectoral theme in the state budget since 2018 (SITRA, 2018; Varis, 2020).

Alleviating child poverty in Finland clearly requires, echoing Head (2022, pp. 40–46), "new thinking." Traditional approaches to public policymaking such as avoidance, denial and minimal responsibility, coercive controls, compartmentalized micromanagement, and technocratic problem-solving (through the "evidence-based" approach) have proven insufficient. New approaches, including greater stakeholder collaboration, are required to promote collective impact at the local level while, in addition, adopting resilience-promoting practices at the microlevel that help to decompose the intergenerational nature of child poverty.

Certain "governance" topics clearly also merit further experimentation, namely, the management of *diverse responsibilities* between different governance (local, regional, and national) levels and institutional arrangements (public, private, and nongovernmental) which clearly affect efficient policymaking. In the context of child poverty, *the role of collaboration and collective sensemaking* between government institutions, policymakers, and the policy implementing agency would make visible the policy problems related to strategic atrophy, resource imprisonment, and diverging commitments. It is important then *to increase strategic sensitivity among policymakers and public institutions* to explore how best to achieve this heightened ambition, potentially embracing, knowledge input diversity, intense dialogs, flexible budgeting, modular public service structures, shared information systems, the reallocation of responsibilities, and better anti-child poverty policies.

5.4 Successful Multilevel Service Delivery

Reforming social security in parallel with family services reform requires multi-stakeholder collaboration across the various branches within the MSAH and KELA. Reforming the family service system has inevitably been made more complex with the introduction of the new regional governance level the Well-being Service Counties where tasks, if not responsibilities, remain fluid during the early stages of a reform process increasingly dominated by fiscal austerity.

Moreover, while Finland has an extensive measurement, compliance, and implementation governance system in place and already implements the multi-stakeholder governance model in its day-to-day business, it remains unclear what impact these *fora* have on the broader recognition of child poverty as a multi-dimensional issue. It is then into this void that street-level implementers could step with new ideas and formulations, independent of both the SDG framework and the drift of national-level declaratory policy.

6. Conclusions

Ending child poverty is recognized as a key facet of both poverty eradication and sustainable development. The intergenerational transmission of poverty remains a key issue, as children growing up in poverty are at increased risk of experiencing a whole host of welfare problems in adulthood, including poverty itself (Duncan et al., 2010; Schmidt et al., 2021). Longitudinal research demonstrates that the intergenerational transmission of poverty introduces complexities to our understanding of the contents and dimensions of child poverty as well as hampering our ability to draw a coherent picture of the causes and consequences of this phenomenon (Ristikari et al., 2018).

As such, the "wickedness" issue remains deeply embedded at the heart of what the SDGs are, as balanced sustainable development is difficult given the role played by deregulation and liberalized social and economic policies generating unsustainable development (Weber, 2017; Swain, 2018). Moreover, "wickedness" is continually generated in the meta-failure of the program's overall coherence, where the pursuit of some SDGs materially endangers the ability to address others (Brown, 2015; Costa et al., 2021).

The salience of the child poverty issue in Finland then presents something of a complex puzzle. In national terms, the issue is confined to certain groups – which, in itself, is a direct result of the "wickedness" flowing from the technical complexity embedded in the institutional set up and the policies it produces. While the issue is generally viewed as "politically" important, featuring in most governmental programs over our review period, public policy has had little impact on the headline figures.

Since the SDGs inception in 2015 moreover, this pattern has not really changed. There are clearly "wicked" aspects here relating to uncertainty and disagreement but the issues around indicators and measurement render "solutions" within the current policy set up difficult, particularly in the context of a welfare system which was not designed to work in the ways required to effectively address multidimensional child poverty. Moreover, in terms of the SDGs themselves, child poverty remains a minor issue for Finland where national attention is focused on other goals relating to development aid, education, and environmental concerns.

This chapter has explored how "rich" Nordic welfare state, Finland, has attempted to cope with the issue of child poverty since the 1990s. The Finnish welfare governance system, specifically those policies addressing child poverty, suggests that it has, simply, "come to terms" with the wickedness aspects of child poverty and effectively "learned to cope" with internationally set targets such as those associated with the SDGs while, in effect, maintaining the policy status quo.

The asymmetries between child policy as a public policy goal and actual public policy interventions remain stark but not however insurmountable. In the context of public policy delivery, Grube (2022) has, for instance, outlined four success factors enhancing the worth of public policy which are relevant to the field of child poverty since they inveigh us not to understand its eradication as "irredeemably wicked."

Accordingly, four elements "need to line up for governments to have a decent shot at winning the politics of policymaking in any given situation" (Grube, 2022, p. 12). Grube (2022, pp. 13–17) outlines these elements as follows: (i) proper *problem definition* (what is the actual problem that this policy is trying to solve? Including an understanding of how to frame the problem and from what kind of perspective?) thus providing the frame of action for actual policymaking; (ii) the *policy narrative* needs to be consistent with the societal problem definition to help explain the policy problem in such a way that connects with service users; (iii) *data and evidence* usage must bring together the facts of what is happening in the context of the policy problem – bearing in mind that evidence can never be totally objective – and finally (iv) *relevant policy interventions* constitute the final chain of alignment that connects the policy problem definition, narrative and evidence as a change mechanism designed to solve the pinpointed policy problem. This approach represents a useful updating of Rittel and Webber's (1973) original task and could be used to develop a comprehensive approach to tackling the determinants of child poverty.

From a Finnish perspective, it is apparent that none of these public policy fundaments have been adequately addressed. Therefore, while government interventions have been insufficient, the role, as actors, of national child welfare and family policy related to nongovernmental organizations has become much more important in terms of bringing the issue of child poverty into societal forums and leading debates in the media.

Anti-poverty policies related to children and families with children need to embody different kinds of policy responses to be effective as one of the primary reasons for the shortcomings in Finnish family policy is the continuing mismatch between financial social security and the implementation, more broadly, of family services. Further problems here relate to the "renewal policies" pursued over the past 30 years in the family policy field where the dominant trend has been to pursue service system renewal by implementing top-down "solutions" without the ability to ensure – given the prevailing governance structure – that policies are effectively implemented at the local level. This may, in part, be addressed in the move toward the recentralization of service delivery, but as the new system of well-being counties only came into force at the beginning of 2023, it is difficult to judge whether this will be the case.

Clearly, while a strong rhetorical consensus around reducing child poverty has existed, in principle, encompassing all national administrations covered in the review period, these government program documents generally lack concrete and innovative policy measures to address child poverty in the context of family services and social security while integration with the SDGs remains weak as piecemeal adjustments to the social security system generate suboptimal solutions to the point where the system is now in need of reorganization to better meet the challenges of child poverty and families at risk of social exclusion.

In sum, while Finland has succeeded in promoting civil society "buy in" to the SDG process in relation to child poverty while also creating a robust system of governance oversight and indicator use – something which could lead to better policy integration – difficulties clearly remain in terms of overall coherence, with siloed thinking and policy implementation still predominating. While value differences do exist, the *locus* of "wickedness" is nevertheless clearly identifiable in the realm of technical and institutional problematics.

References

Arter, D. (2020). When a pariah party exploits its demonised status: The 2019 Finnish general election. *West European Politics*, *43*(1), 260–273.

Berliner, D., & Prakash, A. (2015). 'Bluewashing' the firm? Voluntary regulations, program design and member compliance with the United Nations Global Compact. *Policy Studies Journal*, *43*(1), 115–138.

Bradbury, B., Jäntti, M., & Lindahl, L. (2019). Labour income, social transfers, and child poverty. *Social Indicators Research*, *143*, 251–276.

Brown, J. H. (2015). The oxymoron of Sustainable Development. *BioScience*, *65*, 1027–1029.

Costa, J., Cancela, D., & Reis, J. (2021). Neverland or Tomorrowland? Addressing (in)compatibility among the SDG pillars in Europe. *International Journal of Environmental Research and Public Health*, *18*(22), 11858.

Duncan, G. J., Ziol-Guest, K. M., & Kalil, A. (2010). Early-childhood poverty and adult attainment, behavior, and health. *Child Development*, *81*(1), 306–325.

Finnish National Commission on Sustainable Development. (2016). *The Finland we want by 2050.* https://kestavakehitys.fi/documents/2167391/2186383/FINAL+Kest%C3%A4v%C3%A4n+kehityksen+yhteiskuntasitoumus+20+4+2016_eng-GBs_Final+-+kielenhuolto_EN_rev+(2).pdf/e057e638-507e-464c-a3dd-d3f0826f8950

Gabay, C., & Ilcan, S. (2017). Leaving no-one behind? The politics of destination in the 2030 Sustainable Development Goals. *Globalizations*, *14*(3), 337–342.

Government Communications Department. Finland ranks first in international sustainable development comparison. Ministry of Foreign Affairs (Press Release 14/6/2021).

Government of Finland. (2021). *National child strategy. Committee report. The parliamentary national child strategy committee.* Prime Minister's Office.

Grube, D. C. (2022). *Why governments get it wrong – And how they can get it right.* Macmillan.

Härtull, C., Saarela, J. & Cederström, A. (2017) Income poverty in households with children: Finland 1987–2011. *Research on Finnish Society*, *10*, 43–59.

Hak, T., Janouskova, S., & Moldan, B. (2016). Sustainable Development Goals: A need for relevant indicators. *Ecological Indicators*, *60*, 565–573.

Head, B. W. (2022). *Wicked problems in public policy understanding and responding to complex challenges.* Palgrave MacMillan.

Head, B. W., & Alford, J. (2015). Wicked problems: Implications for public policy and management. *Administration & Society*, *47*(6), 711–739.

Hiilamo, A., Castilla-Rho, J., Ristikari, T., Mäkinen, L., Hirvonen, M., Sissonen, E., Virtanen, P., & Sinclair, D. (2023). *What drives long-term social assistance use among young adults and where are the potential points for intervention? Lessons from a participatory systems mapping exercise and structural network analysis in the Finnish context.* Unpublished article draft that will be submitted during April 2023.

Hiilamo, A., Räsänen, T., Korpela, T., Mukkila, S., Mäkinen, L., & Ristikari, T. (2022, September). Research blog. https://tutkimusblogi.kela.fi/arkisto/6774

Järvinen, A., & Saarela, E. (2021). *Poverty Watch Report Finland 2021.* European Anti-poverty Network Finland.

Kaarakainen, S. S., Virtanen, P., Ristikari, T., Miettinen, A., Saarikallio-Torp, M., & Niemelä, M. (2022). *Suomalainen perhepolitiikka vuosituhannen vaihteen jälkeen* [*Finnish family policy after the turn of the Millennium*]. ITLA Children´s Foundation.

Kangas, O., & Simanainen, M. (2021). The Finnish Social Security System: Background to the Finnish basic income experiment. In *Experimenting with unconditional basic income.* Edward Elgar.

Leino, H., & Åkerman, M. (2022). The politics of making Finland an experimenting nation. *Critical Policy Studies*, *16*(4).

Leppik, I. (2022). *Study report on challenges related to social cohesion in implementing the UN Sustainable Development Goals, targets 1.2 and 11.7*. Council of Europe DG Human Rights and Rule of Law.

Mikkonen, J. (2013). The politics of poverty in Finland. *Social Alternatives*, *32*(1), 24–30.

Newman, J., & Head, B. W. (2017). Wicked tendencies in policy problems: Rethinking the distinction between social and technical problems. *Policy and Society*, *36*(3), 414–429.

Niemelä, M. (2008). Perceptions of the causes of poverty in Finland. *Acta Sociologica*, *51*(1), 23–40.

Noordegraaf, M., Douglas, S., Geuijen, K., & Van Der Steen, M. (2019). Weaknesses of wickedness: A critical perspective on wickedness theory. *Policy & society*, *38*(2), 278–297.

OECD. (2022). *The Short and Winding Road to 2030: Measuring Distance to the SDG Targets*. OECD Publishing, Paris. https://doi.org/10.1787/af4b630d-en

Peters, B. G. (2017). What is so wicked about wicked problems? A conceptual analysis and a research programme. *Policy and Society*, *36*(3), 385–396.

Prime Minister's Office. (2020). *Report on the Implementation of the 2030 Agenda for Sustainable Development*. Voluntary National Review, Finland.

Ristikari, T., Merikukka, M., & Hakovirta, M. K. (2018). Timing and duration of social assistance receipt during childhood on early adult outcomes. *Longitudinal and Life Course Studies*, *9*(3), 312–326.

Rittel, H. W. J., & Webber, M. M. (1973). Dilemmas in a general theory of planning. *Policy Sciences*, *4*, 155–169.

Sachs, J., Kroll, C., Lafortune, G., Fuller, G., & Woelm, F. (2021). *The decade of action for the SDGs: Sustainable Development Report 2021*. CUP, Cambridge.

Schmidt, K. L., Merrill, S. M., Gill, R., Miller, G. E., Gadermann, A. M., & Kobor, M. S. (2021). Society to cell: How child poverty gets "Under the Skin" to influence child development and lifelong health. *Developmental Review*, *61*, 100983.

SITRA. (2018). *Phenomenon-based public administration*. Working Paper, Helsinki.

Swain, R. B. (2018). A critical analysis of the Sustainable Development Goals. In W. Leal Filho (Eds.), *Handbook of sustainability science and research*. Springer.

Termeer, C. J. A. M., Dewulf, A., & Biesbroek, R. (2019). A critical assessment of the wicked problem concept: Relevance and usefulness for policy science and practice. *Policy and Society*, *38*(2), 167–179.

Tiirinki, H., Sulander, J., Sinervo, T., Halme, S., & Keskimäki, I. (2022). Integrating health and social services in Finland: Regional approaches and governance models. *International Journal of Integrated Care*, *22*(3), 18. https://doi.org/10.5334/ijic.5982

Turnbull, N., & Hoppe, R. (2019). Problematizing 'wickedness': A critique of the wicked problems concept, from philosophy to practice. *Policy and Society*, *38*(2), 315–337.

Ungar, M. (2018). The differential impact of social services on young people's resilience. *Child Abuse & Neglect*, *78*, 4–12.

Utting, P., & Zammit, A. (2009). United Nations-business partnerships: Good intentions and contradictory agendas. *Journal of Business Ethics*, *90*(1), 39–56.

Varis, T. (2020). *Development of phenomenon-based budgeting requires a shared understanding and commitment from the public administration*. National Audit Office, Helsinki.

Verho, J., Hämäläinen, K., & Kanninen, O. (2022). Removing welfare traps: Employment responses in the Finnish basic income experiment. *American Economic Journal: Economic Policy*, *14*(1), 501–522.

Virtanen, P., Uusikylä, P., Jalava, J., Tiihonen, S., Laitinen, L., & Noro, K. (2016). *Valtioneuvoston yhtenäisyys – kansainvälinen vertaileva tutkimus*. Valtioneuvoston kanslia.

Weber, H. (2017). Politics of 'leaving no one behind': Contesting the 2030 Sustainable Development Goals Agenda. *Globalizations*, *14*(3), 399–414.

Ylönen, M., & Salmivaara, A. (2021). Policy coherence across Agenda 2030 and the Sustainable Development Goals: Lessons from Finland. *Development Policy Review*, *39*(5), 829–847.

Chapter 3

"Deep Rock Is More Stable Than Society": The Siting of Repositories for High-Level Nuclear Waste in Italy, Germany, and France

Giulio Citroni

University of Calabria, Italy

Abstract

As national governments and international organizations strive to combat climate change and limit greenhouse gas emissions, the energy transition is at the center of the global agenda. Sustainable Development Goal (SDG) 7 of the UN 2030 Agenda calls for affordable, reliable, sustainable, and modern energy for all, but there is ample ambiguity on what is to be considered "sustainable" as opposed to "renewable." This chapter discusses the role of nuclear power in this context, and more specifically the thorny issue of nuclear waste: unless a sustainable strategy for the disposal of nuclear waste is found, the inclusion of nuclear power as a legitimate recipient of Green Deal and other aid will be contested. The cases of Italy, Germany, and France are discussed, showing how these countries have struggled over decades to solve the "wicked problem" of nuclear waste and have dealt with conflict through different mixes of stakeholder engagement, procrastination, or use of scientific expertise for legitimation.

Through the comparative analysis of the three cases, conclusions are drawn on relevant factors that contribute to the policy capacity needed to tackle complex, integrated, super-wicked problems of sustainability policy: issues of problem definition, multilevel coordination, time management, and the engagement of community and science are described and identified as critical.

Keywords: Energy policy; sustainability; nuclear waste; SDG7; policy capacity

Policy Capacity, Design and the Sustainable Development Goals, 49–67

doi:10.1108/978-1-80455-686-320241004

1. Introduction

Sustainable Development Goal (SDG) 7 calls for efforts to "ensure access to affordable, reliable, sustainable, and modern energy for all." Along with a number of initiatives concerning data collection, education, innovation, and coordination, the Global Agenda for SDG7 put forward by the Technical Advisory Group includes major substantive policies to extend access to energy, improve energy efficiency, and accelerate the pace of transition toward renewable energy (United Nations, 2018).

As is inherent in the logic of SDGs (Fukuda-Parr, 2016), SDG7 applies globally to all countries irrespective of their status, size, or performance. However, regional perspectives determine the priorities to be pursued and influence which policies are best suited to pursue the goal in each context; thus, different policy briefs have been published for different world regions by the respective UN Regional Commissions. Universal access to electricity and access to clean cooking fuels and technologies are pressing priorities in Latin America, the Caribbean, and the Asia-Pacific region; the most prominent issues in the European and North-American contexts – on which this chapter is focused – concern in particular the restructuring of the energy industry toward the internalization of environmental costs, the optimization of energy subsidies, the removal of barriers to sustainable energy technology, the transition from "energy products" to "energy services," research into smart(er) networks, and the promotion of investment in renewable energy (UNECE, 2018).

This chapter discusses the problematic implications of the goals of SDG7 through the lens of a specific policy issue that many countries across the world are facing, namely the storage and disposal of high-level nuclear waste (HLW). In translating SDG7 into practice, EU countries face a number of conflicting strategies and views that concern the role of nuclear power as a transition technology (supporting energy security over the period of transition to solar, wind, hydro, and other renewable sources) or as a fully sustainable source itself in the longer term. In this debate, a central role has been played by the issue of nuclear waste, which touches upon all aspects cited above: most importantly, the internalization of environmental costs demands that the cycle is "closed," and that all future impacts are accounted for and compensated; the optimization of subsidies and promotion of investment requires that standards are set as to what constitutes a renewable or sustainable source. As we shall see, the difficulties that states are facing in designing and siting infrastructures for the disposal of nuclear waste radically challenge the fulfillment of these goals.

2. The Taxonomy Regulation and the Debate on Nuclear Power and Nuclear Waste

Among the most relevant – and controversial – initiatives undertaken by the EU in the attempt to promote the transition to sustainable and renewable energy was the so-called "Taxonomy regulation," a set of definitions and criteria intended to standardize environmental reporting and directing investments toward sustainable enterprises. A Technical Expert Group (TEG) was set up in 2018 by the Commission to develop guidelines that would effectively orient all Sustainable finance and Green deal initiatives (EU-TEG, 2020a). The TEG, working with input from numerous stakeholders, published a final report in March 2020 which included nuclear energy among the sustainable sources which may benefit from Sustainable finance and Green deal funding (EU-TEG, 2020a, 2020b):

> Nuclear energy generation has near to zero greenhouse gas emissions in the energy generation phase and can be a contributor to climate mitigation objectives [...] The potential role of nuclear energy in low carbon energy supply is well documented.

As it did so, however, it recognized significant issues in the disposal of nuclear waste. In light of excessive uncertainties in the calculation of risk and damage to the environment, it took the very controversial decision to exclude nuclear waste disposal from its calculation of impact:

> A combination of temporary storage plus permanent disposal in geological formation is the most promising [technical solution] [...]. Yet nowhere in the world has a viable, safe and long-term underground repository been established. It was therefore infeasible for the TEG to undertake a robust DNSH assessment [...].

The inclusion of nuclear energy in the Taxonomy Regulation by the Commission's TEG contradicted the initial attitude of the EU Council and Parliament (Fouquet, 2022), so that a further opinion was asked of the Joint Research Centre (JRC) of the European Commission. The JRC report was even more optimistic about nuclear energy, concluding that "impacts of nuclear energy on the human health and the environment are mostly comparable to hydropower and the renewables, *if non-radiological effects are considered*" (JRC, 2021, p. 182). This final clause about nonradiological effects is the center of the JRC's reasoning: once all measures are taken to avoid radiological contamination, the non-radiological impact is negligible; international regulation, state-of-the-art technology, and geological disposal of high-level waste, all seem sufficient guarantees that radiological risk is averted.

A number of Member States raised concerns and criticism (Fouquet, 2022), all centered on the inclusion of nuclear power in the taxonomy and largely focused on the issue of disposal of nuclear waste. The German government, through its Federal Office for the Safety of Nuclear Waste Management (BASE), published an "expert response" in September 2021 (BASE, 2021); the report emphasizes that it is a mistake not to consider radiological risks and refers explicitly to Agenda 2030 expressing that "considering future generations" and "participative decision-making" are mandatory requirements which are not met by the present advancements in waste disposal. In conclusion, the Do No Significant Harm (DNHS) clause is not safeguarded. Similarly, the Austrian Federal Ministry for Environment published a report reacting to the TEG report (Stagl, 2020), which also called into question the assumption that nuclear power is an effective transition strategy (Stagl, 2020, p. 33).

Further criticism to the TEG and JRC reports came from within the EU institutions as well, when the Commission's own Scientific Committee on Health, Environmental and Emerging Risks (SCHEER) published a review of the JRC report criticizing the interpretation of the DNSH clause by JRC: "with regard to waste recycling, there is limited evidence provided and a more realistic assessment of the actual recyclability in current decommissioning procedures would be useful" (SCHEER, 2021, p. 12).

With the adoption in February 2022 of the Complementary Climate Delegated Act, the Commission ultimately included nuclear (and gas) in the taxonomy, albeit imposing stringent safety and efficiency requirements. As is clear from this brief review of opposing reactions, however, the issue of waste disposal is open and is critical to the very idea of sustainability of nuclear power generation.

3. The Issue of High-Level Radioactive Waste as a Wicked Policy Problem

The disposal of high-level radioactive waste (HLW) has been on the agenda of international institutions and national governments since the early post–second world war times, as witnessed by article 37 of the Treaty establishing the European Atomic Energy Community (EURATOM) in 1957.

Most recently, directive 2011/70/Euratom has defined responsibilities and procedures in the safe management of spent fuel and radioactive waste. Among other things, the directive demands that Member States provide updates on the status of planning and operation of facilities that will host HLW. The analysis of such plans gives an idea of the timescale involved: the infrastructure must guarantee isolation for a long time ("on the order of 100,000 years" according to UNECE (2020, p. 98), but German institution BASE is running safety analysis over a million-year period), and the operation in most countries is expected to start between 2050 and 2070 (European Commission, 2017).

While medical and other uses generate lower level radioactive waste, the problem of HLW disposal is most pressing and ever-increasing in countries with an active nuclear program, like France. However, also countries like Germany, which is phasing out its nuclear power generation, and Italy, which stopped nuclear energy after the 1987 referendum, are left with relevant stocks of waste that they need to dispose of. While France presently hosts a staggering 44.5% of total volumes of radioactive waste in EU Member States, Germany still accounts for 6.5% and Italy for 1.1% (European Commission, 2017).

The problem of HLW disposal has been analyzed over time from several points of view, technical of course but also legal and political, relating to international as well as national and local politics. In addition to a host of more or less detailed case studies, the most recent comparative efforts include the special issue of the *Journal of Risk Research* (Strandberg & Andrén, 2009) and the three-book series by Brunnengräber and colleagues (2015, 2018, 2019), but comparative work has been ongoing over decades to understand the interplay between national and international dimensions of the nuclear waste problem (Blowers et al., 1991; Colglazier, 1982), to discuss the construction of consent and legitimation (Berkhout, 1991), to outline policy contexts and coordinate policy (Eurobarometer, 2005, 2008; OECD NEA, 1999, 2000).

Several aspects of the HLW-disposal problem contribute to its being often used as a prominent example of the wicked problem according to the definition by Rittel and Webber (1973), or the super-wicked problem as posed by Levin et al. (2012). Significantly, Rittel and Webber (1973, p. 163) speak of "long half-lives" of public works when referring to path dependency, thus using nuclear waste as an implicit metaphoric reference.

Many environmental problems (cfr. Crowley & Head, 2017) are indeed inherently uncertain, structured in complex geographical and institutional networks, and requiring specific problem-solving strategies such as argumentative processes, cooperation, and a challenge to rationalism and expert knowledge. The nuclear-waste issue, in addition, calls into question more general value judgments that touch upon nuclear power, energy security and safety, and the limits to growth in energy consumption; its technical complexity and reliance on ongoing research starken the issues of uncertainty and iterative redefinition of the problem, while its almost unfathomable timeframe reinforces the path dependency that makes mistakes inevitably fatal. The issue at hand thus largely fulfills Rittel and Webber's original definition: "every wicked problem can be considered to be a symptom of another problem," "there is no definitive formulation of a wicked problem," "there is no immediate and no ultimate test of a solution," "the planner has no right to be wrong," "there is no opportunity to learn by trial and error." Simultaneously, the HLW issue fits the indicators of "super-wickedness" (Levin et al., 2012) which include a difficulty in calculating and therefore discounting future costs, the absence of a strong central authority, and the fact that the same actors that generate the problem are largely involved in seeking solutions.

The literature suggests that the "wickedness" of the HLW issue is determined by the combination of highly complex and uncertain technical issues and of pressing and articulated political pressures.

On the technical side, as we shall see in the three country cases, decades of research have gone into establishing criteria and solutions to maximize long-term safety (from human access, natural change or disaster, war, etc.) and minimize maintenance in the long run – no existing institution can be expected to monitor the deposit continuously for over one hundred thousand years or even preserve memory of its location, design, and threats. General consensus is focused at present on Deep Geological Repositories (DGRs), deposits in very stable geological environments where barrels can be buried deep and sealed in concrete. The EU "Spent fuel and Radioactive waste Directive" (2011/70/EURATOM) recognizes that "it is broadly accepted at the technical level that, at this time, deep geological disposal represents the safest and most sustainable option"; however, it is recognized that great uncertainty is inherent to the nature and timescale of the projects:

> Since the implementation and development of a disposal facility will take place over many decades, many programmes recognise the necessity of remaining flexible and adaptable, e.g. in order to incorporate new knowledge about site conditions or the possible evolution of the disposal system.

According to the OECD Nuclear Energy Agency, "[t]he world consensus is that there is a basis for confidence in deep geological disposal as a safe solution [...], and there is a sound technical basis for the worldwide consensus that geological disposal is the most practical, practicable, and ethically acceptable way to remove risk from the 'biosphere', the surface of the Earth where people live"; in any case, geology offers a solution to long-term uncertainties since "deep rock is more stable than society" (NEA and OECD, 2017, p. 15).

On the political level, the literature insists on the difficulties of the siting process: references to the nuclear-waste problem are frequent in theoretical discussions of wicked problems, as are single case studies that refer to the wicked-problem concept. A number of proposals have come forward in the literature, including stakeholder and citizen engagement and participation (Di Nucci et al., 2017), participatory research (Fischer, 1993, 1999), or network management (van Bueren et al., 2003). The different proposals converge in identifying several common issues, which participation, deliberation, and network governance are meant to tackle:

- Community engagement and public scientific engagement: the interaction between citizens, politics, and experts should bridge the communication and legitimacy issues raised by processes which are one-sidedly technocratic or political.
- Challenges to problem definition: a key factor is the consensus on problem definition and on the level of its generality, which may range from the very local, Not in my backyard (NIMBY)-type opposition to far-reaching contestation of energy policy and sustainability policy.
- Multilevel coordination: coordination problems between government levels, territories, and public and private stakeholders increase conflict and risk, making it unmanageable.
- Time management: the issue of the long-term management of expectations, attention, postponement, and acceleration is an aspect of power which needs special attention and mediation strategies (Blanck, 2016).

These four dimensions identified in the literature are consistent with the issues raised by the literature on policy capacity, and – as could be expected due to the wide consensus on geologic disposal as the best solution from a technical standpoint – most directly to the political and the system-level skills of legitimation, authorization, political strategy, and governance (Woo et al., 2015). These dimensions will be used in the following sections to test the ability of governments in tackling the wicked problem of HLW disposal through a reconstruction of the siting processes in the three countries. Using published literature, institutional documents, and press reviews, the three cases will be analyzed and discussed in the conclusion highlighting the diverse combinations of political strategy, policy tools, and policy outcomes.

4. Germany: Sixty Years on, the Search has Just Begun

Starting in the early 1960s, Germany was an early mover in research on the disposal of nuclear waste (BMWi, 2008; Hocke & Kallenbach-Herbert, 2015). The federal government begins searching for a rock-salt site in 1964, with the intention of establishing a DGR. Local protest and legal issues with the expropriation of land lead to the interruption of the siting campaign almost immediately, in 1966 (BMWi, 2008); a new campaign starts in 1973, based on a new concept of multifunctional "disposal center" (NEZ), mostly focusing on the region of Lower Saxony, but is stopped again by local protest as soon as three possible sites are named and field research begins (Hocke & Renn, 2009).

In 1976, the Prime Minister of Lower Saxony offers to take over the responsibility to select a site at state level – an offer the federal government gladly accepts (Hocke & Renn, 2009); an interministerial committee is formed, which identifies the Gorleben site through a rather opaque mix of technical and political considerations. This site, which was not included in the federal investigation of 1973, will constitute the object of conflict for the following 40 years. The federal government accepted the proposal, assuming that the bottom-up process would reduce conflict, but protest rapidly arose also in Gorleben as it had in the areas previously identified by the Bund. The local protest rapidly intercepts the antinuclear movement that is rising in Germany, and Gorleben soon becomes a symbol and a site of a more generally antinuclear protest: around 100.000 people gather in 1979 on the "Gorleben Treck," a seven-day march from Gorleben to Hannover and the largest antinuclear demonstration in Western Germany until then (Kirchhof, 2018).

In response to the protest, the "Gorleben-hearing" was initiated, an international workshop on the technical and safety issues raised by the multipurpose center (NEZ) to be established in Gorleben. The doubts raised by the experts were politically translated by the regional administration as concerning the NEZ model, while the mere deep-burial infrastructure was deemed to be still acceptable. Research on-site thus takes place between 1979 and 1983 for the activities above ground and from 1984 also for the underground investigations (Hocke & Renn, 2009).

Between 1984 and 1996, there is substantial stalemate: protest continues, as do rather slow investigation and construction works and lawsuits raised by antinuclear organizations against the project (Hocke & Kallenbach-Herbert, 2015). Meanwhile, the Chernobyl accident, the steady rise of the Green party, and a progressive turn of the Social Democratic Party (SPD) toward antinuclear positions change the political scenario and set the context for a new round of the siting process (Hocke & Renn, 2009).

A new political equilibrium is effectively reached when the Schroeder cabinet is formed in 1998 between SPD and *Bündnis 90/Die Grünen*. Several innovative decisions are made by the new cabinet to buy time and appease protestors:

- In 1999, the AkEnd (group for the selection process of the final repository sites) is created, an autonomous body within the Ministry for Environment tasked with identifying technical criteria and procedural advice for the siting process. The AkEnd produces a final report in 2002 (AkEnd, 2002), setting geological, geographic and social criteria, as well as rather detailed instructions for citizen engagement.
- In 2000, the government and the energy companies agree the so-called "Gorleben-moratorium," stopping the exploration at Gorleben for a minimum of three years and assigning a technical study of the feasibility and risks connected to the project to the Federal office for radiation protection.
- In 2001, the "Atomkonsens" (nuclear consensus) is reached between the energy companies and the federal government: it includes a progressive exit from the production of nuclear power, the *Atomausstieg*, through the gradual shutdown of nuclear power plants over a period of over 30 years.

A new Christian-liberal coalition, however, largely reverses this strategy in 2009, and invests again in the choice of Gorleben to the detriment of a fair and fully open process of siting. At the same time, they plan a "phasing out of the phasing out" process to relaunch atomic energy in the country.

After the Fukushima accident of 2011, the federal government is forced to review again its own pronuclear and pro-Gorleben agenda. A whole new "package" is designed, in substitution of the red-green package of the early 2000s (Tiggemann, 2019):

- In 2013, a new law ("StandAG") on the siting process defines the competences and the criteria for the siting of the *Endlager*: it envisages a "fair, transparent, and science-based" process, largely managed by the BGE, a limited company controlled by the Ministry of Environment and supervised by the Federal Office for the Safety of Nuclear Waste Management (BASE).
- A committee is set up (*Endlagerkommission*), composed of Members of Parliament, representatives of Land governments, scientists, and members of civic organizations; they develop further strategies and criteria and publish a final report in 2016 which leads to a revision of the StandAG law in 2017.
- In 2016, a monitoring committee (*Begleitgremium*) is set up: a neutral, pluralistic committee of 18 members representing citizens, associations, and institutions, entrusted with the monitoring and consultation on the siting process.

BGE has now begun the siting process, which is expected to terminate in 2031 with a final decision on the location of the *Endlager*. The process entails intense collaboration among Land and Bund governments, several channels of public information, and a strict adherence to the criteria set by law. A first "mid-term report" in September 2020 has so far excluded Gorleben from the list of possible siting places, due to geological inadequacy; the search thus begins again from scratch.

Meanwhile, since the onset of the war in Ukraine, the government and Parliament have agreed an extension on the operation of nuclear plants that were planned to shut down, sparking renewed debate between and within parties on the *Automausstieg*, the nuclear exit.[1]

5. From Technocracy to Deliberation: The French Battle Over the Bure Site

The conflict concerning the siting of a radioactive waste repository begins in France in the late 1980s. ANDRA, the National Agency for the Management of Radioactive Waste created in 1979 following over a decade of debate, is a highly technical public enterprise, strongly connected to the industry, supervised by the Ministry for Environment (Blanck, 2016). In the late 1980s, it starts a very technical process of research on four sites (Deux-Sèvres, Maine-et-Loire, Ain, Aisne) hoping to avoid suspicions that a choice is made without proper consideration of local specificities and without proper comparison between viable options (Blanck, 2016). Protest, however, erupts abruptly in 1987, when the Prefects in each area summon the local mayors and communicate the intention of government to begin explorations (Baudron, 2017; Callon et al., 2009). Opposition is immediate in all four areas, and the simultaneity allows for coordination between the local campaigns: a three-year confrontation begins which will include tractor marches, sabotage actions, sit-ins, assemblies of tens of thousands of people, and violent riots with police forces (Baudron, 2017; Blanck, 2016). The mobilization of counter-experts by a composite coalition of farmers, homeowners, local politicians, etc., raises issues about the choice of technology (deep storage) and about the irreversibility of the decision in case new technologies or new knowledge should arise in the long time of planning, construction, and management of the plant.

In the face of such strong local reaction, Mitterrand's socialist Prime Minister Michel Rocard decides in 1990 to establish a moratorium on the exploration of deep geological sites. The moratorium will serve to work on new legislation, leading to the approval of the "Loi Bataille" in 1991.

In essence (D'Allens et al., 2018; Callon et al., 2009, p. 16; Lehtonen, 2015; Prieur, 1992):

[1]https://www.base.bund.de/DE/themen/kt/ausstieg-atomkraft/laufzeitverlaengerung-faq.html

- The law reverts the process to a political dimension, after over a decade of merely technical treatment ("it strives to open the black box of science" [Callon et al., 2009, p. 16]).
- The option of deep burial is no longer treated as the only viable choice but is expected to be discussed and researched alongside transmutation and surface storage.
- In a largely strategic move, the reference to a "burial center" is substituted by a more acceptable "research facility" (see the Italian decree of 2010 below).
- Finally, the law envisages economic incentives and democratic engagement to cultivate relationships with local communities: local administrations will be invited to submit their candidacies to host the infrastructure and will then receive significant compensatory investments; also, local committees will be formed to monitor the process.

The law poses a moratorium of 15 years, demanding that no final solution be decided until 2006.

The implementation of the *Loi Bataille* progresses (Blanck, 2016) as Bataille himself leads negotiations with municipalities and manages to raise as many as 30 candidacies by local administrations to host the research center. ANDRA, now effectively transformed into a research agency, identifies four possible sites in 1995, and the socialist/green government authorizes the Bure (Meuse et Haute Marne) site in 1998. The Laboratory is formally established in 1999, and construction work on site begins.

Over the years, protest has remained active: when Bure is chosen as the final site, a national coordination of protest groups against deep burial has already been established, and summer camps, a squat house, a festival are among the initiatives that create solidarity and identity in the protest movement, while radicalizing the protest which increasingly includes more general antinuclear as well as anti-capitalist positions (D'Allens et al., 2018).

As the deadline of 2006 set by the *Loi Bataille* for a new law establishing a final solution approaches, tensions are high, and a radicalization of the protest pushes for a more general rethinking of the national nuclear strategy: "stop nuclear energy, and we will discuss nuclear waste" is now the position of a number of the groups engaged in the opposition to the infrastructure (CNDP, 2005b).

From now on (2005–2019), a new instrument will be deployed by the authorities to deal with protest and mediate toward the accomplishment of an acceptable solution, namely the *Débat public*. Three successive rounds of deliberation are held with varying degrees of pertinence and success.

In 2005, a Débat Public is held for the first time on a general plan rather than a specific infrastructure: "the general options concerning the management of high-level and medium level/long life nuclear waste." Public meetings take place mostly in the areas surrounding the Bure laboratory and the low-level radioactive waste repository in the northern Manche region. Especially in the Bure area, opposers organize protest actions against the *Débat public* events, but these action are not intended to stop the meetings which take place peacefully (CNDP, 2005a, 2005b). The indications for the new law to be approved in 2006 are effectively limited to reversibility, which must be guaranteed for at least 100 years in view of possible technological innovations and the due consideration of alternatives. Criticisms raised during the debate include that its duration was insufficient, the timing too late, the decisions already made, the geographical scope too limited; some of the opposers demand a referendum, others complain about the absence of their elected Members of Parliament in the debate (CNDP, 2005b).

In 2013, a new *Débat public* takes place, this time on the specific infrastructure to be built in Bure, now defined as "reversible deep-storage center" according to the requirements of the 2006 law, or Cigéo – industrial geological stocking center. This *Débat public* follows the more established procedure of initiative by the company (ANDRA) proposing an infrastructure and is meant to discuss the opportunity and goals of the infrastructure. This time, the opposition is more intense, and the first public meetings are interrupted by local protesters; among the reasons for protest is the lack of attention paid to the results of the previous *Débat public*. The Commission for the *Débat public* decides to increase the number of small territorial meetings (presumably to disperse the protesters, but this only worked when they were held among institutional actors behind closed doors), to hold the larger meetings online to avoid interruption, to start a partnership with local newspapers to promote the process, and to set up a *citizen jury* to integrate the public debate (CNDP, 2013). The results are once again undecisive: "a very deep cleavage" separates the opposing sides on the ethical issues underlying the project (CNDP, 2013).

In 2019, a third *Débat public* is held on a national scale, to discuss the fifth edition of the national plan on management of radioactive materials and waste (PNGMDR). Events are held all over mainland France, and only a handful of meetings are the object of protest actions; only one is interrupted (CNDP, 2019). The difficulties of organizing a debate on a large geographical scale and on a very sensitive subject were tackled by the Commission for Débat Public through (1) the commissioning of a preliminary "clarification of the controversies," (2) the creation of a "mirror group," similar to the citizens' jury of 2013, and (3) the creation of a "workshop of future generations," a jury of 40 students. The Commission notes in the conclusions of the final report that the public keeps raising the same issues across the several editions of Débat public: intergenerational ethics and the governance of decision-making processes where everything seems to be already decided before the consultation.

At present, the situation in Bure and France is characterized by the slow progress of the construction of the deposit, the temporary management of nuclear waste in surface infrastructures, and – as far as the protest is concerned – the trial on seven activists which is attracting the attention and the energies of the local and national movements (Cholez, 2021). In 2022, the project is declared a strategic infrastructure by decree, speeding up the requisition of land and the authorization process, which is planned to be completed by 2027.

Meanwhile, the government has announced the construction of new nuclear power plants, and the National Commission for Public Debate (CNDP) has recommended that a public debate be held on the opportunity of continuing with the national nuclear program.

6. Why Bother? Italy and the Timing of Inaction

Italy is a latecomer in the search for a site for HLW disposal; since the post-Chernobyl 1987 referendum which stopped all nuclear power generation in the country (and a second, post-Fukushima referendum in 2011, which stopped an attempt by the Berlusconi cabinet to reinstate it), the production of waste is limited, and the debate is largely absent in the media and the public opinion (Eurobarometer, 2005, 2008).

Only in 1996 did ENEA, the former nuclear energy commission, now "energy and environment" agency, set up a task force to plan the disposal of nuclear waste and find a suitable site; the government strategy issued in 1999, however, only envisaged temporary sites for high-level waste, postponing any decision or plan concerning their final destination (Di Nucci, 2015). This dilatory strategy holds over time, as SOGIN (see below) now communicates through its dedicated website that a shared international deep geological deposit will be located somewhere "in Europe".[2]

In 1999, in the framework of the reform of the energy sector operated by the center-left coalition, SOGIN is created, which similarly to German BGE is a public-owned company in charge of decommissioning and management of radioactive waste. In 2001, the Ministry for Industry issues guidelines to SOGIN which include the identification of a site for the permanent disposal of low-level waste and the "temporary" storage of high-level waste (SOGIN, 2003).

In 2003, in a more general attempt to expedite infrastructure projects, the center-right Berlusconi cabinet nominates a special commissioner with powers which included the study of options for the temporary nuclear waste deposit site, and a study is commissioned to SOGIN which identifies the village of Scanzano Jonico in the southern region of Basilicata as the perfect site. The immediate protest of the local population brings the proposal to a halt (Zinn, 2007); the protest is largely local but intercepts part of the anti-globalization movement and of political opposition to the center-right government (de Ruggieri, 2004). The government thus starts a new procedure, forming a commission which must find a new site in 12 months; nothing significant emerges from this commission, nor from the one established in the following years by the Ministry for Economic Development (Di Nucci, 2015).

In 2010, a legislative decree (n. 31) is issued, again by a Berlusconi cabinet, which – while reinstating a nuclear program and largely in an attempt to legitimize this choice – sets out the complete procedure for site selection and redefines the infrastructure as a "national repository and technological park." In the first six months after the approval of the decree, SOGIN is expected to publish a "map of potentially suitable areas" (CNAPI), so that a negotiation process can be set in motion between stakeholders and central and local institutions. However, the CNAPI is published 11 years later, in 2021, instead of six months; the scrapping of the nuclear program through a referendum in 2011 reduced the pressure, and successive governments avoided the issue of the disposal site. Based on criteria set

---

[2]https://www.depositonazionale.it/deposito-nazionale/pagine/perche-e-necessario-il-deposito.aspx

by the environmental agency ISPRA in 2014, the CNAPI was handed by SOGIN to the Ministry of the Environment in 2015 and lay unattended by successive Ministers probably wary of the risk of conflict (Giliberto, 2021).

The process outlined by the decree of 2010, notwithstanding the delay, still stands legally. Its design adopts several participatory, deliberative devices in terminology and formal requirements but is also strongly top-down in structure:

- Following the publication of the CNAPI in early 2021, a "public consultation" is opened, whereby all interested stakeholders have access to the relevant data and can express observations. The data, however, are over 1GB of technical tables, with no explanatory material for anyone who is not an expert. Nonetheless, around 400 observations are received from stakeholders and published online.
- At the same time, a "national seminar" is organized, where experts, institutions, trade unions and associations, and a range of well-defined stakeholders discuss (in one-way online webinars) the technical aspects of the project and "the possible economic benefits are illustrated" – so the law states.
- After the public consultation and the national seminar, SOGIN is now expected to publish a final version of the CNAPI, which needs approval by three different Ministries.
- When the CNAPI is finally approved, SOGIN will invite local authorities to offer their candidacy to host the National Repository and Technological Park and hold negotiations that are expected to lead to an agreement. "If an agreement is not reached within 60 days, said agreement is established by decree of the President of the Republic" – so the law states.

At present, after initial reactions by local and regional governments, stakeholders are waiting for the final map before presumably sparking new debate and protest. Meanwhile, the issue of nuclear power has been back on the agenda for the 2022 elections as several parties proposed to restart a nuclear program (Citroni & Campolongo, 2022).

7. Concluding Remarks

The issue of HLW disposal has been identified as a prominent example of wicked problem in the literature, and the description of the three cases has provided ample demonstration of the difficulties encountered by three countries in tackling it notwithstanding the diverse strategies adopted over time.

To conclude, we turn back to the four dimensions of variation that were identified in the literature as strategic assets in the buildup of skills and resources that contribute to policy capacity and may render the problem more manageable. All three countries, as in the Anna Karenina principle, "are unhappy in their own way," and none of them has found a stable, final solution to the problem; however, France seems to be proceeding in the construction of the plant at Bure, Germany has a rather clear roadmap to come to a siting decision, while Italy is lagging behind and permanently postponing a final – or even provisional – decision.

In Table 3.1, the findings of the case studies are analyzed systematically to compare the dimensions identified in the literature and test whether they do in fact contribute to explain different outcomes.

Indeed, the French case most effectively combines the components of potential buildup of systemic policy capacity in its analytical and political components (Wu et al., 2015): community engagement through the Débat public since 2005 is a significant change from the unsuccessful technocratic approaches of the past and contributes to an increasingly consistent clarification and agreement on problem definition; local political mediation, which was present in earlier phases but was in itself insufficient, is still present through the system of local candidacies and compensations; finally, a strategy of time management is always present, as witnessed, for example, by the extremely long moratorium (15 years) decided in 1991, and the inclusion of reversibility among the key characteristics of technical planning.

Germany has witnessed intense antinuclear protest and inconsistent national strategies on the continuation of a nuclear energy program, thus incurring in significant issues of problem definition. However, it engaged in inclusive decision-

Table 3.1. Comparative Analysis of Process Dimensions.

	Germany	**France**	**Italy**
Community engagement and public scientific engagement	Medium (joint committee since 2014)	High (Débat public since 2005)	Absent (2003) Symbolic (2010)
Challenges to problem definition	High (antinuclear protest; contradictory nuclear policy decisions)	Medium (early trans-local protest; Débat public since 2005; atomic consensus)	High (NIMBY protest; anti-globalization protest; contradictory nuclear policy decisions)
Multilevel coordination	Medium (joint committee since 2014)	Medium (system of local candidacies)	Absent (2003) Symbolic (2010)
Time management	Medium (moratorium, clear roadmap since 2013)	High (long moratorium, reversibility)	Absent

Source: Author's original work.

making since 2014 with the establishment of the *Endlagerkommission*, which is a forum for regional governments and civic organizations to participate in the process; time management has been on the agenda, through a brief moratorium between 2000 and 2003, and a clear 20-year roadmap defined by legislation in 2013.

Finally, Italy has adopted top-down, contradictory, and short-term strategies all along. After a failed attempt at siting in 2003 – which ended in a classic "decide-announce-defend" (DAD) syndrome – the 2010 legislation set up a process which is both mostly symbolic in its references to citizen engagement and interinstitutional mediation and highly inconsistent in the timing of its implementation. Local protest and inconsistent decision-making on the nuclear agenda provide significant challenges to consensus in problem definition, and problem pressure is weak and inconsistent as proposals to restart a nuclear program come and go.

While none of the countries have conclusively solved the HLW disposal issue, we find that different strategies in the four dimensions contribute to determine different outcomes; a key factor in a policy that envisages extremely long timeframes is indeed time management: a stable energy agenda and a strategic use of time help France draw very close to the realization of its goals, and the German timing strategy is rather successful in managing conflict; Italy's "wait and see" attitude only seems to focalize and strengthen conflict. At the same time, the strategic planning of multilevel coordination and of the engagement of lay and expert stakeholders contributes to the buildup of governance capacity and legitimation capacity, while top-down, technocratic procedures are confirmed as detrimental to effective formulation and implementation.

Deep rock may well be more stable than society, and this may help maintain HLW safe underground for several millennia; but the relatively shorter term instability of decades-long decision-making processes must be dealt with by designing and adopting more ductile adaptive, negotiated, and concerted strategies.

References

AkEnd. (2002). *Auswahlverfahren für Endlagerstandorte Empfehlungen des AkEnd.* Arbeitskreis Auswahlverfahren Endlagerstandorte.

BASE. (2021). *Expert response to the report by the EU Commission's Joint Research Centre "Technical assessment of nuclear energy with respect to the 'Do No Significant Harm' criteria in Regulation (EU) 2020/852, the 'Taxonomy Regulation'".* Bundesamt für die Sicherheit der nuklearen Entsorgung – The Federal Office for the Safety of Nuclear Waste Management, Berlin.

Baudron, C. (2017). *La Gâtine n'est pas à vendre - Non aux déchets nucléaires: un opposant raconte.* La Crèche (F): La Geste. https://www.fnac.com/a10896819/Charles-Baudron-La-gatine-n-est-pas-a-vendre

Berkhout, F. (1991). *Radioactive waste : Politics and technology, Routledge natural environment–Problems and management series.* Routledge.

Blanck, J. (2016). Gouverner par le temps. Cadrages temporels du problème des déchets radioactifs et construction d'une irréversibilité technique. *Gouvernement et action publique*, *5*(1), 91–116.

Blowers, A., Lowry, D., & Solomon, B. D. (1991). *The international politics of nuclear waste*. St. Martin's Press.

BMWi. (2008). *Endlagerung hochradioaktiver Abfälle in Deutschland – Das Endlagerprojekt Gorleben*. Bundesministerium für Wirtschaft und Technologie (BMWi), Berlin.

Brunnengräber, A., & Di Nucci, M. R. (2019). Conflicts, participation and acceptability in nuclear waste governance. An international comparison volume III. In *Energiepolitik und Klimaschutz [Energy policy and climate protection]* (p. 409). Springer Fachmedien Wiesbaden: Imprint: Springer VS.

Brunnengräber, A., Di Nucci, M. R., Isidoro Losada, A. M., Lutz, M., & Schreurs, M. A. (2015). Nuclear waste governance. An international comparison. In *Energiepolitik und Klimaschutz [Energy policy and climate protection]* (p. 349). Springer VS.

Brunnengräber, A., Di Nucci, M. R., Isidoro Losada, A. M., Lutz, M., & Schreurs, M. A. (2018). Challenges of nuclear waste governance: An international comparison volume II. In *Energiepolitik und Klimaschutz [Energy policy and climate protection]* (Vol. XV, p. 333). Springer Fachmedien Wiesbaden: Imprint: Springer VS.

Callon, M., Lascoumes, P., & Barthe, Y. (2009). *Acting in an uncertain world: An essay on technical democracy, inside technology*. MIT Press.

Campolongo, F., & Citroni, G. (2022). Attori e frames nella transizione energetica: mappare il conflitto in Italia e Spagna. In Convegno SISP - Società Italiana di Scienza Politica. Roma. https://www.sisp.it/convegno2022/?pagename=cms&name=session tracks&trackname=scienza-politica-e-politiche-pubbliche

Cholez, L. A. (2021). *Après une enquête démesurée, sept antinucléaires en procès à Bar-le-Duc*. Reporterre le quotidien de l'écologie (01.06.2021). https://reporterre.net/Apres-une-enquete-demesuree-sept-antinucleaires-en-proces-a-Bar-le-Duc

CNDP. (2005a). *Bilan du débat public sur les options générales en matière de gestion des déchets radioactifs de haute activité et de moyenne activité à vie longue*. Commission nationale du débat public – Commission particulière du débat public Gestion des déchets radioactifs.

CNDP. (2005b). *Compte-rendu du débat public sur les options générales en matière de gestion des déchets radioactifs de haute activité et de moyenne activité à vie longue*. Commission nationale du débat public - Commission particulière du débat public Gestion des déchets radioactifs.

CNDP. (2013). *Compte-rendu*. CNDP Commission particulière du débat public Projet de centre de stockage réversible profond de déchets radioactifs en Meuse/Haute-Marne (Cigéo).

CNDP. (2019). *Compte-rendu du Débat Public: Plan national de gestion des matières et des déchets radioactifs, 5e édition 2019–2021*. CNDP Commission particulière du débat public Projet de centre de stockage réversible profond de déchets radioactifs en Meuse/Haute-Marne (Cigéo).

Colglazier, E. W. (1982). *The politics of nuclear waste, Pergamon policy studies on energy*. Pergamon Press.

Crowley, K., & Head, B. W. (2017). The enduring challenge of 'wicked problems': Revisiting Rittel and Webber. *Policy Sciences*, *50*(4), 539–547.

D'Allens, G., Fuori, A., & Jarrige, F. (2018). Politiser les infrastructures nucléaires: les résistances au projet Cigéo à Bure. Entretien avec Gaspard D'Allens et Andrea Fuori, auteurs militants de Bure, la bataille du nucléaire. *Tracés. Revue de Sciences humaines*, *35*(2), 229–249.

de Ruggieri, R. (2004). Il problema delle scorie radioattive: il caso di Scanzano Jonico. *Economia della Cultura*, *14*(1), 83–92.

Di Nucci, M. R. (2015). Breaking the stalemate. The challenge of nuclear waste governance in Italy. In A. Brunnengräber, M. R. Di Nucci, A. M. Isidoro Losada, L. Mez, & M. A. Schreurs (Eds.), *Nuclear waste governance. An international comparison* (pp. 300–322). Springer VS.

Di Nucci, M. R., Brunnengräber, A., & Isidoro Losada, A. M. (2017). From the "right to know" to the "right to object" and "decide". A comparative perspective on participation in siting procedures for high level radioactive waste repositories. *Progress in Nuclear Energy*, *100*, 316–325.

EU-TEG. (2020a). *Taxonomy Report: Technical Annex. Updated methodology & updated technical screening criteria.* EU Technical Expert Group on Sustainable Finance, Brussels.

EU-TEG. (2020b). *Technical Report. Taxonomy: Final report of the Technical Expert Group on Sustainable Finance.* EU Technical Expert Group on Sustainable Finance, Brussels.

Eurobarometer. (2005). *Radioactive waste. Special Eurobarometer 227/Wave 63.2.* TNS Opinion & Social.

Eurobarometer. (2008). *Attitudes towards radioactive waste. Special Eurobarometer 297/Wave 69.1.* TNS Opinion & Social.

European Commission. (2017). *Report from the Commission to the Council and the European Parliament on progress of implementation of Council Directive 2011/70/ EURATOM and an inventory of radioactive waste and spent fuel present in the Community's territory and the future prospects.* Brussels.

Fischer, F. (1993). Citizen participation and the democratization of policy expertise: From theoretical inquiry to practical cases. *Policy Sciences*, *26*(3), 165–187.

Fischer, F. (1999). Technological deliberation in a democratic society: The case for participatory inquiry. *Science and Public Policy*, *26*(5), 294–302.

Fouquet, D. (2022). The healing force of renewables calls for a nuclear free taxonomy in times of aggression. *Renewable Energy Law and Policy Review*, *10*(3–4), 1–3.

Fukuda-Parr, S. (2016). From the Millennium Development Goals to the Sustainable Development Goals: Shifts in purpose, concept, and politics of global goal setting for development. *Gender and Development*, *24*(1), 43–52.

Giliberto, J.. (2021). Svelata la mappa del deposito nucleare. Da Nord a Sud, ecco le zone idonee. *Il Sole 24 Ore* (05.01.2021). https://www.ilsole24ore.com/art/svelata-mappa-deposito-nucleare-nord-sud-ecco-zone-idonee-ADQX2XBB

Hocke, P., & Kallenbach-Herbert, B. (2015). Always the same old story? Nuclear waste governance in Germany. In A. Brunnengräber, M. R. Di Nucci, A. M. Isidoro Losada, L. Mez, & M. A. Schreurs (Eds.), *Nuclear waste governance. An international comparison* (pp. 177–201). Springer VS.

Hocke, P., & Renn, O. (2009). Concerned public and the paralysis of decision-making: Nuclear waste management policy in Germany. *Journal of Risk Research*, *12*(7–8), 921–940.

JRC. (2021). *Technical assessment of nuclear energy with respect to the 'do no significant harm' criteria of Regulation (EU) 2020/852 ('Taxonomy Regulation')*. JRC Science for Policy Report. Joint Research Centre – European Commission/ European Atomic Energy Community.

Kirchhof, A. M. (2018). East-West German transborder entanglements through the nuclear waste sites in Gorleben and Morsleben. *Journal for the History of Environment and Society*, (3), 145–173.

Lehtonen, M. (2015). Megaproject underway. Governance of nuclear waste management in France. In A. Brunnengräber, M. R. Di Nucci, A. M. Isidoro Losada, L. Mez, & M. A. Schreurs (Eds.), *Nuclear waste governance. An international comparison* (pp. 117–138). Springer VS.

Levin, K., Cashore, B., Bernstein, S., & Auld, G. (2012). Overcoming the tragedy of super wicked problems: Constraining our future selves to ameliorate global climate change. *Policy Sciences*, *45*(2), 123–152.

NEA and OECD. (2017). *Communication on the safety case for a deep geological repository. Radioactive waste management*. Nuclear Energy Agency/Organisation for Economic Co-operation and Development, Paris.

OECD Nuclear Energy Agency. (1999). *Geological disposal of radioactive waste: Review of developments in the last decade, radioactive waste management*. Nuclear Energy Agency, Organisation for Economic Co-operation and Development, Paris.

OECD Nuclear Energy Agency. (2000). *Geologic disposal of radioactive waste in perspective*. Nuclear Energy Agency/Organisation for Economic Co-operation and Development, Paris.

Prieur, M. (1992). Les déchets radioactifs, une loi de circonstance pour un problème de société. *Revue juridique de l'Environnement*, (1), 19–47.

Rittel, H. W. J., & Webber, M.M. (1973). Dilemmas in a general theory of planning. *Policy Sciences*, *4*(2), 155–169.

SCHEER. (2021). *SCHEER review of the JRC report on Technical assessment of nuclear energy with respect to the 'do no significant harm' criteria of Regulation (EU) 2020/852 ('Taxonomy Regulation')*. SCHEER - EU Scientific Committee on Health, Environmental and Emerging Risks.

SOGIN. (2003). *Deposito nazionale centralizzato per i rifiuti radioattivi. Studio per la localizzazione di un sito di deposito*. SOGIN Società Gestione Impianti Nucleari.

Strandberg, U., & Andrén, M. (2009). Editorial: Nuclear waste management in a globalised world. *Journal of Risk Research*, *12*(7–8), 879–895.

Tiggemann, A. (2019). The elephant in the room. The role of Gorleben and its site selection in the German nuclear waste debate. In A. Brunnengräber & M. R. Di Nucci (Eds.), *Conflicts, participation and acceptability in nuclear waste governance: An international comparison volume III* (pp. 69–87). Springer Fachmedien Wiesbaden.

UNECE. (2018). *Policy brief #20: Achieving Sdg 7 in the UNECE Region (Central Asia, Europe and North America)*. United Nations Economic Commission for Europe (UNECE), Washington DC.

UNECE. (2020). *The role of nuclear energy in sustainable development – Entry pathways*. Draft report: Application of UNFC and UNRMS. United Nations Economic Commission for Europe (UNECE), Washington DC.

United Nations. (2018). *Accelerating SDG 7 achievement: Policy briefs in support of the first SDG 7 review at the UN high-level political forum 2018*. United Nations Department of Economic and Social Affairs, Washington DC.

van Bueren, E. M., Klijn, E. H., & Joop Koppenjan, F. M. (2003). Dealing with wicked problems in networks: Analyzing an environmental debate from a network perspective. *Journal of Public Administration Research and Theory*, *13*(2), 193–212.

Woo, J. J., Ramesh, M., & Howlett, M. (2015). Legitimation capacity: System-level resources and political skills in public policy. *Policy and Society*, *34*(3–4), 271–283.

Wu, X., Ramesh, M., & Howlett, M. (2015). Policy capacity: A conceptual framework for understanding policy competences and capabilities. *Policy and Society*, *34*(3–4), 165–171.

Zinn, D. L. (2007). Il caso di Scanzano: La ragione di stato e le ragioni di una ribellione. *Quaderni di sociologia*, *44*, 151–174.

Chapter 4

Gas Flaring Reduction in Iran: A Super-Wicked Policy Problem on the Way to Sustainability

Javad Keypour

Tallinn University of Technology, Estonia

Abstract

Gas flaring is a crucial issue in the energy transition era, as it is a major source of carbon emissions in the gas production chain. The reduction of flaring could potentially contribute to eliminating energy poverty, as the amount of gas currently flared each year could power the entirety of Sub-Saharan Africa. Despite Iran's zero-clearing target, the country ranks third in gas flaring globally, with 12% share. This case study examines the reasons behind gas flaring in Iran within the Sustainable Development Goals framework. The study reveals that while technological and economic difficulties were the primary obstacles in early years, policy malfunctioning has demonstrated the wicked nature of a sustainability problem in recent years. The traditional top-down institutional structure has led to interference from public agencies and Operations and Maintenance (O&M) companies, complicating decision-making. The lack of precise criteria for finding best solutions, as well as the absence of appropriate control and monitoring mechanisms, has further paralyzed efforts to reduce flaring. The intensification of conflict between interest groups has added complexity to the situation. The issue has been further complicated at higher levels due to economic sanctions. This study offers practical solutions for reducing flaring in Iran based on global experiences and policies and programs of some selected countries. These suggestions address the policy, technological, and institutional aspects of the problem and aim to pave the way for sustainable and responsible energy transition. By reducing gas flaring, Iran can contribute to global efforts to mitigate climate change and create a more equitable and sustainable energy future.

Keywords: Gas flaring; Iran; wicked policy; SDG; sustainability

Policy Capacity, Design and the Sustainable Development Goals, 69–88

doi:10.1108/978-1-80455-686-320241005

1. Introduction

Producing oil releases dissolved or separated natural gas, a by-product known as associated petroleum gas (APG). While nowadays natural gas is a precious energy source, it was not in the early years, especially before the oil crisis of the 1970s. Therefore, it was not uncommon to flare APG in oil fields, mainly in remote areas and on offshore platforms where transportation was costly. Although different methods, such as power generation or direct usage of treated APG, have been introduced over time, flaring has remained a convenient practice in many areas. This is mainly attributed to market and economic constraints, lack of appropriate regulation, and political will.

Reducing APG flaring has become a significant concern by international organizations in recent decade, especially as it contributes to the achievement of the United Nations Sustainable Development Goals (SDGs), and most importantly, in the goal 3 (good health and well-being), 7 (affordable and clean energy), and 13 (climate action) as follows. The continuation of APG flaring has resulted in incompletely combusted methane and black carbon, which are detrimental to human health causing asthma, cough, breathing difficulty, eye/skin irritation, and structural deformation, change in hematological parameters of humans, and lung malfunctioning, increase in gamma radiation level, and environmental degradation (Caulton et al., 2014; Giwa et al., 2019; Lack et al., 2014). Since several studies have also shown that the flared gas can be captured and utilized to provide power or valuable energy carrier products such as synthesis crude and methanol, it can supply affordable and clean energy to remote areas along with SDG7 targets (Mansoor & Tahir, 2021). Finally, APG flaring produces over 400 million tons of CO_2 emissions annually (The World Bank, 2022), which is estimated to be a significant climate forcer within the Arctic environment (Noe et al., 2022). Thus, APG reduction can greatly contribute to the achievement of SDG13's targets, especially "adaptive capacity to climate-related hazards" and integrating "climate change measures into national policies, strategies, and planning".[1]

Statistics indicate that half of global gas flaring occurred in Russia, Iraq, Iran, and the United States in 2021 (The World Bank, 2022). In the United States, the growth in oil and gas production and the regulations curtailing natural gas venting led to flaring growth until 2019. However, thanks to strict regulations and the use of technology, the United States succeeded in halving its flaring level to reach 8.8 bcm in 2021 (Allen et al., 2016; Murphy, 2022). Iran's flaring level has been impacted by the 2012 and 2018 sanctions on its oil exports. Lower exports and production resulted in flaring reduction for a while. However, as no

[1]In addition to the above-mentioned explicit contributions, Ajugwo (2013) observes that APG flaring leads to the escalation of poverty in Nigeria and thereby retards output growth. While his argument can be applied in some other states flaring APG, it can also show how flaring reduction can have a role in SDG1, i.e., poverty reduction. Other studies have also claimed that flaring reduction impacts SDGs 2, 5, and 11 (Romsom & McPhail, 2021). Considering the strong connections with the abovementioned goals, APG flaring reduction contributes to SDGs.

significant flaring reduction project has been initiated in recent years, it has remained a chronic problem, which could potentially worsen if Iran's oil production level returns to its presanction stage. For a country with more than a hundred years of experience in the oil industry, this is a policy problem symptom, as will be discussed further, which justifies its selection as a suitable case study for wicked policy problems.

Considering the importance of APG flaring in SDG goals, this study's objective is to make recommendations to the energy policymakers concerning flaring reduction by providing a theoretical overview applying the wicked policy problem concept in the Iran case. It also contributes empirically by providing proposals for achieving the SDG goals, in particular climate change reduction. The importance of this research is evident given the growth in attention to climate issues within the SDG frameworks in recent years and Iran's ranking in global gas flaring. Iran's gas flaring level will rise if sanctions against Iran's oil exportation are relaxed.

Gas flaring in Iran has been discussed by scholars before. Many scholars like Soltanieh et al. (2016), Khalili-Garakani et al. (2021), and Tahmasebzadehbaie and Sayyaadi (2022) have discussed it from a technical perspective to address the relevant reduction technologies. Taherifard et al. (2016) and Zayer Kabeh and Khoshkhoo (2021) also elaborated on the economic assessment of different flaring cases. PourMirza (2017) approached the issue using comparative studies on Iran and other Persian Gulf countries. Nevertheless, these studies did not address policy issues from a theoretical policy perspective. Therefore, this research aims to analyze Iran's flaring problem from the wicked policy problem theoretical perspective while also considering the SDG framework to address the research gap. The related research question is formulated as "to what extent is wicked policy problem framework capable of stipulating policy recommendations in the Iran gas flaring problem?" The study claims that structural, economic, and monitoring flaws have turned gas flaring into a wicked problem in Iran and have paralyzed the existing legal and regulations designed to solve the issue.

The study starts with a theoretical briefing on wicked and super-wicked policy problems. The second part provides background about Iran's oil industry structure and an overview of the flaring situation in Iran. The next part renders an analytical debate showing how APG flaring in Iran is a policy problem. Moreover, it discusses to what extent Iran's APG flaring has the main features of a super-wicked policy problem. This chapter ends with some suggestions for solving the issue.

2. Theoretical Framework and Methodology

Rational comprehensive planning entails planning consecutive steps of objective formulation, making programs delineating the objectives, setting out clear outcomes for each program, drawing up action plans for achieving those outcomes, and measuring the extent of achievement at regular intervals (McConnell, 2018). Such a model assumes that each public organization has set goals, a supportive political environment, and control over the resources and capabilities necessary to deliver on the goals – none of which necessarily apply in the presence of wicked problems (Head & Alford, 2015). While social policy professionals are expected to improve education, welfare, and equality by relying on such a planning style, their failure to achieve the goals in the late 1960s led to Rittel and Webber coin the "wicked policy problem" concept (as opposed to "tame problems") arguing that some policy problems were not amenable to being put into clearly defined boxes labeled "the problem," "desired outcome," and "optimal solution." Since then, the concept has been criticized and developed[2]; however, wicked policies are still mainly identified by Rittel and Webber's 10 characteristic definition addressed in their initial paper (Rittel & Webber, 1973).

Various examples have been cited as wicked policies such as climate change (Ross et al., 2022), energy security (Chester, 2009), poverty (Spicker, 2016), and biodiversity conservation (Brennan, 2004), while the level of wickedness is not essentially the same. Roberts (2001) has articulated a helpful taxonomy for distinguishing wicked problems. In type 1, or tame problems, the problem definition and the potential solution are clear to the decision-maker. In type 2, or complex problems, the problem definition is clear, but there is no consensus about the solution. Finally, in type 3, both the problem definition and the solution are unclear, and more extensive learning and discussion are required for all concerned. Moreover, conversely to the complex problems, the relationship between variables comprising the policy areas is essentially linear in wicked problems, and although challenging, it is ultimately more tractable (Peters & Tarpey, 2019).

In addition to Robert's taxonomy, the super-wicked problem has also been recognized as an extreme case of wicked ones. This concept is defined by several additional characteristics, including (Peters, 2017):

- Time is running out.
- There is no central authority, or only a weak central authority, to manage the problem.
- The same actors causing the problem seem to solve it.
- The future is discounted radically so that contemporary solutions become less valuable.

According to Levin and colleagues (Levin et al., 2012), time is critical in super-wicked problems. Once overtime is reached, there is a tipping point; a fundamental shift may essentially change the issue and leave no capacity for a solution. Peters and Tarpey (2019) believe that, unlike wicked policies, variable connections are not linear in super-wicked ones, making it more complicated than complex

[2]For instance, Funke (1991) redefined the concept and counted six other features for the wicked policy problems, including intransparency, polytely, situational complexity, connectivity of variables, dynamic developments, and time-delayed effects. Nevertheless, his conceptualization still has substantial conformity with Rittel and Webber. The wicked policy concept has also been criticized by Noordegraaf and colleagues (2019), among scholars arguing it is ambiguous and often used rhetorically rather than analytically.

and wicked policies. Nonlinearity in variable connections implies that the relationships between factors and variables are not straightforward and can exhibit complex, often unexpected interactions. Unlike linear systems, where changes in inputs lead to proportional and predictable outputs, nonlinear systems, such as super-wicked problems, are characterized by intricate, nonproportional relationships. This peculiarity of nonlinearity adds an extra layer of complexity to super-wicked problems, making them inherently more challenging to decipher and address compared to situations where linear relationships prevail.

Methodologically, this research undertakes an integrative review of sources to "benefit from holistic conceptualisation and synthesis of the literature to date" (Torraco, 2005) and evaluate the applicability of the wicked policy problem theory in Iran's APG flaring case. The five-stage integrative review process includes (1) problem formulation, (2) data collection or literature search, (3) evaluation of data, (4) data analysis, and (5) interpretation and presentation of results (Russell, 2008). Having the wicked policy problem theory in mind, the research extracts supporting data from sources deductively. To this end, the primary sources, i.e., governmental documents and the secondary sources, including relevant reports from think tanks, government departments, and research projects, have been scrutinized. While the former sources encompass the decisions and policies regarding Iran's APG flaring, the latter can provide analytical insight into the consequences of such decisions or the main reasons behind them.

3. APG Flaring in Iran as a Super-Wicked Policy Problem

3.1 Iran Oil Industry: Background

Oil exploration began in Iran when William D'Arcy obtained the concession for oil exploration in 1901, followed by oil production in Iran's southwest four years later. Today, the oil and gas industry is one of the largest and most important industries in Iran, with state-owned, private, foreign, and the so-called quasi-private entities simultaneously playing important roles. The main actors in this industry include[3]:

- The Ministry of Petroleum, which was established to exercise Iran's national ownership and sovereignty over the country's oil, gas, and petrochemical

[3]No precise legal definition exists for quasi-private institutions in Iran, leading to challenges in regulating and managing these entities. On the other hand, quasi-public institutions are privately owned entities with strong affiliations and connections to the government or other public institutions, often perceived as state-owned or state-controlled enterprises. This status allows them to circumvent extensive government regulations and bureaucratic layers, while their ongoing connections with influential government figures enable them to access state resources, such as government rents, when necessary. Many economic enterprises, such as some banks, oil refineries, transportation companies, oil and gas companies, can be run as quasi-private companies.

resources, industries, and facilities, and is responsible for various tasks, including policymaking, planning, monitoring operations, and activities of various units in these industries. This ministry has four main subsidiaries, including the National Iranian Oil Company (NIOC). In addition, companies whose more than 50% of their shares are owned by the Ministry of Petroleum's main subsidiaries are known as subsidiary companies under the Ministry of Petroleum.

NIOC, whose responsibilities mainly include exploration, production, and supply of crude oil, has divided its operational areas into three onshore and one offshore zone headed by its subsidiaries, including National Iranian South Oil Company (NISOC), Iranian Central Oil Fields Company (ICOFC), Arvandan Oil and Gas Company (AOGC), and Iranian Offshore Oil Company (IOOC) (NIOC, 2022).

- Private and foreign companies, which include hundreds of small and large companies operating in various segments of the oil value chain, such as production, refining, supply, and ancillary services. Despite in the first round of US secondary sanctions against investment in Iran's oil and gas industries in the early 1990s, some non-US companies decided to continue their business and only left with the intensification of sanctions on the pretext of Iran's nuclear program by the end of 2000s (Stevens, 2015, p. 5).[4]
- Quasi-private companies. They also engage in commercial activities, similar to private companies. However, their opaque ownership structure and political connections have led to concerns about rent-seeking and distortion of market competition. Three distinct types of such companies can be identified.

First are those established by individuals with political influence or close connections to them but whose capabilities originate from these connections and the main source of rents, namely the government. In contrast to those founded by political elites using their personal assets, these companies may have been established informally through a government official's decree to operate under the guise of being entirely private entities, to bypass legal limitations on governmental institutions. Nevertheless, their primary purpose is to fulfill needs predetermined by the government.

---

[4]The Iran and Libya Sanctions Act (ILSA) under P.L. 104–172 on August 5, 1996, (later, Iran Sanctions Act) after it ceased to apply to Libya in 2006, aimed initially to counter Iran's move to open its energy sector to foreign investment. ISA was the first significant extraterritorial sanction imposed on Iran, which authorized US penalties against third-country firms involved in investment in Iran's petroleum sector. For more details, see SEC. 5. IMPOSITION OF SANCTIONS in an archived version of the Act in https://www.govinfo.gov/content/pkg/STATUTE-110/pdf/STATUTE-110-Pg1541.pdf.

Second are the companies found by nongovernmental public institutions (especially the foundations or the so-called "bonyad").[5] In terms of Article 5 of Iran's Public Accounts Law, nongovernmental public institutions and organizations are those who are established to perform tasks and services that are essentially for public interests. However, since some of these institutions have significant financial turnover and budgets, in recent decades, they have penetrated in giant business activities, including in the oil and gas industry through their subsidiaries (Saeidi, 2004). For instance, the "Social Security Organisation (SSO)" is affiliated with the Ministry of Cooperatives, Labour, and Social Welfare. SSO's primary responsibilities are implementing, generalizing, and expanding various types of social insurance, as well as establishing a coordinated and appropriate system for social security programs. However, the organization is authorized to invest and exploit funds and deposits for social and investment purposes, and one of its significant investment companies is Tamin Petroleum & Petrochemical Investment Co (TAPPICO), which is specifically involved in the petroleum industry. SSO has 165 subsidiary companies as well proves its considerable power in the oil industry.[6]

Third are the Islamic Revolutionary Guard Corps (IRGC)–affiliated organizations. The prevalence of IRGC-affiliated companies has surged notably since the 2000s when international companies began withdrawing from Iran due to sanctions. The aim was to compensate for the absence of foreign firms while implementing a top-down economic development model enabling the government to control and advance the economy. As a result, these companies have been assigned multiple oil industry projects (Saidi, 2020).

As anticipated, the imposition of sanctions on Iran resulted in mounting financial pressures, leading to a surge in the magnitude of Iran's informal economy despite the economic reforms undertaken between 1997 and 2005 (Farzanegan, 2013). This, in turn, facilitated the consolidation of the quasi-private sector's dominance in the oil and gas industry. Fig. 1.1 shows the involved actors in Iran's oil industry.

3.2 APG Flaring

APG burning in Iran is a chronic problem that developed significantly since the early 1950s to the mid-1970s when excess natural gas was burnt in place due to its

---

[5]Foundation ("bonyad" in Farsi) refers to charitable foundations or organizations that play a significant role in various aspects of the country's economy, society, and welfare. Bonyads were initially established after the Iranian Revolution in 1979 to manage the assets and wealth that were confiscated from the Pahlavi dynasty and its associates. These foundations were intended to redistribute wealth, provide social services, and promote Islamic principles. It's important to note that bonyads are a complex and multifaceted aspect of Iran's socioeconomic landscape, and their role and influence have evolved over the years. While they were initially created to serve charitable and social welfare purposes, their activities have expanded into various sectors of the economy, making them a subject of ongoing debate and scrutiny within Iranian society.

[6]For more information, see https://en.tappico.com/at-a-glance and https://www.ssic.ir/en/.

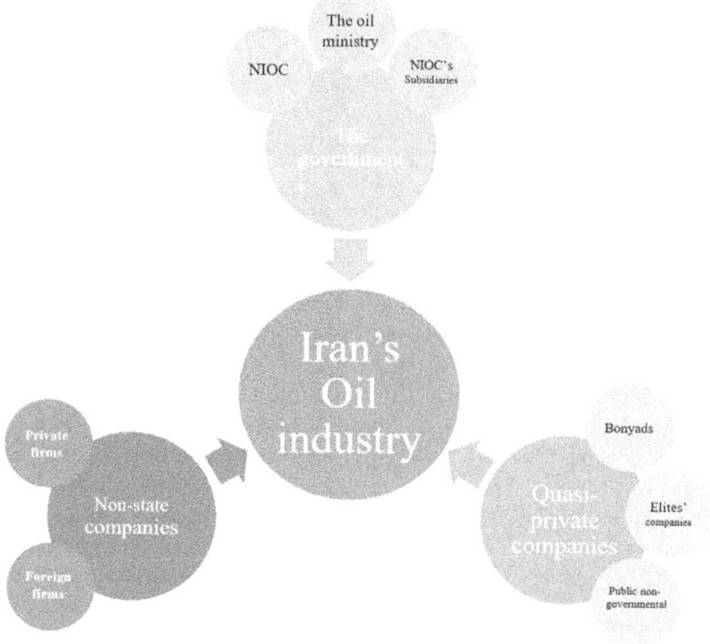

Fig. 1.1. Major Actors in Iran's Oil Industry. *Source:* Designed by author.

low value compared to oil. Attention to natural gas over time, especially after the oil crises in the 1970s, encouraged NIOC to plan to utilize APG. Since then, NIOC's plans for using produced APG have been mainly based on collecting APG streams to a specific point to refine and produce more valuable products, especially natural gas liquids (NGL). Such units are simply called NGL units (Babaei, 2020). Nevertheless, establishing the capital-intensive NGL plants was hampered mainly by consecutive political factors in the coming decades, from the revolution and military invasion of Iraq in the early 1980s to the sanctions against investment in Iran's oil and gas industry, limiting Iran's access to foreign direct investment. Therefore, the APG reduction goals were postponed several times (Soltanieh et al., 2016). Fig. 2.2 shows the persistence of the APG burning problem in Iran since 2007.

3.3 The Persistence of the APG Flaring

Despite the availability of different technical options which could be implemented instead of capital-intensive NGL units, the APG flaring problem has continued due to malfunctioning policies as follows.[7]

[7]Such as in-place gas-to-power, gas treatment, and reinjection to oil wells.

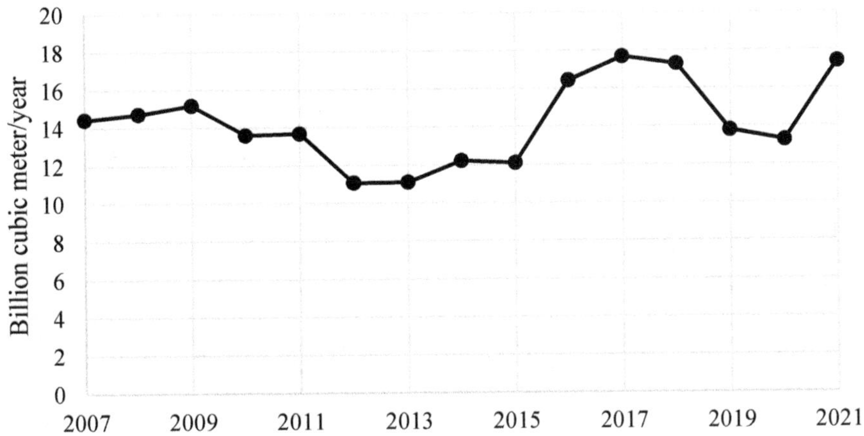

Fig. 2.2. APG Flaring Volume in Iran 2007–2021. *Source:* World Bank, Iran energy balance sheet 2015.

Adopting solutions for Iran gas flaring is still dependent on how decision-makers perceived APG flaring as a "problem" or how they prioritize it, besides other issues. In an oil exporting country dealing with sanction-generated challenges, there have always been more prioritized issues comparing to gas flaring reduction. While a strategic plan started with a careful and balanced definition of gas flaring as a problem is missing, opting for the best solution depends on decision-makers' personal opinions as to whether flaring is a significant problem (Mahdavi, 2016). According to Qayyoumi (2014), despite being established in the early 20th century, the administrative structure of the Iranian oil industry remains highly "traditional," meaning that it continues to be heavily influenced by personal relationships rather than bureaucracy, among other factors.[8] Managers are

[8]In the absence of modern institutional structures, the traditional bazaar is governed by time-honored practices, where each stall is presided over by its owner along with a select group of trusted confidants and relatives. Daily issues are handled traditionally; for instance, transactions in the bazaar are often conducted based on virtual credit, with the creditworthiness of a stall owner being assessed based on criteria such as age, religious faith, and the length of time they, or their ancestors, have operated within the bazaar. Moreover, the ability to advance within the bazaar is closely tied to an individual's capacity to quickly and effectively address issues and seize opportunities for personal gain rather than relying on established mechanisms. The bazaar's hierarchical structure is significantly influenced by the principle of "respect for elders," which comes into play especially when collective decisions, such as a decision to go on strike, need to be made. An institutional analysis addressing the relation between religion and the economy in Tehran bazaar has been provided by Ghomi et al. (2016). Keshavarzian (2007) has also presented a comprehensive book elaborating on different aspects of the bazaar as an institution, particularly before and after the Islamic Revolution of 1979.

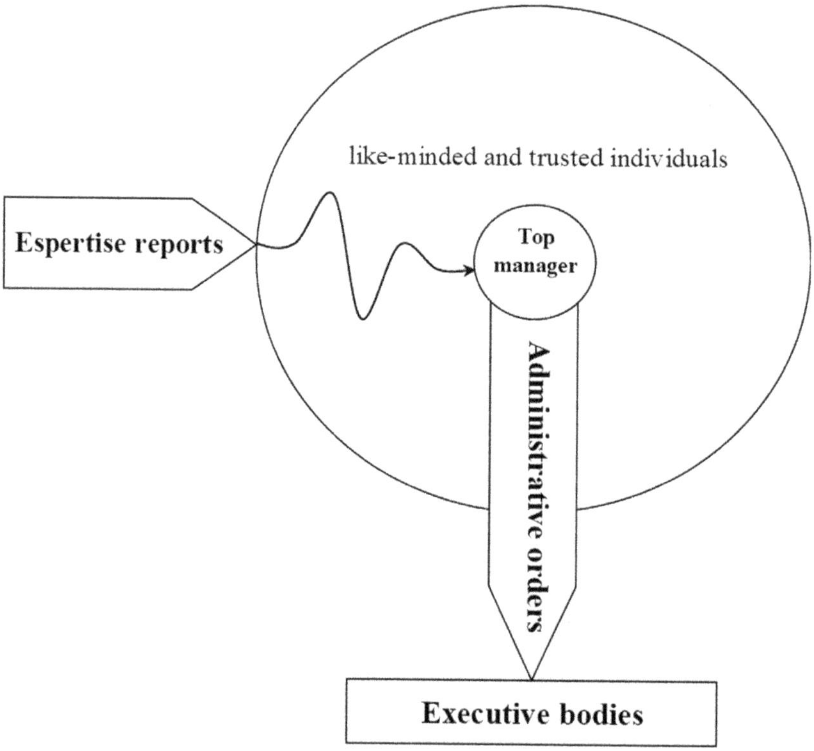

Fig. 3.3. Administrative Model in Traditional, Individual-Oriented Organizations. *Source:* Based on Qayyoumi (2014).

surrendered by their own designated like-minded and trusted individuals for decision-making, depicted symbolically in Fig. 3.3 by a surrounding circle. Although expertise departments and think tanks may submit reports, their outputs must pass through this surrounding ring – consisting of individuals who may lack expertise – to reach the center. Consequently, these reports may fail to reach the top manager, leaving the final decision at the discretion of the central individuals.

Given the described structure, solving the gas flaring issue depends on how the problem and the corresponding solution are understood by these individuals. Is it best to follow the "collecting in one-point option to feed them into the giant NGL units (added-value policy approach)"? Should they be refined and used in place (regional development approach)? Is it possible to export APG abroad (enhancing terms of trade policy)? Should they be directly converted into electricity (improving regional energy security approach)? Is injecting them into oil wells the best solution to increase oil production (oil industry development as a strategic priority)? Hence, the APG flaring has the first wicked policy characteristic as defined by Rittel and Weber, namely no definitive understanding of the problem or the solution is clear.

In the highly politicized Iranian oil industry (Hassanzadeh, 2014, p. 74), finding a transparent evaluation system for assessing the decisions is challenging. Opposite interest groups may highlight the adverse side effects of actions to demonize industry managers who have strong connections to one or more political groups. A relevant example can be the infamous unfulfilled Crescent gas export contract supposed to export gas from Iran to UAE in 2005. Political opposition parties heavily criticized and lobbied against the contract, accusing the government of "fire-selling" national wealth and calling the contract a "blatant betrayal" (Mozaffari, 2022; Torbat, 2020, p. 265). Although the contract was canceled due to political pressures, some experts argued that critics were not well-founded. Such a polarized perception was not an ordinary opinion gap, but it stems from different value judgments in accord with the group or personal interests, values, and ideological preferences. Therefore, every decision can later be realized as good or bad or as a "betrayal." This could imply the third feature of wicked policy problems where there is good or bad rather than true or false.

Since implementing technical solutions, i.e., establishing APG utilization plants, is costly and time-consuming, it cannot be practically undone once implemented. Although this is true, the complexity of the Iranian oil industry depicted in 2.1 makes the expenses of undoing decisions even higher; implementing a decision at high levels requires mobilizing resources and aligning the preferences of interest groups, which makes reversing a decision highly problematic, if not impossible. Furthermore, as a rentier state, the Iranian government is heavily dependent on oil and gas revenue; the oil rents are also a core element in the competition between major political factions interested in the rents or direct profits they earn from it (Kuhn, 2014, pp. 188, 338). In a polarized and politicized system of oil governance, undoing a decision can make decision-makers lose face and, more importantly, destroy their supporting groups. A reversal decision in major projects exposes the corresponding faction to harsh critics accusing them of incompetency and is highly detrimental to their fame. Hence, not only because of the nature of technical decisions in the oil industry but also because of the decision-making structure, undoing is expensive. In the same way, one can argue that decision-making about flaring reduction policies in Iran is sensitive enough that no one may dare to be wrong as they will be held accountable and blamed for the consequences of the decision. This proves the fifth and tenth features of wicked policies, according to Rittel and Weber, the "one shot" essence of the APG flaring problem in Iran and "no right to be wrong" for planners.

Iran's oil industry is plagued with significant governance problems, from privatization and corruption (Mehregan et al., 2019) to a high attrition rate (Hadi-Peykani & Khanifar, 2017) and sanctions. There is no reason to assume an already experienced successful solution for one area, if there is any at all, can inspire a solution for another, e.g., APG flaring. Moreover, even inside the APG flaring problem, one can never be sure that the particulars of a flaring case do not override its commonalities with other cases already dealt with. This could mean that the conditions in one specific flaring case may look similar, but transferring the former's solutions directly to the latter is neither advisable nor possible. This stems not just from the technical considerations but from contextual differences and the approaches that need to be adopted to convince corresponding decision-makers (given the complexities of decision-making in Iran's oil industry). For instance, local governments may expect one flaring reduction plan to reduce pollution and stimulate local job creation, but in another case, making higher profits is more desirable, even if gained by less job creation. The situation becomes more complicated, knowing that the preferences are sometimes not explicit. Therefore, different contextual conditions or local authorities' expectations may far outweigh similarities in general technical features. This could mean that the direct transference of engineering solutions into social policy might be dysfunctional in flaring reduction policies, which recalls the seventh characteristic of wicked policy problems; according to Rittel and Webber (1973), every wicked problem is essentially unique.

Further evidence shows that the APG flaring problem is extensively a symptom of higher level challenges, including repercussions of sanctions, structural flaws, and regulatory issues. Sanctions have limited Iran's access to technologies and industrial instruments, especially rotary equipment, e.g., compressors, needed for flaring reduction. In one case, the NGL project in Siri Island in the vicinity of the Hormuz Strait in the Persian Gulf has been repeatedly prevented from becoming fully operational because of imposed sanctions causing problems with the gas compression units. Additionally, Iran had to reduce its oil production level in 2012 due to international sanctions, which forced NIOC to extract oil from the shared fields, mainly offshore, with fewer plans for collecting the associated gas (Soltanieh et al., 2016). While the international sanctions against Iran's oil export were suspended after the 2015 Iran nuclear deal, the re-emergence of US sanctions against Iran in 2018 has hampered flaring reduction plans.[9]

Nevertheless, the repercussions of sanctions should not be interpreted only as barriers to foreign investment. They have also intensified the historical pessimism against foreign investment, especially among Iranian conservatives. Two opposite tendencies emerged in the late 1980s when the government aimed at economic development after the Iraq–Iran war: the conservatives' view prescribing robust government control over upstream resources and activities and the reformists who sought to create a more attractive environment for foreign investors. While the latter approach backed Iran's first and second five-year development plan (1989–1999), it coincided with the US secondary sanctions, especially the Iran–

[9]The Iran nuclear deal, or officially, the Joint Comprehensive Plan of Action (JCPOA), is an agreement reached between Iran and E3/EU+3 (Germany, the UK, France, China, Russia, and the US) and became operationalized in January 2016. According to it, Iran accepted partial restrictions on its nuclear program instead of E3/EU+3 manage to lift and suspend international and primary nuclear-based sanctions against Iran. Nevertheless, in the aftermath of Trump's decision to withdraw unilaterally from the deal in 2018, the United States resumed and intensified sanctions against Iran, including Iran's oil exports. Consequently, this hampered Iran's commercial relations with third parties.

Libya Sanctions Act (ILSA) (GovInfo, 1996). The ILSA aimed to punish American and third parties who cooperated or invested in Iran's oil and gas industry by more than $40 million (and later, $20 million) except for ad hoc exemptions. Since then, the US economic sanctions against Iran have been tightened as a punishment for alleged international transgressions. While sanctions influenced foreigners' intentions for investment adversely (van Bergeijk, 2015), Iranian conservatives took advantage to consolidate their narrative against the West. At the same time, IRGC and quasi-private companies tried to increase their penetration in the petroleum industry, as described in 2.1 section. Conservatives' narrative aimed to designate private foreign (Western) investment too unreliable for economic development in contrast to the sufficient indigenous resources also supported this trend. Such an approach was visible in the political discourse of conservatives, who have taken over the parliament and executive power since 2020. These political changes put the Islamic Republic's current foreign policy in opposition to the previous president, Hassan Rouhani, whose policy was characterized by his effort to improve economic conditions through lifting the sanctions and opening the economy for foreign investment (Mousavi et al., 2020).

In addition to sanctions, whose elimination depends on decisions at higher levels, recent research has shown that other significant problems, such as a high degree of politicization, corruption, and political group competition, have prevented Iran from effectively tackling its persistent domestic oil and gas problems (Damianova, 2018, p. 178). In the APG flaring case, the lack of incentive and punitive laws and regulations to reduce flaring, lethargic bureaucracy in decision-making, and restrictions on access to technical data needed for the private sector are among the most critical challenges at higher levels hindering flaring reduction plans in Iran (Taherifard et al., 2019). Such a description of the causes and origins of problems indicates that Iran's APG flaring problem is a symptom of problems at a higher level as discussed; sanctions, corruption, regulatory system, structural problems (rentier system), the role of interest groups, and even development policies and approaches which are all decided at the highest governmental level (wicked policy problem eighth feature), according to Rittel and Weber's taxonomy.

In addition to the characteristics of the wicked policy, four super-wicked policy features can also be seen in Iran's APG flaring problem. First, time is running out. From a technical point of view, Iran's oil wells are in the second half of their life (Emami-Meybodi et al., 2020), which means that with time, the ratio of their gas production to oil will increase and, as a result, the issue will become more complicated. In the current situation, it is possible to reinject the produced APG into the reservoir, which increases the oil production efficiency and solves the flaring problem. However, a further delay may mean the oil fields will reach the point where, from a technical point of view, the reinjection of APG will become useless, if not impossible.

Second, NIOC is expected to deal with the flaring pollution happening in its operational areas. Considering that the NIOC is a state-owned company, and the government is also the actor who should monitor, control, and reduce pollution, one realizes that the same actor causing the problem is responsible for resolving it. This is exacerbated when we note that the governmental environment agencies have weak authority to oblige NIOC to reduce flaring since the existing laws and regulations impose negligible environmental punishments against NIOC for flaring (Majlis Research Center, 2017). As quasi-private companies have gained a more significant role and dominance in the oil and gas industry, ensuring accountability for oil production and reducing flaring has become increasingly challenging. Thus, it is not surprising that NIOC's plans targeting zero-flaring have never been realized. Finally, as discussed earlier, flaring is a long-term and large-scale policy problem which has never been realized as an absolute priority. In such a situation, the public sector has not been able to tackle the problem, implying the last super-wicked policy problems feature.

The foregoing analysis reveals that Iran's APG flaring predicament exhibits several characteristics of a wicked problem. However, it does not display the second characteristic (lack of a clear endpoint), the fourth feature (absence of mechanisms to measure the effectiveness of proposed solutions), the ninth feature (existence of differences among stakeholders), and to some extent, the sixth feature (proliferation of potential solutions). From a "classical conceptualization" perspective (Sartori, 1970), Rittel and Weber's taxonomy defines wicked problems as possessing all 10 characteristics. While the strict classical framework can enhance the accuracy and precision of the wicked policy problem concept and discourage excessive labeling by governments, it also raises doubts about the existence of wicked problems at all (Peters & Tarpey, 2019). Thus, it is more appropriate to view wickedness as a variable that may assume varying degrees depending on the situation, rather than an all-or-nothing criterion.

Scholars have approached applying the wicked policy problem differently, even to the recent challenges like climate change and environmental problems, where gas flaring can also be classified. Many researchers have recognized climate change as a super-wicked problem, partly due to the time urgency and because those who caused the problem are now expected to solve it (Lazarus, 2008; Levin et al., 2012). On the contrary, Peters and Tarpey (2019) found that the statement "the same actors causing the problem seem to solve it is not descriptive of climate change in their research respondents" view, making it questionable to apply the wicked policy term. They suggested that environmental challenges can be better explained by the conceptual framework of complex than wicked. Similarly, Selman (2002) says that environmental issues are complex not for technical reasons but also for the multiple arenas where they are contested and debated.

Despite this division of opinion, it is still possible to consider the problem of gas flaring in Iran as a super-wicked problem by adopting a flexible approach. Iran's flaring problem has the key characteristics of a super-wicked policy problem so firmly that it makes the lack of inclusion of others less critical. Remarkably, considering that many wicked problems can lurch from crisis to crisis, this increases the need to recognize and act on them in time (Head, 2019). Moreover, the APG problem has all four features of super-wicked policy problems, so we can confidently classify it as belonging to this category. This can also be beneficial in emphasizing time sensitivity. Thus, recognizing gas flaring as a super-wicked policy urges decision-makers to step into action.

4. Conclusion: Policy Instruments and Strategies

This study investigated different dimensions of APG flaring in Iran as a problem that can be classified in the framework of sustainable development goals. The results showed that the APG flaring in Iran has the main characteristics of super-wicked policies, such as the absence of a definitive formulation, the irreversibility of decisions, and the causes of problems at higher levels, in addition to all four additional features that indicate its super-wickedness, especially since time is working against it, and we may reach the point of no return. Thus, one conclusion is that the continuation of flaring is due to its super-wicked nature rather than merely technical difficulties.

As discussed under the eighth feature of the APG flaring problem, it is a symptom of flaws in higher policymaking levels which are highly resistant to reform. Hence, until other major bad governance problems have been dealt with, we may alleviate the APG flaring issue within the current organizational structure instead of solving it completely. This point resonates with the similar view of Rittel and Webber about chronic conditions of wicked problems; they can only be settled, never solved (Rittel & Webber, 1973, p. 160). Such an approach also resembles coping strategies in dealing with wicked policy problems: to keep and run the organizations to maintain service provision within the limits of acceptability yet improve it at best, as Wallace (2008) suggests.

While their wickedness makes it impossible to present a one-fit-for-all solution, some proposed outlines from the previous research could be recommended for the Iran APG case. Tackling the wicked policy problems requires dealing with their complexity and the disagreements among actors, among other things (Head & Alford, 2015). Several researchers point to the role of discursive methods in forming a shared value vision among stakeholders and helping them adopt and implement a coherent action in line with these shared values (Head, 2019). Despite this, the circle of actors in the APG flaring problem is so closed that the same actor causing the problem (the state-owned NIOC) is expected to solve it, reflecting the third super-wicked policy problems' features. Therefore, the first step should be to open this closed circle by relying on a new actor, e.g., the private sector. This resembles one of Roberts' actor-oriented solutions for wicked problems, namely the authoritative strategy in which more stakeholders are encouraged to be involved. Creating pseudo-brainstorming among the actors is expected to reduce the complexity and achieve a suitable solution acceptable to the majority (Roberts, 2000).

Nevertheless, a key question is whether NIOC is motivated to accept a new player in the APG flaring issue, given the complex landscape of actors described in section 2.3. Addressing this concern involves assuring NIOC that it will not be unfairly accused, especially by other influential bodies, such as the judiciary, of conducting a "fire sale" of the national wealth if the private sector or foreign companies purchase APG for utilization as a feedstock (see section 3.3 for similar cases). Additionally, legal punitive instruments, i.e., specific environmental fines, should be outlined by which NIOC is faced considerable environmental punishments if it does not solve the APG flaring issue. This will set the stage for creating new true-or-false criteria where negligence in flaring reduction results in a direct loss for the NIOC, which demands decision-makers' "true" actions as the wicked policy problem theory defines.

Simultaneously, a shared value framework should be established in which NIOC decision-makers are persuaded to find solving the APG flaring problem in collaboration with the private sector as a beneficial solution, for instance, by accentuating the relative benefits. NIOC's annual income from Iran's oil exports could be around $65.7 billion. The expected income from selling all currently burning flared gases will not exceed $400 million, which is not comparable with oil export revenue. As mentioned before, NIOC's performance has been historically assessed by its success in maintaining or increasing Iran's oil production and export level rather than APG utilization.[10] Therefore, handing over the exploitation of these gases to the private sector does not threaten NIOC's income or performance but saves it from punishment. At the same time, the pricing and contract terms and conditions must be attractive enough to reduce uncertainties for the private sector and provoke them to contribute, as its fundamental goal is profit-making.

Nevertheless, the implementation of such an idea will have its difficulties. NIOC managers, especially conservative ones, may resist handing over flaring APG streams to the private sector. Particularly, in the absence of a robust private sector, such a decision may lead to an increased dominance of quasi-private companies, thereby exacerbating the aforementioned vicious cycle of monitoring. The urgency and significance of flaring issues must be comprehended by high-level decision-makers, who must recognize that continuing the current situation is a pure loss. One can initiate the private sector's contribution from the younger NIOC's subsidiaries, where such conservatism is usually less.

However, it is simplistic to assume that other significant problems do not influence the implementation of such decisions. This research suggests that higher policy structures, although highly influential, are too sluggish to change; therefore, their flaws will remain. For instance, implementing environmental fines requires transparent financial structures free of corruption. In addition, the sanctions will continue to curtail procurement of the necessary equipment, even if the private sector is involved. Finally, the flaws of the regulatory system can still exacerbate uncertainties for the private sector and make it reluctant to contribute. Considering all the challenges, solving the flaring problem is not straightforward on paper, as the nature of super-wicked problems entails.

[10] The estimation assumes Iran's oil export is in its nonsanctioned conditions, i.e., almost 2.4 million barrels per day, and the average oil price is $75 per barrel. The untreated APG is priced at $20 per 1,000 cubic meters.

References

Ajugwo, A. O. (2013). Negative effects of gas flaring: The Nigerian experience. *Journal of Environment Pollution and Human Health*, *1*(1), 6–8.

Allen, D. T., Smith, D., Torres, V. M., & Saldaña, F. C. (2016). Carbon dioxide, methane and black carbon emissions from upstream oil and gas flaring in the United States. *Current Opinion in Chemical Engineering*, *13*, 119–123.

Babaei, Z. (2020). ISNA. www.isna.ir/news/99013118510. Accessed on August 27, 2022.

Brennan, A. (2004). Biodiversity and agricultural landscapes: Can the wicked policy problems be solved? *Pacific Conservation Biology*, *10*(10), 124–142.

Caulton, D. R., Shepson, P. B., Cambaliza, M. O., McCabe, D., Baum, E., & Stirm, B. H. (2014). Methane destruction efficiency of natural gas flares associated with shale formation wells. *Environmental Science & Technology*, *48*(16), 9548–9554.

Chester, L. (2009). *Does the polysemic nature of energy security make it a 'wicked' problem?* (pp. 159–171). World Academy of Science, Engineering and Technology.

Damianova, K. K. (2018). Iran's post-sanctions oil and gas management. In S. Raszewski (Ed.), *International political economy of oil and gas* (pp. 175–192). Palgrave Macmillan.

Emami-Meybodi, A., Dashab, M., & Akbari-Birgani, M. (2020). Examining the challenges and attractiveness of international service contract models in financing the upstream projects of the oil industry of Iran and Iraq. *Iranian Energy Economics Research Journal*, *9*(36), 11–48.

Farzanegan, M. R. (2013). Effects of international financial and energy sanctions on Iran's informal economy. *The SAIS Review of International Affairs*, *33*(1), 13–36.

Funke, J. (1991). Solving complex problems: Exploration and control of complex systems. In R. Sternberg & P. Frensch (Eds.), *Complex problem solving – Principles and methods* (pp. 185–222). Lawrence Earlbaum Associates.

Ghomi, M. H., Bagheri, S., & Mansouri, F. (2016). An institutional approach to the Tehran Bazaar. *International Journal of Religious Education*, *4*(4), 16–31.

Giwa, S. O., Nwaokocha, C. N., Kuye, S. I., & Adama, K. O. (2019). Gas flaring attendant impacts of criteria and particulate pollutants: A case of Niger Delta region of Nigeria. *Journal of King Saud University-Engineering Sciences*, *31*(3), 209–217.

GovInfo. (1996). *United States Government Publishing Office (GPO)*. https://www.govinfo.gov/content/pkg/STATUTE-110/pdf/STATUTE-110-Pg1541.pdf. Accessed on September 17, 2022.

Hadi-Peykani, M., & Khanifar, A. (2017). Explanation and prioritization of the factors affecting key employees' turnover intention in privatized firms of National Oil Company (case study: Ahvaz pipe industrial company). *Strategic Studies in the Oil and Energy Industry*, *8*(31), 153–175.

Hassanzadeh, E. (2014). *Iran's natural gas industry in the post-revolutionary period: Optimism, scepticism, and potential* (1st ed.). Oxford University Press.

Head, B. W. (2019). Forty years of wicked problems literature: Forging closer links to policy studies. *Policy and Society*, *38*(2), 180–197.

Head, B. W., & Alford, J. (2015). Wicked problems: Implications for public policy and management. *Administration & Society*, *47*(6), 711–739.

Keshavarzian, A. (2007). *Bazaar and state in Iran: The politics of the Tehran marketplace*. Cambridge University Press.

Khalili-Garakani, A., Iravaninia, M., & Nezhadfard, M. (2021). A review on the potentials of flare gas recovery applications in Iran. *Journal of Cleaner Production*, *279*, 123345.

Kuhn, M. (2014). *Enabling the Iranian gas export options* (1st ed.). Springer.

Lack, D. A., Moosmüller, H., McMeeking, G. R., Chakrabarty, R. K., & Baumgardner, D. (2014). Characterizing elemental, equivalent black, and refractory black carbon aerosol particles: A review of techniques, their limitations and uncertainties. *Analytical and Bioanalytical Chemistry*, *406*, 99–122.

Lazarus, R. J. (2008). Super wicked problems and climate change: Restraining the present to liberate the future. *Cornell Law Review*, *94*, 1153.

Levin, K., Cashore, B., Bernstein, S., & Auld, G. (2012). Overcoming the tragedy of super wicked problems: Constraining our future selves to ameliorate global climate change. *Policy Sciences*, *45*(2), 123–152.

Mahdavi, R. (2016, March). *Associated petroleum gas is not a priority in the Iran Ministry of Oil* (pp. 101–104). Energy Diplomacy.

Majlis Research Center. (2017). *The experience of selected states in APG gathering: Lessons for Iran*. Majlis Research Center.

Mansoor, R., & Tahir, M. (2021). Recent developments in natural gas flaring reduction and reformation to energy-efficient fuels: A review. *Energy & Fuels*, *35*(5), 3675–3714.

McConnell, A. (2018). Rethinking wicked problems as political problems and policy problems. *Policy & Politics*, *46*(1), 165–180.

Mehregan, M. R., Hosseinzadeh, M., & Foroushani, M. S. (2019). Strategic modeling of the corruption in the oil industry of Iran: An application of system dynamic approach (original text in Farsi: مدل سازی استراتژیک مبارزه با فساد در صنعت نفت ایران: کاربردی از رویکرد پویایی سیستم). *Iranian Public Policy Journal* (فصلنامه سیاستگذاری عمومی), *5*(3), 165–187.

Mousavi, S. Q., Azin, A., & Jafarinejad, M. (2020). Discourse analysis of the foundations of development in the government of Hassan Rouhani. *Humanidades & Inovação*, *7*(4), 282–292.

Mozaffari, F. (2022). The controversial crescent contract. https://legamart.com/articles/the-controversial-crescent-contract/. Accessed on August 27, 2022.

Murphy, J. (2022). Gas pathway. https://gaspathways.com/pioneer-halves-methane-intensity-from-2019-baseline-1090. Accessed on August 13, 2022.

NIOC. (2022). *National Iranian oil company*. www.nioc.ir/fa-IR/nioc/4958/page. Accessed on August 27, 2022.

Noe, S. M., Tabakova, K., Mahura, A., Lappalainen, H. K., Kosmale, M., Heilimo, J., Salzano, R., Santoro, M., Salvatori, R., Spolaor, A., & Cairns, W. (2022). Arctic observations and sustainable development goals – Contributions and examples from ERA-PLANET iCUPE data. *Environmental Science & Policy*, *132*, 323–336.

Noordegraaf, M., Douglas, S., Geuijen, K., & Steen, M. V. D. (2019). Weaknesses of wickedness: A critical perspective on wickedness theory. *Policy and Society*, *38*(2), 278–297.

Peters, B. G. (2017). What is so wicked about wicked problems? A conceptual analysis and a research program. *Policy and Society*, *36*(3), 385–396.

Peters, B. G., & Tarpey, M. (2019). Are wicked problems really so wicked? Perceptions of policy problems. *Policy and Society*, *38*(2), 218–236.

PourMirza, A. (2017). Gas flaring status, trend and policy around the Persian Gulf. *Energy Sources, Part B: Economics, Planning and Policy*, *12*(3), 250–259.

Qayyoumi, A. (2014). *A historical analysis of Iran's oil and gas industry*. I.R.Iran Vice-Presidency for Science and Technology.

Rittel, H. W., & Webber, M. M. (1973). Dilemmas in a general theory of planning. *Policy Sciences*, *4*(2), 155–169.

Roberts, N. (2000). Wicked problems and network approaches to resolution. *International Public Management Review*, *1*(1), 1–19.

Roberts, N. (2001). Coping with wicked problems: The case of Afghanistan. In J. G. L. Jones & P. Steane (Eds.), *Learning from international public management reform: Part B* (pp. 353–375). Emerald publishing Limited.

Romsom, E., & McPhail, K. (2021). *Capturing economic and social value from hydrocarbon gas flaring and venting: Solutions and actions*. WIDER Working Paper, Helsinki.

Ross, D., Leonard, B., & Inayatullah, S. (2022). Leadership beyond the great pause: Climate change and other wicked problems. *Journal of Futures Studies*, *24*(4), 15–22.

Russell, C. L. (2008). An overview of the integrative research review. *Progress in Transplantation*, *15*(1), 8–13.

Saeidi, A. A. (2004). The accountability of para-governmental organizations (bonyads): The case of Iranian foundations. *Iranian Studies*, *37*(3), 479–498.

Saidi, H. (2020). *The political economy of the IRGC's involvement in the Iranian oil and gas industry: A critical analysis*. University of Amsterdam.

Sartori, G. (1970). Concept misformation in comparative research. *American Political Science Review*, *64*(4), 1033–1053.

Selman, P. (2002). Three decades of environmental planning: What have we really learned? In M. Kenny & J. Meadowcroft (Eds.), *Planning sustainability* (pp. 158–184). Routledge.

Soltanieh, M., Zohrabian, A., Gholipour, M. J., & Kalnay, E. (2016). A review of global gas flaring and venting and impact on the environment: Case study of Iran. *International Journal of Greenhouse Gas Control*, *49*, 488–509.

Spicker, P. (2016). *Poverty as a wicked problem*. CROP Secretariat.

Stevens, P. (2015). *Prospects for Iran's oil and gas sector*. Chatham House for the Royal Institute of International Affairs.

Taherifard, A., Mahdavi, R., Sahebhonar, H., Keypour, J., & Kamali, M. (2019). *Associated petroleum gas gathering in Iran* (1st ed.). Talab.

Taherifard, A., Mahdavi, R., Sahebhonar, H., Khakpour, M. A., & Keypour, J. (2016). Designing model of associated petroleum gas pricing with emphasis on sale of gas to Ngl Units: Case study of feed pricing of Ngl-3200. *Iranian Energy Economics*, *5*(20), 187–225.

Tahmasebzadehbaie, M., & Sayyaadi, H. (2022). Technoeconomical, environmental, and reliability assessment of different flare gas recovery technologies. *Journal of Cleaner Production*, *367*, 133009.

The World Bank. (2022). *Gas flaring explained*. https://www.worldbank.org/en/programs/gasflaringreduction/gas-flaring-explained#:~:text=Gas%20flaring%20is%20the%20burning,appropriate%20regulation%20and%20political%20will

Torbat, A. E. (2020). *Politics of oil and nuclear technology in Iran* (1st ed.). Palgrave Macmillan.

Torraco, R. J. (2005). Writing integrative literature reviews: Guidelines and examples. *Human Resource Development Review*, *4*(3), 356–367.

van Bergeijk, P. (2015). *Sanctions against Iran-A preliminary economic assessment*. European Union Institute for Security Studies (EUISS).

Wallace, M. (2008). *The dynamics of coping: Maintaining normal public service while orchestrating complex change*. Management (IRSPM XII), Brisbane.

Zayer Kabeh, K., & Khoshkhoo, R. H. (2021). Economic feasibility of small-scale gas to liquid technology in reducing flaring in Iran and case study of implementing the technology at the third South Pars refinery. *Energy Equipment and Systems*, *9*(4), 317–330.

Chapter 5

State Capacity and Wicked Problems: Examining the Agri-Environmental Topic Through Media Framing and the Legislative Agenda in Brazil

María Alejandra Costa and Éric Montpetit

University of Montreal, Canada

Abstract

This chapter explores how the capacity of different sectors of the government influences which topics are prioritized in the legislative agenda. We focus on the complex and challenging topic of agriculture and the environment in Brazil and analyze how it's framed in both the media and the legislature. Our analysis shows that, in normal circumstances, the governmental actors with the highest state capacity prevent threatening topics from entering the legislative agenda, biasing it toward the status quo. However, we find that the media can act as a tool for sectors with lower capacity to bring their priorities to the forefront and trigger a legislative response.

Keywords: State capacity; wicked problems; agriculture and environment policy; legislative agenda; media framing

1. Introduction

Contemporary democracies face intricate issues that do not have straightforward solutions, as evidenced by the literature. To facilitate prosperity and growth, advanced democratic societies need to incorporate Sustainable Development Goals (SDGs) into their policymaking processes, prioritizing fundamental aspects such as the economic and social welfare of nations. However, governments encounter "wicked problems" that require reconciling conflicting interests to achieve comprehensive development (Maidin, 2022). Policymakers and stakeholders engage

Policy Capacity, Design and the Sustainable Development Goals, 89–117

Published under exclusive licence by Emerald Publishing Limited
doi:10.1108/978-1-80455-686-320241006

in debates on the most pressing topics of modern life, often interpreting and proposing solutions that align with their prior beliefs, leading to disagreements. The "wicked problem" literature identifies state capacity as one of the significant challenges for democratic governments in tackling complex and challenging topics, referring to the skills, resources, and capabilities necessary to achieve political goals (Wu et al., 2015).

However, while most of the studies on wicked problems are focused on advanced democracies (Capano et al., 2020; Head & O'Flynn, 2015; Pattyn & Brans, 2015), little is known about policy definitions (Rochefort & Cobb, 1993) in unconsolidated democracies, in which state capacities to address complex problems vary significantly from one policy field to the next. In these countries, traditional policy fields, defense, for example, tend to enjoy disproportionately high capacity in comparison with newer fields. Brazil provides an ideal case study due to the uneven distribution of capabilities across policy fields. Our study focuses on the SDGs that seek to promote *Economic Growth* and *Life on Land.* Our case study is particularly relevant because these objectives seem to conflict with each other. On the one hand, the agricultural sector prioritizes economic growth without considering the environmental degradation it causes, which contradicts the objective of progressively enhancing global resource efficiency in terms of consumption and production, while ensuring that economic growth does not lead to environmental harm (Goal 8.4). Secondly, our analysis considers Goal 15 (Life on Land), which advocates for sustainable forest management, the cessation of deforestation, the restoration of degraded forests, and a significant increase in global afforestation and reforestation.

Since the country has the biggest exportation of raw materials and its economic growth was mainly focused on exporting primary materials such as soybeans and corn, the agricultural field has been the sector with the most significant influence on political priorities for much of Brazilian history (Escobar, 2011). However, during the last decades, the environmental damages produced by the proliferation of agribusiness and the environmental impacts related to Amazon deforestation and the use of pesticides have gained a pride of place among ecological advocates, who are concerned about environment preservation (Nasrala Neto et al., 2014; Sauer, 2018). Environmental capacity within the state, however, is extremely weak, especially when compared with state capacity in agriculture.

Thus, Brazil constitutes a case of particular interest since the debate about the wickedness of the agri-environmental topic has been structured around the opposition between agribusiness who advocate for economic growth and affordable food and the environmental groups which defend the preservation of the environment and the implementation of sustainable practices, which are aligned with the SDGs (Hochstetler & Keck, 2007).

Because policymakers have a large amount of information and the time and attention are limited resources (Jones & Baumgartner, 2005), they must decide how to prioritize and integrate this information into the policy process. State and nonstate experts are useful resources in the process of prioritization (Nutley et al., 2007). However, scholars have shown that relying on expertise could fail at finding solutions for complex problems, which requires the integration of information from different expert sources and stakeholders (Rittel & Webber, 1973; Schön & Rein, 1995). While dealing with wicked problems, a search for diverse information, known as "entropic search," appears more appropriate than a narrower one (Baumgartner & Jones, 2015). However, the result of information diversity is the opposite of clarity. The more the government searches for information to address a problem, the more information will be found, which likely brings confusion in the policymaking process. Entropic search is likely to put on the agenda divergent frames and problem perceptions, generating debates rather than a consensual solution to a given problem.

In policy fields with high state capacity, governmental experts are more likely to influence problem definition and limit information search to their community of like-thinking experts, resulting in policy solutions that represent, at best, modest departures from the status quo. Nevertheless, the public policy literature has shown that inertia in policy, while being the norm, can be broken, that policy debates and actor mobilization can occasionally be expanded, triggering large policy changes (Schattschneider, 1960). To achieve debate expansion, the media is a valuable resource. Groups whose concerns are weakly represented in the distribution of state capacities among policy fields can turn to the media to present their own understandings of problems, encourage nongovernmental experts to speak out, and hope to attract the attention of policymakers (Baumgartner & Jones, 1993; Majone, 1989; Walgrave & Vliegenthart, 2010).

In this chapter, we study the wicked problem of environmental harms caused by agriculture in Brazil. We ask, under what conditions can this problem arise on the legislative agenda, given weak environmental state capacity and strong agricultural state capacity in the country? We argue that wicked problems characterized by weak state capacity in one problem dimension require a media coverage that will encourage a mobilization of interests likely to attract the attention of policymakers. Specifically, we test the hypothesis that an increase in the media coverage of agri-environmental problems in Brazil will increase the presence of agri-environmental problems on the legislative agenda. To add complexity to the argument, reactions are not a one-way street: the media also reacts to legislative activity, reducing its attention to a topic when it gets the sense that legislators have satisfactorily addressed the concerns on which the coverage had focused its attention. When this happens, capacity imbalances within the state return as a factor inducing biases in the ways wicked problems are addressed. In this regard, once the less influential groups perceive their need to have been met and incorporated to the legislative agenda, the pre-existing power imbalance between agricultural and environmental groups tends to resurface as a dominant factor.

2. Data

For this study, we built an original database of media coverage and legislative bills in Brazil between 2000 and 2020. We limit our analysis to this period because of the availability of information. The data are compiled by year. We have conducted an inductive analysis to select the most frequent agri-environmental topics in the media and legislative agendas. We found that *Amazon deforestation* and *pesticide use* are by far the most frequent topics on both agendas. We used a text analysis technique to classify press articles and bills on each topic, in view of comparing the media and legislative agendas.

2.1 Legislative Agenda

In this chapter, we focus on the legislative agenda, Brazil having a presidential system that enables legislators to be responsive to problems prioritized in the media coverage. Legislative bills are readily available and have been frequently used in studies of political agendas (Baumgartner & Jones, 1993; Soroka, 2002; Wilkerson et al., 1999). Therefore, the dependent variable in this chapter is the number of bills on Amazon deforestation and pesticide use introduced into the Brazilian Chamber of Deputies.

2.2 Media Agenda

Newspaper coverage has been extensively employed in scholarly investigations concerning public opinion and media agenda dynamics (Baumgartner & Chaqués Bonafont, 2015; Erbring et al., 1980; Shaw & Martin, 1992). The media agenda, which serves as the primary independent variable in this study, encompasses the number of news articles related to Amazon deforestation and pesticide utilization, as featured in Brazil's newspaper with the largest circulation: *Folha de S. Paulo*.

It is worth noting that the Brazilian media landscape is characterized by market-driven conglomerates (Matos, 2008). While the ideological orientation of media outlets could conceivably influence their coverage of events, as suggested in existing literature (Weaver & Scacco, 2013), recent studies (Mourão, 2019) have provided compelling insights into the uniformity of Brazilian media in covering protest events. The insights underscore the consistent nature of media reporting across a range of outlets, justifying our reliance on a single major newspaper.

2.3 State Capacity

As previously mentioned, state capacity is defined in this chapter as the set of skills, resources, and capabilities necessary to achieve political goals. This definition of state capacity takes into consideration three dimensions: analytical, operational, and political (Wu et al., 2015). Firstly, *analytical capacity* refers to the use of information in each sector and is measured through the number of employees per ministry. According to the data collected from the Brazilian government: the Ministry of Agriculture (MAPA) has an annual average of 36.300 employees, while the Ministry of Environment (MMA) has an annual average of 5.300 employees.[1] From this statistic, we can confidently conclude that state capacity in agriculture is much stronger than it is in the environment.

[1]See Table A1 in the Annex.

Secondly, *operational capacity* involves the process of transforming information from each political sector into public policy instruments that can effectively address identified topics. *Operational capacity* was measured using two indicators: the overall federal budget allocated to each ministry and the distribution of federal funds toward agri-environmental policies within each ministry, particularly those related to regulating deforestation practices and the use of pesticides. Firstly, our analysis demonstrates that the MAPA is significantly larger than the Ministry of Environment. However, the funds allocated to programs by the MAPA primarily focus on agribusiness and do not take into account public policies aimed at regulating deforestation and the use of pesticides. On the contrary, the Ministry of Environment invests in agri-environmental policies.[2]

Finally, *political capacity* refers to the power of a government entity to garner public support for its preferred public policies (Mukherjee et al., 2021). Literature suggests that achieving political capacity involves prioritizing a particular topic on the political agenda (Batley & Mcloughlin, 2015). Therefore, supra-party groups or informal caucuses emerge in the National Congress to advocate for specific and sectoral causes, ideas, and interests. These groups organize debates and aim to influence decisions in support of the public policy agenda they defend. Throughout history, the *ruralist caucus* has been one of the most prominent caucuses in Brazilian Congress, with a significant number of parliamentarians who have direct and formal connections to the agribusiness sector (Departamento Intersindical de Asesoria Parlamentar, 2015). Therefore, the overrepresentation of economic interest groups linked to the agribusiness sector in the Brazilian Congress has hindered the development of public policies that effectively serve the interests of society as a whole (Machado, 2018).

We measured the *political capacity* by counting the number of legislators who are part of the informed caucuses.[3] Although the composition of the caucuses may change over time due to changes in legislatures, our analysis shows that the *ruralist caucus*, linked to the agro-sector, has historically been among the most important in the Brazilian Congress.

2.4 The Framing of Media and Legislative Topics

To analyze the two topics, deforestation and pesticide use in the two agendas, the media and the legislature, we made a random selection of 50% of the full database. Coding the entire body would have been resourceful and would have added very little precision in comparison to a representative sample. Concerning *Deforestation* in the media agenda ($N = 686$), we distinguished four framings:

(1) *Environment activism:* the coverage mostly speaks about environmental advocates' manifestations and actions.

---

[2]See Tables A2 and A3 in the Annex.
[3]See Table A4 in the Annex.

(2) *Environment preservation:* here, the coverage mostly speaks about pollution, water crisis, climate change, animal preservation, forest preservation, illegal deforestation, and indigenous topics.
(3) *Sustainable practices:* here, the coverage mostly speaks about practices to preserve the environment and make it more sustainable.
(4) *Agribusiness:* here, the coverage emphasizes agribusinesses.

A framing refers to a particular emphasis, giving an angle to a news story on a topic, deforestation here. Framings are not mutually exclusive, news articles sometimes reporting on the various angles of a topic, activism versus agribusiness, for example. Here, we associated each article to a single framing, the one that is dominant in the article. We distinguish between framing as they enable us an analysis of the correspondence between the media and legislative agendas that is far more detailed than if we had stayed at the level of topics.

For the legislative agenda ($N = 40$), we used the same framings, but *Environment Activism.* Instead, we added a framing that we labeled *Illegal Deforestation*, which emphasizes deforestation that exceeds the limits allowed by the *Forest Code* law.[4] Note that given the total number of legislative bills, we did not have to rely on random sampling here and coded the entire body of bills.

For *Pesticides*, we used a similar process. We distinguished the same four framings for the media ($N = 279$) and legislative agendas ($N = 69$), excluding environmental activism from the latter.[5]

3. Method

Our study's central argument is that environmental groups' influence over the legislative agenda will be more significant in periods when their arguments are more visible in the media. We conducted a systematic and chronological descriptive statistical analysis of our variables of interest, legislative bills and media coverage. This statistical analysis was complemented by an in-depth qualitative analysis of the topics in the news media and legislative bills.

Our analysis focuses on the bills introduced in the Chamber of Deputies. This choice is based on the institutional design of the Brazilian legislative system, which deserves some explanation. Brazil has a symmetrical bicameral legislative system, and the individual members of both chambers, the deputies and senators, have equal rights to present bills. The Chamber of Deputies in Brazil comprises 513 deputies, while the Senate consists of 81 senators. As a result, most legislative discussions in Brazil take place in the Chamber of Deputies. This is not only because the lower house has more representatives but also because bills proposed by the Executive Branch are initially voted on by the deputies (Schneider & de Marques, 2016). Therefore, the cost of information is inversely proportional to

[4] See Tables A5 and A6 in the Annex.
[5] See Tables A7 and A8 in the Annex.

the size of the chamber, which implies that the upper house has fewer motivations to propose legislation compared to the lower house (Rogers, 1998).

The president has the right to introduce bills on any topic. In addition, the president enjoys exclusive rights to initiate legislation on public administration, tax and the budget, as well as having veto powers. Through powers to introduce provisional decrees, the president can exercise direct control over the legislative process (Neto et al., 2003). However, there is a debate in the literature regarding the actual legislative participation of the president, who might exercise some restraint depending on the fragmentation of the chamber and the ideological distance between parties (Pérez-Liñán & Rodríguez-Raga, 2009).

Because media activity is much more voluminous than legislative activity, each variable in the descriptive statistical analysis was scaled to an indicator ranging from 0 to 100 and measures the saliency of the framings. This method enables comparisons between legislative and media agendas, but it is worth underlining that the relatively small frequency of legislative bills in comparison to news articles makes saliencies in the legislative agenda much more volatile than the saliency in the media agenda. The introduction of just 2 or 3 bills with a particular framing can produce a large variation on the legislative agenda while 2 or 3 news articles would make the variation on the media agenda barely visible.

To avoid bias in the study, we dismissed news articles reporting legislative activities in strict factual matter, failing to address the topic in any particular framing. The quantitative analysis reflects the quantity of news articles and legislative bills that match each topic: *deforestation* and *pesticides use*.

In qualitative analysis, we focus on periods characterized by the highest levels of environmental activism, as evidenced by media coverage. Regarding deforestation, two periods were selected: 2011–2012, during the debate over the Forest Code, and the first two years of Jair Bolsonaro's presidency: 2019–2020. For pesticides use, we selected the year 2019.

4. Results and Discussion

Brazilian deforestation and the use of pesticides and agrochemicals represent two of the most complex agri-environmental challenges in Brazil's history. The issue's intricacy stems from the diverse range of interests at play. Agribusiness advocates for economic growth and accessible food, while environmentalists oppose the excessive exploitation of natural resources in favor of environmental preservation (Hochstetler & Keck, 2007).

Throughout our analysis, we observed that media coverage and legislative actions are intricately linked, underscoring the strong connection between these two agendas. It's crucial to note that the capacity of the agricultural sector within the state significantly surpasses that of the environmental sector. Consequently, under typical circumstances, this discrepancy does not result in substantial changes in the status quo or public policy. However, when the environmental sector effectively extends the conflict beyond the state's borders through their advocates, they can mobilize allies who question the legitimacy and credibility of the agricultural sector. It's only after the conflict escalates that the agricultural sector makes limited concessions.

As our analysis demonstrates, both sectors hold contrasting interests regarding deforestation and pesticide use. Nevertheless, the environmental sector, through the expansion of conflicts and heightened media visibility, can challenge the legitimacy of the agricultural sector and secure concessions.

In the case of the *Forest Code* debate, the Chamber of Deputies introduced legislation to address illegal deforestation only after activists initiated a series of actions to expose the government's alignment with the agricultural sector (see Fig. A1 in the Annex). Moreover, during the inaugural year of Jair Bolsonaro's presidency, actions advocating for agriculture and adverse to environmental concerns witnessed a notable proliferation. Concerning deforestation, it wasn't until the end of 2019, following media attention and international credibility concerns about the government, including figures like the Pope, that the Chamber of Deputies introduced several bills to combat deforestation (see Fig. A2 in the Annex).

Finally, the pesticide issue follows a similar pattern. In 2019, the media published numerous studies reflecting public concern about the adverse effects of pesticides and agrochemicals on both health and the environment. Only after these events did the Chamber of Deputies respond by introducing bills to regulate these actions (see Fig. A3 in the Annex).

In summary, our findings uncover the intricate interplay of political, economic, and environmental forces in shaping policy outcomes in Brazil. This chapter highlights that the inertia of public policy can be transformed through the ability of environmental stakeholders to escalate conflicts and gain visibility, which has proven pivotal in driving change within these agri-environmental issues.

4.1 Qualitative Analysis 2011–2012: The Forest Code Debate in Brazil and a Partial Victory for Agribusiness

When looking at framings, we observe that environmental activism and preservation were particularly important in 2011–2012 and in 2019–2020. In May of 2011, the Brazilian Chamber of Deputies approved a bill to update the regulation of the *Brazilian Forest Code*. Among the bill's main points was the implementation of an amendment that makes the protection of the country's extensive forests more flexible, enabling further advances of agricultural land in the Amazonian Forest. The bill also granted amnesty to those responsible for illegal deforestation before 2008.

Following the introduction of the bill, environmental and ecological interest groups began publicly expressing their discontent with government intentions. In our descriptive statistics for 2011, we observe that the framings in the media were distributed disproportionately in favor of environmental advocates and environmental preservation: 43% of the news concentrated on *Environment preservation*, 38% on *Environment activism*, 10% on *Agribusiness*, and 10% on *Sustainable practices*. In contrast, *Environment activism* was about 22% in the previous period, which means it grew by 16% in only 1 year.

The environmental activists' framing underlines the need for a proper debate about the *Forest Code* while criticizing Dilma's government for not reaching a consensus with the whole of society. Activists, as reported by the media, carried out demonstrations calling for society to wake up to the problems with the code. The following citations are representative of the media coverage of deforestation at the time:

> The #florestafazadifença is a communicative arm, a way to present to society the need for this debate. **They say that the code results from a consensus, which is not true**.
>
> *Source:* https://www1.folha.uol.com.br/poder/2011/12/1017109-organizacoes-civis-protestam-contra-novo-codigo-florestal-no-rio.shtml

> Let us show that we are not few and we are willing to change this situation. Let us wake up those still sleeping. **Let us march for a better future** for our children and us.
>
> *Source:* https://www1.folha.uol.com.br/cotidiano/2011/07/944930-manifestantes-marcham-contrabelo-monte-e-codigo-florestal-em-sp.shtml

The agribusiness framing was also present in the media in 2011, but with much less intensity. As stated above, it represented 10% of the coverage. The agribusiness framing was related to the necessity of deforestation as a means of food production, as we can see in the citation below:

> According to Kátia Abreu, president of CAN (National Confederation of Agriculture), **the project puts an end to the agony of Brazilians**. More than 24,000 farmers came here to demonstrate the desperation of each one. **Of them, 99% are with their food production in illegality**.
>
> *Source:* https://www1.folha.uol.com.br/ambiente/898878-protestos-esquentam-debate-sobre-novo-codigo-florestal.shtml

4.2 The Forest Code Debate in Brazil

As the months passed and the conflict expanded, the environmental groups intensified their protest. Under the slogan: "Veta Dilma," they built their narrative against the implementation of the *Forest Code*. Among the points most criticized by environmental activists was the controversial provision of the bill that granted amnesty to illegal deforesters prior to 2008.

In 2012, 40% of the media coverage about deforestation matched the *Environment activism framing*, and the activism was more specifically against the *Forest Code*. The news stories reminded the Brazilian president about the promises made during the presidential campaign not to give amnesty and denounced the advantages of the bill for the agricultural sector at the expense of deforestation.

> **She assumed a campaign commitment**. She said she did not favour the amnesty and would not reduce the legal reserve area. Let us see if she will comply, said the Atlantic Forest Network coordinator of NGOs, Renato Cunha. For him, the code passed in the House of Representatives **was more like an agricultural code than a *Forest Code*.**
>
> *Source:* https://www1.folha.uol.com.br/ambiente/920706-ambientalistas-apostam-em-veto-de-dilma-ao-codigo-florestal.shtml

> Master of ceremonies at an event in Rio this Friday, the actress Camila Pitanga addressed President Dilma Rousseff. She said: I will break the protocol. **Veta the law, Dilma**!
>
> *Source:* https://m.folha.uol.com.br/poder/2012/05/1085608-camila-pitanga-pede-veta-dilma-em-cerimonia-no-rio.shtml

As the debate expanded in the media, environmental nongovernmental organizations (NGOs) and members of the scientific community joined in, criticizing the government for its lack of support for environmental protection.

> **It is not possible that farmers oligarchies in Brazil decide** [on the *Forest Code*] **and the population remains quiet**. We do not give up; the game is not over, said Mário Mantovani of SOS Mata Atlântica. **The current government is acting in the opposite direction** to the path we were following in environmental public policies, said João Paulo Capobianco, president of the Board of Directors of IDS (Democracy and Sustainability Institute).
>
> *Source:* https://www1.folha.uol.com.br/poder/2011/12/1017109-organizacoes-civis-protestam-contra-novo-codigo-florestal-no-rio.shtml

The environment organization *Greenpeace* denounced that the Brazilian president was an ally of agribusiness:

> The so-called amnesty for deforesters is the main point of environmental activists' anger at the march. The *Forest Code* creates a dangerous precedent for the continued deforestation of Brazilian

> forests, said Sergio Leitao, campaign director of Greenpeace. Signs carried by protesters said: **Dilma, a puppet of the rural sector**.
>
> *Source:* https://www1.folha.uol.com.br/ambiente/2012/06/1107724-protesto-de-ongs-ocupa-principal-avenida-do-centro-do-rio.shtml

4.3 Dilma's Veto and the Environment Policy Field Victory

After a long debate that lasted several months and under pressure from environmental groups, Brazilian President Dilma Rousseff finally vetoed the *Forest Code* bill on May 25, 2012. The presidential veto removed 12 articles from the original bill, and more than 30 modifications were made. The main modification to the original bill was that those who illegally destroyed the forest before 2008 would not benefit from an amnesty.

> "**The veto was decided to avoid an amnesty for those who deforested**. We will not allow environmental protection to be reduced", said Izabela Teixeira, Minister of the Environment. (NBC, 2012)

The victory of the environment over the agricultural policy field does not only rest on the presidential veto. It also manifested itself in the framing of bills introduced in the Chamber of Deputies between 2011 and 2012. Three agri-environmental bills were introduced with the preservation of the environment as their primary objective.

> According to the study, through the analysis of public policies implemented in the Cerrado, it is observed that there has been progress in recent years, with the survey of vegetation cover and also with the priority areas for conservation, and the beginning of monitoring and the removal of native vegetation in the biome. **However, the study warns that important actions still need to be developed**.
>
> *Source:* https://www.camara.leg.br/proposicoesWeb/prop_mostrarintegra?codteor=1018213&filename=PL+4307/2012

After the media pressure exerted during the forestry code debate and according to our argument, the legislative agenda in 2013 was focused exclusively on regulating illegal deforestation.

> **Illegal deforestation is an extremely serious problem** in Mato Grosso, the Amazon, the Cerrado and many other places in our country. Expanding agriculture and cattle raising in our territory is

> beneficial and must be increased. However, **environmental conservation** for the improvement of the quality of life of the population **cannot be forgotten**.
>
> *Source:* https://www.camara.leg.br/proposicoesWeb/fichadetramitacao?idProposicao=589598

4.4 Environmental Public Policy in the Bolsonaro Era

Jair Bolsonaro assumed the presidency of Brazil on the first of January 2019; the right-wing candidate pledged to reduce government commitments to environmental conservation. He notably promised access to an environmental license facilitating corporate investments. Among the most controversial measures was the closing down of the Environment Ministry, which is also responsible for the Brazilian Institute of Environment and Renewable Natural Resources (Ibama) and the Chico Mendes Institute for Biodiversity Conservation (ICMBio). After facing criticism, Bolsonaro ultimately decided to keep the Ministry (Pereira et al., 2019).

The measures taken by Jair Bolsonaro were directly associated with the preservation of agribusiness interests. In Brazil, 24% of the gross domestic product (GDP) comes from agribusiness; moreover, the trade war between the United States and China has increased the demand for Brazilian commodities and facilitated Amazon deforestation (Arruda et al., 2019). During the general debate of the 74th session of the General Assembly, Bolsonaro declared that: "it is a fallacy that the Amazon is the heritage of humanity or the lungs of the planet" (BBC, 2019).

As a result of the president's measures and declarations, as well as the environmental disasters during the first 2 years of his mandate, social movements and civil organizations demonstrations gained momentum. In 2019, the media coverage related to *Environmental Activism* represented 27% and reached the peak in the period covered in this chapter. Consequently, the news related to *Environment Preservation* and *Sustainable Practices* occupied 49% and 16%, respectively, while those associated with *Agribusiness* were only 9%.

In August 2019, the Amazon rainforest was devastated by fires, and land use for cattle ranching and soya planting was partly to blame. Jair Bolsonaro was under intense international pressure to control these fires and avoid an environmental catastrophe (BBC, 2019). The expansion of the conflict by environmental groups even found an echo in the Catholic Church, as we can see in the quotation below of the message of Pope Francisco:

> As has been customary since the beginning of his pontificate, Pope Francisco emphasized attention to the poor as a priority for the church. In this synod, **we have had the grace to listen to the voices of the poor** and reflect on the precariousness of their lives, **threatened by predatory models of progress**.
>
> *Source:* https://www1.folha.uol.com.br/poder/2019/10/saque-desfigura-o-rosto-da-amazonia-diz-papa-francisco-ao-encerrar-o-sinodo.shtml

Brazilian artists also joined the demonstrators through art expression. They wrote a song, *We are the World*, whose main objective was to denounce the relationship between government and corporations and to alert the population about the loss of vegetation in the Amazon at the hands of deforesters.

> "It is not a problem that has to be solved by us alone. The biggest problem is in the hands of big corporations," he says. "If we do our part, we take the attention away from holding big corporations accountable. **We need to address political issues and pressure governments and big corporations**, which make us believe that we have to solve the problem by recycling our waste, eating organic, and riding bicycles. Moreover, it is not enough."
> *Source:* https://www1.folha.uol.com.br/ambiente/2019/12/artistas-lancam-musica-para-alertar-sobre-crise-climatica.shtml

As we have shown with the *Forest Code*, President Jair Bolsonaro's public policy decisions about Amazon preservation were the targets of environmental groups during his first 2 years of mandate. However, at the outset of 2019, and as a result of pressure from NGOs and media exposure, the president ultimately reversed his policy of merging ministries. The government's decision was influenced by the balance of power between agribusiness, which was under pressure from raw material importers that had previously refused to purchase products originating from the deforested Amazon, and the pressure from global public opinion. Bolsonaro's statement came after criticism from the then ministers of the environment, Edson Duarte, and agriculture, Blairo Maggi, who was also an investor in the soybean sector. Maggi declared that the measure could have consequences for the agribusiness sector (Menezes, 2020). As Greta Thunberg mentioned: "activism threatened the Brazilian government."

> They feel they should silence us because we have become too noisy compared to what they can handle; **we have become a threat**.
> *Source:* https://www1.folha.uol.com.br/ambiente/2020/06/viramos-uma-ameaca-diz-greta-thunberg-em-encontro-virtual-com-jovens-brasileiros.shtml

4.5 Deforestation on the Legislative Agenda

Despite Jair Bolsonaro's controversial policies and the environmental crises of his mandate, between 2019 and 2020, the legislative agenda registered the highest introduction rates of bills on environment preservation. And this increase followed an intensive media coverage of deforestation. The framing of illegal deforestation accounted for 66% during this period. Below is a good illustration of the content of the bills.

> A study published in July in the journal Science, called *The rotten apples of Brazilian agribusiness*, concluded that **2% of properties in the Amazon and Cerrado regions are responsible for more than 60% of illegal deforestation alone practiced in these biomes.**
>
> *Source:* https://www.camara.leg.br/proposicoesWeb/prop_mostrarintegra?codteor=1938219&filename=PL+5014/2020

4.6 The Use of Pesticides: Economic Growth Versus Environment Preservation

Brazil is the world's largest importer of pesticides and has also been one of the primary consumers during the last 20 years. According to the *New York Times* (2019), the Brazilian market is not only attractive because of its potential as the world's third largest exporter of agricultural products, but also because it is cheap to obtain permission to sell pesticides.

In 2019, the number of pesticides and the rate of registration in Brazil were the highest since the MAPA started documenting them in 2005. Since the beginning of 2016, under the government of Michel Temer, the increase in the use of pesticides in Brazil has accelerated, reaching a historic peak in 2019 with 474 registrations, representing an increase of 356% in comparison with the situation 10 years before.[6] MAPA and the agribusiness sector insist that legislation must encourage pesticide use by maintaining their cost at the lowest possible level, thereby keeping the agricultural sector competitive on the world markets and securing affordable food.

As we have shown with deforestation, the increasing use of pesticides in Brazil has generated controversy, with environmental activists warning about the consequences of pesticide use on health and the environment. In 2019, the media coverage of pesticide use reached a maximum, peaking at 13%. Moreover, 92% of this coverage was framed in terms of environmental preservation. The specific distribution was as follows: *Healthy and Environmental Consequences* 67%, *Environmental Activism* 17%, *Sustainable Practices* 8%, and *Agribusiness* 8%.

The news related to environmental activism started on January 2019 and was led by young Brazilians who objected to the environmental policies of Jair Bolsonaro. Below is a quotation showing the tone of the media coverage:

> Extinct species, **the risks of pesticides**, the impact of livestock on the emission of Brazilian greenhouse gases. Even with the focus on macro climate change topics, the universe closer to young people was also part of the discussion.
>
> *Source:* https://www1.folha.uol.com.br/ambiente/2019/05/protesto-pelo-clima-em-sp-pede-acoes-imediatas-e-tem-encontro-com-autoridade.shtml

---

[6] https://www.canalrural.com.br/noticias/nacional/ministerio-da-agricultura-apreende-fertilizantes-e-agrotoxicos

> **These problems in the river's headwaters compromise the entire basin**, not just locally. It is a river that was already born with problems, with loss of water availability, in a critical situation, comments Malu Ribeiro, the water specialist at the SOS Mata Atlântica Foundation.
>
> *Source:* https://www1.folha.uol.com.br/cotidiano/2019/09/mancha-de-poluicao-no-rio-tiete-volta-a-crescer-apos-tres-anos.shtml

As with deforestation, the government's actions have been at the center of criticisms by environmental groups. Precisely, in August 2019, rural workers joined indigenous and fisherwomen in a protest to pressure the Brazilian government, asking for gender equality, sustainable agriculture, and restrictions on the use of pesticides.

> **We built a platform with the model of society. It is not aligned with what the government is doing, which is to remove the rights of workers and women**, says Mazé Morais, general coordinator of the March.
>
> *Source:* https://www1.folha.uol.com.br/poder/2019/08/marchas-de-mulheres-indigenas-e-camponesas-se-unem-em-pressao-a-bolsonaro.shtml

As we have already mentioned, the use of pesticides is a highly complex problem and its framing is sometimes counterintuitive. The *Agribusiness* framing, for example, includes native people who appreciate their new found prosperity owing to good jobs in agri-food corporations.

The indigenous perspective on the agri-environmental topic is multifaceted and complex. While the Bolsonaro administration has prioritized economic growth over environmental conservation, some indigenous communities have surprisingly benefited from these policies. The indigenous population of the Utiriati locality in the Mato Grosso region has formed contracts with agricultural producers who offer them technical expertise and equipment for the economic exploitation of their lands. However, this activity is prohibited by the Constitution as it constitutes a "land lease," whereas indigenous lands are intended for the exclusive use of indigenous peoples. Therefore, the pro-agribusiness framings have more than one twist. While mostly oriented toward economic growth, it sometimes integrates social concerns.

The quotation below provides a good illustration:

> "Here, 20 years ago, guards were at the supermarket doors because they thought Indians would steal. **Today they open their doors to us**; they know we will buy", says Arnaldo, a member of the Paresi indigenous group in the Mato Grosso region.
>
> *Source:* https://www1.folha.uol.com.br/ambiente/2019/05/indios-pro-bolsonaro-querem-ampliar-lavoura-de-soja-e-desafiam-fiscalizacao.shtml

4.7 Pesticide Uses on the Legislative Agenda

The primary aim of this chapter is to investigate the correlation between how the media portrays agri-environmental issues and the legislative agenda. As such, we've identified periods of heightened environmental coverage, specifically focusing on two agricultural practices: deforestation and pesticide use. It's noteworthy that the coverage of pesticide use and the introduction of pesticide-related bills in the legislature exhibit similar patterns, in alignment with our hypothesis. In 2019, a peak of 92% of bills related to pesticides introduced in the Chamber of Deputies was framed in terms of their health and environmental implications. The following quotation provides insight into the bill contents and serves as an illustrative example of this framing:

> According to the Brazilian Agricultural Research Corporation (Embrapa), **the contamination of water, land, animals, and workers by pesticides is potentiated by area spraying**, as the practice results in a strong runoff of the chemical product beyond the application target.
>
> *Source:* https://www.camara.leg.br/proposicoesWeb/prop_mostrarintegra;jsessionid=node09e427diu3glw118g483sc2hj599876.node0?codteor=1786145&filename=PL+4302/2019

5. Conclusion

While our analysis is preliminary, we have found that in policy fields with limited state capacity, the media can play a significant role in raising awareness of key issues and shaping the legislative agenda. By giving voice to civil society actors whose concerns are not adequately represented in government, the media can prompt legislators to introduce bills that address these issues. However, we have also observed that legislators aligned with environmental interests, particularly those in the Workers' Party (PT), are more likely to take advantage of media momentum to push their preferences to the legislative agenda. Given the over-representation of agribusiness interests in the Brazilian Congress, this suggests that leveraging media attention may be a key strategy for promoting environmental preservation in public policy. Nevertheless, addressing complex "wicked problems" such as the environmental impact of agriculture requires careful analysis of contradictory information from multiple sources.

On the one hand, agribusiness, which is essential for the economy and affordable food, pleads for moderation when it comes to the adoption of environmental constraints. On the other hand, environmental activists are concerned that some agricultural practices, such as deforestation and pesticide use, will harm the environment and human health. Policymakers have scarce resources and limited time and, therefore, struggle to obtain all the information from the wide range of experts and stakeholders needed to make the best possible decisions (Baumgartner & Jones, 2015). Most of the time, they will satisfy themselves with the information provided by the strongest group of government experts and legislators, which is the agricultural sector in this case. Furthermore, as we have demonstrated through the analysis, policymakers are often entrenched and aligned with powerful agricultural interests. Therefore, the over-representation of the agribusiness sector in Congress makes it difficult for pro-environmental legislators to shift the balance of power and the dynamic of the agenda. The result will be, at best, minor adjustments from the status quo and continued dissatisfaction among people who disapprove of the way the topic is framed and addressed by these actors.

These people, environmental activists, for example, will not easily let go, trying to mobilize as many people as possible against the governmental approach. And in their effort to mobilize people, the media plays an important role. In fact, when the topic about which they are concerned, agricultural pollution, for example, gets sufficient coverage and when the topic is framed in ways that capture their concerns, the legislative agenda can change in their favor. This is precisely what happened in 2019 with the topic of pesticide use. After intense media coverage, framing the topic in ways that echoed the concerns of environmental activists, Brazilian legislators introduced bills in Congress that addressed these concerns. In a sense, the media made up for the weakness of governmental environmental actors. However, as Witko et al. (2021) has pointed out, weaker policy fields require herculean efforts to shift the balance of power and influence public policy change, particularly when compared to stronger policy fields. Introducing environmental bills will not necessarily strengthen governmental capacity on the environment. If it fails to do so, the attention of legislators to agricultural pollution is likely to fade. In fact, government reactivity, as Soroka and Wlezien (2009) have shown, works a little like a thermostat. Legislative activity that stems from intense media coverage of agricultural pollution is likely to reduce media attention to the topic at the benefit of other topics. Media attention to these other topics is likely to alter the legislative agenda, attracting it to these other topics just as it once was attracted to agricultural pollution. Having fallen outside the span of attention, the strong group of agricultural experts within government is likely to become again the major source of information of policymakers whenever topics in relation to agriculture, including pollution, emerge. The resulting policy adjustments might even undermine any progress made on the front of agricultural pollution when the topic was on top of the legislative agenda. And this situation will likely prevail until agricultural pollution becomes again a major topic of media attention.

In this chapter, we have shown that the process whereby wicked problems are addressed by government requires an account of relative state capacities in the policy fields relevant to the problem, as well as to media coverage. We have shown that when state capacities are strong in one field and weak in the others, turning the attention of legislators toward the concerns in these latter fields can be achieved through media attention. As media attention diminishes once legislators have addressed the concerns previously put forth in the press, imbalances in the distribution of state capacities are likely to regain a pride of place as a factor influencing how legislators address the wickedest of problems.

References

Amazon rainforest belongs to Brazil, says Jair Bolsonaro. (2019, September 24). *BBC News.*

Arruda, D., Candido, H. G., & Fonseca, R. (2019). Amazon fires threaten Brazil's agribusiness. *Science*, *365*(6460), 1387. https://doi.org/10.1126/science.aaz2198

Artistas brasileiros lançam 'We are the World' do clima; veja clipe. (2019, December 20). Folha de S.Paulo. https://www1.folha.uol.com.br/ambiente/2019/12/artistas-lancam-musica-para-alertar-sobre-crise-climatica.shtml

Azevedo, G. (2022, September 6). *Ministério da Agricultura apreende fertilizantes e agrotóxicos.* Canal Rural. https://www.canalrural.com.br/noticias/nacional/ministerio-da-agricultura-apreende-fertilizantes-e-agrotoxicos/

Baumgartner, F. R., & Jones, B. D. (1993). *Agendas and instability in American politics.* University of Chicago Press.

Baumgartner, F. R., & Chaqués Bonafont, L. (2015). All News is Bad News: Newspaper Coverage of Political Parties in Spain. *Political Communication*, *32*(2), 268–291.

Baumgartner, F. R., & Jones, B. D. (2015). *The politics of information: Problem definition and the course of public policy in America.* University of Chicago Press.

Brazil's Rousseff enacts forest law in blow to farm lobby. (n.d.). *NBC News.* https://www.nbcnews.com/id/wbna49469259. Accessed on November 15, 2022.

Camila Pitanga pede 'veta, Dilma' em cerimônia no Rio–04/05/2012–Poder–Folha de S.Paulo. (n.d.). https://m.folha.uol.com.br/poder/2012/05/1085608-camila-pitanga-pede-veta-dilma-em-cerimonia-no-rio.shtml. Accessed on April 15, 2024.

Capano, G., Howlett, M., Jarvis, D. S. L., Ramesh, M., & Goyal, N. (2020). Mobilizing policy (In)capacity to fight COVID-19: Understanding variations in state responses. *Policy and Society*, *39*(3), 285–308.

Erbring, L., Goldenberg, E. N., & Miller, A. H. (1980). Front-page news and real-world cues: A new look at agenda-setting by the media. *American Journal of Political Science*, *24*(1), 16–49.

Escobar, A. (2011). *Encountering development: The making and unmaking of the third world.* Princeton University Press.

Folha.com–Ambiente–Ambientalistas apostam em veto de Dilma ao Código Florestal –25/05/2011. (n.d). https://www1.folha.uol.com.br/ambiente/920706-ambientalistas-apostam-em-veto-de-dilma-ao-codigo-florestal.shtml. Accessed on April 15, 2024.

Folha.com–Ambiente–Protestos esquentam debate sobre novo Código Florestal–06/04/2011. (n.d). https://www1.folha.uol.com.br/ambiente/898878-protestos-esquentam-debate-sobre-novo-codigo-florestal.shtml. Accessed on April 15, 2024.

Head, B. W., & O'Flynn, J. (2015). Australia: Building policy capacity for managing wicked policy problems. In *The international handbook of public administration and governance* (pp. 341–368). Edward Elgar.

Hochstetler, K., & Keck, M. E. (2007). *Greening Brazil: Environmental activism in state and society.* Duke University Press.

Índios pró-Bolsonaro querem ampliar lavoura de soja e desafiam fiscalização. (2019, May 20). *Folha de S.Paulo.* https://www1.folha.uol.com.br/ambiente/2019/05/indios-pro-bolsonaro-querem-ampliar-lavoura-de-soja-e-desafiam-fiscalizacao.shtml

Jones, B. D., & Baumgartner, F. R. (2005). *The politics of attention: How government prioritizes problems.* University of Chicago Press.

Machado, M. (2018). *Doação ou investimento? Financiamento e atuação da bancada ruralista: O comportamento legislativo dos parlamentares da bancada ruralista e o financiamento de campanhas eleitorais no Brasil*. Novas Edições Acadêmicas.

Maidin, A. J. (2022). Governance of SDGs: Solving the wicked problem. In *Good governance and the sustainable development goals in Southeast Asia*. Routledge.

Majone, G. (1989). *Evidence, argument, and persuasion in the policy process*. Yale University Press.

Mancha de poluição no rio Tietê volta a crescer após três anos. (2019, September 18). *Folha de S.Paulo*. https://www1.folha.uol.com.br/cotidiano/2019/09/mancha-de-poluicao-no-rio-tiete-volta-a-crescer-apos-tres-anos.shtml

Manifestantes marcham contra Belo Monte e Código Florestal em SP - 17/07/2011—Cotidiano. (2024, April 15). *Folha de S.Paulo*. http://www1.folha.uol.com.br/cotidiano/944930-manifestantes-marcham-contra-belo-monte-e-codigo-florestal-em-sp.shtml

Marchas de mulheres indígenas e camponesas se unem em pressão a Bolsonaro—14/08/2019—Poder—Folha. (n.d.). https://www1.folha.uol.com.br/poder/2019/08/marchas-de-mulheres-indigenas-e-camponesas-se-unem-em-pressao-a-bolsonaro.shtml. Accessed on April 15, 2024.

Matos, C. (2008). *Journalism and political democracy in Brazil*. Lexington Books.

Menezes, T. C. C. (2020). Environmental governance and regularization of land ownership: Development and multiple territorial dynamics in the Amazon. *Vibrant: Virtual Brazilian Anthropology*, *17*.

Ministério da Agricultura, Pecuária e Abastecimento—Português (Brasil). (n.d.). https://www.gov.br/pt-br/orgaos/ministerio-da-agricultura-pecuaria-e-abastecimento. Accessed on November 14, 2022.

Mourão, R. R. (2019). From mass to elite protests: News coverage and the evolution of antigovernment demonstrations in Brazil. *Mass Communication and Society*, *22*(1), 49–71.

Mukherjee, I., Coban, M. K., & Bali, A. S. (2021). Policy capacities and effective policy design: A review. *Policy Sciences*, *54*(2), 243–268.

Nasrala Neto, E., Lacaz, F. A. de C., & Pignati, W. A. (2014). Health surveillance and agribusiness: The impact of pesticides on health and the environment. *Danger ahead! Ciência & Saúde Coletiva*, *19*, 4709–4718.

Neto, O. A., Cox, G. W., & McCubbins, M. D. (2003). Agenda Power in Brazil's Câmara Dos Deputados, 1989–98. *World Politics*, *55*(4), 550–578.

Nutley, S. M., Walter, I., & Davies, H. T. O. (2007). *Using evidence: How research can inform public services* (1st ed.). Bristol University Press.

Organizações civis protestam contra novo Código Florestal no Rio–05/12/2011–Poder. (2024, April 15). http://www1.folha.uol.com.br/poder/1017109-organizacoes-civis-protestam-contra-novo-codigo-florestal-no-rio.shtml

Pattyn, V., & Brans, M. (2015). Organisational analytical capacity: Policy evaluation in Belgium. *Policy and Society*, *34*(3), 183–196.

Pereira, E. J., Silveira Ferreira, P. J., de Santana Ribeiro, L. C., Sabadini Carvalho, T., & de Barros Pereira, H. B. (2019). Policy in Brazil (2016–2019) threaten conservation of the Amazon rainforest. *Environmental Science & Policy*, *100*, 8–12.

Pérez-Liñán, A., & Rodríguez-Raga, J. C. (2009). Veto players in presidential regimes: Institutional variables and policy change. *Revista de Ciencia Política (Santiago)*, *29*(3).

Protesto de ONGs ocupa principal avenida do centro do Rio–20/06/2012–Ambiente. (2024, April 15). *Folha de S.Paulo*. http://www1.folha.uol.com.br/ambiente/1107724-protesto-de-ongs-ocupa-principal-avenida-do-centro-do-rio.shtml

Protesto pelo clima em SP pede ações imediatas e tem encontro com autoridade–24/05/2019–Ambiente–Folha. (n.d.). https://www1.folha.uol.com.br/ambiente/2019/05/protesto-pelo-clima-em-sp-pede-acoes-imediatas-e-tem-encontro-com-autoridade.shtml. Accessed on April 15, 2024.

Radiografia do Novo Congresso—DIAP – Departamento Intersindical de Assessoria Parlamentar. (n.d.). https://www.diap.org.br/index.php/publicacoes/category/13-radiografia-do-novo-congresso. Accessed on March 10, 2023.

Rittel, H. W. J., & Webber, M. M. (1973). Dilemmas in a general theory of planning. *Policy Sciences*, *4*(2), 155–169.

Rochefort, D. A., & Cobb, R. W. (1993). Problem definition, agenda access, and policy choice. *Policy Studies Journal*, *21*(1), 56–71.

Rogers, J. R. (1998). Bicameral sequence: Theory and state legislative evidence. *American Journal of Political Science*, *42*(4), 1025–1060.

Sauer, S. (2018). Soy expansion into the agricultural frontiers of the Brazilian Amazon: The agribusiness economy and its social and environmental conflicts. *Land Use Policy*, *79*, 326–338.

Schattschneider, E. E. (1960). *The Semisovereign People: A Realist's View of Democracy in America*. Holt, Rinehart and Winston.

Schneider, M., & de Marques, A. A. B. (2016). Green or grey: Origin, bias and fate of environmental bills in the Brazilian National Congress. *Journal of Legislative Studies*, *22*(4), 528–539.

Schön, D. A., & Rein, M. (1995). *Frame reflection: Toward the resolution of intractable policy controversies*. Lexington Books.

Shaw, D. L., & Martin, S. E. (1992). The function of mass media agenda setting. *Journalism Quarterly*, *69*(4), 902–920.

Soroka, S. N. (2002). Issue attributes and agenda-setting by media, the public, and policymakers in Canada. *International Journal of Public Opinion Research*, *14*(3), 264–285.

Soroka, S. N., & Wlezien, C. (2009). *Degrees of democracy: Politics, public opinion, and policy*. Cambridge University Press.

The Chamber of Deputies. (n.d.). *Portal da Câmara dos Deputados*. https://www2.camara.leg.br/english/copy_of_index_html. Accessed on November 11, 2022.

Walgrave, S., & Vliegenthart, R. (2010). Why are policy agendas punctuated? Friction and cascading in parliament and mass media in Belgium. *Journal of European Public Policy*, *17*(8), 1147–1170.

Weaver, D. A., & Scacco, J. M. (2013). Revisiting the protest paradigm: The tea party as filtered through prime-time cable news. *The International Journal of Press/Politics*, *18*(1), 61–84.

Wilkerson, J. D., Feeley, T. D., Schiereck, N. S., & Sue, C. (1999). *Policy interest and legislative responsiveness: Bill introductions as indicators of topic salience*. Presented at the American Political Science Association Annual Meeting, Atlanta.

Witko, C., Morgan, J., Kelly, N. J., & Enns, P. K. (2021). *Hijacking the agenda: Economic power and political influence*. Russell Sage Foundation.

Wu, X., Ramesh, M., & Howlett, M. (2015). Policy capacity: A conceptual framework for understanding policy competences and capabilities. *Policy and Society*, *34*(3–4), 165–171.

Annex

JANUARY 2010	Negotiations between political parties regarding the text of the new forest code have begun, which pits environmentalists against the agricultural sector.
JANUARY TO FEBRUARY 2011	***Media Coverage***: There is ongoing tension in the region where Dorothy Stang, an American nun and Amazon activist who advocated for land rights and environmental protection in Brazil, was tragically assassinated. Additionally, scientists have voiced criticism against the recently enacted Forest Code.
APRIL TO JULY 2011	***Media Coverage***: Intense protests and debates over the new Forest Code. Environmentalists hope for Dilma's veto.
NOVEMBER TO DECEMBER 2011	***Media Coverage***: Demand for Dilma's promises regarding deforesters. Civil organizations protest against the new Forest Code in Rio de Janeiro.
MARCH TO MAY 2012	The Chamber of Deputies initiates the Forest Code vote. ***Media Coverage***: Protests escalated during March, April, and May 2012, involving environmental activism, Greenpeace actions, and criticism of the Forest Code. Activists accuse Dilma of being aligned with the agricultural sector.
MAY 25, 2012	***Dilma vetoed deforestation*** forgiveness in APPs but allowed amnesty for small rural properties. She permitted reserve compensation in degraded areas, raising conservation concerns.
AFTER MAY 25, 2012	***Media Coverage***: Continuing protests, agreements, and incidents related to environmental issues, including Greenpeace activities and criticism of the Forest Code, occurred from June 2012 onward.
SEPTEMBER 2012	The Brazilian Deputies Chamber insisted on Dilma Rousseff's vetoes to the Forest Code.
JUNE TO AUGUST 2013	This marks the first instance since 2009 in which two legislative bills have been presented in the Chamber of Deputies with the objective of ***legislating against illegal deforestation***.

Fig. A1. Deforestation Bills and News During the Forest Code Debate.

JANUARY 2019

***Media Coverage*:** Scientists affirmed that the Amazon rainforest is worth more standing due to its environmental benefits. Deforestation threatens its transformation into a savanna and desert, **with government inaction linked to industry influence**.

Public opinion protests **Bolsonaro's agribusiness alliance**, urging him to fulfill his commitment to reduce deforestation in the Amazon and Cerrado, emphasizing the need for oversight if agribusiness is truly sustainable.

APRIL TO JULY 2019

***Media Coverage*:** Public opinion protests that there were no major efforts combat deforestation, and IBAMA imposed the lowest number of fines since 1995.

An Ibama report declared that at least part of the cerrado was **illegally deforested**. states that the condominium deforested 38,100 hectares through fraudulent authorizations.

Public opinion is critical of the manipulation of deforestation statistics by Jair Bolsonaro (PSL).

AUGUST TO DECEMBER 2019

***Media Coverage*:** Environmental protests gained momentum between August and December 2019 with the appearance of 18 articles related to illegal deforestation and government credibility.

The protests were primarily motivated by apprehensions regarding government actions that were perceived as detrimental to the nation's reputation and natural resources. These concerns encompassed issues such as tampering with deforestation data in the Amazon and the endangerment of critical financial mechanisms designed to address deforestation.

The ongoing deforestation crisis significantly contributes to Brazil's greenhouse gas emissions**, impacting its international reputation**.

Additionally, the alignment of Brazilian diplomacy with climate change deniers and **the erosion of government credibility** due to doubts in statistics from the National Institute for Space Research (INPE) have exacerbated the situation.

Imazon NGO's Forest Monitoring System (SAD) data reveals a significant rise in Amazon deforestation, **sparking international concerns about environmental consequences**, as voiced by business leaders and Pope Francis.

AUGUST 2019 TO DECEMBER 2020

Between mid-2019 and 2020, five bills were introduced in the Deputy Chamber **to tackle illegal deforestation comprehensively**, amending existing laws with penalties like land forfeiture, conversion into legal reserves, a 20-year ban on agricultural or urban use in affected areas, and special tax regulations. This marked a significant milestone in the ongoing time series analysis.

Fig. A2. Deforestation Bills and News During 2019–2020.

JANUARY TO APRIL

Media coverage: Media coverage prominently highlights the harmful impact of pesticide use in agriculture. It also includes critical scrutiny of government policies and their impact on the agricultural sector's growth, emphasizing the need for a balanced approach to ensure both sector expansion and environmental protection.

APRIL

Two bills were introduced in the **deputy's chamber**: one addresses pesticide use in agriculture and its impacts, while the other focuses on the consequences of water pollution in parks caused by agrochemicals and its effects on public health and the environment.

MAY TO JUNE

Media coverage: A scientific investigation highlights environmental concerns, specifically the adverse effects of cigarette butt and plastic pollution on public parks. It underscores the critical importance of conserving these green spaces for the well-being of the public and the integrity of ecosystems.

Media spotlights climate activism with a significant climate strike in São Paulo, where students engaged with government representatives on pressing climate and environmental issues.

The media spotlights a satirical environment art exhibition by acclaimed cartoonists Angeli and Laerte, known for their incisive social and political commentary. Additionally, Paula Lavigne introduces an eco-awareness app with a focus on Amazon preservation and ecological awareness.

JULY

Media coverage: A scientific report shows that pesticides caused the deaths of millions of bees, crucial for food production, near soy farms in Rio Grande do Sul. The intensive use of agrochemicals in agriculture has raised concerns among the use of pesticides and their safety in Brazil.

AUGUST

In August 2019, **deputy's chamber** introduced four bills. One aimed to prohibit pesticides due to environmental and health concerns, while another revoked registration of glyphosate-based agrochemicals and halted new registrations until safety is proven.

These legislative actions were prompted by widespread public concerns, as media reports indicated that 78% of surveyed Brazilians considered pesticide-contaminated foods unsafe.

Fig. A3. Pesticides Bills and News During 2019.

Table A1. Ministry Employees.

Year	Agriculture	Environment
2011	34,142	6,083
2012	33,727	6,120
2019	42,053	5,934
2020	40,303	5,789

Table A2. Ministry Federal Budget and Agri-Environmental Public Policy Program Budget.

Year	Agriculture	Environment
2011	9,291,563,048	3,338,859,340
2012	10,376,929,928	3,647,818,647
2019	11,902,358,634	3,797,362,978
2020	17,052,639,889	2,853,045,254

Table A3. Agricultural Public Policy Program Budget and Environment Public Policy Program Budget.

	2011	2012	2019	2020
Agriculture Public Policy Program				
Research and development of technologies for the sustainability of the agribusiness and its adaptation to global environmental changes	1.847.051	35.306.358	–	–
	1.847.051	**35.306.358**	–	–
Environment Public Policy Program				
Deforestation surveillance	3,601,667	44,120,000	–	–
Monitoring and control of deforestation and forest fire	2,019,166	28,506,288	–	–
Policies and strategies to prevent deforestation	–	–	253,000	–
Support for the implementation of agri-environmental policies	–	475,000	285,000	–
Environmental control of potentially polluting products, substances, waste and activities	–	–	2,500,000	449,922
	5,620,833	**73,101,288**	**3,038,000**	**449,922**

Note: *The currency in the report is the Brazilian Real (BRL) R$1.00.

Table A4. Congressional Caucuses Composition.

Congressional Caucuses	2011–2015 Legislature	2019–2023 Legislature	Prioritized Issues
Business	273, comprising 246 deputies and 27 senators	242, comprising 204 deputies and 38 senators	Labor rights reform, outsourcing, competitiveness, reduction of charges for the sector, 'Brazil cost', tax reform, tax breaks and incentives, credit and monetary policies.
Family	105, comprising 78 deputies and 27 senators	199, comprising 175 deputies and 24 senators	Avoiding restrictions in electoral legislation that prevent candidacies based on family relationships.
Ruralist	160, comprising 142 deputies and 18 senators	107, comprising 80 deputies and 27 senators	Environmental issues, regulation of Constitutional Amendment 81/2014 on Slave Labor, regulation of foreign land acquisition, demarcation of indigenous lands, and amnesty for rural producers' debts.
Evangelical	73, comprising 70 deputies and 3 senators	92, comprising 85 deputies and 7 senators	Same-sex union, stem cell research, defense of the family, School without Party, gender ideology, abortion.
Union	72, comprising 64 deputies and 8 senators	40, comprising 35 deputies and 5 senators	Defense of labor, union, and social security rights, maintenance of the national minimum wage policy, reduction of working hours.

(Continued)

Table A4. *(Continued)*

Congressional Caucuses	2011–2015 Legislature	2019–2023 Legislature	Prioritized Issues
Women's	58, comprising 45 female deputies and 12 female senators	89, comprising 77 female deputies and 12 female senators	Extension of maternity leave, representation of women in decision-making bodies, combatting violence against women, political reform with gender equality.

Table A5. Deforestation Media News.

Year	Environment Activism	Agribusiness	Sustainable Practices	Environment Preservation	Total
2000	1	2		2	5
2001	9			4	13
2002	1	1	2	5	9
2003	5	1	4	4	14
2004	6		3	4	13
2005	7	2	5	9	23
2006	10		2	8	20
2007	6	1	4	6	17
2008	9	9	7	17	42
2009	19	7	9	21	56
2010	9	4	7	21	41
2011	15	4	4	17	40
2012	18	6	4	16	44
2013	8	2	9	1	20
2014	8	1	4	25	38
2015	5	1	8	10	24
2016	7	2	3	2	14
2017	9	9	2	35	55
2018	6	10	1	18	35
2019	25	8	15	46	94
2020	15	12	15	27	69
Total	**198**	**82**	**108**	**298**	**686**

Table A6. Deforestation Political Bills.

Year	Agribusiness	Environment Protection	Ilegal Deforestation	Sustainable Practices	Total
2000				1	1
2003				3	3
2004		2			2
2006		1			1
2007	1	3			4
2008		4		1	5
2009		1	2		3
2010	1	2			3
2011		3			3
2012		2			2
2013			2		2
2015		1			1
2016		2			2
2017		3			3
2019		2	1		3
2020		1	4	1	6
Total	**2**	**27**	**9**	**6**	**44**

Table A7. Pesticides Media News.

Year	Environment Activism	Healthy and Environmental Consequences	Agribusiness	Sustainable Practices	Total
2000		4			4
2001	1	4	1	3	9
2002		12	1	1	14
2003		10			10
2004	1	2	1		4
2005	1	5		2	8
2006	1	8			9
2007	2	2			4

(Continued)

Table A7. *(Continued)*

Year	Environment Activism	Healthy and Environmental Consequences	Agribusiness	Sustainable Practices	Total
2008	1	9	1		11
2009	8	3	1	1	13
2010	2	1	3		6
2011	10	11		2	23
2012	10	6	3	3	22
2013	5	7	2	5	19
2014	1	7		1	9
2015	2	8	4	1	15
2016	2	4	3	3	12
2017	1	5	5	6	17
2018	3	6	5	11	25
2019	6	24	3	3	36
2020	3	4	1	1	9
Total	**60**	**142**	**34**	**43**	**279**

Table A8. Pesticides Political Bills.

Year	Healthy and Environmental Consequences	Agribusiness	Sustainable Practices	Total
2000	2			2
2001		1		1
2002	3			3
2004	3			3
2005	1	1		2
2006	2			2
2008	1		1	2
2009	2			2
2010			1	1
2011	4			4
2012	5			5

Table A8. *(Continued)*

Year	**Healthy and Environmental Consequences**	**Agribusiness**	**Sustainable Practices**	**Total**
2015	12		3	15
2016	5	1		6
2017	3			3
2018	1	1	1	3
2019	12	1		13
2020	2			2
Total	**58**	**5**	**6**	**69**

Chapter 6

Organizing Wicked Policy Fields: A Strategic Framework for Capacity-Building in Cross-Border Transport Megaprojects

Giovanni Esposito[a] *and Andrea Terlizzi*[b]

[a]Université Libre de Bruxelles, Belgium
[b]University of Florence, Italy

Abstract

In this chapter, we propose a strategic framework for capacity-building in cross-border transport megaprojects. First, we make the case for infrastructure megaprojects as wicked policy fields marked by a complex web of stakeholders' interests and characterized by uncertainty and entrenched value divergence and conflict. Second, inspired by Pettigrew's contextualism and by drawing evidence from the case of the Lyon-Turin high-speed railway megaproject, we suggest that strategic management involves the analysis of three different albeit interconnected dimensions: the content of change, the process of change, and the context of change. Our study shows that variations in performance (content) are determined by and determine variations in (1) the openness or closure of national institutional contexts to civil society stakeholders (inner context), (2) the intensity of supervision and control functions realized by actor seating in the supranational institutional context (outer context), and (3) national and supranational actors' capability of making agreements over contested megaprojects aspects (process). We suggest that, from a strategic point of view, there is not a linear relationship between the content, context, and process of change in megaproject development. This is rather a complex nonlinear relationship that varies over time with little predictability. Time is a key factor in understanding these interactions between the content, context, and process. We claim that the capacity for organizing wickedness in megaprojects should rest on a socio-economic logic and, in particular, on three core governance features: (1)

Policy Capacity, Design and the Sustainable Development Goals, 119–141

doi:10.1108/978-1-80455-686-320241008

open decision-making systems, (2) bottom-up performance management, and (3) active dialogue between proponents and opponents.

Keywords: Megaprojects; infrastructure policy; strategic management; capacity; change

1. Introduction

Megaprojects are large-scale ventures that take many years to develop, involve multiple public and private stakeholders, and have a long-lasting impact on the economy, environment, and society (Flyvbjerg, 2017). Examples of megaprojects include special economic zones, infrastructures (e.g., dams, airports, seaports, bridges, highways, tunnels, railways, wastewater projects, oil and natural gas extraction projects), major investments (e.g., COVID-19 relief plans), large-scale high-cost initiatives in scientific research, as well as projects of various sort undertaken to tackle sustainable development and climate change. In this regard, megaprojects play a crucial role in the efforts to meet the United Nations (UN) Sustainable Development Goals (SDGs) (Corazza, Cottafava, et al., 2022; Sankaran et al., 2020; The Economist Intelligence Unit, 2019). In particular, SDG9 specifically refers to building resilient infrastructures, including cross-border transport megaprojects. Governing sustainable infrastructure poses important concerns in terms of governance given the short-termism that often characterizes policy development and the interdependence between SDG9 and other SDGs (Sankaran et al., 2020). Moreover, whereas major infrastructures may have positive impacts in terms of sustainable development, they can also have negative consequences for the environment as well as disrupt and displace communities (Di Maddaloni & Davis, 2017; Esposito et al., 2022; The Economist Intelligence Unit, 2019).

Megaprojects are therefore wicked policy fields marked by a complex web of stakeholders' interests and characterized by uncertainty and entrenched value divergence and conflict. In order to deal with the wicked nature of megaprojects, we argue for the importance of building what we call *capacity for organizing*. Such capacity should rest upon three governance features: (1) open decision-making systems, (2) bottom-up performance management, and (3) active dialogue between proponents and opponents. To illustrate our argument, we provide an in-depth analysis of the development of a cross-border transport megaproject: the Lyon-Turin high-speed railway (hereafter, the LT). The case is analyzed under the lenses of Pettigrew (1987) contextualist approach, which is suitable to make sense of complex, uncertain, and conflictual processes. We use Pettigrew's scheme as analytic tool for presenting evidence. In fact, as pointed out by Pichault (2013), rather than an explanatory theory, contextualism is an analytical framework which places emphasis on three key concepts and their interrelations: content, context, and process. We use contextualism to highlight what aspects to intervene on to improve the governance capacity of megaprojects. Empirical material is drawn from 79 semi-structured interviews, conducted between 2014 and 2016 with megaproject promoters, public institutional actors, lobbyists, and organized groups opposing the megaproject. We triangulated interviews with key documents including legal texts, press releases, financial agreements, policy papers, and third-party studies.

This chapter is organized as follows. In the next section, we discuss the concept of capacity in relation to megaprojects understood as wicked policy fields. Section 3 introduces Pettigrew's analytical tool to study complex, uncertain, and conflict-ridden policy environments. In section 4, the analysis of the LT case is presented. Finally, Sections 5 and 6 provide discussion and conclusions, respectively.

2. Megaprojects' Wickedness and Capacity

Megaprojects can be seen as inherently wicked policy fields marked by a complex web of stakeholders and populated by problems which are resistant to a clear and agreed solution (see also Lippi & Tsekos, this book; Head, 2022; Rittel & Webber, 1973). These are indeed policy fields involving a great variety of governmental and nongovernmental actors holding different interests, preferences, attitudes, visions, imaginaries, cultures, and logics of collective action (Esposito et al., 2022). Esposito and Terlizzi (2023) discern three defining features of megaprojects: complexity, uncertainty, and conflict.

Complexity derives from the fact that megaproject development involves several interorganizational layers spanning across geographical, cultural, and institutional boundaries. Sources of complexity can be technical (e.g., megaproject scale), political and administrative (e.g., involvement of multiple governments and administrations), social and cultural (e.g., stakeholders' multiple interests, visions, interpretations about the megaproject), and legal and regulatory (e.g., changing legislation and regulations). Uncertainty is related to the views of the future held by the actors involved in and concerned by the megaproject development. Uncertainty can stem from either the lack of knowledge about the consequences of a megaproject on the economy, society, and environment (epistemic uncertainty), or it can originate from the divergent meanings that the different stakeholders participating in the policy process attach to the megaproject. This is all related to the notion of ambiguity, which refers to the many different ways of thinking about the same circumstances (Fowler, 2021). Finally, conflict arises from divergence in actors' beliefs, visions, and objectives. Conflict-ridden dynamics may involve internal stakeholders (e.g., megaproject teams, contractors), external actors (e.g., governments, citizens, social movements), or both (Esposito et al., 2022). The wickedness of megaprojects is apparent in relation to the efforts to achieve the UN SDGs. As pointed out by Sankaran et al. (2020), it is imperative the development of a more integrated and holistic view of UN SDGs and the establishment of a workable governance structure for megaprojects supporting their delivery (see also Corazza, Torchia, et al., 2022). Sustainable infrastructures are a core issue also at the European Union (EU) level, with the *Green Deal* adopted by the European Commission in 2019, emphasizing the construction of infrastructures for sustainable mobility (Corazza, Cottafava, et al., 2022).

In this chapter, we focus on the Lyon-Turin high-speed railway. This is a cross-border transport megaproject which is part of the Trans-European Transport Network (TEN-T). TEN-T is an infrastructure policy directed toward the development of a Europe-wide transport network aimed to eliminate barriers that hamper the free movement of people and freight across EU member states. The LT consists of a 270 km high-speed railway line connecting Lyon and Turin. The rail line requires the construction of a 57 km tunnel traversing the Alps between Susa Valley in Italy and Maurienne in France. Completion of the planned megaproject has been postponed several times with the most recent forecast predicting completion in 2030. The megaproject delay has largely been caused by the opposition of local communities of the Susa Valley. The complex, uncertain, and conflictual nature of the LT is given by its multilevel, transnational, and pluralistic nature (Table 6.1): (1) multilevel because decision-making is dispersed from the national to the supranational level, (2) transnational because it is implemented within two countries having different domestic institutions, and (3) pluralistic because of the coexistence of divergent actor groups, each with its own legitimate set of beliefs and objectives.

To deal with wicked policy fields such as the LT, several capacities are needed. These capacities should go beyond a narrow domain of traditional managerial action, which conceive of megaproject development as a rational, linear process. Capacity-building in megaprojects should instead embrace a comprehensive socioeconomic logic – as opposed to a techno-economic one – to deal with the complex, uncertain, and conflictual nature of a wider set of policy processes and subsystems that all organizational players have to confront with (Esposito & Terlizzi, 2023).

In general terms, the concept of capacity refers to the ability any public authority does or should possess to deal with policy problems (Lippi & Tsekos, this book). In the literature, the concept of capacity has been articulated in several ways (for a review, see Brenton et al., 2022; Lippi & Tsekos, this book). In this chapter, we integrate the notions of governance capacity and policy capacity. Policy capacity is the "set of skills and resources – or competences and capabilities – necessary to perform policy functions" (Wu et al., 2018, p. 3). These capabilities can be analytical (knowledge generation and mobilization), operational (know-how to act upon policy intentions and achieve policy goals), and political (mobilization of concerned stakeholders to increase the acceptability of policy measures). Governance capacity includes formal structural features of the governmental apparatus as well as "informal elements, that is, how these features work in practice" (Christensen et al., 2016, p. 888). In this respect, relevant capacities are the capacity to coordinate (bringing together diverse organizations), analyze (collecting information as well as measuring and monitoring performance), and regulate (control, surveillance, and oversight) (Christensen et al., 2016; Lodge & Wegrich, 2014).

In integrating these perspectives, in what follow, we propose a strategic framework for building capacity for organizing. The capacity for organizing rests upon a socioeconomic logic of megaproject governance and involves a wider set of public management and policymaking skills to interact with the megaproject

Table 6.1. Complexity, Uncertainty, and Conflict in the LT.

Complexity	Uncertainty	Conflict
Construction of a 57 km tunnel – one of the longest in history – traversing the Alps between Susa Valley in Italy and Maurienne in France (*Technical complexity*). The megaprojects involve supranational (EU), national (France and Italy), and subnational administrations and authorities (*Political, administrative, financial, legal, and regulatory complexity*). The construction is the responsibility of the two national railway infrastructure managers, which are in turn subsidiaries of two state-owned holding companies (*Organizational complexity*).	Almost 30 years after the announcement of the project, the megaproject is still incomplete. The original forecast cost of 12€ billion has increased to 26€ billion. The projected completion date has been postponed several times. The most recent forecast predicts completion in 2030.	Delays in the megaproject development are the result of construction stoppage brought about by the opposition of civil society groups in the Susa Valley (This is liked to *social and cultural complexity*). In the early-2000s, the Italian Parliament passes a law that includes the LT in a list of strategic infrastructures to be completed before 2013. For such infrastructures, the law introduces a fast-lane procedure directing concerned administrative authorities to approve related works without any obligation to consult local citizens. When expropriation letters to acquire the local lands and set the construction site work are sent, the locals mount a protest campaign called NOTAV (*No Treno ad Alta Velocità*, No High-Speed Train)

environment made of a great variety of actors, structures, and informal practices. The framework is based on the assessment of three governance dimensions which relate to both structural and agentic factors: (1) national institutions' openness or closure to civil society stakeholders, (2) supranational intensity of supervision and control, and (3) actors' capability of making agreements.

3. Capacity for Organizing: A Strategic Framework for Capacity-Building

Capacity for organizing needs to take context seriously. Context does matter in public policy and management (Pollitt, 2013). A contextualist framework of analysis distinguishes between three dimensions of change: content, process, and context (Pettigrew, 1987). The content refers to *what* is changed as expressed in terms of objectives, purpose, and goals of change. The process refers to *how* change is implemented, whereas the context refers to the internal and external environment *where* change is implemented. Pettigrew and Whipp (1991) emphasize the continuous interplay between these dimensions and hold that change is an iterative and cumulative process. Against this background, we conceive of strategic management as relational (D'Amato & Terlizzi, 2022). This means that in aligning aspirations and capabilities with a view to achieve certain goals (Bryson & George, 2020), actors – individuals or collective – strategically interact within a nonlinear relationship between content, process, and context.

Contextualism offers an analytical framework within which different theoretical lenses may be mobilized, allowing researchers to unpack change processes and describe them as a result of multiple content-process-context interactions (Pichault, 2013). In what follows, we integrate three theoretical lenses: (1) neo-institutionalism, (2) Foucauldian theory of power, and (3) Boltanski & Thévenot's (1991) justification theory. We choose these three theories because, although separately, they have already been used to analyze and explain change in the LT development. Therefore, they particularly fit the LT empirical settings. Firstly, relying on institutional work theory, Esposito et al. (2021) have shed light on the relationship between national institutions (inner context) and change, focusing on the participants' purposive actions to shape the broader national overarching institutional contexts in which the megaproject is implemented in France and Italy. This research shows that different national administrative structures and legal systems differently affect LT implementation performance within the national (inner) contexts. Particularly, it shows that national institutional settings open to civil society participation facilitate and streamline implementation, whereas difficult and conflictual conditions emerge in the opposite case (Esposito et al., 2023). Secondly, scholars have also mobilized Foucault's Panopticon theory to shed light on how performance in France and Italy is influenced and steered by supranational institutional frameworks (outer context), with EU-level actors using corporate-style metrics and indicators to exert control over the LT participants operating within the national contexts (Esposito, Terlizzi, et al., 2023; Sargiacomo et al., 2022). This research stream particularly shows that, in global megaprojects such as the LT, actors operating within supranational administrative structures (EU institutions) use performance-based systems of financial incentives and sanctions to exert supervision and control over actors operating within national structures (Italian and French institutions). Thirdly, relying on Boltanski and Thévenot's justification theory, Esposito et al. (2022) show that the LT implementation performance is not only influenced by (inner and outer) contextual variables but also by processual ones such as the sequence of events triggered by the dialectical interactions (and controversies) between agents with adversarial interests and logics of action. This work brings the focus on the conflicts and dialectics between the opposing arguments conveyed through narratives by proponents and opponents of the LT.

The above-mentioned three theoretical lenses shed light on three different dimensions that ought to be considered when organizing wickedness in cross-border megaprojects such as the LT. Firstly, the lens of institutional work theories (Biesenthal et al., 2018; Tonga Uriarte et al., 2019) suggests to bring the focus of analysis on the work of actors as they attempt to shape the institutional contexts within which megaprojects are implemented. Thus, mobilizing neo-institutionalist theories within the contextualist framework may help shed light on the first governance dimension of the capacity for organizing, i.e., the national institutions' openness or closure to civil society stakeholders.

Secondly, the lens of Foucault's (1980) Panopticon theory suggests that, using performance management systems (PMSs), nested tiers of public managerial personnel seating in supranational institutional bodies can establish clear lines of command across the organizational hierarchy of national public administrations enabling the constitution of a pyramidal field of visibility wherein supranational officers can exert direct functions of supervision and control over national officers. Such hierarchical observation is enabled by several procedures and techniques of notation, computation, calculation, and reporting of megaproject performance that help promoters to increase or decrease the intensity supervision and control functions in order to effectively manage the megaproject "at a distance" (Berdayes, 2002). Mobilizing Foucauldian theory within the contextualist framework may help improving our understanding of performance-measurement techniques and procedures turning the supranational context into organizational constraints that shape the collective behavior of national administrative bodies. Therefore, it helps us shedding light on the second dimension of the capacity for organizing, namely, the supranational intensity of supervision and control functions.

Thirdly, the lens of Boltanski and Thévenot's justification theory provides a useful analytical toolkit to understand actors' behaviors within organizational contexts. In fact, this theoretical approach offers insights into situated disputes among actors and the different forms of conflict which are likely to emerge among them. On the one hand, this theory focuses on actors' discursive justifications about their practices and, therefore, allows understanding the multiple moral stances which compete in a controversy. On the other hand, it provides a taxonomy of practices that actors may deploy to solve a controversy, either making agreements with actors espousing competing moral stances or dropping the dispute without making any agreement. Mobilizing Boltanski and Thévenot's theory within the framework of contextualism allows assessing the third dimension of the capacity for organizing, namely, actors' capability of making agreements.

Fig. 6.1 shows how our model integrating the theoretical lenses discussed above applies to the LT case. We suggest that, in the case of LT, variations in performance objectives (content) are determined by, and determine variations in, (1) national institutions' openness to civil society stakeholders (inner context), (2) supranational intensity of supervision and control functions (outer context), and (3) actors' capability of making agreements (process).

4. Content-Process-Context Interactions in the LT Megaproject

As explained above, existing empirical research on the LT governance (Esposito et al., 2021, 2022, 2023) suggests that the performance of LT (content) is variously correlated with three key governance dimensions. Table 6.2 summarizes how, according to this literature, these variables have evolved through the time span under examination (1990s, 2000s, and 2010s) and across jurisdictions involved (Italy, France, and EU).

Performance – in the sense of achieving planned objectives – in France is relatively better than in Italy. Additionally, we see that its trajectory in the French context is different from the Italian one (Fig. 6.2). In France, performance steadily goes well until the early-2010s and then it slightly decreases. In Italy, it decreases between the 1990s and 2000s and increases during the 2010s. In both contexts, delays in the realization of plans emerge as local opposition to the project increases. In France, planned geognostic works concerning the base tunnel are accomplished by the late-2000s. However, in the 2010s, the opposition of local stakeholders leads the project promoters to review the plans for the development of the national route giving access to the base tunnel. As of today, while the implementation of the base tunnel timely goes on, no plan is envisaged yet for the construction of the access routes. In Italy, planned geognostic works concerning the base tunnel stop in the mid-2000s because of the strong opposition of local stakeholders. In the 2010s, following the militarily occupation of the construction site, the geognostic works restart. As of today, the geognostic works are ongoing, but they are late compared to the initial plans. Similar to France, no plan is envisaged yet for the construction of the access routes to the base tunnel.

In the next sections, we first separately present the content, inner context, the outer context, and the process. Secondly, we discuss their interactions and relationships with the content.

4.1 National Institutions' Openness or Closure to Civil Society Stakeholders (Inner Context)

Italy and France have different institutional systems regulating the decision-making process of large infrastructure project like the LT. A key difference

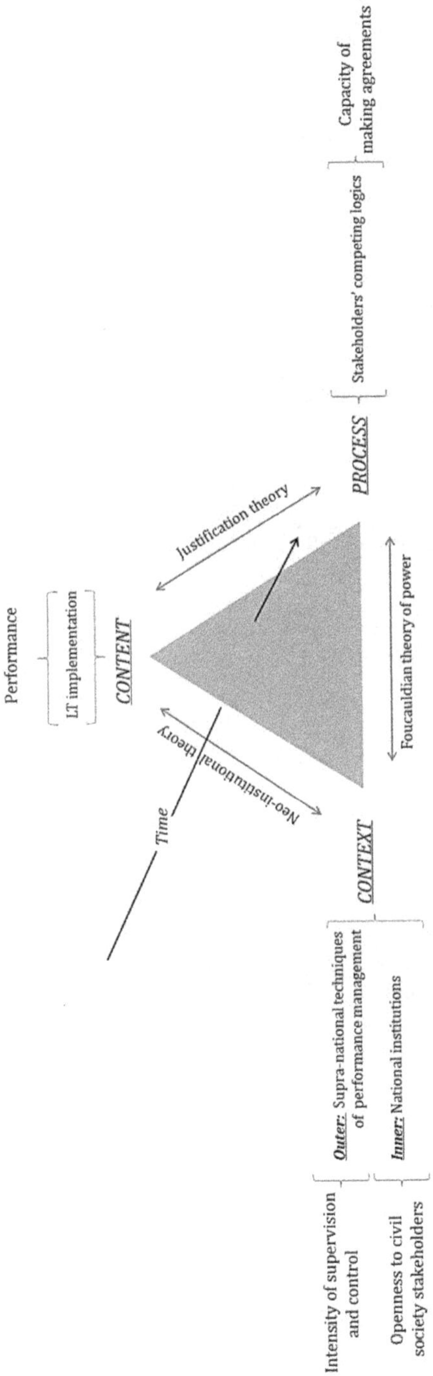

Fig. 6.1. Assessing Capacity for Organizing in the LT Case.

Table 6.2. Performance and Governance Dimensions Across Time and Jurisdictions.

Performance and governance dimensions	Jurisdictions	Time		
		1990s	2000s	2010s
Performance objectives *(content)*	IT	+	-	+ -
	FR	+ +	+ +	+
Intensity of supra-national supervision and control functions *(outer context)*	EU	+ -	+ +	+ +
National institutions' openness or closure to civil society stakeholders *(inner context)*	IT	-	+	- -
	FR	+	+	+ -
Capability of making agreements *(process)*	IT	-	- +	- -
	FR	+	+	-

Legend	
+ +	High
+	Moderately high
+ -	Slightly high
- +	Slightly low
-	Moderately low
- -	Low

between the two national systems concerns their openness to stakeholders with divergent views of the project. The French system is more opened than the Italian one (Esposito et al., 2021, 2022, 2023). As explained by a French local public officer, "there is a whole legal process that must be complied with when carrying out a project like [the LT]. The railway company is in charge of the administrative setting up [which] involves a public inquiry procedure."[1] Instead, in Italy, a participatory venue was extraordinarily set up to deal with the local protest

[1]Interview with a public officer of the Savoie Department, 18/03/2015.

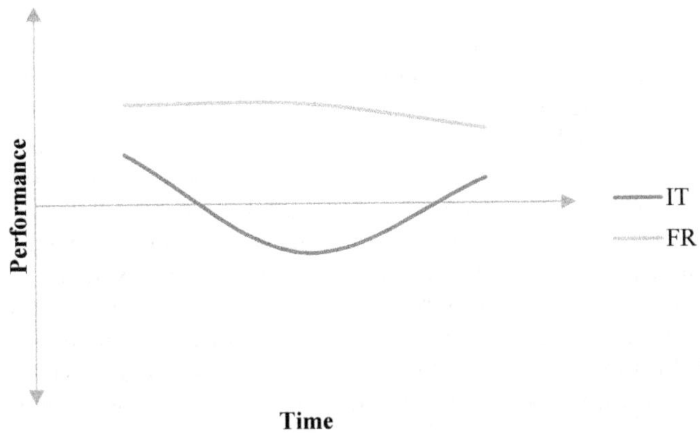

Fig. 6.2. Performance Objectives Across Time and National Contexts.

movement against the LT.[2] Whereas the French system can be defined as a moderation system (open to the requests of different stakeholders), the Italian one can be seen as an either/or closed system (Hargrave & Van de Ven, 2009).

In France, openness was high throughout the 1990s and 2000s, and then, it slightly decreased in the 2010s (Fig. 6.3). In the 1990s, the project promoters set

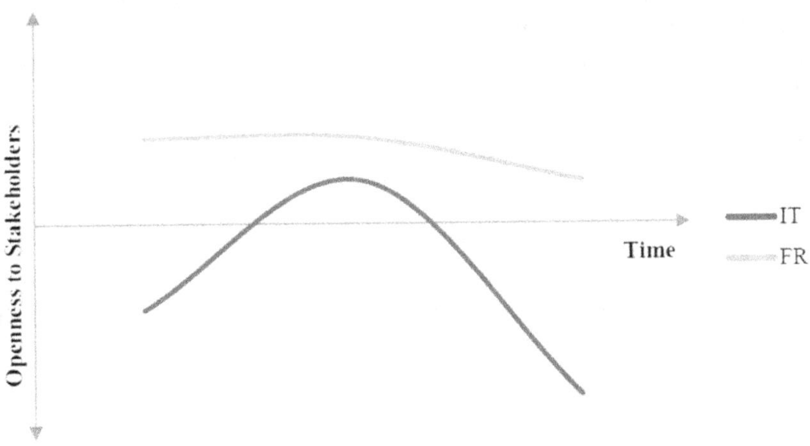

Fig. 6.3. Openness of National Institutional Systems to Civil Society Stakeholders.

[2]Interview with a technical expert representing the local administrations of the Susa Valley in the Observatory, 05/11/2014.

up a public debate with the local stakeholders on the social and economic interest of LT. In the 2000s, the Public Inquiry procedure imposed the creation of a public enquiry committee in charge of consulting the local stakeholders before the project is officially declared of public interest. The Public Inquiry procedure was the occasion for inhabitants of the municipalities to inform public authorities about their opinions and concerns. Anyone could write her opinion about the project in a dedicated register made available in the municipality: "These opinions will be examined by the members of the public inquiry committee who will decide which one is legitimate or not".[3] In 2010s, a group of local stakeholders – in the light of new information available about the LT – ask to stop the project implementation call for a new public debate on the social and economic interest of the project. Promoters refuse and prosecute their spokesperson while continuing the consultation with those local actors who do not oppose the implementation of the LT.

In Italy, openness was low during the 1990s, then – after a slight increase in the 2000s – it dramatically worsened during the 2010s (Fig. 6.3). In the 1990s, local stakeholders have no place in the decision-making concerning LT. In the 2000s, Law 443/01 intensifies the marginalization of local stakeholders who thus strengthen their protest campaign against the LT. Vis-à-vis local stakeholders' mass mobilization, the project promoters create an extraordinary body – the so-called *Osservatorio Torino-Lione* (OTL) – to have public consultations with the representatives of the opposition groups. The OTL was the place where the administrations "had to go to talk about the new high-speed line by putting all possible alternatives on the table: Do we do it? If yes, how do we do it? Do we do it in this way or we do it in alternative way?" Nevertheless, the consultations fail because of extremely divergent views between the local stakeholders and the project promoters. It is important to highlight that, after initial discussions, the so-called "zero option" – namely "the option of not doing the LT" – was excluded on the basis of a cost–benefit analysis.[4–6] In 2010s, as local protests do not stop, the national government approves Law 180/2011 and permanently mobilizes the army in the Susa Valley to discourage further protests against the implementation of the LT.

4.2 Supranational Intensity of Supervision and Control (Outer Context)

EU's actors use a complex PMS to steer the TEN-T program toward planned objectives. This is done through indicators representing the project performance in terms of objectives achieved by state-level project promoters against the initial plans agreed with the European Commission (Esposito et al., 2022).

---

[3]Interview with the mayor of a municipality concerned by Lyon-Turin construction, 22/03/2016.

[4]Interview with the mayor of a Susa Valley's municipality concerned by Lyon-Turin construction, 19/10/2015.

[5]Interview with the mayor of a Susa Valley's municipality concerned by Lyon-Turin construction, 19/10/2015.

[6]Interview with a public officer of the Piedmont Region, 28/10/2014.

PMSs are very important instruments that allow EU managers and officials to evaluate the implementation of the TEN-T program, to uncover the factors that led to success in achieving planned objectives and to decipher the strategic errors that led to failure. These instruments may be described as "intellectual technologies" (e.g., written reports, drawings, pictures, charts, graphs, and statistics) allowing the managerial staff to make judgments as to whether and why this or that project succeeded or failed, or to devise remedies for alleged deficiencies across all actors in the field. These technologies enable managers to represent the TEN-T reality in a form amenable to managerial and political deliberation, argument, and scheming.

The intensity of TEN-T PMS's control and supervision functions increases over time (Fig. 6.4). In the 1990s, there is no system to manage the implementation of projects funded within the Member States. During the 2000s, the number of planned projects realized throughout the EU fall behind the optimistic plans of the 1990s. The European Coordinator and an executive agency are thus appointed by the European Commission to assure the timely completion of funded projects. As commented by a public officer:

> …the European Coordinator works to promote the development of corridors and plays a political role to tell governments: 'Look, it's really time now!' […]. Because of their reputation, personality and experience, they have the capability to speak with high-level politicians from the member states.[7]

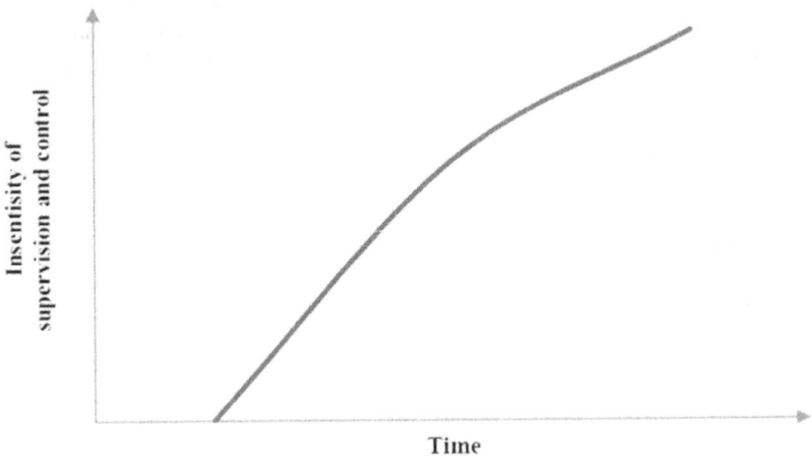

Fig. 6.4. Intensity of Supranational Functions of Supervision and Control.

[7]Interview with a public officer, DG MOVE – European Union.

In the 2010s, the plans are reviewed, and the EU financial contribution is concentrated on the 9 core network corridors. Each of these corridors is placed under the governance of the so-called the "corridor forum." This is a dedicated body where all the national industries and public authorities concerned by the construction of a corridor collaborate to the timely implementation of funded projects under the supervision of the European Coordinator. However, civil society actors have no right to participate in the "corridor forum":

> ...if the European Coordinator thinks that it is useful they can establish a dialogue with them [...]. We do not include opponents because if they do not want to work with us constructively it does not really make sense to involve them.[8]

4.3 Actors' Capability of Making Agreements (Process)

The LT can be described as an organizational field where the competing institutional logics of contradicting groups (proponents vs opponents of LT) generate controversies whose evolution variously impact on change. Differences in the evolution of these controversies may be explained as a consequence of differences in national proponents' capacities of making agreements with opponents. Innovatively building on Boltanski and Thévenot's (1991) justification theory, Esposito et al. (2022) show that, on the one hand, proponents' justificatory arguments mobilize the industrial, green, and civic orders of worth, thus narrating the megaproject as a form of: (a) technological progress, (b) sustainable innovation, and (c) an infrastructure of collective interest. On the other hand, opponents challenged these arguments from within the same industrial, green, and civic orders of worth, thus centering their resistance strategy on state-of-worth criticisms and unveiling the technical, environmental, and democratic inconsistencies of proponents' narratives. They thus depict the Lyon-Turin railway as a (technically and environmentally) useless megaproject, undemocratically imposed from the top. Such a counternarrative succeeded to mobilize tens of thousands of individuals against the megaproject construction.

We argue that an important aspect for the successful design and implementation of megaprojects like the LT is therefore the proponents' ability to cope with the multiplicity of visions that contradictorily coexist in the field. Particularly, in France – where proponents have most often worked to make agreements with the opponents – resistance to change is weaker than in Italy – where proponents have most often ignored opponents' critiques. Making agreements with stakeholders outside the project team is thus a key factor for the smooth conduct of cross-border transport megaprojects.

Despite different capacities of making agreements, Italian and French proponents' posturing toward opponents' requests has similarly evolved over time

---

[8] Interview with a public officer, DG MOVE – European Union.

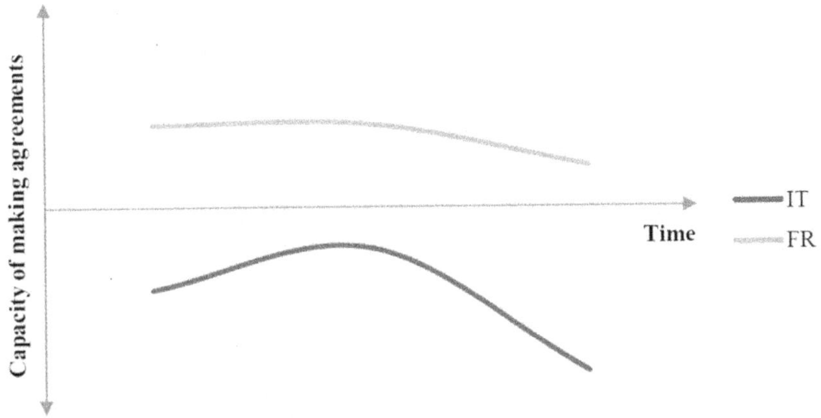

Fig. 6.5. Capability of Proponents to Make Agreements With Opponents.

(Fig. 6.5). In France, proponents' capacity is relatively high throughout the 1990s and 2000s when opponents' criticisms do not question the overall feasibility of the project. In the early-2010s, while the French Court of Audit releases a report that casts doubt on the economic feasibility of LT, local opposition groups appoint a new spokesperson, Daniel Ibanez. Under the leadership of Mr. Ibanez, the opponents ask to stop the implementation of LT and set up a new public debate on the social and economic interest of the project. Proponents refuse and file a claim for defamation against Mr. Ibanez. However, upon reaching the court, the lawsuit is dismissed on insufficient legal ground.

In Italy, proponents' capacity is low during the 1990s, and it significantly deteriorated during the 2010s. In the 1990s, proponents avoid local opponents' criticisms of the project by ignoring their requests of taking part in the decision-making of LT. In the 2000s, after a mass mobilization of Susa Valley's populations, proponents accept to establish a dialogue with the opponents on condition that they accept to limit the discussion to how implementing the project rather than whether implementing it or not. Opponents interpret this condition as a way of the proponents to avoid again their criticisms and impose de facto the planned project. As a consequence, they decide to stop the ongoing dialogue and occupy the construction site of the base tunnel as a form of protest. As a response, in the 2010s, the proponents mobilize the army to evacuate the opponents. They thus militarily occupy the construction site and prosecute the activists of the opposition groups.

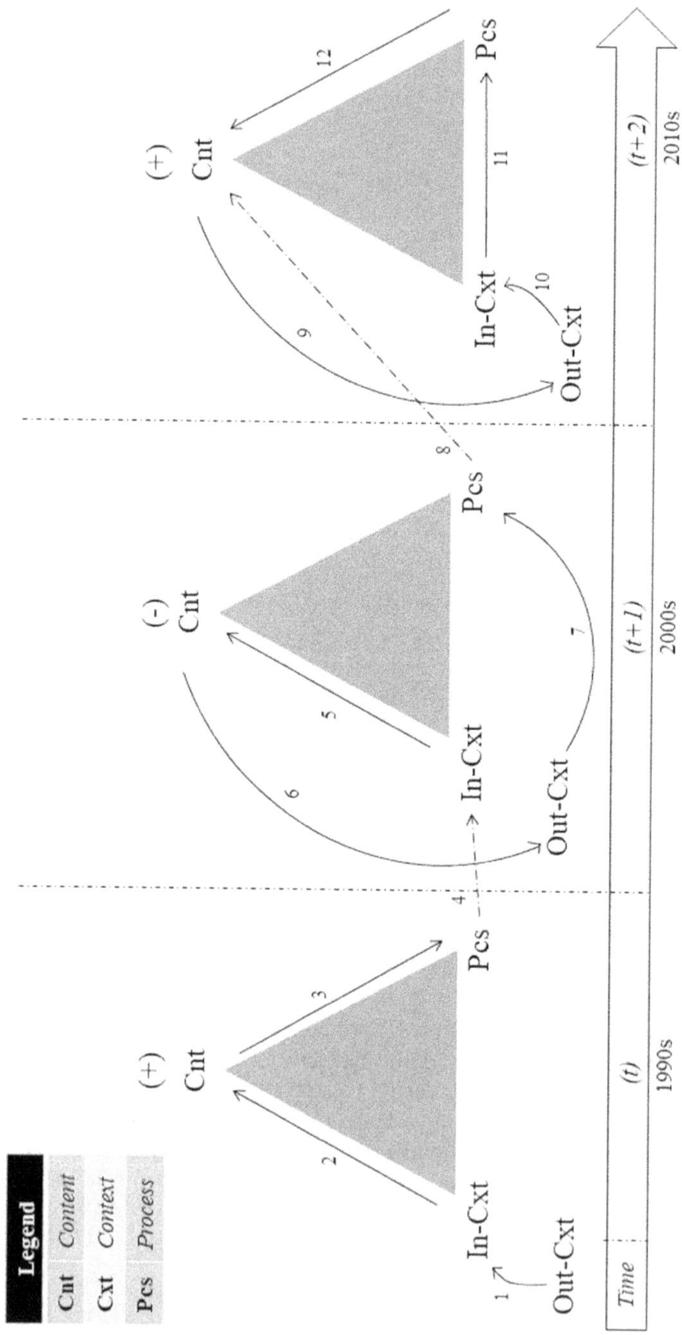

Fig. 6.6. Interactions Between Content, Context, and Process Through Time.

4.4 Content, Context, and Process on the move

Time is a key factor to understand the continuous interactions between the content, context, and process of change. In the case of the LT, we identified three periods (*t*, *t+1*, and *t+2*) through which we could observe important variations in the contextualist interactions (Fig. 6.6). Our analysis suggests 12 key interactions which unfold over time.

In the early 1990s, the Treaty of Maastricht introduces the TEN-T policy to stimulate Member States' investments in seamless trans-European transport chains for passenger and freight, while keeping up with the latest technological trends such as high-speed railway technology in the rail sector. In Italy and France, this policy framework provides economic incentives that lead both national governments and railways to invest public funds in the construction of LT (interaction n°1). Within each national context, different institutional systems are in place to govern the project implementation. The French system is opened to stakeholder participation whereas the Italian one is not. These different systems produce two different implementation strategies. In France, the project proponents establish a dialogue with the local communities, whereas in Italy, they ignore them. Despite these different strategies, LT experiences a relatively positive performance in both contexts (interaction n°2). By the end of the 1990s, the first preliminary studies are accomplished, and both national governments and railways declare their official commitment to the construction of the new infrastructure. However, the implementation of the project at the national levels produces different processes where local communities differently oppose the project (interaction n°3). In France – where proponents implement the LT while making agreements with the opponents (moderation strategy) – resistance to change is weaker than in Italy – where proponents implement the LT while ignoring opponents' critiques and avoiding agreements (either/or strategy).

In Italy, the systematic exclusion of local stakeholders from the decision-making process leads to popular protests and to the occupation of the base-tunnel construction site. The turmoil of these events – and the pressures of the public opinion – leads the government to reform the national institutions in charge of the LT and make them more open to local participation (interaction n°4). An extraordinary body (OTL) is thus created to involve the local communities in the decision-making system and dialogue with them. Because of proponents' and opponents' divergent views, the OTL consultations take long, and the implementation of LT is further delayed (interaction n°5). Performance worsens and the mid-term review of the TEN-T's executive agency provides a negative assessment of LT (interaction n°6). Alarmed by the negative assessment, the European Coordinator puts pressure on the national authorities to take up the implementation again in accordance with the planned agenda, otherwise financial support to LT might be reduced (interaction n°7). To comply with the EU requests, the Chairman of the OTL unilaterally adopts the "Agreement of Pracatinat." The Chairman does so in the name of all OTL participants although none among the local stakeholders has signed it. This document imposes OTL members to shift the focus of their meetings from debating the project feasibility to project implementation. As a consequence, the representatives of the local communities quit the OTL.

In the 2010s, local protests intensify in Italy and revitalize in France. As a consequence, performance worsens (interaction n°8). In Italy, the local communities occupy the construction site and impede the start of the geognostic works. In France, the works do not stop, but the opposition of local stakeholders leads the project promoters to review the plans and objectives for the development of the national route giving access to the base tunnel. At the supranational level, the poor performance of several projects funded by TEN-T leads the EU to strengthen its supervision and control functions on the Member States (interaction n°9). The new investment guidelines introduce the corridor forum that imposes to all the Member States involved in TEN-T to provide a work plan of funded projects (interaction n°10). Moreover, any further delay at the national levels in the implementation of funded projects will imply new reductions of EU's financial support (so called "use it or lose it" principle). As a consequence, Italian and French proponents introduce new institutional practices (e.g., Law 183/2011 and prosecution of opponents) which reduce the margin to maneuver of local opponents (interaction n°11). In both contexts, proponents overtly manifest their will to make agreements only with those actors who support the implementation of the LT. In Italy, they get to the point of militarily occupying the construction site to discourage any further opposition and secure the timely implementation of planned objectives. The project performance improves but at the expenses of important-but-unmeasured democratic values (interaction n°12).

5. Discussion

In this chapter, we have proposed a strategic framework for capacity-building in cross-border transport megaprojects. By focusing on the LT case, we have shown how the interactions between content, process, and context have unfolded over time. In particular, we find that LT performance (content) has been affected by (1) national institutions' openness to civil society stakeholders (inner context), (2) supranational intensity of supervision and control (outer context), and (3) actors' capability of making agreements (process). The framework has proved useful to unravel the complex, uncertain, and conflictual nature of megaprojects, the latter being critical to sustainable development design.

Our analysis of the LT invites to reflect on the capacities that are needed in dealing with wickedness in cross-border transport megaprojects. We have analyzed the governance scheme of the LT in the complex settings of the TEN-T, an infrastructure policy at supranational level with the overall aim of improving the functioning of the internal market through continuous and efficient transnational networks in transport flows. As we have shown, the governance of TEN-T is centered on the notion of performance, in the sense of achievement of planned objectives. This is done through indicators representing the project performance in terms of objectives achieved by state-level project promoters against the initial plans agreed with the European Commission. The rationale behind these tools is rooted in technical rationalism and in the belief that public organizations work better when they are oriented toward results, rather than being focused on processes. However, this research has shown that, when translated into practice, this belief may lead the management to strengthen the supervision and control of planned outputs while reducing its openness to stakeholders and ability to make agreements with opponents.

From our perspective, this occurs because the promoters had a rather linear conception of change. This conception sees collective decision-making as a rational choice process where all stakeholders share the same set of values and hold homogenous preferences. Our study suggests that this is a simplistic view of collective decision-making as stakeholder groups may behave on the basis of contradicting logics (proponents vs opponents of change) and by responding to different institutional pressures (French vs Italian institutions). As a consequence, change is rather the result of conflicting interests, politics, and institutional cultures which, all at the same time, make management a social process, meandering and developing over time.

According to our findings, performance management instruments narrow the focus of supranational managerial action on the supervision and control of project outputs – as measured by performance numbers – but overlook the process unfolding over time within the national contexts involved. This narrow focus may have inescapably disciplinarian effects which improve performance at the expenses of important-but-unmeasured democratic values.

Additionally, our study suggests that, at the state level, change in trans-European megaprojects is an uncertain process whose direction may vary across the national contexts involved. In fact, the institutional systems of the Members States may be characterized by different degrees of openness to stakeholders and capacity of making agreements, which in turn may affect performance by producing resistance to change. It therefore indicates that, other than content, more attention should be paid to national contexts and processes. As suggested by Pichault (2013), when managers' over-rely on the content, they tend to prioritize planning and control activities (e.g., plans and programs, performance targets and evaluation). Change is thus understood as a linear process in which the manager has full control over the decision-making process. In the case of trans-European megaprojects, this linear perspective may be detrimental as EU managers and officers might be required to adapt their practices to the evolution of national contexts and processes – and not merely implement planned objectives. Most traditional planning and control approaches are unable to cope with the diversity of viewpoints that characterize trans-European megaprojects.

This research suggests that, at the supranational level, the planning approach should be softened to give more importance to the different processes and contexts structuring the national level. Due attention is to be paid at the complex interplay between supranational and national levels as we show that supranational initiatives of performance management may interfere with the institutions and social relationships at the national levels. Particularly, we have showed negative effects in terms of institutional openness to civil society stakeholders and actors' capability of making agreements with opposing groups in society.

We suggest EU actors to invest more efforts in the design of mechanisms enabling a better alignment between national and supranational organizational processes. Time is also an important aspect as we see that viewpoints on and attitudes toward public initiatives may change over time as new information is disclosed.

6. Conclusions

The findings of this study invite us to think the governance of TEN-T projects beyond the traditional planning logic based on technical rationalism and reflect more on alternative managerial paradigms aimed at reconciling stakeholder participation and performance management. In order to deal with the wicked nature of megaprojects, we argue for the importance of building capacity for organizing. The latter is rooted in a socioeconomic logic directed to achieve public value (Bryson et al., 2014; Moore, 1995), conceived here as "a way of measuring progress towards the achievement of broad and widely accepted societal goals" (Mazzucato & Ryan-Collins, 2022, p. 346).

Capacity for organizing should rest upon three governance features: (1) open decision-making systems, (2) bottom-up performance management, and (3) active dialogue between proponents and opponents. It needs to favor decision-making systems widely opened to the participation of all stakeholder groups, also those having a negative view of the initiative. In this respect, we call for a deliberative approach to megaproject development, which demands that governance is based on truly inclusive discursive practices that engage in an authentically deliberative and consequential way (Corazza, Cottafava, et al., 2022; Esposito et al., 2023). Capacity for organizing also rests upon the belief that performance indicators matter in public management. However, we need to escape a discipline-and-punish type of logic and practices of top-down hierarchical control. Top-down performance management may well hit the target but miss the point (Bevan & Hood, 2006). Traditional PMSs are unable to cope with wickedness of nonlinear policy processes (Noto et al., 2023). Accordingly, we argue that alternative systems of performance management ought to be envisaged to monitor the progress made over the implementation process. In line with an approach grounded in democratic and participatory evaluation (House, 2006; Murray, 2002), our study suggests that the plans and objectives against which performance of megaprojects is assessed ought to be collectively cocreated, debated, and approved (bottom-up) rather than decided from the top management (top-down).

Strategic management is relational, and it is about aligning aspirations and capabilities with a view to achieve certain goals (Bryson & George, 2020; D'Amato & Terlizzi, 2022). If the goal is to build a cross-border high-speed railway line, capacity for organizing wickedness needs to be developed. As the evidence reported in this chapter suggests, this capacity cannot but rest on inclusiveness and cocreation.

References

Berdayes, V. (2002). Traditional management theory as panoptic discourse: Language and the constitution of somatic flows. *Culture and Organization*, *8*(1), 35–49. https://doi.org/10.1080/14759550212102

Bevan, G., & Hood, C. (2006). What's measured is what matters: Targets and gaming in the English public health care system. *Public Administration*, *84*(3), 517–538. https://doi.org/10.1111/j.1467-9299.2006.00600.x

Biesenthal, C., Clegg, S., Mahalingam, A., & Sankaran, S. (2018). Applying institutional theories to managing megaprojects. *International Journal of Project Management*, *36*(1), 43–54. https://doi.org/10.1016/j.ijproman.2017.06.006

Boltanski, L., & Thévenot, L. (1991). *De la Justification. Les Economies de la Grandeur*. Gallimard.

Brenton, S., Baekkeskov, E., & Hannah, A. (2022). Policy capacity: Evolving theory and missing links. *Policy Studies*, 1–19. https://doi.org/10.1080/01442872.2022.2043266

Bryson, J. M., Crosby, B. C., & Bloomberg, L. (2014). Public value governance: Moving beyond traditional public administration and the new public management. *Public Administration Review*, *74*(4), 445–456. https://doi.org/10.1111/puar.12238

Bryson, J. M., & George, B. (2020). Strategic management in public administration. In B. G. Peters & I. Thynne (Eds.), *The Oxford encyclopedia of public administration*. Oxford University Press. https://doi.org/10.1093/acrefore/9780190228637.013.139

Christensen, T., Rykkja, L. H., & Lægreid, P. (2016). Organizing for crisis management: Building governance capacity and legitimacy. *Public Administration Review*, *76*(6), 887–897.

Corazza, L., Cottafava, D., & Torchia, D. (2022). Toward sustainable infrastructural megaprojects. In W. L. Filho, M. A. P. Dinis, S. Moggi, E. Price, & A. Hope (Eds.), *SDGs in the European Region* (pp. 1–25). Springer. https://doi.org/10.1007/978-3-030-91261-1_14-1

Corazza, L., Torchia, D., Cottafava, D., & Tipaldo, G. (2022). Considering the social and economic implications of infrastructure megaprojects: Theoretical contributions, practical challenges and managerial implications. In R. Kudłak, R. Barkemeyer, L. Preuss, & A. Heikkinen (Eds.), *The impact of corporate social responsibility*. Routledge.

D'Amato, S., & Terlizzi, A. (2022). Strategic European counterterrorism? An empirical analysis. *European Security*, *31*(4), 540–557. https://doi.org/10.1080/09662839.2022.2029847

Di Maddaloni, F., & Davis, K. (2017). The influence of local community stakeholders in megaprojects: Rethinking their inclusiveness to improve project performance. *International Journal of Project Management*, *35*, 1537–1556. https://doi.org/10.1016/j.ijproman.2017.08.011

Esposito, G., Felicetti, A., & Terlizzi, A. (2023). Participatory governance in megaprojects: The Lyon–Turin high-speed railway among structure, agency, and democratic participation. *Policy and Society*, *42*(2), 259–273. https://doi.org/10.1093/polsoc/puac029

Esposito, G., Nelson, T., Ferlie, E., & Crutzen, N. (2021). The institutional shaping of global megaprojects: The case of the Lyon-Turin high-speed railway. *International*

Journal of Project Management, *39*(6), 658–671. https://doi.org/10.1016/j.ijproman.2021.06.001

Esposito, G., & Terlizzi, A. (2023). Governing wickedness in megaprojects: Discursive and institutional perspectives. *Policy and Society*, *42*(2), 131–147. https://doi.org/10.1093/polsoc/puad002

Esposito, G., Terlizzi, A., & Crutzen, N. (2022). Policy narratives and megaprojects: The case of the Lyon-Turin high-speed railway. *Public Management Review*, *24*(1), 55–79. https://doi.org/10.1080/14719037.2020.1795230

Esposito, G., Terlizzi, A., & Pichault, F. (2023). The Panopticon reloaded: A critical analysis of performance management systems in the trans-European transport network policy. *Environment and Planning C: Politics and Space*, 1–23. https://doi.org/10.1177/23996544231208546

Flyvbjerg, B. (Ed.). (2017). *The Oxford handbook of megaproject management*. Oxford University Press.

Foucault, M. (1980). Truth and power. In C. Gordon (Ed.), *Power/Knowledge: Selected interviews and other writings 1972–1977* (pp. 107–133). The Harvester Press. https://doi.org/10.1038/433570a

Fowler, L. (2021). How to implement policy: Coping with ambiguity and uncertainty. *Public Administration*, *99*(3), 581–597. https://doi.org/10.1111/padm.12702

Hargrave, T. J., & Van de Ven, A. H. (2009). Institutional work as the creative embrace of contradiction. In T. B. Lawrence, R. Suddaby, & B. Leca (Eds.), *Institutional work: Actors and agency in institutional studies of organizations* (pp. 120–140). Cambridge University Press.

Head, B. W. (2022). *Wicked problems in public policy: Understanding and responding to complex challenges*. Palgrave Macmillan.

House, E. R. (2006). Democracy and evaluation. *Evaluation*, *12*(1), 119–127. https://doi.org/10.1177/1356389006064196

Lodge, M., & Wegrich, K. (Eds.). (2014). *The problem-solving capacity of the modern state: Governance challenges and administrative capacities*. Oxford University Press.

Mazzucato, M., & Ryan-Collins, J. (2022). Putting value creation back into "public value": From market-fixing to market-shaping. *Journal of Economic Policy Reform*, *25*(4), 345–360. https://doi.org/10.1080/17487870.2022.2053537

Moore, M. H. (1995). *Creating public value: Strategic management in government*. Harvard University Press.

Murray, R. (2002). Citizens' control of evaluations. *Evaluation*, *8*(1), 81–100. https://doi.org/10.1177/1358902002008001488

Noto, G., Prenestini, A., Cosenz, F., & Barresi, G. (2023). Tackling wicked problems in performance management and governance of public health: An empirical analysis of COVID-19 vaccination strategies. *International Journal of Public Sector Management*, *36*(2), 130–151. https://doi.org/10.1108/IJPSM-07-2022-0163

Pettigrew, A. M. (1987). Context and action in the transformation of the firm. *Journal of Management Studies*, *24*(6), 649–670. https://doi.org/10.1111/j.1467-6486.1987.tb00467.x

Pettigrew, A. M., & Whipp, R. (1991). *Managing change for competitive success*. Blackwell. https://www.wiley.com/en-us/Managing+Change+for+Competitive+Success-p-9780631191421

Pichault, F. (2013). *Change management. Towards polyphony*. De Boeck.

Pollitt, C. (Ed.). (2013). *Context in public policy and management: The missing link?* Edward Elgar.

Rittel, H. W. J., & Webber, M. M. (1973). Dilemmas in a general theory of planning. *Policy Sciences*, *4*, 155–161. https://doi.org/10.1080/01636609209550084

Sankaran, S., Müller, R., & Drouin, N. (2020). Creating a 'sustainability sublime' to enable megaprojects to meet the United Nations sustainable development goals. *Systems Research and Behavioral Science*, *37*(5), 813–826. https://doi.org/10.1002/sres.2744

Sargiacomo, M., Corazza, L., D'Andreamatteo, A., & Torchia, D. (2022). Megaprojects and hybridity. Accounting and performance challenges for multiple diverse actors and values. *The British Accounting Review*, 101152. https://doi.org/10.1016/j.bar.2022.101152

The Economist Intelligence Unit. (2019). *The critical role of infrastructure for the Sustainable Development Goals*. The Economist Intelligence Unit.

Tonga Uriarte, Y., DeFillippi, R., Riccaboni, M., & Catoni, M. L. (2019). Projects, institutional logics and institutional work practices: The case of the Lucca Comics & Games Festival. *International Journal of Project Management*, *37*(2), 318–330. https://doi.org/10.1016/j.ijproman.2018.09.001

Wu, X., Ramesh, M., & Howlett, M. (Eds.). (2018). *Policy capacity and governance: Assessing governmental competences and capabilities in theory and practice*. Palgrave Macmillan. https://doi.org/10.1007/978-3-319-54675-9_1

Chapter 7

Wicked Nature of Sustainability Problems in Latvia

Iveta Reinholde, Inese Abolina and Ilze Auliciema

University of Latvia, Latvia

Abstract

This chapter examines how Latvia manages Sustainable Development Goals (SDGs) within a policymaking process in Latvia – how SGDs are interpreted into policy actions in Latvia. This chapter is based on the two cases to reveal a link between SDGs and wicked problems. The case of education is about policy and strategic planning considering the high priority of the education sector in society. At the same time, climate change reflects the opposite perspective – limited public attention and fewer policy actions. Thus, both cases reveal actual policy implementation with several uncertainties. In the meantime, both topics are essential to identify strategies for solving wicked agendas related to policy coherence and interconnection among goals. As a result, the implementation of SDGs needs more institutional mechanisms for future-oriented policymaking where the present development needs are met without compromising the ability of future generations to meet their needs.

Keywords: Sustainable Development Goals; Latvia; public administration; governance; implementation failures

1. Introduction

Sustainable Development Goals (SDGs) are accepted as a part of the management practice at the organizational levels and have become an integral part of policy design. The approach "SDGs in every policy" has been integrated into all national policies, shaping their substance and challenging implementation. The SDGs reporting is a national responsibility; thus, any country tries to outline their progress.

Policy Capacity, Design and the Sustainable Development Goals, 143–160

Published under exclusive licence by Emerald Publishing Limited
doi:10.1108/978-1-80455-686-320241010

Two selected cases for analysis in the article – education (4th SGD) and climate change (13th SDG) – are appropriate to outline their wickedness and policymakers' strategies to cope with it, where policy coherence and interconnection among goals are essential. The Latvian point is interesting as it illustrates the complexity of sustainability problems and the challenges of achieving SDGs in a decentralized bureaucratic system.

The dual subordination of the education system at the national and municipal levels in combination with a long-lasting search for optimal solutions affected by the recent municipal amalgamations demonstrate the conditions capable of creating wicked problems at the primary level of education (Rittel & Webber, 1973). The case study shows how the wickedness of the problem manifests itself not only at the institutional but also at the social and personal level: society begins to distrust the work of educational institutions, but young people avoid choosing to be employed in this system.

Meanwhile, such complex problems as climate change and green policy have yet to be high on either the political agenda or societal concerns. International pressure to mitigate the adverse effects of climate change forced Latvian policymakers to take some steps. Latvia is a signatory to global climate change agreements like the Paris Agreement. However, Latvia has yet to join the International Energy Agency, which works with countries worldwide to shape energy policies for a secure and sustainable future. However, climate change is perceived more as a complex problem with no responsible authority yet, but it can affect the national economy's future.

Additionally, the Latvian Sustainable Development Strategy 2030, a long-term planning document necessary for bureaucratic routine, expresses the shared vision toward the sustainable future of the state. The Strategy was widely discussed with society during its design stage. However, policy problems related to sustainable development, such as aging society, globalization of the economy, crises of democracy, and poverty risks related to urbanization, are complex enough to create implementation failures and gaps and label them "wicked" as they fall into different bureaucratic authorities and bureaucratic image of the same problems differs.

2. SGD in Latvia: Place and Perception

Latvia started its road toward achieving SDGs in 2002 when the policy paper on sustainable development of Latvia was formally approved. The political commitment was tailored to set out activities for achieving goals defined in 1992 by the UN.

The planning system in Latvia is decentralized, meaning that each institution should do a certain number of activities toward sustainability. In this context, the national government provides a framework and general guidelines, while national and local agencies ensure implementation. Overall, the planning system means that Latvia plans its policy action at the national level, where the ministries are the critical authorities for policy planning. At the same time, agencies and municipalities are the key stakeholders in policy implementation.

For planning purposes, Latvia has designed a planning system where all policy papers are placed in a specific line of hierarchy. The policy papers are an essential component of Latvia's planning process to provide detailed policies and strategies needed to implement broader objectives outlined in the Latvian Sustainable Development Strategy 2030. By aligning development plans, Latvia aims to ensure its policies and actions are coherent and directed toward achieving long-term sustainability goals. Policy papers serve as the bridge between high-level vision and practical implementation, helping to guide Latvia's policy decisions and actions. Latvian Sustainable Development Strategy 2030 is a crucial long-term document, sometimes labeled as the first document for all policies. National plans are approved for 7 years and are assumed to be medium-term with a high degree of coherence with Strategy 2030 (Saeima, 2011).

The planning system with a strong hierarchy of documents and steps to follow is well established in Latvia. A particular law also regulates the planning system and the whole approach. Thus, it provides all preconditions for tackling problems once they are in the system. However, such a planning system has a shortcoming – problems should already be well-defined before they are expanded in analytic papers.

All in all, the Sustainable Development Strategy 2030 (Saeima, 2011) is both a long-term planning document necessary for bureaucratic routine and a document expressing the shared vision toward the sustainable future of the state, discussed widely with society. The design process of the Strategy was unique as the community groups were commonly involved in designing the vision. Meaningful public engagement involves consultations with various stakeholders, including government agencies, civil society organizations, businesses, and the general public, to gather diverse perspectives and ensure that the Strategy reflects the priorities and concerns of the population. So, a strategy being a "public agreement" discussed what sustainability means for Latvians and how much effort the nation is ready to invest in achieving goals.

According to the Strategy, the Latvian vision toward sustainability is based on a shared understanding expressed by the UN. However, the Latvian Strategy emphasizes such issues as an aging society, globalization of the economy, continuous demand for new competencies, climate changes, increasing demand for resources, crises of democracy, and poverty risks related to urbanization (Saeima, 2011, p. 6). The wickedness picture is structured by placing the Latvian complex problems in the typology grid of difficulties.

Value divergence regarding wicked problems plays a vital role. Wicked problems are usually complex, loaded with uncertainty and different societal perceptions among politicians. Thus, communication during the policy design stage and following policy coordination during the implementation may substantially decrease value divergence. Recent data from the security index collected by the insurance company ERGO reflect that the top problems of societal concern are – physical security and job and financial security (ERGO, 2022). The research on subjective perception demonstrated similar results – Latvian citizens are more concerned about personal, economic, and political security (Ozoliņa et al., 2021). However, climate change is not among Latvians' critical areas of concern. While education, health care, and social insurance have always been sectors with relatively high public trust and areas for concern (LU SPPI, 2021; Ozoliņa et al., 2021), in fact, according to Table 7.1, education is a tame problem requiring continuously inputs and improvements to react to needs of society and industries.

Lack of ex ante and ex post assessment limits communication among stakeholders in building a shared understanding of wicked problems and limits in identifying the problems and solutions (OECD, 2018). Even though Latvia is improving in an ex ante and ex post analysis of draft laws and policy papers, assessment tools are not fully utilized and cannot provide a systemic impact (European Commission, 2022). Latvia needs to conduct more policy assessments (ex ante and ex post) to capture wicked problems at the early stages. Thus, policymakers have limited information regarding wicked problems and their solutions. In a way, this is a process in the education and climate changes where limited policy assessment does not provide an in-depth illustration of the sector, resulting in invalid solutions.

Meanwhile, the assessment of the implementation of SDGs reflects critical challenges – the transition toward innovation and an eco-efficient economy, including climate commitments (PKC, 2022a, p. 32). Latvia is progressing in the implementation of goals related to education (4th SGD), and the overall status is better than in the EU on average; regarding climate change (13th SDG), Latvia's performance is improving, but the situation is worse than in EU (Eurostat, 2022). The national report recognized that Latvia is also improving in the education

Table 7.1. Typology of Problems.

	Actors Willing to Cooperate or Avoid Conflict	**Multiple Actors, Each With Relevant Useful Knowledge**	**Multiple Actors With Conflicting Values and Interests**
Both the problem and solution known	*Demand for new skills and competencies* (Tame problem)	*Disproportional regional development* (Communicatively complex problems)	*Globalisation of economy* (Politically wicked problem)
The problem is known; the solution is not known	*Weak urban-rural interaction* (Analytically complex problem)	*Demand for energy resources and energy safety* (Complex problem)	*Climate changes Ageing society* (Wicked problem)
Neither problem nor solution known	*Demographic changes* (Cognitively complex problem)	*Poverty risks related to urbanisation* (Wicked problem)	*Crisis of democracy* (Very wicked problem)

Source: Adopted from Head (2022, p. 32), the policy problems from Saeima (2011).

sector. Recently, the State Audit Office found out Latvia needs to significantly improve its actions toward achieving SDG by coordinating policies, allocating budget and raising awareness of SGDs (LRVK, 2023). According to the State Audit Office, the key reason for the weak performance toward SDG is its fragmented governmental approach, assuming that implementing agencies will perform their tasks. In reality, Latvia has no real operational plan and responsible authority. Thus, it only motivates the bureaucratic agencies to implement the Strategy if translated into the bureaucratic language. In addition, the State Audit Office also identified a severe implementation gap – SGDs are not a part of the planning system. They are not incorporated into the system for sectoral planning (LRVK, 2023). Thus, they are bringing together multiple actors and their diverse interests.

Most often, policymaking faces wicked problems due to knowledge gaps: poor learning processes of stakeholders and researchers and nonparticipatory or limited negotiations of solutions (Pham-Truffert et al., 2020). In light of SGD, if there is long-term public concern and trust (like for education), policymakers will probably try to solve the issues despite uncertainties and complexities. While climate change has limited public attention, it receives less policy and political engagement. Media coverage, major climate events, and public awareness campaigns affect public interest and engagement with climate change. When public attention is limited, policymakers may prioritize other issues more salient to their constituents.

As Andersson and Törnberg (2018) pointed out, acknowledging the wickedness of the problems seems like opening a black box where more incoming and related problems challenge any attempts to resolve complex issues. In a way, this is the case that characterizes Latvia in the context of SDGs; having no clear interpretation of SDGs in the national context, policymakers are afraid to come up with actions as this may put more issues on the agenda, especially if causality of cases are not transparent or analyzed before. Although the wicked problems are usually related to the three types of uncertainties – cognitive, strategic, and institutional (Van Bueren et al., 2003), adverse effects of those uncertainties are minimized by cooperation within networks and communication with stakeholders. However, the common understanding and perception of a complex problem are of the same importance as the process during which networks and stakeholders innovate, debate, and compromise for the results.

3. Case Study: Latvia 2030 and Inclusive Preschool Education

The case aims to discover why the SDGs should be evaluated complexly and why assumptions about sustainability in the education sector should not be made based on a few exclusive and good-performing criteria. The case demonstrates that some reasons for wicked problems seem relatively straightforward – a limited capacity and multiple actors in one stage of policy implementation result in difficulties afterward. At the same time, the case study reveals a more profound problem facing the modern education system: it is impossible to simultaneously provide an inclusive environment for students with special needs and a developmental environment for students who develop faster. One of the parties will always suffer because it will not be possible for educators to devote enough attention to either one or the other, and the working methods will be different in both cases. Society will have to choose one of the directions – an inclusive environment that adapts to the needs of the weakest students (including students with special needs) or an environment that develops the most capable students in pursuit of excellence. When choosing an inclusive solution, one must be aware of its strengths and weaknesses and be able to stop in time to align all interests of multiple actors.

Inclusive education, as initially defined by the Salamanca Statement (UNESCO, 1994), refers to schooling in which all children, including children with severe disabilities, have access to regular classrooms with the help of adequate support (Saloviita, 2020). Modern inclusive education includes preschool, general secondary, vocational, and higher education establishments. It provides not only the active inclusion and participation of children with special educational needs in the educational process of the general education school but also, to a greater extent, the restructuring of the entire educational process as a system to meet the educational needs of all children (Bogush et al., 2022). Realizing this idea means significant changes in the education system – starting with policymaking, industry management, curricula and methods, teachers, students, and parents. In this broader sense, inclusion is comparable to equality as a social value relating to all aspects of social disadvantage, oppression, and discrimination (Avramidis & Norwich, 2010). Thus, these issues also affect questions of societal values and human rights.

The studies consider the attitude of teachers as the most important key point in the implementation of inclusive education, along with the attitude of parents (Avramidis & Norwich, 2010; Štemberger & Kiswarday, 2018). Undoubtedly, the teachers face the most significant challenges in this process, as they must ensure that all students learn the program, regardless of their ability.

David Armstrong points to several groups of wicked problems: (1) Achieving a curriculum which is fit for purpose in meeting the holistic needs of learners with disabilities – this wicked problem involves, for example, designing a curriculum which can "respect and respond to human differences in ways that include rather than exclude learners," (2) the adverse, flow-on effects of neoliberal educational policies on children or young people with disabilities (unhelpful calls for return to what might be described as traditional teaching practices and a regressive return to the "normative center" of education, greater segregation), (3) responding effectively to behaviors by students with a disability which warrant adult concern or action and in a manner which avoids educational exclusion, (4) ensuring that special and inclusive education is a progressive space which adopts ethical and research-informed practices, and (5) ensuring that special and inclusive education is a progressive space which adopts ethical and research-informed practices (Armstrong, 2017).

The above indicates that the set goal of creating an inclusive education system contains many challenges, including wicked problems. The situation is made even more complicated by the need to measure the effectiveness of an inclusive education system so that the chosen indicators of goal achievement reflect the actual situation. Brian G. Cook et al., analyzing evidence-based indicators of inclusive education, found that these indicators should be comprehensive. Special educators must validate their effectiveness for each child (Cook & Odom, 2013). Change cannot be unidimensional to succeed in schools. Still, it must be adopted across the political, social, cultural, psychological, and behavioral dimensions of complex educational institutions' everyday, routine fabric (Armstrong, 2017).

At the same time, the goal achievement indicators chosen in the political planning documents practically do not reflect the impact of wicked problems on the education system. The National Development Plan of Latvia uses two indicators that describe the creation of an inclusive environment in educational institutions – the proportion of children and young people who continue their education after obtaining compulsory education and the number of children with special needs who study in general educational institutions and programs about the total number of children in these institutions (PKC, 2020). Many initiatives have been financed by the government and EU funds to promote inclusive education and decrease the risk of social exclusion in Latvia. However, data reflect that in 2016, only 40.9% of special needs students were fully integrated into general education (PKC, 2018).

3.1 Process and Stakeholders

The policy paper "Latvian Education Development Guidelines 2021.–2027" offers several measures for inclusive education. These measures include:

- implementation of early diagnosis for children who start compulsory preschool education at the age of five,
- availability of support staff in the school and kindergarten to strengthen the inclusive approach,
- capacity building of schools and kindergartens regarding cooperation and communication with parents,
- involvement of the municipality and coordination of local strategic investments in the education process at all stages. (MoE, 2021)

Following the hierarchy line established in development planning, the policy paper is translated into the Education Law, which sets out the responsibilities of stakeholders. So, the Ministry of Education has developed guidelines and methodological materials explaining the process of assistance for each child with special needs should be provided. However, all functions related to diagnosing children with special needs are classified and protected by data protection regulations and requirements. Latvia's Report on Sustainable Development (2022) and PKC (2022b) observed good progress achieved in education. According to the Report, education for children at the age of five is compulsory, access to preschool education is constantly improving, and an increasing number of children with special needs are integrated into general education schools. The available system so far is formally in line with sound governance principles.

However, the picture regarding the implementation is different. Local municipalities tended gradually to reduce the number of specially designed schools as a part of budgetary saving mechanisms (MoE, 2022), according to the policy paper "Latvian Education Development Guidelines 2021.–2027 (MoE, 2021), many reforms are taking place in the educational system, covering topics like management, organizational structure, and content. At the same time, the lack of staff (especially teachers and supporting team) and the aging staff are urgent challenges to the education system. Thus, achieving quick changes and results in this area will be problematic.

The administrative-territorial reform of 2021 significantly reduced the number of local governments, reducing the number of schools. This is how municipalities reacted to depopulation (Saeima, 2010, p. 19).

Generally, there is a sound preschool education system with qualified teachers and experienced management. At the same time, some significant shortcomings in the system are also identified in two similar cases in different preschools.[1] Parents have observed a relatively common situation: children who previously enjoyed attending school no longer want to. It was discovered that most cases of aggression are related to an individual child having a negative influence over others. The whole learning process was disturbed. Educators refrained from commenting on this situation under the pretext of confidentiality requirements. Information about a person's state of health cannot be disclosed to third parties. Only when parents directly ask the school administration if a particular child has special needs or a learning disability do they receive approval.

Meanwhile, parents were informed that the preschool was understaffed (i.e., teachers, teaching assistants, social workers, and psychologists) to handle all inquiries, and full assistance would only be provided when additional staff were brought in, even the unique learning plan for a child with special needs. Parents' observations and preschool staff's explanations were documented in the parents' submission to the preschool management. It should also be noted that the administration could not refuse to accept a child with special needs in a preschool educational institution even if there were no conditions and support.

The situation was even more complicated from the "special" child's and his family's perspective.[2] The policy aims to integrate "special" children into the public preschool, creating hope that their children will be integrated into society. At the policy level, the support scheme is designed. However, when it comes to the implementation – the family of the child with special needs are left alone as teachers are overloaded with assignments, and supporting staff is unavailable. In this case, a well-intentioned policy facing failures resulted in a wicked problem:

[1]The cases have been recorded in the records of educational institutions following the procedures specified in the Law on Submissions of the Republic of Latvia.

[2]Parents' opinion was confirmed during the anonymous interview.

the "special" child and his family were excluded, not included. The story ended with the fact that kids with special needs do not attend preschool anymore.

Besides the ethical dilemma of each involved stakeholder, the case reveals severe systemic failures – the municipal finances municipal preschool education. As demand for preschool is high and there is a lack of physical capacity, temporary solutions were offered – municipal allowance for children who attend the privately run preschool. However, for parents earning an average salary (in the third quote of 2022 in Latvia, it was 1,369 eur per month (Statistical office, 2022)), the cost of private preschool is unbearable. From the SDG perspective, this aspect impacts the indicators that characterize the depth of poverty and gender equality (despite equal rights according to the regulation, more often mothers stay with children).

The wickedness or the problem is inherited in the education system as well. The law requires accepting the kid while coping with conditions that are not functioning well. The school administration tends to look for the simplest solution – to move a child with special needs to another class in the same age group. As a result of the failed implementation of inclusive education, the child with special needs and their future classmates will receive psychological trauma. Such a result will contradict the goals in the policy paper "Latvian Education Development Guidelines for 2021.–2027."

The details of planning and the number of finances affect the municipality and the Ministry of Education. The task of these institutions is to ensure the implementation of SDGs, to finance schools, and to react to the needs of society, including children (both with and without special needs) and their parents, even when resources are scarce. While the desire to reduce the number of specialized schools and integrate children into the general education system allows for an inclusive society, the wish is constrained by the short-term benefits of saving money and the long-term benefits of education quality for everyone.

Extremal pressure on educational institutions has far-reaching consequences for preschool administration, teachers, supportive staff, children, and their families. The SDGs and their achievement indicators are a large-scale planning tool demonstrating the overall picture at the national level. Evaluating the policy's success might include several perspectives depending on how these indicators are defined. Since the problem is wicked, policy effectiveness could be measured with the indicator (the number of children with special needs who attend the general preschool) as the issue's complexity is related to stakeholders' capability to compromise over the solution.

In this specific case, the SDG regarding inclusive education was adopted by the government and accepted by society. High-level plans and regulations (the policy paper "Latvian Education Development Guidelines 2021.–2027." and the Education Law) reflected these objectives adequately. Problems turn into wicked when it comes to implementation. It does not necessarily mean that inclusive education policy has failed. Insufficient funding for the education system, the unbalanced workload of staff, and staff burnout – are primarily managerial issues to be solved coherently at the national and local levels.

3.2 The Wickedness of Inclusive Preschool Education Policy

The inclusive preschool education policy demonstrates the wickedness of problems, mainly in the implementation phase of inclusive education. The problems occur at different levels:

- Individual (in this case – children) level – safety and understanding are primary prerequisites for an inclusive attitude. This is important for children who meet the "special" child and must interact with society acceptably.
- Family level – a family expectation toward inclusive education and their readiness to contribute to inclusiveness.
- Education agency level – they are expected to provide the best possible solutions for all parties involved, even if resources are insufficient. Society must accept that the educational agency may refuse to take responsibility for a child with special needs if there are no available staff to deliver the service.
- Inter-sectoral policy implementing level – policy coordination is essential to avoid sector-driven and fragmented solutions. Teacher salary and family support issues are tasks of the Ministry of Education and the municipality.

The number of "special" children attending public preschools indicates a well-implemented sustainable policy. Achieving this indicator requires a high price – teacher burnout, lack of staff, and a decrease in public sympathy toward "special" children and their families, superficially seen as a wicked problem. While from the process perspective, it is all about managing the process with many stakeholders and shared authorities.

4. Case Study on Climate Change Policy

Another interesting case for Latvia is climate change, pointing to the strengths and weaknesses of the implementation process of SDG at the different stages of implementation. Climate change is explored from the policy perspective by considering policy tools, measures, and uncertainties. Climate change is the 13th SDG, which has been positively assessed nationally, while public perception indicates a different perspective (Ozoliņa et al., 2021).

Action related to climate permeates all UN SGD and Latvian sectoral policies. Latvia is committed to reducing the greenhouse gas emissions produced by the national economy and has a political commitment to achieve climate neutrality by 2050. By 2030, Latvia is expected to improve energy efficiency in electricity production and transport infrastructure. At the same time, Latvia is required to take the necessary steps to prepare for the impact of the climate risks, including the prevention of possible disasters – floods, coastal erosion, heat waves and heavy rains, as well as the effects of extreme weather on various sectors of the economy.

4.1 Process and Stakeholders

Latvia has established measures to reduce the impact of climate change. Currently, Latvia's mitigation of climate change is designed as a national-level policy with such measures as – reduction of greenhouse gas (GHG) emissions and increase in carbon dioxide capture, increase in the proportion of renewable energy sources, improvement of energy efficiency, ensuring energy security, maintenance and improvement of energy market infrastructure. Climate goals are also included in the long-term strategies of local governments (Halkos & Gkampoura, 2021). Extensive work is being done to improve societal understanding of climate change, its impact and adaptation, and regular public campaigns are organized. The involvement of Latvia's scientific potential in international studies and forecasts, in evaluating Latvia's natural capital and conducting practical research, is ensured. In Latvia's National Energy and Climate Plan 2021–2030, Latvia has set targets to reduce GHG emissions. Also, Latvia has increased renewable energy sources such as wind, solar, and hydropower to reduce carbon emissions. Latvia significantly reduces GHG emissions by improving energy efficiency in buildings, transportation, and industries.

There are several policy papers designed. So far, Latvia has adopted its climate change adaptation plan for up to 2030. Also, Latvia's Strategy for achieving climate neutrality by 2050 has been approved. The government has approved the National Energy and Climate Plan for 2021–2030. A regular assessment of flood risks has been carried out, and measures have been taken to reduce flood risks. The National Civil Defense Plan was approved after the early warning system was substantially improved. A climate change portal has been created to raise public awareness of climate change. The portal has an analytic tool that allows us to forecast and visualize Latvia's current and future climate through maps and graphs. Also, as a member of the European Union (EU), Latvia has committed to reducing the EU's emissions by at least 55% by 2030 compared to 1990. Until 2027, 30% of the bilateral development cooperation funding managed by the Ministry of Foreign Affairs in mitigating climate change offers to strengthen the capacities of society and institutions and integrate climate change into policies and planning.

Meanwhile, the climate change policy is facing a lack of horizontal and vertical coordination. Climate change is a complex problem that requires a coordinated response from various sectors and levels of government. However, coordination of SDGs, especially ownership, is the critical factor in why goals will not be achieved (LRVK, 2023). There are some specific challenges that Latvia may face with SDG13:

- Insufficient financing: Addressing climate change requires significant investments in renewable energy, energy efficiency, and other climate-related measures. There are plans to invest in EU structural funding for climate change mitigation and adaptation activities, but more is needed, considering climate change mitigation includes changing citizens' behaviors. Insufficient financing is related to each institution; once the managerial decisions are made, the institutions allocate a budget for the functions entrusted and issues relevant to society. Thus, if the implementation of SDG is not defined as a function and problems do not apply to the community, the implementation will likely be pending.

- Limited public awareness and engagement: Public awareness and engagement are essential for creating support for climate change policies and actions (Sree Kumar et al., 2020). Without public attention, any issue of SDG will reach the stage of cognitive uncertainty (Van Bueren et al., 2003).
- Limited institutional capacity: Addressing climate change requires technical expertise, data, and analytical skills. The institutional ability to design, implement, and monitor climate change policies and actions is still limited as politicians or citizens do not recognize climate change as a priority.

Considering the actual policy capacity, Latvia could decide on several strategies to react to the challenges, like setting institutional ownership for the particular SDG (including climate change) to set multidisciplinary cooperation platforms and partnerships with research institutions and international organizations. For climate change SDG, the meta-governance approach is helpful in guidance for coping with the different governance traditions (He et al., 2023). For example, energy issues are currently dominated by the market in Latvia. It is linked to climate action, often leaning toward hierarchical solutions (legally binding agreements). Air pollution policy is also rules-based, while transport policies are often market-based. Bottom-up network-style innovation fuels the circular economy in synergy with industry policy, which frames market rules. Thus, climate change is a complex mix of policy tools and approaches that fuels institutional uncertainty as bureaucratic practices differ from case to case.

Fast-track SDG implementation includes taking risks, trials, and failures. However, the risk-taking culture is not well-developed in the Latvian public sector. Public agency's first reaction to external shocks is usually the "freeze" approach – stop and wait. Nevertheless, to be prepared for crises, the Latvian public sector is expected to combine stability with flexibility, where institutional innovation is rewarded instead of punishment.

The SDGs and their achievement indicators are a large-scale planning tool that somehow describes the overall picture. Communication is essential to tackle issues which arise during the climate crisis. For example, Latvia has also been affected by climate change. In the summer of 2018, it was dry and hot in Latvia. High temperatures contributed to the spread of fire in peat (52% of Latvia is covered by forests, and 9.9% are peat bogs) fields of Sala. The fire quickly spread underground and into the woods. Neighboring countries helped overcome this natural disaster with helicopters, drawing public attention to the environmental dimension of sustainability and constructive international cooperation (Martín-Blanco et al., 2022).

Several policy failures have contributed to the slow progress of achieving SDG13 in Latvia. One of the main reasons is the low political prioritization of climate change issues at the national level. Social prioritization is critical in policy formulation and implementation, especially when addressing complex global challenges like climate change. As a result, climate policies in Latvia lack more consistency and cohesion, with limited coordination between different sectors and levels of government. Another policy failure is low public awareness and engagement on climate change issues. To accelerate progress on climate action and SDG13, Latvia is expected to increase awareness, more substantial political commitment, and more excellent societal prioritization of climate change in Latvia.

Finally, international cooperation and coordination on climate change provide external pressure on Latvia. Despite signing the Paris Agreement, Latvia has struggled to participate effectively in international climate negotiations and coordinate its policies with other countries. These policy failures have contributed to the slow progress of achieving SDG13 internally. Latvia's ability to achieve SDG13 is closely linked to participation in international climate agreements and its capacity to coordinate policies with other nations. Challenges in this regard can slow down progress toward climate action goals. To address these issues, Latvia engage in diplomatic efforts, seek assistance from international organizations (for example, International Energy Agency), and update domestic policies to align with global commitments.

Climate change is perceived more as a global, geographically distant challenge than a local one. The population survey conducted in 2021 shows that a relatively large proportion of respondents (38%) agree that Latvia could influence climate change mitigation. Implementing Latvia's climate change adaptation plan requires extensive involvement and cooperation of institutions and society. Measures and tasks are planned to be implemented using state and local government budget funding and attracting financial resources from the EU and other sources and private capital. When forecasting GHG emissions, Latvia may not achieve the goals set for 2030 and 2050, which means that additional measures, tasks, actions, and finances must be planned to achieve them. The expected legislative changes include actions like the gradual cessation of coal and oil extraction and use, the reduction of their subsidies, the promotion of renewable energy production, restrictions on the sale of internal combustion engines, energy efficiency requirements, the development of a circular economy, the reuse of waste, the condition of the use of chemical substances in agriculture industry. This is an opportunity for sustainable and inclusive development, which does not leave negative consequences for the environment and human health and improves the quality of life of all people living in Latvia. Particular attention should be paid to society's low-income and socially excluded part.

One major factor contributing to the wickedness of climate change policy in Latvia is the country's heavy reliance on fossil fuels. Latvia is highly dependent on imported oil and gas, and these fuels significantly contribute to GHG emissions. However, transitioning to renewable energy sources is a complex and expensive process that requires substantial political will, investment, and stakeholder engagement.

Another factor contributing to the wickedness of climate change policy in Latvia is the difficulty of coordinating and integrating approaches across different sectors and levels of government. Climate change policy requires collaboration between multiple stakeholders, including government agencies, civil society organizations, and private sector actors. However, these stakeholders often have conflicting interests and priorities, making developing and implementing effective policy a high-stakes game.

As new research emerges, policymakers must continually update their understanding of the causes and impacts of climate change, as well as the most effective ways to address it. This ongoing process of learning and adaptation makes climate change policy inherently complex and challenging.

The wickedness of climate change policy in Latvia is driven by a combination of factors, including the country's heavy reliance on fossil fuels, the difficulty of coordinating policy across different sectors and levels of government, limited government capacity, and the uncertain nature of climate science. Addressing these challenges will require significant investment in renewable energy, stakeholder engagement, and capacity building for effective policy design and implementation.

5. Conclusions

The two case studies selected describe how Latvia moves toward achieving SDGs in two fields – education and climate change.

The case on education corresponds to conditions when both problem and solution are known. However, due to implementation failures and a lack of political priorities, the issues in education might jeopardize national growth. The education case demonstrates how factors accumulate at the local level of governance and organization. However, as education is among the critical concerns of populations and politicians, they will still search for potential solutions, whatever the factors affect stakeholders.

The second case of climate presumptively refers to the situation where the problem is known. Still, the solution involves many activity areas and affects various interests and actors. From Latvia's perspective, climate change issues require diverse policy actors to cooperate. Problems related to reducing carbon emissions, producing "green" energy, and preventing floods, droughts, and hurricanes are applied to climate change. In addition, it is difficult to determine the causes of these natural phenomena in each case. From this point of view, the second case study can be described as a situation when the problem is not thoroughly investigated in each specific instance. The case of climate change reflects a top-down approach when climate change is tackled at the national level due to global liabilities and pressure. However, there is slow progress due to cognitive, strategic, and institutional uncertainties. Challenges arise when addressing the specific impacts and policy responses at the national or local level, where detailed investigations of local environmental conditions are ongoing and require further research.

The education case study is where we can follow how shortcomings in policy implementation led to wicked problems both in the process itself and related processes. The selected SDG achievement indicator (the number and percentage of "special" children who study in general education establishments) shows the operational result but does not demonstrate its quality. The relatively small scale of the problem allows us to see how the wickedness of the problem is formed. In the case of education, the root of the problem was an incorrectly defined form of training and insufficient help for the any child with special needs to fit into general education. However, issues in the education sector are familiar and unique; they have already existed for a long time. This indicates that the root of the problem is to be inherited at the planning and decision-making level. At the beginning of the policy implementation, the impacts and risks inside and outside the sector still need to be sufficiently evaluated. While, society generally supports the integration of "special" children at the earliest possible age suffers. The most important thing, in this case, is that people need to catch up to the SDG goals, thus forming a gap between the administration and society.

The second case study is a macro-level case with a global dimension. Climate change affects all countries; therefore, international coordination and agreements are essential. Some countries assume certain obligations toward other countries, thus trying to improve the situation by working together. Communicating SDGs and their achievement indicators is significantly more complicated in this case. SDGs should be understood and accepted both within each country and globally together. Creating a common understanding among all involved parties is made difficult both by the diverse forms of climate change, which are different in different parts of the world, and by the fact that the causes and consequences of human activity are shifted in time.

Consequently, measures to be taken should be agreed upon both at the national and global levels. It is of utmost importance to reach an agreement between the government, businesses, and people at the national level. The most confronting part of this arrangement is at the national level, where government, business, and people's (as individuals) interests must be aligned. Building such awareness takes time, but climate change requires immediate action. In addition, there needs to be more trustful and reliable information to be provided on a broad spectrum overview to judge the causality of climate change. Thus, the problem interaction takes place in a dynamic system that is constantly changing, and this system has different levels and dimensions: (1) global and national, (2) business, government, and people. In such a situation, capturing all interactions of problems at all levels and assessing risks for every policy is difficult, if possible. However, issues should still be solved.

Wicked policy problems are complex and ambiguous issues that are difficult to define, measure, and solve. Climate change and education are two examples of wicked policy problems, and their solutions require a collaborative effort among multiple stakeholders. In the case of Latvia, climate change is a significant policy problem exacerbated by the country's high dependence on fossil fuels. To address this issue, Latvia needs to increase its policy capacity by investing in renewable energy sources and improving energy efficiency. Moreover, Latvia should develop policies that promote sustainable transportation, such as public transit and biking.

Similarly, education is a wicked policy problem in Latvia. The country's education system faces challenges such as unequal access to quality education, high dropout rates, and a shortage of skilled teachers. To address these issues, Latvia should focus on improving policy capacity by investing in teacher training and professional development, promoting equity in access to education, and creating policies that support student success and retention.

A diagnostic approach to analyzing wicked policy problems and policy capacity in Latvia identified critical stakeholders' involvement in addressing the issue, such as government agencies, civil society organizations, and private sector actors. Also, policy capacity gaps were identified to tackle the wicked policy problem effectively. Developing a strategy for enhancing policy capacity and addressing the wicked policy problem is needed by developing new policies, investing in training and capacity building, and collaborating with stakeholders to create shared solutions. Monitoring and evaluating the progress in addressing the wicked policy problem and enhancing policy capacity over time is crucial to track progress and conduct regular assessments to identify new challenges and opportunities.

SDGs are based on universal human values, but indicators of their achievement cannot entirely reflect the actual situation. While aiming to achieve specific, measurable values, which could prove the improvement of the case, one should maintain the importance of the people for whom these goals need to be set in the first place.

Acknowledgment

The work on which this chapter is based was funded by the Latvian Ministry of Education and Science, project "Innovative and Inclusive Governance for the Promotion of Social Involvement, Trust, and Communication," project No. VPP-LETONIKA-2021/3-0004.

References

Andersson, C., & Törnberg, P. (2018, January). Wickedness and the anatomy of complexity. *Futures*, *95*, 118–138. https://doi.org/10.1016/j.futures.2017.11.001

Armstrong, D. (2017). Wicked problems in special and inclusive education. *Journal of Research in Special Educational Needs*, *4*, 229–236. https://doi.org/10.1111/1471-3802.12402

Avramidis, E., & Norwich, B. (2010). Teachers' attitudes towards integration/inclusion: A review of the literature. *European Journal of Special Needs Education*, 129–147. https://www.tandfonline.com/doi/abs/10.1080/08856250210129056

Bogush, A., Kovshar, O., Knyazheva, I., Suiatynova, K., & Drevniak, L. (2022). Analysis of the key theoretical frameworks of the organization of inclusive education in a preschool establishment. *International Journal of Early Childhood Special Education*, 253–259. https://doi.org/10.9756/INT-JECSE/V14I1.221031

Cook, B. G., & Odom, S. L. (2013). Evidence-based practices and implementation science in special education. *Exceptional Children*, *79*, 135–144.

ERGO. (2022). *ERGO Drošības indekss: vairāk nekā puse Latvijas iedzīvotāju baidās nonākt nabadzībā*. https://www.ergo.lv/lv/par-ergo/jaunumi/ergo-drosibas-indekss-vairak-neka-puse-latvijas-iedzivotaju-baidas-nonakt-nabadziba

European Commission. (2022). *2022 country report – Latvia*. https://commission.europa.eu/content/eu-economic-governance-monitoring-prevention-correction/european-semester/european-semester-your-country/latvia/european-semester-documents-latvia_en

Eurostat. (2022). *Sustainable development in the European union: Monitoring report on progress towards the SDGs in an EU context*. https://ec.europa.eu/eurostat/web/products-flagship-publications/-/ks-09-22-019

Halkos, G., & Gkampoura, E. (2021). Where do we stand on the 17 sustainable development goals? An overview of progress. *Economic Analysis and Policy*, *70*, 94–122. https://doi.org/10.1016/j.eap.2021.02.001

He, X., Khan, S., Ozturk, I., & Murshed, M. (2023). *The role of renewable energy investment in tackling climate change concerns: Environmental policies for achieving SDG-13*. Sustainable Development. https://doi.org/10.1002/sd.2491

Head, B. W. (2022). *Wicked problems in public policy. Understanding and responding to complex challenges*. Palgrave Macmillian.

LRVK. (2023). Vai Latvijā ir izveidoti priekšnosacījumi ANO ilgtspējīgas attīstības mērķu sasniegšanai? https://lrvk.gov.lv/lv/revizijas/revizijas/noslegtas-revizijas/vai-latvija-ir-izveidoti-prieksnosacijumi-ano-ilgtspejigas-attistibas-merku-sasniegsanai

LU SPPI. (2021). *Latvijas vērtības salīdzinošā skatījumā*. Rīga.

Martín-Blanco, C., Zamorano, M., Lizárraga, C., & Molina-Moreno, V. (2022). The impact of COVID-19 on the sustainable development goals: Achievements and expectations. *International Journal of Environmental Research and Public Health*, *19*(23). https://doi.org/10.3390/ijerph192316266

MoE. (2021). *Izglītības attīstības pamatnostādnes 2021.–2027. gadam "Nākotnes prasmes nākotnes sabiedrībai"*. https://likumi.lv/ta/id/324332-par-izglitibas-attistibas-pamatnostadnem-20212027-gadam

MoE. (2022). *Par speciālās izglītības iestāžu tīkla izvērtējumu*.

OECD. (2018). *OECD regulatory policy outlook 2018*. OECD Publishing. https://doi.org/10.1787/9789264303072-en

Ozoliņa, Ž., Reinholde, I., & Struberga, S. (2021). Subjektīvā drošības uztvere- izpētes ietvar konstruēšana. In Ž. Ozoliņa, I. Reinholde, & S. Struberga (Eds.), *Latvijas iedzīvotāju subjektīvā drošības uztvere: ietekme uz drošības politikas veidošanu*. Rīga, LU Akadēmiskais apgāds.

Pham-Truffert, M., Metz, F., Fischer, M., Rueff, H., & Messerli, P. (2020). Interactions among sustainable development goals: Knowledge for identifying multipliers and virtuous cycles. *Sustainable Development*, 1–15. https://doi.org/10.1002/sd.2073

PKC. (2018). *Latvia. Implementation of the sustainable development goals*. http://pkc.gov.lv/lv/LV-zinojums-ANO

PKC. (2020). *Latvijas Nacionālais attīstības plāns 2021.–2027.gadam*. https://pkc.gov.lv/sites/default/files/inline-files/NAP2027_apstiprināts%20Saeimā_1.pdf. Accessed on September 01, 2023.

PKC. (2022a). *Latvia. Implementation of the sustainable development goals – 2022*. http://pkc.gov.lv/lv/LV-zinojums-ANO

PKC. (2022b). *Latvijas Ziņojums Apvienoto Nāciju Organizācijai par ilgtspējīgas attīstības mērķu ieviešanu*. https://pkc.gov.lv/sites/default/files/inline-files/Latvia%202nd%20VNR_2022_2pg%20%281%29.pdf

Rittel, H. W., & Webber, M. M. (1973). Dilemmas in a general theory of planning. *Policy Sciences*, *4*(2), 155–169.

Saeima. (2010). *Sustainable development strategy of Latvia until 2030*. https://www.pkc.gov.lv/sites/default/files/inline-files/LIAS_2030_en_1.pdf

Saeima. (2011). *Sustainable development strategy of Latvia until 2030*. https://www.pkc.gov.lv/sites/default/files/inline-files/LIAS_2030_en_0.pdf

Saloviita, T. (2020). Attitudes of teachers towards inclusive education in Finland. *Scandinavian Journal of Educational Research*, *64*(2), 270–282. https://doi.org/10.1080/00313831.2018.1541819

Sree Kumar, S., Banerjee, B., Duarte, F. D. P., & Dadich, A. (2020). The business – Government nexus: Impact of government actions and legislation on business responses to climate change. *Journal of Management and Organization*, *26*(6), 952–974. https://doi.org/10.1017/jmo.2020.21

Statistical Office. (2022). https://data.stat.gov.lv/pxweb/lv/OSP_PUB/START__EMP__DS__DSV/DSV010m/table/tableViewLayout1/

Štemberger, T., & Kiswarday, V. R. (2018). Attitude towards inclusive education: The perspective of Slovenian preschool and primary school teachers. *European Journal of Special Needs Education*, *33*(1), 47–58. https://doi.org/10.1080/08856257.2017.1297573

UNESCO. (1994). The Salamanca statement and framework for action on special needs education. In *World conference on special needs education*. UNESCO.

Van Bueren, E., Klijn, E.-H., & Koppenjan, J. (2003). Dealing with wicked problems in networks: Analysing an environmental debate from a network perspective. *Journal of Public Administration Research and Theory*, *13*(2), 193–212.

B

Institutional Tools to Steer Wicked Policies in Sustainable Development

Chapter 8

Jurisdictional Approaches to Managing Wicked Problems: The Contribution of the PROAmazonia Program to Tackling Deforestation in Ecuador

Paul Cisneros[a], *Kate Macdonald*[b] *and Cristhian Parrado*[b]

[a]Instituto de Altos Estudios Nacionales, Ecuador
[b]University of Melbourne, Australia

Abstract

Global demand for agricultural commodities, including beef, soy, and palm oil, has driven tropical deforestation throughout the 21st century, threatening biodiversity and ecosystem services while contributing significantly to greenhouse gas emissions. Deforestation in the tropics is a wicked problem because there is no consensus on its solution, conflicting moral and political considerations among stakeholders, and uncertainty about the potential effects of intended solutions. Faced with such complex policy challenges, jurisdictional approaches (JAs) are being increasingly embraced as potential means of increasing policy capacity to tackle deforestation and support the Sustainable Development Goals. JAs integrate tools such as public and private regulations, collaborative planning processes, and payments for ecosystem services to respond to the complexity that characterizes deforestation. In this chapter, we study PROAmazonia, an anti-deforestation JA implemented in Ecuador's Amazon region since 2017.

Our study shows that enhancing policy capacities to manage wicked problems associated with deforestation requires confronting the inherent complexity of these problems and the wider socio-environmental system in which they emerge. However, this requires integrated policy strategies that exceed the scope of JAs, also demanding support from wider governance structures.

Policy Capacity, Design and the Sustainable Development Goals, 163–181

doi:10.1108/978-1-80455-686-320241012

Keywords: Tropical deforestation; jurisdictional approaches; policy capacity; wicked problems; complexity

1. Introduction

Global demand for agricultural commodities, including beef, soy, and palm oil, has driven tropical deforestation throughout the 21st century, threatening biodiversity and ecosystem services while contributing significantly to greenhouse gas (GHG) emissions (see Lyons-White et al., 2021). Problems like tropical deforestation are often called "wicked," meaning they are complex, dynamic, contextually unique, and engage diverse and often competing stakeholder values (Head, 2008; Rittel & Webber, 1973). Because they present high levels of uncertainty and lack clear solutions, wicked problems require real-time, flexible, and ongoing responses (Peters, 2017).

Jurisdictional approaches (JAs) emerged in the last decade and a half to manage tropical deforestation and other wicked problems (Boyd et al., 2018; Seymour & Harris, 2019). JAs stem from the conviction that individual programs and projects run by governments, international cooperation, or business initiatives are insufficient to protect forests, reduce emissions, and enhance livelihoods over the long term. Their proponents also recognize that a high level of government involvement is required to scale up initiatives and convene multiple stakeholders while integrating overlapping sectoral tasks and levels of decision-making (Bishai et al., 2022; Boyd et al., 2018; Hovani et al., 2018; Reed et al., 2020; Stickler et al., 2018). Other authors argue for the need to consider the capacities built within JAs to achieve sustainable interventions over time (Oorthuizen et al., 2018; Stroh, 2018). To this end, JAs often deploy multiple policy tools to deal with the main features of wicked problems. Standard mixes to tackle deforestation include commitments to zero deforestation (Lambin et al., 2018), payments for ecosystem services, extension support, and regulatory enforcement (Azevedo et al., 2017; Börner et al., 2017).

In principle, JAs enhance multiple stakeholders' capacities to manage wicked problems. However, more needs to be said about how experimental approaches such as JAs help to build capacities. In this chapter, we use the Programa PROAmazonía (PPA) as an example of a JA designed to tackle the wicked problem of deforestation in the Ecuadorian Amazon. PPA intends to contribute to several Sustainable Development Goals (SDGs): SDG13 by reducing GHG emissions from deforestation and SDG15 by protecting, restoring, and promoting the sustainable use of terrestrial ecosystems and sustainable forest management. Indirectly, PPA works on SDG1 by supporting small producers to adopt more sustainable and economically viable models, SDG8 through the promotion of environmental certifications that improve income generation, and SDG12 by promoting the consumption of sustainable agricultural products.

The main argument of this chapter is that to generate adequate policy capacities to tackle wicked problems, JAs must engage the inherent complexity of such problems. This engagement is necessary for JAs to surpass the linear logic of conventional strategies for local development that work on one or a few aspects of the development challenges contained in the SDGs. If JAs embrace complexity, they may be better equipped to tackle the interrelationships between the SDGs, taking stock of their mutually reinforcing and often conflicting nature (see Fu et al., 2019).

This chapter is based on an abductive review of secondary sources complemented by primary interview data. Official documents from the institutions in charge of designing and implementing PPA and material including academic papers and institutional reports from actors linked to the program were extensively reviewed. This review allowed us to reconstruct the program's design, understand the context for its implementation, and identify outcomes. In addition, during September 2021, September 2022, and from January to March 2023, 20 interviews were conducted with key informants related to the design and implementation of the PPA at the national level.

This chapter is structured as follows. The first section serves as a theoretical background where the relevance of embracing complexity in the context of JAs and policy capacity is justified. The second section presents the context of the case study referring to the public policies related to conservation, agricultural development, forest conservation, and land-use planning in the Amazon. The third section examines how PPA's four components have mobilized policy capacities and the extent to which they embrace complexity and produce the desired outputs and outcomes. This chapter concludes with a reflection on the relevance of studying designs for solutions to complex problems such as deforestation under the analytical lens of wicked problems.

2. Wicked Problems, Jurisdictional Approaches, Complexity, and Policy Capacity

According to Head (2008, p. 101), wicked problems present three main characteristics: complexity, uncertainty, and divergence. Complexity relates to the number of elements, subsystems, and interdependencies embedded in a public problem. As the number of agencies, stakeholders or rights holders, and communities involved in a problem increases, the challenge of securing coordinated action among the elements also increases and potentially unveils disagreements in priorities, interests, and beliefs that could lead to inaction or protracted conflict.

Uncertainty about risks, consequences of actions, and changing patterns is also a common trait of wicked problems. Their presence can also justify inaction or incrementalism until the problem becomes intractable under normal circumstances. However, external or internal shocks can create conditions for policy actors to reassess their approach to a wicked problem, thus generating opportunities opportunity to tackle the problem by new means. Finally, wicked problems are characterized by deeply embedded disagreements about the nature of the issues, their relative importance, and appropriate responses (Head, 2018). Their management requires learning processes and intra- and inter-coalition building that are often lengthy and costly.

New process responses to wicked problems have been increasingly tested in the past three decades. These include joined-up government and cross-sectoral collaboration (Head, 2008, p. 101). In a context of intensified preoccupations about the contribution of commodity production to climate change, JAs have emerged to help policy actors promote transitions to more sustainable resource use. JAs relating to agricultural commodity sourcing involve the participatory creation of a land-use plan that maintains forest ecosystems while promoting commodity production under strict social and environmental standards (Boshoven et al., 2021). One of the most widely recognized JAs was implemented in the Brazilian state of Acre in 2012 to implement the Program on Reducing Emissions from Deforestation and Forest Degradation (REDD1) (von Essen & Lambin, 2021).

These approaches recognize that fragmentation in public action reduces the effectiveness of policy delivery, thus demanding efforts to tackle interdependencies across sectors and levels. Common elements of JAs include strong involvement from a jurisdictional government, broad multi-stakeholder and rights-holder participation, attempts to reconcile competing social, economic, and environmental objectives, and a focus on monitoring at the jurisdictional scale. At the same time, JAs recognize that actors often lack a uniform understanding of the problem or the potential ways to manage it. Thus, they are required to (a) secure the broad-based participation of legitimate interests and (b) establish collective mechanisms for decision-making. Some JAs also attempt to anticipate the (unintended) consequences of actions by adopting tools that increase the political-administrative system's capacity to enforce safeguards and enhance co-benefits (see Boshoven et al., 2021; Stickler et al., 2018; von Essen & Lambin, 2021). These tools, according to the cited authors, involve promoting improved consultation and benefit-sharing mechanisms throughout the system, as well as strengthening stakeholder commitments. These characteristics of JAs may lead us to think they are well equipped to deal with wicked problems; however, as Boyd et al. (2018, pp. 1–14) report, an evidence gap remains regarding JAs' record on implementation, particularly concerning how they strengthen capacities to achieve deforestation targets.

Policy capacity has become a significant concern as governments are called upon to address increasingly complex problems (Bridgman & Davis, 2000; Fellegi, 1996; Parsons, 2004). Wu et al. (2018) developed an integrative framework to study policy capacity that combines theoretical insights about the skills and competencies that are put to work, often in combination with one another and across different governance levels to perform policy functions (agenda-setting, formulation, decision-making, implementation, and evaluation). The framework includes analytical, operational, and political policy capacities that operate at the individual, organizational, and systemic levels, as shown in Fig. 8.1.

Analytical capacity refers to knowledge and skills used in the tasks of policy formulation that include diagnosing problems and constructing evidence-based plans and supportive systems for implementation and evaluation. Operational

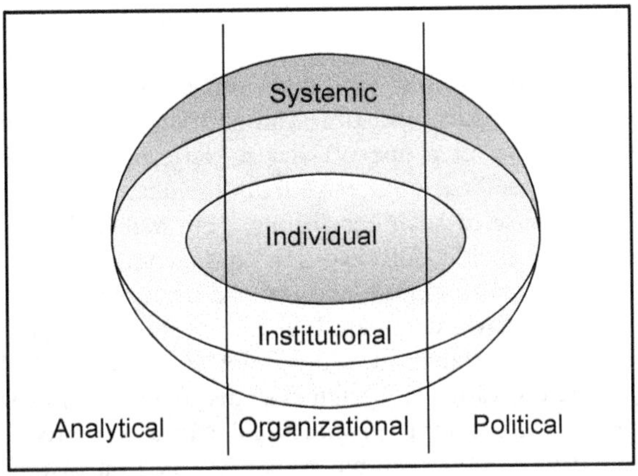

Fig. 8.1. Levels and Dimensions of Policy Capacity's Framework. *Source:* Authors.

capacity refers to expertise in running effective organizations and managing constellations of organizations and their policy environments. Lastly, political capacity refers to securing legitimacy for the policy process and processes for stakeholder engagement and access to policymakers. These capacities are used at the individual or service delivery level, the organizational or governmental institution implementation level, and the systemic level or wider arena where policymaking occurs.

This framework offers the possibility to specify the type of policy capacities related to tackling wicked problems. As Mueller (2020, p. 311) puts it, "If a public policy is recognized as taking place within a complex system, it is necessary to use instruments that can work within those informational and epistemological constraints." Given the experimental nature of most JAs (Boyd et al., 2018, pp. 1–14), identifying general contributions to capacity development is beyond the aims of this paper. However, we believe that a more detailed understanding of the dynamics of policy capacity within individual governments and their partners would provide the basis for a more nuanced and realistic assessment of what can feasibly be achieved within particular jurisdictions and timeframes.

Complex systems are characterized by several features, some of which have been highlighted as relevant for public policy: emergence, nonlinearity and feedback, and path dependence (see Cairney, 2012; Furtado et al., 2015). In simple terms, emergence refers to the characteristic where the action of the whole system is more than the action of its parts. Goldstein (2011, p. 66) identifies different types of emergent phenomena with common characteristics that include: radically novel macro-level entities and properties with respect to a microlevel substrate, integrated coordination characterizing the macro-level, and dynamical in the sense of coming to be over time. In this sense, tropical deforestation can be linked to emergent conditions involving the decisions made by multiple actors across space and time that, for instance, affect patterns of land-use change (an emergent property). These patterns occur without central control, and their existence does not derive from the agency of those involved at the microlevel. In response to such conditions, approaches for monitoring and evaluating programs to tackle deforestation and generate local development must take stock of emergent phenomena and the multiple recombinations and associations of existing resources, capabilities, symbols, language, and work patterns that bring the emergent order into being (Goldstein, 2011, p. 67).

Complexity in socio-ecological systems stems from nonlinearities. Unlike linear systems, these don't exhibit proportional cause-and-effect relationships. Small changes can trigger unpredictable responses, as seen in the link between deforestation and disrupted river discharge (Lima et al., 2014). This necessitates managing for both diversity and dynamism within the integrated landscape approach (Ros-Tonen et al., 2018). Jurisdictional approaches (JAs) must account for these feedback effects, considering how changes like agricultural expansion influence the system as a whole.

Complex systems are also susceptible to initial conditions producing long-term momentum or "path dependence" (Cairney, 2012). Path dependence means that "current and future states, actions, or decisions depend on the path of previous states, actions, or decisions" (Page, 2006, p. 88). The suggestion is that the history of an institution and the roles previously played by its actors, within the context of a larger society that also influences the institution, impact its future outcomes. In the case of deforestation and illegal logging in Indonesia, Atkinson (2014) shows that path dependence created by regulations adopted before the 1980s served to protect and empower timber and plantation interests. These regulations spurred groups with control to engage in self-serving behavior while limiting the entry of those who might seek to compete in the industry. Although the regulatory system being supported was clearly inefficient and lacking in benefit for the broader public interest due to the continuation of illegal logging, burning, and potential for haze events, its elements were 'locked in' and even resisted exogenous shocks of considerable significance, such as the influence of globalization and the fall of Suharto in 1998.

3. Case Study: Deforestation in the Ecuadorian Amazon and the Emergence of PPA

The Ecuadorian Amazon has an approximate extension of 120,000 km^2, corresponding to 43% of Ecuador's continental land surface. This area hosts around 97% of the country's forest cover (RAISG-MapBiomas, 2021) and its largest and most biodiverse protected areas. This region is administratively divided into five provinces: Sucumbíos, Orellana, Napo, Pastaza, Morona Santiago, and Zamora Chinchipe. The Andes mountain range marks its limits to the west, which separates it from the Sierra region – dominated by the Andes mountains; Peru and Colombia constitute the southeastern and northern limits, respectively (Fig. 8.2).

Deforestation in Ecuador's Amazon is driven by socioeconomic dynamics associated with multiple factors at different scales. Official documents indicate that expanding extensive agricultural systems based on low-productivity monocultures has generated a high degradation of native forests and overexploitation of natural resources (ST-CTEA, 2021). The Ecuadorian environmental authority (Ministry of Environment, Water and Ecological Transition or MAATE) points out that additional causes of deforestation are the absence of adequate territorial planning, population growth, and rural land fragmentation (MAE, 2015, 2016). On the other hand, the indirect factors of deforestation include agricultural tax incentives, oil and mining exploitation, weak multi-sectoral dialogue, and almost no coordination between institutions that manage competencies in forests and land use (MAE, 2016). Extractive activities have also left their footprint in the Amazon. Oil extraction began in the 1970s and is the primary source of state revenue. Legal and illegal mining has grown in importance since the 2003 commodities boom. The latter, in particular, is spreading quickly through protected areas, rapidly increasing deforestation.

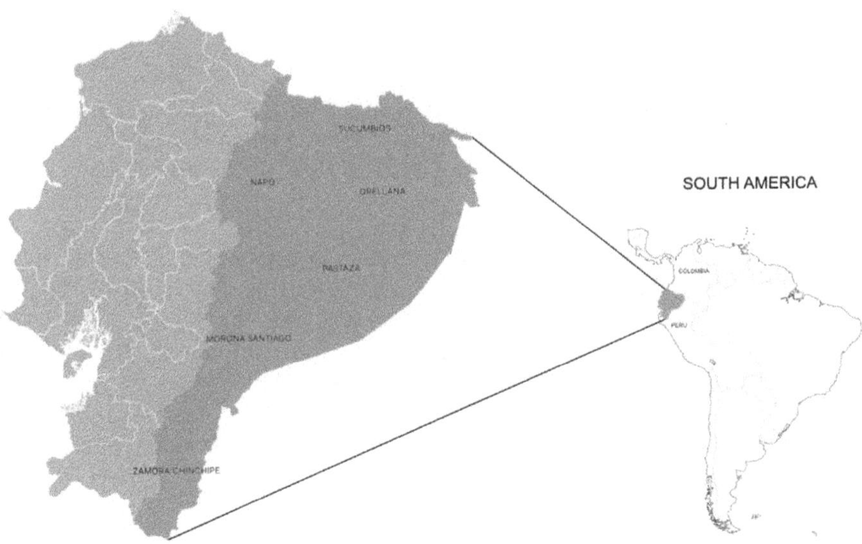

Fig. 8.2. The Provinces of the Ecuadorean Amazon. *Source:* Authors.

Approximately 99% of the deforested area between 1990 and 2008 was transformed into crops and pastures (MAE, 2016). Of the sites that lost forest between 2008 and 2014, 64.9% became pasture land for livestock, 11.8% agricultural mosaics, 3.7% cocoa, 3.1% hard corn, 3% African palm, and 2% coffee (MAE, 2016, p. 47). The products with the largest cultivated area are oil palm (43,357 ha), cocoa (59,572 ha), plantain (21,111 ha), coffee (14,895 ha), and cassava (8,281 ha). Livestock occupies 10% of the region's total area. Despite these changes, the Ecuadorian Amazon maintains 84% of its forests (ST-CTEA, 2021).

PROAmazonía (PPA) is a JA led by the MAATE and the Ministry of Agriculture and Livestock (MAGAP) that has supported the implementation of Ecuador's REDD+ Action Plan (or "Bosques para el Buen Vivir") in the Ecuadorian Amazon since 2017. PPA represents a change of strategy to reduce deforestation based on the coordination of multiple initiatives focusing on the Amazon that include several agricultural subsectors (coffee, cocoa, palm oil, and livestock).

The first has the explicit objective of implementing the priority measures and policies identified in the REDD+ Action Plan of Ecuador.[1] The second seeks to catalyze the transformation of land-use planning and management in the Amazon by establishing a governance and sustainable production framework.

PPA has four strategic components. The first component tackles the coherence of public policies across different levels, ranging from land-use plans and community-level planning instruments to forming regional platforms behind interinstitutional (interministerial) agreements. The second promotes adopting improved production practices and new technologies and strengthens producers' associations in all four sectors: coffee, cocoa, oil palm, and livestock. The third component promotes sustainable forest management, biodiversity-based entrepreneurship, conservation, and restoration of ecosystems. Finally, the fourth component supports the implementation of REDD+ working with the enabling context of the beneficiaries.

PPA intervenes in a special jurisdiction, the Amazon Special Territorial Circumscription (CTEA), created by the 2008 constitution. The CTEA's main planning tools are the Amazon Productive Transformation Agenda (APTA), which started in 2011, and the Comprehensive Plan for the Amazon (PIA). APTA's design includes three components closely related to the REDD+ Action Plan: (1) mechanisms for information and management of land tenure and use, (2) promoting sustainable agro-productive development, and (3) strengthening productive chains and equitable trade. PIA's actions also contribute to the establishment of a sustainable development model. This model prioritizes the

---

[1]The REDD+ Action Plan seeks to articulate the measures and actions inside and outside the forest sector to national and local policies, programs, and initiatives, as well as to generate multiple environmental and social benefits (MAE, 2016, p. 19). Its main goal is to reduce gross emissions by at least 20% by 2025 from the national reference levels for the 2000–2008 period. It contains a set of strategic lines that seek to promote climate change mitigation actions and that are aimed at the convergence of the country's environmental and development agendas with a territorial approach (MAE, 2016, p. 16).

preservation of the Amazon's natural and cultural heritage, ensures the full exercise of the rights of its population with territorial relevance and co-responsibility, strengthens local capacities, and promotes the diversification of the production framework within the context of sustainable use of its renewable and nonrenewable resources (ST-CTEA, 2021, p. 88). PIA is implemented by the CTEA's Technical Secretariat (STCA) under the mandate to coordinate with the different levels of government and other public and private entities.

4. PROAmazonía, Policy Capacities and the Management of Complexity Within a Jurisdictional Approach

The following sections analyze how the three elements of complexity – emergence, nonlinearity, and feedback – play out in PPA's attempt to tackle the wicked problem of deforestation in the Ecuadorian Amazon. It identifies how the components of PPA contributed to different policy capacities in the 2017–2023 period. It does not present a complete revision of all PPA's actions but uses information on some programmatic to illustrate progress and limitations in implementing this JA.

4.1 Emergence and Institutional Development

Embracing the complexity of wicked problems requires intra and inter-institutional arrangements to surpass conventional sectoral approaches that reproduce the fragmentation of public action. As complexity theory reminds us, a complex system has emerging properties that are more than the sum of its parts; therefore, managing the parts through siloed arrangements will lose sight of the emerging properties and threaten any significant progress.

PPA's first component seeks to influence the causes of deforestation in a cross-cutting manner and enables the implementation of the other components. Its objective is to support the articulation of intersectoral and governmental policies to mainstream climate change and REDD+ in national public policies and the main land-use planning instruments at local and community levels. To this end, this component aspired to the following outputs: (a) mainstreaming climate change, sustainable production, and REDD+ in 28 Development and Territorial Management Plans (PDOT) and (b) strengthening local capacities for the supervision of land-use planning and zoning.

By mid-2022, PPA reported an 86% cumulative progress on this component. The main results obtained at the beginning of 2023 involved 28 finalized PDOTs with climate change and sustainable production criteria; 17 plans for land management and use, including protected areas and sustainable production zones; five proposals for local ordinances on sustainable production and conservation; and five plans that were prepared and approved by local communities (interview # 17, March 2023).

As of early 2023, there is evidence that PPA has strengthened organizational capacities at the individual and organizational levels. This output is reflected in PPA's work with decision-makers in local governments to support the adoption of territorial planning instruments. This support focused on incorporating climate change and sustainable production criteria to access international funds, which constitute the only reliable source of resources on these topics. On the other hand, at the national level, efforts have been made to formalize collaboration processes between the involved ministries through ministerial agreements that generate a framework for permanent action between the environment and agriculture sectors to implement PPA (interview # 17, March 2023).

In addition, six institutional articulation platforms were created to update the PDOT documents, addressing topics such as climate change, sustainable production, gender, and interculturality. The platforms have contributed to enhancing political capacity at the institutional level. In 2021, the platforms supported the STCA in updating the PIA. This action set a common framework for discussing the region's main chellenges faced by the Amazon. Since 2021, these platforms have continued supporting the implementation of PPA through information exchange and the definition of priorities for intervention. They have mainly served as spaces that allow for navigating the political and social environment in which local policies are developed. In addition, PPA has provided support for financing 'life plans' for indigenous communities and peoples, with the support of the UNDP, to mobilize international funds for community conservation and sustainable production (interview # 17, March 2023).

These outcomes are important in their own right but leave open a question as to whether these capacities are sufficient to respond to the emerging properties that affect the capacity of forests and ecosystems to provide services. A review of the PIA 2021–2025 shows that although emergent properties of the Amazon region are identified in its diagnostic section, such as the reduction of water availability caused by the increase of nonconsumptive water uses (such as hydroelectric projects), no specific mechanisms have been put in place to monitor their development. These issues remain under the exclusive control of national institutions, which have traditionally imposed decisions in the Amazon region.

Another instance of emergence relates to the conversion of the Ecuadorian Amazon into a hub for the expansion of illegal and informal mining. Despite training local practitioners to strengthen policy capacity across all its components, the PPA curriculum reportedly omitted addressing illegal mining and its impact on conservation efforts (interview #20, March 2023). Interviewees have asserted during regional training sessions that illegal mining is a recurrent issue. However, the MAATE has repeatedly stated that dealing with illegal mining requires capacities at levels in which PPA cannot and will not act (interviews # 19 and # 20, March 2023). The main constraint for controlling illegal mining resides in that the competence is distributed among multiple national-level entities but coordination capacity was reduced in 2017 due to the adoption of austerity measures.

Emergent properties are also only partially tackled by intra institutional arrangements defined in local planning tools. A review of a random sample (about 20%) of the 28 updated PDOTs shows that although the emerging properties noted above are identified as the main challenges for the transition to a more sustainable state where deforestation is controlled and ecosystems recovered and adequately managed, no specific actions are identified to tackle them. It is as if no or only marginal effects are attributed to emerging properties.

4.2 Nonlinearity and Feedback and the Transition to Sustainable Systems

Managing wicked problems demands interventions that transcend linear thinking by incorporating assessments of the unintended consequences and co-benefits generated by the multiple actions taken under JAs. In this regard, and in addition to strengthening capacities related to planning, PPA supports the implementation and strengthening of forest control and traceability processes for forest products included in Ecuador's REDD+ Action Plan (interviews # 3, September 2021; # 14, February 2023; and # 18, March 2023).

PPA recognizes the expansion of the agricultural frontier as one of the leading causes of deforestation in Ecuador. Therefore, it is critical to adopt mechanisms that provide traceability of production and allow access to international markets with higher prices for deforestation-free commodities. Certifications incentivize producers to adopt new technologies that guarantee traceability (interview # 14, February 2023). These transformations require the development of supporting individual and organizational analytical capacities for measurement and evaluation (usually as equivalent tonnes of CO_2), organizational capacity to deliver technical assistance and strengthen local organizations and networks within the value chains, and political capacity to diversify the resources to sustain the intervention in the jurisdiction.

To date, PPA has made progress in supporting oil palm producers to adopt sustainable and deforestation-free production practices proposed by the Roundtable on Sustainable Palm Oil (RSPO). In addition, PPA is currently working with the Agrocalidad Program from the Ministry of Agriculture to adopt RSPO at the jurisdictional level; for this, a national interpretation of RSPO rules must first be produced (interview # 4, September 2021). This goal has been pursued with the support of the Interinstitutional Committee for Sustainable Palm Production (CISPS). However, organizational and political capacities to build a network of stakeholders to apply deforestation-free certifications to the jurisdictional level have yet to meet the goals set by PPA. As of early 2023, the last full year of PPA implementation, Ecuador's plan for RSPO jurisdictional certification remained at early stages of progression, with the definition of the mechanisms and standards for guaranteeing deforestation-free status yet to be finalized. In addition to the political instability that affected the Ministry of Agriculture and the effects of the COVID-19 pandemic, the lack of progress in the adoption of the jurisdictional RSPO can be explained by the limited political capacity at the systemic level to secure the inclusion of small producers in the CISPS.

PROAmazonía also supports the development of the 'Buenas Prácticas Agrícolas' or Good Agricultural Practices (BPA+) certification, a local effort to produce a deforestation-free certification that will be mandatory for all Ecuadorean exports. BPA+ is Ecuador's strategy to maintain its position in the European market (interview # 14, February 2023). The adequate deployment of this strategy requires developing analytical capacities to implement this certification (baselines for measuring deforestation, demarcation of plots, improving collection centers, labeling, and reporting) at the individual and institutional levels. Also, at the institutional level, PPA is supporting the adoption of a BPA+ focus within the local development plans of the provincial governments and directly with producer associations to enhance their organizational capacity through field schools and technical tables for each one of the prioritized products (coffee, cocoa, oil palm, and livestock). To complement these actions, PPA has worked to improve access to lines of credit for producers developing targeted financial products with local cooperatives and a state-owned bank. Progress on this front has been possible because of the political capacity to mobilize support from the national government deployed at the systemic level by international organizations, mainly the UNDP and Food and Agriculture Organization (FAO).

The objective of PPA's fourth component is to increase carbon stocks by maintaining areas under conservation and increasing areas under reforestation. The proposed outputs for this component are: (a) supporting the implementation of activities concerning mitigation actions in the forest sector, including institutional arrangements under the Warsaw Framework for REDD+ and other operational processes and (b) operationalizing the financial architecture for the REDD+ Action Plan (interview # 18, March 2023). As of mid-2022, 44% cumulative progress is reported for this component.

Regarding the first expected output, the most significant results relate to creating analytical and organizational capacity to implement safeguards associated with REDD+, mainly around collective knowledge and rights and local participation. These mechanisms have generated a positive response from local populations during the implementation of the other components of PPA, as exemplified by several outcomes. First, the agreement on the guidelines for prior and informed consultation establishes protocols for implementing REDD+ actions in collective territories. Any activity in these territories must be socialized with the communities, respecting their forms of social organization and decision-making processes. In this case, all interventions must first pass through the filter of the regional indigenous organization CONFENIAE, the confederation that brings together different organizations of indigenous nationalities of the Ecuadorian Amazon (interviews # 17 and # 19, March 2023). Another mechanism seeks to respect collective rights and enhance local participation in community forest monitoring (interview # 18, March 2023). This has been implemented in eight indigenous territories to foster a sense of belonging, territorial governance, and knowledge of the negative impacts caused by land change among local populations. In addition, a "complaint management" mechanism has been adopted, consisting of an online form that registers conflicts generated around the implementation of PPA. This mechanism has shown that lack of information and requests for clarification of the program's actions are the complaints registered most frequently to date; these inform ongoing marginal adjustments to the program's design.

4.3 Path Dependence: The Extractive Industries Versus Conservation and Sustainable Forest Management

The contribution of JAs to transforming territorial dynamics toward sustainability is greatly limited by existing institutional barriers to implementing program activities. The barriers relate to how the State has approached the expansion of extractive activities and the formalization of land tenure in the past.

Commenting on such enduring legacies, Lovejoy and Nobre (2018) point out that for the last two decades, the Amazon development debate has been torn between attempts to reconcile two somewhat opposing views: on the one hand, a vision of setting aside large tracts of the Amazon forests for conservation purposes, and on the other hand, seeking a "sustainable" resource-intensive development, mainly through agriculture/livestock, energy, and mining. However, reality shows that a "convergent reconciliation" is not happening. High-input agriculture/livestock drives a rapid expansion of the commodity frontier, especially for beef production, and mining and oil require infrastructure to generate energy and transportation, which in turn attracts more people to the region and fuels further deforestation for agriculture/livestock purposes to feed the increasing urban population.

Oil has been extracted from the Ecuadorian Amazon since le early 1970s and quickly became the main source of State revenue. Since 2010, large-scale mining is growing with foreign investments in the southern provinces of Zamora Chinchipe and Morona Santiago. The advance of these extractive industries has produced two main effects regarding deforestation. First, both activities require opening roads to construct infrastructure and transport the extracted materials. These roads provide access to the last primary forests in the region, some inhabited by uncontacted tribes, mainly in the central portion of the Amazon that borders Peru. Second, mining is based on the effective possession of land by the developers, which incentivizes local communities to sell their land or clear the surrounding forests to prospect or extract minerals using technology that harms their health and pollutes water bodies and soil.

According to interviewees, the expansion of mining both legal and illegal, is one of the primary considerations for local communities to decide whether they enter conservation programs related to REDD+, as the incentives offered by the government in support of conservation are low in comparison with the short-term cash provided by mining operators to access or buy their lands (interviews # 17 and # 19, March 2023). The existence of collective titles limits land sales, but communities nonetheless search for legal ways to make individual sales of plots to secure income. Money from legal and illegal mining is one of the drivers of urbanization and increased consumption in the Amazon which in turns spurs further land-use change for grazing and commercial crops (Cabrera et al., 2023).

PROAmazonía lacks the political capacity to push the authorities responsible for controlling illegal mining to strengthen their interventions. Instead, it has focused on working along with indigenous organizations to raise awareness about the nefarious effects of local community participation in illegal mining activities (interview # 17, March 2023).

The lack of land titles and credit for small-scale producers also illustrates how PPA struggles with path dependency created by previous policy decisions that promoted the colonization and development of the Amazon in the 1970s. As part of this legacy, progress is limited by policies regarding access to credit that demand proof of tenure in deforestation-reduction, which somewhat perversely is more accessible after clearing the forest for pasture and then introducing cattle, which can be used as collateral (Armenteras et al., 2019). Although the Ministry of Agriculture has the authority to grant land titles, PPA still needs to be able to increase its organizational and political capacity to support small producers to access those titles through improved engagement with both stakeholders and policymakers (interviews # 17 and # 19, March 2023). Fixing the land title bottleneck is crucial for PPA as the BPA+ certification for deforestation-free products is set only to work with producers with land titles (interview # 14, February 2023). However, the requirement to have a land title is itself not based on a deep understanding of the drivers of deforestation in the Ecuadorean Amazon, as multiple studies show that land titles can sometimes incentivize deforestation (Buntaine et al., 2015; Probst et al., 2020), incentivize hoarding and speculation of land (Armenteras et al., 2019), or have no effect if clear restrictions on deforestation are not introduced along with titles (Holland et al., 2017).

5. Concluding Remarks

Public policies fail when complex problems are addressed using linear and reductionist approaches that presuppose more knowledge and control than can practically be achieved (Head, 2018). Complex systems can be managed, harnessed, influenced, constrained, tweaked, hedged, and (to a certain extent) understood (Hoppe, 2010). The key is for policy actors to repeatedly assess how much they can manage complex problems (Mueller, 2020); thus, they require "greater awareness of complexity to encourage more informal, inquiring attempts to understand how the policy is being realized – rather than simple performance monitoring" (Cairney, 2012, p. 354).

JAs have been proposed to help actors deal with wicked problems effectively. In principle, they could aid the localization of the SDGs, which has been highlighted as one of the most critical challenges for implementing Agenda 2030 (Reddy, 2016). However, policy actors must adopt a holistic and multidimensional view of development to truly use the SDG framework to localize the global agenda. Hence, synergies and trade-offs among the SDGs must be identified and leveraged or negotiated (International Council for Science, 2017; Pradhan et al., 2017).

The evidence gathered in this study highlights that addressing the complexity of deforestation requires comprehensive attention to its primary components. While PROAmazonía has made considerable strides in enhancing policy capacities at various levels – individual, organizational, and systemic – its sustainability progress faces considerable challenges. These challenges include disconnection from emerging properties, limitations in fostering positive feedback for its endeavors, and the obstacles presented by path dependence. Consequently, despite notable progress, this disconnect with complexity hinders the JA's ability to nurture capacities for a sustainable transition effectively (Hovani et al., 2018; Oorthuizen et al., 2018; Stroh, 2018).

Significant drivers of deforestation, such as oil extraction and infrastructure development, remain at arms length of PPA's efforts to tackle deforestation. This weakens its capacity to contribute to protecting forests (SDG15), reducing inequalities (SDG10), and promoting sustained, inclusive, and sustainable economic growth (SDG8) in its jurisdiction.

The study also highlights the need for JAs to build and mobilize policy capacities in ways that fully embrace the properties of the complex problem at hand. From the PPA case, we learn that the most salient shortcoming relates to the development of analytical capacities at the individual, organizational, and political levels. These capacities are critical to understanding and framing the socio-ecological system under intervention and its changes and to purposedly shape interactions with other systems. When analytical capacity is effectively deployed to identify different perspectives, needs, cultures, issue definitions, and potential frictions, organizational capacity can be activated to process these differences to reduce uncertainty and divergence. In addition, mobilizing organizational and political capacities at all levels (individual, organizational, and systemic) can help create the conditions to respond to intended and unintended system changes influenced by the intervention of JAs. Organizational and political capacities are crucial to organizing learning at more complex levels, where not only procedures and routines must be subject to changes but also the normative assumptions that drive the definition of problems and the courses of action.

Finally, JAs cannot tackle the challenges presented by path dependence, emergence, nonlinearity, and feedback on their own. They require support from other governance structures, complicating the task of governing wicked problems even further. However, increased awareness of complexity's role in wicked problems could help design mechanisms for interaction with such structures for whenever they may be required. Furthermore, following Reed et al. (2020) and Stroh (2018), for these approaches to embrace complexity, it is necessary to incorporate evaluation designs within them that focus on observing the short-term effects of their implementation and measuring the evolution of their efforts over time. In this way, it would be possible to understand how these efforts are contributing more effectively to addressing wicked problems sustainably.

Interviews

Number	Role of the Person Interviewed	Date
1	Implementation personal PROAmazonía component 3	September 4, 2021
2	Implementation personal component 2	September 7, 2021
3	Implementation personal component 2	September 28, 2021
4	Implementation personal component 2	September 29, 2021
5	Implementation personal component 3	September 30, 2021
6	Independent consultant	September 27, 2022
7	Researcher in cocoa and biodiversity conservation	January 12, 2023
8	Professor in spatial analysis and Amazon region	January 17, 2023
9	Professor in public policy and Amazon region	January 18, 2023
10	Professor in agricultural development	January 18, 2023
11	Rural development technician of the provincial government	January 22, 2023
12	Executive director of a national association of cocoa exporters	January 24, 2023
13	Communications director of a national cocoa platform	January 25, 2023
14	Implementation personal PROAmazonía component 2	February 6, 2023
15	Executive director of an export company of agricultural products	February 9, 2023
16	Consultant of the international technical assistance team to the Ministry of Agriculture	February 22, 2023
17	Implementation personal PROAmazonía component 1	March 2, 2023
18	Implementation personal PROAmazonía component 4	March 3, 2023
19	Implementation personal FAO-PROAmazonía	March 10, 2023
20	Implementation personal PROAmazonía component 3	March 15, 2023

References

Armenteras, D., Negret, P., Melgarejo, L. F., Lakes, T. M., Londoño, M. C., García, J., Krueger, T., Baumann, M., & Davalos, L. M. (2019). Curb land grabbing to save the Amazon. *Nature Ecology & Evolution*, *3*(11), 1497. https://doi.org/10.1038/s41559-019-1020-1

Atkinson, C. L. (2014). Deforestation and transboundary haze in Indonesia: Path dependence and elite influences. *Environment and Urbanization ASIA*, *5*(2), 253–267. https://journals.sagepub.com/doi/10.1177/0975425315577905

Azevedo, A. A., Rajão, R., Costa, M. A., Stabile, M. C. C., Macedo, M. N., dos Reis, T. N. P., Alencar, A., Soares-Filho, B. S., & Pacheco, R. (2017). Limits of Brazil's Forest Code as a means to end illegal deforestation. *Proceedings of the National Academy of Sciences*, *114*(29), 7653–7658. https://doi.org/10.1073/pnas.1604768114

Bishai, N., Sirait, H., & Pedroza, N. (2022). *Landscape and jurisdictional approaches in Indonesia*. Policy brief. CDP, Disclosure insight Action. https://www.cdp.net/pt/reports/downloads/6098

Börner, J., Baylis, K., Corbera, E., Ezzine-de-Blas, D., Honey-Rosés, J., Persson, U. M., & Wunder, S. (2017). The effectiveness of payments for environmental services. *World Development*, *96*, 359–374. https://doi.org/10.1016/j.worlddev.2017.03.020

Boshoven, J., Fleck, L. C., Miltner, S., Salafsky, N., Adams, J., Dahl-Jørgensen, A., Fonseca, G., Nepsted, D., Rabinovitch, K., & Seymour, F. (2021). Jurisdictional sourcing: Leveraging commodity supply chains to reduce tropical deforestation at scale. A generic theory of change for a conservation strategy, v 1.0. *Conservation Science and Practice*, *3*(5). https://doi.org/10.1111/csp2.383

Boyd, W., Stickler, C., Duchelle, A. E., Seymour, F., Nepstad, D., Bahar, N. H. A., & Rodriguez-Ward, D. (2018). *Jurisdictional approaches to REDD+ and low emissions development: Progress and prospects*. World Resources Institute. https://www.cifor.org/knowledge/publication/6933/

Bridgman, P., & Davis, G. (2000). *The Australian policy handbook. A practical guide to the policy-making process*. Allen & Unwin. https://doi.org/10.4324/9781003117940

Buntaine, M., Hamilton, S., & Millones, M. (2015). Titling community land to prevent deforestation: An evaluation of a best-case program in Morona-Santiago, Ecuador. *Global Environmental Change*, *33*, 32–43. https://doi.org/10.1016/j.gloenvcha.2015.04.001

Cabrera, M., Capparelli, M. V., Ñacato-Ch, C., Moulatlet, G. M., López-Heras, I., González, M. D., & Rico, A. (2023). Effects of intensive agriculture and urbanization on water quality and pesticide risks in freshwater ecosystems of the Ecuadorian Amazon. *Chemosphere*, 139286.

Cairney, P. (2012). Complexity theory in political science and public policy. *Political Studies Review*, *10*(3), 346–358. https://doi.org/10.1111/j.1478-9302.2012.00270.x

Essen, M., & Lambin, E. (2021). Jurisdictional approaches to sustainable resource use. *Frontiers in Ecology and the Environment*, *19*(3), 159–167. https://esajournals.onlinelibrary.wiley.com/doi/10.1002/fee.2299

Fellegi, I. (1996). *Strengthening our policy capacity*. Deputy Ministers Task Force.

Fu, B., Wang, S., Zhang, J., Hou, Z., & Li, J. (2019). Unraveling the complexity in achieving the 17 sustainable-development goals. *National Science Review*, *6*(3), 386–388. https://doi.org/10.1093/nsr/nwz038

Furtado, B., Sakowski, P., & Tóvolli, M. (2015). *A complexity approach for public policies*. Institute for Applied Economic Research. Discussion Paper, No. 205. https://www.econstor.eu/bitstream/10419/220293/1/dp_205.pdf

Goldstein, J. (2011). Emergence in complex systems. In P. Allen, S. Maguire, & B. McKelvey (Eds.), *The Sage handbook of complexity and management* (pp. 65–78). SAGE Publications. https://philpapers.org/rec/GOLEIC-2

Head, B. (2008). Wicked problems in public policy. *Public Policy*, *3*, 101–118. https://espace.library.uq.edu.au/view/UQ:167582/UQ167582OA.pdf

Head, B. W. (2018). Forty years of wicked problems literature: Forging closer links to policy studies. *Policy and Society*, *38*(2), 1–18. https://doi.org/10.1080/14494035.2018.1488797

Holland, M. B., Jones, K. W., Naughton-Treves, L., Freire, J.-L., Morales, M., & Suárez, L. (2017). Titling land to conserve forests: The case of Cuyabeno Reserve in Ecuador. *Global Environmental Change*, *44*, 27−38. https://doi.org/10.1016/j.gloenvcha.2017.02.004

Hoppe, R. (2010). *The governance of problems: Puzzling, powering and participation*. Policy Press.

Hovani, L., Cortez, R., Hartanto, H., Thompson, I., Fishbein, G., Madeira, E. M., & Adams, J. (2018). *The role of jurisdictional programs in catalyzing sustainability transitions in tropical forest landscapes*. The Nature Conservancy. http://doi.org/10.13140/RG.2.2.34252.67205

International Council for Science. (2017). *A guide to SDG interactions: From science to implementation*. International Council for Science. https://council.science/publications/a-guide-to-sdg-interactions-from-science-to-implementation/

Lambin, E. F., Gibbs, H. K., Heilmayr, R., Carlson, K. M., Fleck, L. C., Garrett, R. D., Waroux, Y. le P. de, McDermott, C. L., McLaughlin, D., Newton, P., Nolte, C., Pacheco, P., Rausch, L. L., Streck, C., Thorlakson, T., & Walker, N. F. (2018). The role of supply-chain initiatives in reducing deforestation. *Nature Climate Change*, *8*(2), 109–116. https://doi.org/10.1038/s41558-017-0061-1

Lima, L. S., Coe, M. T., Filho, B. S. S., Cuadra, S. V., Dias, L. C. P., Costa, M. H., Lima, L. S., & Rodrigues, H. O. (2014). Feedback between deforestation, climate, and hydrology in the southwestern Amazon: Implications for the provision of ecosystem services. *Landscape Ecology*, *29*(2), 261–274. https://doi.org/10.1007/s10980-013-9962-1

Lovejoy, T., & Nobre, C. (2018). Amazon tipping point. *Science Advances*, *4*(2). https://doi.org/10.1126/sciadv.aat2340

Lyons-White, J., Jespersen, K., Gallemore, C., Catalano, A. S., Ewers, R. M., & Knight, A. T. (2021, February 3). Tackling the "wicked" conservation problem of tropical deforestation in global commodity supply chains using mixes of mechanisms. https://doi.org/10.31235/osf.io/gan7w

MAE – Ministerio de Ambiente del Ecuador. (2015). *Estadísticas del Patrimonio Natural del Ecuador Continental*. Ministerio del Ambiente.

MAE. (2016). *Plan de Acción REDD+ del Ecuador "Bosques para el Buen Vivir" (2016–2025)*. http://reddecuador.ambiente.gob.ec/redd/wpcontent/uploads/2017/08/MAE_2016_11_21_ART_LIBRO_REDD_17_nov%202016.pdf

Mueller, B. (2020). Why public policies fail: Policymaking under complexity. *Economia*, *21*(2), 311–323. https://doi.org/10.1016/j.econ.2019.11.002

Oorthuizen, J., Vermaak, H., Dalmau, C. R., & Papaemmanuel, E. (2018). *Collaborative transformation: The art of making international trade more sustainable*. IDH. https://www.idhsustainabletrade.com/collaborative-transformation/

Page, S. (2006). Path dependence. *Quarterly Journal of Political Science*, *1*(1), 87–115. http://doi.org/10.1561/100.00000006

Parsons, W. (2004). Not just steering but weaving: Relevant knowledge and the craft of building policy capacity and coherence. *Australian Journal of Public Administration*, *63*(1), 43–57. https://doi.org/10.1111/j.1467-8500.2004.00358.x

Peters, B. (2017). What is so wicked about wicked problems? A conceptual analysis and a research program. *Policy and Society*, *36*(3), 385–396. https://doi.org/10.1080/14494035.2017.1361633

Pradhan, P., Costa, L., Rybski, D., Lucht, W., & Kropp, J. P. (2017). A systematic study of sustainable development goal (SDG) interactions. *Earth's Future*, *5*, 1169−1179. https://doi.org/10.1002/2017EF000632

Probst, B., BenYishay, A., Kontoleon, A., & dos Reis, T. N. P. (2020). Impacts of a large-scale titling initiative on deforestation in the Brazilian Amazon. *Nature Sustainability*, *3*, 1019−1026. https://doi.org/10.1038/s41893-020-0537-2

RAISG-MapBiomas. (2021). https://plataforma.amazonia.mapbiomas.org/stats

Reddy, P. (2016). Localising the sustainable development goals (SDGs): The role of local government in context. *African Journal of Public Affairs*, *9*(2), 1–15. http://hdl.handle.net/2263/58190

Reed, J., Ickowitz, A., Chervier, C., Djoudi, H., Moombe, K., Ros-Tonen, M., Yanou, M., Yuliani, L., & Sunderland, T. (2020). Integrated landscape approaches in the tropics: A brief stock-take. *Land Use Policy*, *99*, 104822. https://doi.org/10.1016/j.landusepol.2020.104822

Rittel, H., & Webber, M. (1973). Dilemmas in a general theory of planning. *Policy Sciences*, *4*(2), 155–169. https://link.springer.com/article/10.1007/BF01405730

Ros-Tonen, M. A. F., Reed, J., & Sunderland, T. (2018). From synergy to complexity: The trend toward integrated value chain and landscape governance. *Environmental Management*, *62*, 1–14. https://doi.org/10.1007/s00267-018-1055-0

Seymour, F., & Harris, N. L. (2019). Reducing tropical deforestation. *Science*, *365*(6455), 756–757. https://pubmed.ncbi.nlm.nih.gov/31439784/

ST-CTEA – Secretaría Técnica de la Circunscripción Territorial Especial Amazónica. (2021). *Plan Integral para la Amazonía 2021–2025*. Secretaría Técnica de la Circunscripción Territorial Especial Amazónica. Puyo, Ecuador.

Stickler, C. M., Duchelle, A. E., Ardila, J. P., Daniel, N., David, O., Chan, C., Rojas, J. G., Rafael, V., Bezerra, T., Pritchard, L., Simmonds, J., Joanna, D., Simonet, G., Peteru, S., Komalasari, M., María, D., & Warren, M. (2018). The State of jurisdictional sustainability: Synthesis for practitioners and policymakers.

Stroh, D. (2018). *Systems thinking for jurisdictional sustainability*. The Nature Conservancy. https://www.nature.org/content/dam/tnc/nature/en/documents/TNC_SystemsThinking_JurisdictionalSustainability_2018.pdf

Wu, X., Ramesh, M., & Howlett, M. (2018). Policy capacity: Conceptual framework and essential components. In *Idd., policy capacity and governance assessing governmental competences and capabilities in theory and practice* (pp. 1–25). London Palgrave Macmillan. https://link.springer.com/chapter/10.1007/978-3-319-54675-9_1

Chapter 9

Old Institutions Dealing With the Challenge of Sustainability: Water Planning in Spanish Inter-Regional Basins as a Wicked Problem

Alberto De la Peña Varona and Jaione Mondragón

University of the Basque Country, Spain

Abstract

The management of inter-regional basins in the Spanish case is a clear example of the complexity of water policy. The entry into force of the Water Framework Directive changed the objective and design process of public policy, prioritizing the conservation of river ecosystems and establishing the mandate for participation and inter-administrative coordination. This expanded the number of participants, creating a network of public and private actors with different interests and perceptions, bringing the water issue closer to what is often referred to in public policy as a wicked problem. In this chapter, we highlight how the Spanish political sphere has approached water policy in this new context, paying special attention to the role played by river basin organizations. To this end, we deal with two conflicts: the first concerning the Ebro Delta and the second on the water transfer between the Tajo and Segura rivers. Both cases show the inability of the central bodies of the State, the autonomous communities, and private agents to reach a consensus on water policy, which ends up shaping a decision-making system in which, although the legislative resources of the stakeholders are key, and the policy capacity of the basin organizations is reduced.

Keywords: Water planning; multilevel governance; policy capacity; wicked problems; sustainability

Policy Capacity, Design and the Sustainable Development Goals, 183–200

doi:10.1108/978-1-80455-686-320241015

1. Introduction

In the final decades of the 19th century and into the 20th, Spain took its first systematic actions in water planning and management against a backdrop of widespread crisis and regenerationism, seeking a framework of specific actions to mitigate Spain's relative late arrival on this scene with respect to other European countries. During that time, this sectoral policy was dominated by what could be called a developmentalist approach that views water availability as a strategic objective within the process of modernization. The most visible outcome of this approach throughout the years has been the construction of large-scale reservoirs and the harnessing of energy, coupled with decisions that follow a classic top-down model driven by the authoritarian environment in which these policies were usually designed and implemented.

The European Water Framework Directive (WFD), approved in 2000, has a dual purpose of fostering collaboration between different actors and prioritizing conservation objectives. In that sense, water policies were clearly aligned with the other sustainable development policies, placing Spain at a political conjuncture that was more complicated than ever, given the need to satisfy both the old interests represented by socioeconomic actors with other interests coming from competing definitions, such as environmentalist concerns and the obligation to integrate the subnational level within decision-making. In short, Spanish authorities had to move away from the previous top-down paradigm that saw the water supply as an input for economic development to a newer paradigm related to sustainability, governance, and interinstitutional cooperation, making water policies fall into the group of wicked public problems.

In recent times, water policies have also been influenced by the approval of the 2030 Agenda for Sustainable Development. There is broad consensus that the fulfilment of the 2030 Agenda requires an approach linked to the so-called global public goods that, by their very nature, transcend state capacities. Among these, we find, for example, the preservation of the environment and specifically the sustainable management of water and the protection of life in terrestrial ecosystems (SDGs 6 and 7), whose provision requires the establishment of transnational collective action frameworks and a multilevel approach (from the local to the global, including the state and the regional). These objectives, although internationally agreed, will be dependent upon adequate implementation within the member states, which will have to guide political action toward more sustainable policies. All this logically has a great impact on water planning and management.

In this chapter, we highlight how the Spanish political sphere has addressed water policies, given the new context defined by European law and the 2030 Agenda. We will examine two inter-regional basins – the Ebro and Tajo hydrographic demarcations – insofar as they bring together a complex array of interests and actors: the first basin has the greatest regional diversity and comprises nine autonomous communities (ACs); the second has experienced the most significant interbasin transfer, which in itself has caused a multitude of conflicts between different territorial administrations.[1] In both cases, planning and decision-making have been conditioned not only by divergent proposals from the various regions but also by the conflicting interests of a large number of private actors. This takes us sometimes to the field of intergovernmental relations, sometimes to pay attention at the governance systems. In any case, all this has manifested in the planning cycles defined by the WFD, and every time, strategic decisions must be taken regarding the distribution and management of existing resources.

From a methodological standpoint, this analysis draws upon a previous study by De la Peña Varona et al. (2022) and from which we have extracted much of the empirical data, in particular those arising from the analysis of the official documentation generated in water planning processes and which reflect the positions and perceptions of the various actors involved. Of particular interest are the minutes of the meetings of institutions such as the National Water Council, the committees of competent authorities, and the water councils of the Ebro and Tajo demarcations. These institutions formalize the participation of the respective government networks in both basins.

2. Dimensions of Water Planning as a Wicked Problem

The concept of a wicked problem coined by Rittel and Webber (1973/1993), as opposed to those which are tame or benign (1993, p. 170), draws on the perceived complexity of such problems. The discourse relating to wicked problems criticized the insufficiency of technical, rational, and top-down approaches and addressed new challenges such as environmental policy, town planning, and social policies (Head, 2010). What is more, technical approaches tend to overlook the values, perspectives, and experience of the stakeholders, as well as the citizens directly or indirectly involved in these interventions.

According to this critique, scientific and technical knowledge alone cannot resolve political problems, since these involve opposing values and must be observed from different viewpoints. Addressing these problems requires deliberation and wide-reaching debate on their very nature. This deliberative process of finding solutions, and its recognition of perspectives and values that "frame" the definition of a problem, is very different from the top-down imposition of technical solutions or those based on experiences arising from expanding empirical knowledge (Head, 2010, p. 11).

As a general rule, "The greater the disagreement among the stakeholders, the more wicked the problem" (Camillus, 2008). In that respect, Rittel and Webber (1973/1993) point out that this concept concerns problematic social situations

[1]Throughout this chapter, we have kept the Spanish name when referring to the Tagus river, contrary to what is the norm in English-written literature. This is for a number of reasons, the most important being that other rivers are also cited without any translation, and we have therefore decided to take a systematic approach to the naming of such geographical features.

involving different circumstances: there is no obvious solution; many individuals and organizations are involved out of necessity; the solution requires behavior changes in certain actors. Similarly, Head (2019) stresses that disagreements arise because stakeholders' viewpoints are rooted in different assumptions, values, interests, and abilities. This difference of perspectives has significant consequences insofar as the way a problem is defined will influence the policy actions taken to address it.

According to Head (2010), the fundamental challenges for researchers lie in developing a new approach to the multiple causes of problems. The same author (2022, p. 102) maintains that many aspects of environmental policy and the way natural resources are managed have been seen as wicked problems in which complexity and conflict can only be managed effectively with collaborative approaches.[2] Consequently, when studying the complexity inherent in issues such as water planning, we must consider other crucial dimensions of the way in which different actors address problems and devise solutions. Covarrubias (2022) highlights how the study of a problem must look at how difficulties increasingly call into question the traditional benchmarks of government organization and action, since an issue spreads through different levels – local, regional, national, and global – and pays no heed to existing political and administrative borders. The author examines how problems develop their own geography and create a complex map of "scale overflow" that vexes public administrations, accustomed as they are to operating from a territorial standpoint.

As already mentioned, the WFD represented a seminal moment in water policy across the European member states in general and in Spain in particular, in that it requires inter-administrative coordination and cooperation reflecting the multi-scale context of a river basin. All of this has an impact on intergovernmental relations overcoming what has been termed as "complex intergovernmental problem."[3] However, the most crucial aspect of this significant and procedural about-turn in water policies, and one which we wish to highlight, is its growing complexity. Since the WFD came into force, it has generated a new set of

---

[2]In his 2022 paper, Head looks at regulation of water basins in the United States. Though traditionally the responsibility of public agencies the planning processes involved have gradually expanded to include multiple stakeholders and the general public to achieve greater cooperation in water management. This change arose in part from pressure from various actors and from persistent underlying problems concerning water quality, biodiversity conservation, and coastal zone protection.

[3]"Complex intergovernmental problems (CIPs) are defined as a type of public policy problems that are inherently intergovernmental in nature and are characterized by three typical features: (1) addressing their root causes is not something that can be done through the actions of a single level of government; (2) the very nature of CIPs requires high levels of coordination and collaboration among the governments involved; and (3) these problems challenge existing norms and venues of intergovernmental relations, requiring the close collaboration of bodies and governments that traditionally do not work together, sometimes making joint interventions necessary despite the existing distribution of competencies (Colino, 2022).

actors and relationships (Perez de los Cobos, 2021, p. 79 *et seq.*) that, together, bring the question of water closer to what is often known in public policy as a "wicked problem," principally on account of the diversification of interests, multiplication of axes of conflict, and even the emergence of disagreements when defining the very objective of public policy. The introduction of the WFD has given rise to diverse settings for the aforementioned diversification of interests. The number of actors has increased in practically all areas, since new conservation interests and those of users once scarcely involved now have to be factored in. In addition, while the WFD directly involves the various intermediate and local authorities under the principle of inter-administrative cooperation, these have diverse territorial interests – as is to be expected in a country with massive domestic water imbalances. The ACs become the champions of these interests and, in turn, often become policy entrepreneurs (Font & Subirats, 2010, p. 10).

In short, we believe that water planning in Spain meets the criteria for a wicked problem, particularly following the approval of the WFD. The directive engages a greater number of public and private actors and examines alternative ways of approaching the water problem, in turn making it more difficult to take decisions and reach agreements. Furthermore, the challenge of creating new shared strategies and processes will require organizational learning and a degree of cultural change (Head, 2022).

3. An Attempt to Classify the Actors in Water Planning

The different framings of public policy problems generate conflict regarding their nature and how to address them (Head, 2022, p. 8). In water planning, we may consider two main conditioning factors when actors examine a public good that is to be protected: first, the regional scope or the scale of the action; second, the overall objective of the public policy (Table 1.1). While the first alludes to how public and private actors imagine the area affected by public decisions in the context of the absolutely critical principle of basin unity, the second is about how to approach the problem and the purposes of the public intervention, establishing a basic dichotomy between water as an economic resource (developmentalism) and the fluvial ecosystem as habitat and natural heritage (conservationism). We believe that it is possible to distinguish up to five large framings, which we describe further on.[4]

Starting with those actors that mostly fit within the current management framework established by the WFD, we have the conservationist framing in which water planning is, above all, a question of rational resource use and preservation of quality – not just of water but of the water environment. Planning here is primarily a tool for achieving sustainability in the basin, which is an

[4]The WFD establishes the principle of basin unity in identifying the geographical scope of river management and defines a basin as the entire region over which a principal watercourse and its tributaries flow. This provides the regional scope for decision-making regarding water policy.

Table 1.1. Water Planning Framings Based on the Actors' Positions.

Conflict Dimensions	**Substantive: Overall Objective of the Policy**	
Territorial: Scale of the Policy	**Conservationist**	**Developmentalist**
Respect for the principle of basin unity	• FNCA • Ecologist organizations • Recreational associations	• Energy companies • Irrigation groups in surplus basins
Pro-ACs water decentralization	• ACs with no water deficit (Basque Country)	• ACs with water risk (Cantabria, Aragon, Castilla and León, Andalusia)
Centralization of water policies (National Hydrological Plan)	–	• ACs with a water deficit (Murcia, Valencia) • SCRATS

Source: Authors.

indisputable geographical area insofar as it clearly reflects the interdependencies in such a fragile and complex ecosystem as the river environment. In line with this view, we can cite the New Water Culture Foundation (FNCA), environmentalist concerns and interests related to the recreational use of fluvial ecosystems.[5] From their perspective, upholding the principle of basin unity guarantees that planning will be undertaken at the appropriate scale to provide comprehensive solutions that respect the natural cycles of the river course.

Still maintaining the principle of basin unity but with a more developmentalist approach to its objectives, we have a number of private organizations, such as irrigation associations like the National Federation of Irrigation Communities (FENACORE) in basins not subjected to high water stress, as well as energy corporations (ENDESA, Iberdrola, etc.) that depend on a minimum water flow for their activity. For these actors, water planning must ensure a reasonable distribution of resources throughout the basin. Here, the priority is not conservation of river ecosystems but water demand.

Now, we come to ACs at varying ends of the conservation-development scale, calling into question, at least partially, the principle of basin unity as a result of interests in the acquisition of political competences. The Basque Country, for instance, faces no water deficit while enjoying significant competences in water policy. This AC takes a more rigorous conservationist stance, perhaps because it does not have extremely large irrigation areas or because agriculture is less important to its economy as a whole. By contrast, some ACs challenge the

[5]https://fnca.eu/en/

principle of basin unity by demanding more regulatory power and pursue a developmentalist use of water. This is true for autonomous governments with significant river basins around which the autonomous authorities base most of their economic strategies and production plans.[6]

In terms of the territorial magnitude of water policy, we can envisage a higher level of centralization which overlooks the principle of basin unity to stress the advantages of national-scale planning, as envisaged by the National Hydrological Plan (NHP). While theoretically this approach could be combined with conservation objectives, we find no significant actors here since a national water policy is not easily compatible with the environmental argument for respecting natural scales or with the WFD itself. What we do find, however, are actors who reconcile this regional principle with a more developmentalist approach to water. This is the case for some ACs with a water deficit or for the Central Irrigation Union of the Tajo-Segura Aqueduct (SCRATS)[7] which support, at least partially, a redistribution of water from regions considered as "surplus." This is one particular interpretation of the principle of inter-regional solidarity, based on the competences of the central administration to implement an NHP. Clear examples of this type of discourse can be found in the public statements made by the regional governments of Murcia and Valencia when defending the Tajo-Segura water transfer (Del Moral & Hernandez-Mora, 2016, p. 1044).

In short, we can see that the governance system implemented since the approval of the WFD is based on the existence of relevant actors who not only have different views regarding the desirable objective of planning but also regarding the scale at which it should be projected.

4. The Difficult Interactions Between Water Use, Regional Interests, Feelings of Identity, and Basin Unity

4.1 The Ebro Delta Problem

Given the number of actors and the media impact of the movements involved, management of the Ebro Delta is surely the greatest conflict in the history of the River Ebro basin. The focus has largely been on the issue of environmental flows. That is, the number of cubic hectometers of water needed to maintain river ecosystems in a good state in accordance with the WFD. This is particularly important in the final stretch of the Ebro, where the cumulative demand for

---

[6]The case of the Autonomous Community of Aragon and the Ebro is relevant here. Aragon attempted to secure stronger competences in water planning via statutory reform (in other words, through the change of its self-government statute, a regulation that is, to a certain extent, similar to subnational constitutions in federal countries). This supposed Aragon emerging as the main antagonist of the central government when the latter attempted to introduce the National Water Plan (NWP) in 2001 and particularly when PM Aznar's first cabinet proposed diverting the "extra" water from the Ebro to south-east Spain.

[7]Sindicato Central de Regantes del Acueducto Tajo-Segura (https://www.scrats.es/).

irrigation, urban water supply, and industrial usage must be balanced with the sustainability of the area.

The fact that the Delta is part of the final course of the river complicates decision-making and increases the environmental significance of the various planning alternatives. The main problem in recent years has been the rising level of the Mediterranean Sea as a result of climate change, in addition to the Ebro's inability to transport sediment due to progressive reservoir creation and diversion to meet different demands. In other words, water management in the upper sections of the river course prevents the river from supplying the materials needed to maintain the fragile Delta ecosystem. Hence, the need to set environmental flows (minimum amounts of water) becomes a crucial aspect of water planning if the latter is to uphold the environmental parameters set out in the WFD. It is not only natural resources at stake here but all human settlements and economic activities tied to a coastal region threatened with disappearance.

This problem brings two ACs into conflict: Catalonia and Aragon, located, respectively, at the mouth of the river and on the course immediately prior to this. Catalonia's strong sense of identity is illustrated by the impact of Catalan nationalism in the political and electoral spheres and its control of the autonomous government throughout various administrations. Aragon, on the other hand, has developed a strong water policy discourse and sees the resources of the River Ebro as crucial to its regional development options. It is in the context of these two extremes that the Ebro Hydrographic Confederation has had to take forward successive water plans that have clashed time and again with the issue of how to regulate the flow of the Ebro Delta.[8]

The interests of the ACs in that respect would appear to be determined by the position of the regional actors on the river course. This calls into question the extent to which said actors have truly internalized the concept of basin unity and leads to problems manifesting, for example, as obstructive and negative positioning by the AC of Catalonia in terms of water planning in the Ebro basin. This is in line with the more general and publicly formulated position of the Catalan government that focuses on defending the Delta against the loss of surface area and salinization (La Vanguardia 27/05/2016).[9] Discrepancies around environmental flows raised by the Government of Catalonia feature in all debates preceding the approval of the successive river basin water plans. Approval of the second such plan was supported by the arguments of the European Commission in relation to the evaluation of the first plan, specifically that the latter did not

[8]The hydrographic confederations plan and manage the various basins or water demarcations. In Spain, they are considered as river basin authorities, accountable before the central government, assuming this role when the WFD set out the principle of basin unity.

[9]https://www.lavanguardia.com/local/terres-de-l-ebre/20160527/402092335727/govern-compromete-frenar-perdida-superficie-salinizacion-delta-ebre.html

align with the environmental requirements of the WFD, particularly in terms of the absence of environmental flows in the Ebro.[10]

Other nongovernmental organizations with a great capacity for mobilization have joined in this opposition to the hydrological plans. This is the case, for example, of the Platform in Defence of the Ebro, which brings together local irrigation organizations, conservationists, political parties, trade unions, etc., and forms part of the Network for a New Water Culture (*Xarxa per a una nova cultura de l'Aigua*). On the approval of this second plan, the Platform's main criticism was the plan's provision for a total of 56 reservoirs, which would worsen the situation of the Delta, because of which it called for demonstrations and protests.[11]

Disagreements between the ACs continue. Efforts to boost competences over water in the reforms of the self-government statutes initiated in 2005 have, to a certain extent, "dismantled" the water management model based around the basin management body. Some of these attempts have led other ACs to accuse the River Basin Authority of "tepidness" in its intervention or of seeking bilateral solutions with some ACs without achieving a model of shared multilateral governance. Conflicts such as these take place against a backdrop of more widespread divisiveness regarding the distribution of regional competences over water policy, stirred up by reforms to autonomous statutes, which will lead to other ACs bringing successive appeals before the Constitutional Court. Some authors have dubbed this the "water wars" (Perez de los Cobos, 2021, p. 33), and the Ebro Delta boasts its own chapter on the matter. In fact, an appeal was brought by the AC of Murcia against the comprehensive protection plan for the Delta approved by the Government of Catalonia, on the grounds that it violated the abilities of the Ebro River Basin Authority to plan in accordance with the principles of basin unity and, in turn, the competences of the State over inter-community water resources recognized in Article 149 of the Constitution.[12]

Overall, we can see that shared planning by all actors involved in the Delta conflict seems to be a zero-sum game in which it is difficult to find a middle ground. The interests of upriver regions cause grievances at the mouth of the river, and these cannot be contained without successive local conflicts which are not completely free from identity politics. In addition to a lack of agreement on the matter of environmental flow levels, the AC of Catalonia has brought to light an institutional-level disagreement by stating that no consensus or alignment of positions has been sought and that, ultimately, the Hydrographic Confederation fails to acknowledge that the regional entities have joint responsibility for water

[10]Committee of Competent Authorities for the Ebro Hydrographic Demarcation. Meeting minutes 02/09/2015.

[11]https://www.heraldo.es/noticias/nacional/2016/05/17/la-plataforma-defensa-del-ebro-recuerda-que-nuevo-plan-hidrologico-hace-peligrar-delta-861732-305.html

[12]In 2012, the Constitutional Court dismissed the appeal on the grounds that the comprehensive plan does not modify per se the planning by the national administration, but rather is an acceptable form of cooperation in an area with a unique overlapping of competences (Perez de los Cobos, 2021, pp. 244–251).

management. In other words, the political relationship between institutional authorities should be different to the model that is traditionally applied, recognizing equal status for any of the subnational governments involved in the process.

In short, the question of environmental flows in the Delta does not appear to be approaching a consensus between the regional actors affected, despite the significant environmental damage occurring. The recurring decision to date has been to establish certain flows based on criteria set by the Hydrographic Confederation, which are seen as incorrect by the region at the mouth of the river. It is difficult to see a path toward bilateral negotiation, since this would immediately trigger opposition from the ACs in the middle course of the river, one of which – Aragon – typically uses water as a key political and administrative issue. Given the urgency with which measures must be taken to halt the disappearance of the Delta, in the near future, this problem is likely to continue being a sticking point in the water governance system and in water planning.

4.2 The Tajo-Segura Water Transfer

In Spain, there are currently more than forty active water transfers comprising a supply capacity of 1300 cubic hectometers annually (Morote Seguido et al., 2018, p. 3). While some serve the urban water supply, the most controversial are those clearly intended for irrigation and tied to developmentalist values driven by early water policies. In addition, interbasin transfers such as the one we are concerned with pose an added difficulty in that they reveal another dimension of water policy. That is, national-level water planning subjects the river basin authorities to an external context which conditions the actual effects of their planning activity, generating conflict with the principle of basin unity enshrined in the WFD. There is surely no other basin management body in Spain more directly exposed to this inter-regional conflict that the one pertaining to the Tajo-Segura Water Transfer (TSWT).

The transfer was originally planned in the 1930s and eventually approved by the Spanish Council of Ministers in 1979. The age of the project is, in itself, key to understanding its relative lack of legitimacy today, since a significant number of actors already feel that the original approach and the analysis upon which it was based are now redundant. Initial planning for the TSWT was conducted through the lens of water as an economic resource. This stands in contrast to the environmental shift reflected in the WFD (Escudero Gómez & Martín Trigo, 2020, p. 335). The project was undertaken based on now outdated calculations on rainfall, internal basin demands, urban pressure on the basin, and the very idea of a surplus upon which transfer is based. This situation is no surprise given climate change and the growing pressure on the resource.

As already mentioned, the question around the benefits of the transfer is part of a wider political debate on the relevance of the National Water Plan (NWP). The latter is often defended with allusions to solidarity between the ACs or to the need to rebalance and unite the Spanish territory – allusions which do not sit well with the principle of basin unity outlined in the WFD. The debate over the TSWT has even brought in regions which are less directly affected. Aragon, for example, has a very small percentage of its territory in the Tajo basin but is fiercely opposed to the idea of transfers, since it is an issue that would ultimately affect the principal river in this AC: the Ebro. Moreover, the WFD consolidates the concept of environmental flows as the guarantee of the good state of water bodies and as a factor restricting other uses and demands in the basin. This calls into question the suitability of the TSWT: how the transfer of water to another basin can be acceptable if environmental flows in the middle course of the river are not guaranteed (Escudero Gómez & Martín Trigo, 2020, p. 340; Gallego, 2013, p. 36).

Estimations suggest that the TSWT diverts around 75% of the water resource from the reservoirs at the top of the basin (Gallego, 2013, p. 36) for a variety of uses, particularly irrigation, which consumes up to 86% of the flow in the recipient basin (Morote Seguido et al., 2018). This illustrates the developmentalist view implicit in a project geared toward providing resources to transform a semi-arid region – in this case south-eastern Spain – into prime agricultural land. The economic contribution of agriculture and its role in national gross domestic product (GDP) are often raised in defense of the transfer.

The environmental impacts of the transfer are aggravated in this case by the fact that it starts at the source of a river and connects two basins subjected to similar climate conditions. This causes clear water stress in the middle course of the Tajo, which also supplies water to Madrid, one of Europe's largest conurbations (Escudero & Martín, 2020, p. 338). Given the limited reach of waste water purification and the salinity problem in the river's waters, the TSWT significantly exacerbates issues with water quality, which is one of the guiding principles established in the WFD (Gallego, 2013, p. 55). The problem is particularly serious in the Aranjuez-Toledo-Talavera stretch (Hernández Mora, 2019), as evidenced in discussions during meetings of the Tajo Water Demarcation Council. Such interventions often come from conservation organizations though are also made by the leaders of the Tajo River Basin Authority.[13,14] Some of those who support the transfer have argued the need for novel water treatment approaches to improve the state of waste water from Madrid without reducing the amount of water the city receives (Cámara, 2021), though leaders of the Tajo River Basin Authority warned of the limits of this approach during the first planning cycle.[15,16] These justifications stoke the radical opposition to this public intervention by conservation organizations and those representing the territorial interests of the ACs in the donor basin.

---

[13]https://fnca.eu/73-boletin/titulos/567-a-vueltas-con-el-trasvase-tajo-segura

[14]Minutes of the Tajo Water Demarcation Council, 15/06/2012 (Point 7 of the Agenda: "Appeals and Questions".

[15]https://murciaplaza.com/a-vueltas-con-el-trasvase-tajo-segura-por-que-se-quiere-reducir

[16]Meeting of the National Water Council 26/12/2013 (Point 2 of the Agenda: "Mandatory report on the Tajo Water Plan").

The problems concerning the transfer are no less serious in the purely legal and political sense. As already discussed, the WFD shook up early approaches to water as a development resource and openly established the need to maintain water bodies and river ecosystems in a good state. This requires a radical change in approach which, among other things, means that the water plan itself should determine the level of transferable surpluses in a basin. This is no small detail in the case concerning us here, insofar as this role has been assigned in recent years either to the Central Commission for Exploitation of the Tajo-Segura Aqueduct or to the Council of Ministers in times of water scarcity, both of which are outside of the basin.

The regulations governing the TSWT were modified in 2015 to align management of the transfer with the WFD. Previously, in March 2013, the "Memorandum Agreement" was signed between the central government and those in Valencia and Murcia, and subsequently the ACs in the Tajo hydrographic demarcation, taking advantage of the political climate in that the Popular Party was in power in Madrid as well as Valencia, Murcia and Castilla-La Mancha – the latter contains the donor reservoirs and was historically critical of the TSWT. Since the governments in these three regions held, at that time, an absolute parliamentary majority in their respective assemblies, the central government was able to tackle legislative change from a position of strength and with fewer incentives to seek consensus among conflicting interests. The negotiations lacked significant public participation, as noted by some observers (Escudero Gómez & Martín Trigo, 2020, p. 335) and as is clear in the precursor documentation to the agreement.[17] What this means is that aside from the central administration and the aforementioned ACs, only the irrigation groups participated in the negotiations. The resulting agreement thus adapts, in a highly controversial way, management of the TSWT to the new regulatory framework defined by the WFD but removes it from water planning and includes it in a new and wider-reaching law that lacks legitimacy.

In terms of its content, the agreement established a new system with different usage rules based on the water supplies in the reservoirs at the top of the basin. The Central Commission for Exploitation of the Tajo-Segura Aqueduct approves water transfers under certain hydrological conditions which either determine the transfer quantity or rule out a transfer during water shortages. Voting and decision-making rights in this committee pertain exclusively to representatives of the central administration; delegates from the ACs involved (those from the donor basin and recipient basins [Madrid, Castilla-La Mancha, Extremadura, Murcia, Valencia, and Andalusia]) have a voice but no vote. Likewise, the representative of the SCRATS has voting rights, while there is no representation from the local administration or from other organizations that usually have a seat on water

---

[17]https://tajotoledo.es/wp-content/uploads/2017/05/Acta%20y%20Memor%C3%A1ndum%20Tajo-Segura.pdf

councils, such as user associations and conservation organizations, etc.[18] Moreover, the resolutions of the commission are based on nonpublic documentation and reports (Gallego, 2013, p. 57, note 25).

The central government's interpretation of this process and of the new management system was clear in the intervention by then Minister Arias Cañete in response to criticism from Ecologists in Action:

> …what has been done in the transfer is to objectify how it works, to eliminate political discretion. That is, what we need to do within a set of objective parameters is to give a regulation the scope of a law to objectify the criteria, which is what the irrigation groups wanted, legal security, which is always good… What has been specifically sought is to avoid putting territories in opposition, approving a regulation with the scope of a law that provides peace of mind to everyone. A regulation based on objective parameters… What has been attempted is to remove politics and introduce objective parameters.
>
> (National Water Council Meeting minutes 26/12/2013, p. 15)

The advantageous political backdrop is also reflected in the positive interpretation given by the representative of Castilla-La Mancha when discussing the mandatory report on the second Tajo water plan during a meeting of the National Water Council in December 2013. It contradicts the fierce criticism of the TSWT traditionally seen in this region:

> From the perspective of Castilla-La Mancha, the TSWT agreement is a significant achievement because... the allocations and reserves for Castilla-La Mancha constitute an 18% increase in the water resource compared with the current plan. It also constitutes an increase in the minimum non-transferable reserve from the source… for the first time guaranteeing a minimum flow of 10m3/s through Talavera with all the resources in the basin, including those at the top… All this has been achieved with the utmost openness to dialogue, collaboration, and above all, the principle of solidarity in which CLM has played a vital role.
>
> (National Water Council Meeting minutes 26/12/2013, p. 8)

The argument used to justify the agreement is clear: the need to make the management criteria "technical" and to depoliticize decisions by invoking the principle of solidarity between the ACs. Politically speaking, however, the Memorandum Agreement is highly controversial since it was initially a bilateral

[18]SCRATS approaches management of the TSWT as a representative of the irrigation groups and bases its primary argument on the average profitability of the water resources provided by the Tajo in the Segura basin (Escudero Gómez & Martín Trigo, 2020, p. 339).

negotiation between the central government and the ACs of Valencia and Murcia, both of which are beneficiaries of the transfer and use developmentalist discourse. This criticism comes to the fore with respect to basin planning in that the agreement forces the TSWT off the list of questions to consider and limits the impact of the planning process to such important matters as environmental flows:

> Lastly, the approach to the Tajo-Segura Water Transfer and the justification for not including a specific record on a matter as important as water planning in the Tajo basin is an error. The ongoing justification for rejecting requests to include a record on the matter is that it is outside the competence of the Tajo River Basin Authority, which is wrong, since we are not talking about the competences of said Authority but of water planning in a basin, meaning this should be a subject of discussion. We all know the role of this factor in reducing environmental flows, loss of water quality, meaning it is an error to consider that the matter cannot be addressed because it is not within the competence of the Authority.
>
> (Tajo Water Demarcation Council. Meeting minutes, 28/10/2014. Intervention by a representative from Ecologists in Action.)

Similarly, following the change in political power in Castilla-La Mancha with the Socialist Party returning to government, support once again gives way to criticism, appealing to arguments similar to those we have just examined and illustrating beyond doubt the fragile legitimacy of decisions taken around the TSWT:

> They criticise the non-inclusion of the Tajo-Segura Water Transfer as a pressure in the Plan and question all the recent legislation in that respect (Memorandum, Environmental Assessment Law, Forests Law). As per the WFD, they state that the quality and quantity of water in the middle Tajo could be improved were there greater provision at the headwaters, thus avoiding the transfer.
>
> (Committee of Competent Authorities for the Tajo Hydropgraphic Demarcation. Meeting minutes 02/09/2015, Point 2 on the Agenda: Proposed Tajo Water Plan. Intervention by the representative for Castilla-La Mancha)

In other words, presenting the TSWT as a national planning matter requires more direct ministerial intervention and, in turn, a rescaling of water policy toward the national dimension. This would reduce the organizational autonomy of a River Basin Authority stifled by a lack of necessary resources to address the multiple factors involved in this matter and in the political dimension of the conflict.

The ultimate reasons for the radicalization of the transfer, beyond the controversial nature of its initial approach, surely lie in the crystallization of perceptions and discourses both for and against the TSWT. These often go hand in hand with matters concerning national identity, drawing on feelings of collective grievance that either perceive the transfer as "water theft" or view the demand for conservation of the resource at the source as a "lack of solidarity." With respect to the latter, a clear "hegemonic water discourse" has emerged in the recipient basin. Under the premise of "water for all," a widespread view has formed around a series of factors such as the vital nature of water, the structural deficit in south-east Spain, the exemplary nature of water management, sustainability as the balance between supply and demand, and the rights of the people of Murcia to have the State ensure the water supply, all while appealing to inter-regional solidarity (Del Moral & Hernandez-Mora, 2016, p. 1044). While this discourse has been weakened by domestic issues such as the growing water demand for tourism and residential use, it still has the "ability to prevent dissent" (Del Moral & Hernandez-Mora, 2016, p. 1051) in the TSWT recipient region by structuring a form of regional identity around water demand and, by extension, in defense of the transfer.

In any case, these discourses result in rigid approaches little disposed to negotiation. This seems to generate a certain overlap with the national partisan conflict such that the Socialist Party and the Popular Party – the main representative political parties in Spain – support one approach or the other.

5. Conclusions: A Wicked Problem Affecting Policy Capacity

Throughout this chapter, we have described the variety of interests and interpretive frameworks in water planning processes in Spain, illustrating these using two of the perhaps most significant conflicts in terms of media attention and the mobilization of actors: the Ebro Delta and the TSWT. The ultimate consequence of all this complexity has been the difficulty in making decisions and the practical impossibility of achieving and consolidating consensus to enable a degree of stability of the interventions in a sectoral policy which, more than any other, requires sustained actions over time.

Analyzed from a historical perspective, we must necessarily see the WFD as a break-point moment in water policies: the general definition of the public problem changed, at the same time as new values and interests were included in a renewed, more pluralistic, and multilevel governance system. Undoubtedly, the difficulty in finding common frames of reference and assessments in the discourses means, among other things, that the legislative resources of the different actors become more important, in turn reinforcing the definitive role of those actors that have legal/constitutional control over the different political competences. In these circumstances, the constitutional principle that grants the final say to a specific political or administrative actor becomes crucial – the central administration in the case of Spanish water policy, namely the hydrographical confederations. These bodies thus become the target for pressure from the actors involved in the governance processes, reproducing something now almost commonplace in the

Spanish territorial model: a tendency toward clear bilateralism in intergovernmental relations.

As previous cases have shown, however, an administrative hierarchy is no guarantee of the legitimacy and much less of the effectiveness of policies which are often closely linked to inter-regional tensions. This is why, with respect to planning processes, alternative discourses arise related to identity (Catalonia), stronger views regarding the competences of the central government (Murcia) or inter-regional solidarity (Valencia). These arguments not only question the appropriateness of the decisions but challenge the assessments made by the opposing parties, all of whom are involved in a game resembling a dialogue involving different languages and no hope of understanding. Given this lack of common ground and the significance of the legislative resources, it is no wonder the various ACs have tried to improve the latter via their self-government statutes. The corresponding litigiousness – various ACs have presented appeals to the Constitutional Court to try to rebalance relations – also comes as no surprise.

The ultimate consequence is that the underlying problems persist, be it the disappearance of the Ebro Delta, the problems of water availability in the Tajo basin or other issues arising from a planning approach that does not effectively integrate the principle of basin unity. The wicked nature of these problems therefore arises in the form of inefficient and ineffective planning of water resources.

Consequently, throughout history, we can point to a relative reduction in the policy capacity of the decision-makers in Spain's water administration, possibly more visible in the hydrographic confederations but not exclusive to them. Given the fact that these were the institutions responsible for water policies in the golden days of developmentalism, it is by no means surprising that they have encountered many difficulties in overcoming path dependency after the WFD was transposed into Spanish law. However, the level of success has not been any greater when the Environment Ministry has been involved (the TSWT), evidencing the same difficulties in reaching consensus exhibited by the confederations. We therefore believe that both cases illustrate how some of the resources depicted as enjoyed by public administration, such as expertise or control over the decision-making process (Peters, 2015, pp. 220–221), seem to have been eroded as a consequence of the establishment of new water policies. This loss of capacity is particularly significant in those institutions with formal powers to control water policies. They are not alone in this, however, since sustainable water policies pose a challenge for all the actors involved.

In fact, the aforementioned lack of skills and capabilities is also due to a certain political-administrative culture that goes beyond the confederations being present both at a national and subnational level, including some noninstitutional stakeholders. This culture is based on an old approach that finds it difficult to adapt its territorial view and give more say to the subnational level, as well as establishing water policies at their natural river-basin scale. Certainly, the two cases discussed here are representative of both aspects: in the case of the Ebro Delta, the inability of the central administration and the ACs to reach a consensus (also a problem between the different ACs themselves) and, in the case of the

TSWT, the reluctance to abandon a national perspective, even at the cost of going against the spirit of the WFD. Perhaps these should be the first steps on the road to more legitimate and effective water planning.

From a broader, theoretical point of view, the basis of our argument is that the WFD establishes a new approach that changes water policy, turning it into what we know as a "wicked problem." In fact, this directive changed the objective of public policy since it established the conservation of river ecosystems as the goal, rather than the mere provision of water resources. Likewise, its entry into force also resulted in procedures being modified, with the result that the number of intervening actors multiplied and new conceptions and concepts regarding the object of water policy were integrated into decision-making. We therefore argue that the public problem, the planning and management of river ecosystems, has become a key challenge for the analytical and management capacities of both individual and organizational actors. In other words, it is becoming increasingly difficult to conceive of and manage the public problem, since the preservation of ecosystems requires the complicated reconciliation of diverse and often contradictory factors, based on complex scientific knowledge and the demanding new visions of water. At the same time, the decision-making process involves a greater number of divergent interests, which generates a higher level of organizational responsiveness. What all this ultimately leads to is a reduction in policy capacity, visible especially at an individual and organizational level but also ultimately detectable at a systemic level (Wu et al., 2015), especially because of a lack of ultimate legitimacy of public decisions.

References

Cámara, J. M. (2021). A vueltas con el trasvase Tajo-Segura ¿Por qué se quiere reducir? *Murciaplaza*. https://murciaplaza.com/a-vueltas-con-el-trasvase-tajosegura- por-que-se-quiere-reducir. Accessed on May, 2022.

Camillus, J. C. (2008). Strategy as a wicked problem. *Harvard Business Review*, *86*, 98–101.

Committee of Competent Authorities for the Ebro Hydrographic Demarcation. Meeting minutes 02/09/2015. http://www.chebro.es/contenido.visualizar.do?idContenido=63803&id-Menu=6405

Committee of Competent Authorities for the Tajo Hydrographic Demarcation. Meeting minutes 02/09/2015. *Minutes from the Water Council and from the Committee of Competent Authorities*. Provided by the Tajo River Basin Authority.

Covarrubias Moreno, O. M. (2022, March). Problemas complejos y políticas públicas: el caso de la epidemia de obesidad en México. *GAPP*, (28), 81–98. https://doi.org/10.24965/gapp.i28.10886

De La Peña Varona, A., Mondragón Ruiz de Lezana, J., Ramos Gallarin, J. A., & Alda, M. (2022). *Gobierno multinivel y compartido en España. La interacción entre Comunidades Autónomas y Administración General del Estado en la planificación hidrológica*. Instituto Nacional de Administración Pública. Colección INNAP INVESTIGA. Serie ESTUDIOS TERRITORIALES. ISBN 978-84-7351-748-5.

Del Moral, L., & Hernandez-Mora, N. (2016). Nuevos debates sobre escalas en política de aguas. Estado, cuencas hidrográficas y comunidades autónomas. *Ciudad y Territorio. Estudios Territoriales, 190*, 563–583.

Escudero Gómez, I. A., & Martín Trigo, A. (2020). La gestión pública de una obra hidráulica compleja, entre el marco internacional y los intereses regionales privados: el caso del trasvase Tajo-Segura (España). *Relaciones internacionales: Revista académica cuatrimestral de publicación electrónica*, (45), 327–344.

Font, N., & Subirats, J. (2010). Water management in Spain: The role of policy entrepreneurs in shaping change. *Ecology and Society*, *15*(2), 21.

Gallego, M. S. (2013). *El abastecimiento de Madrid y el trasvase Tajo-Segura en la planificación y gestión de la Demarcacion Hidrográfica del Tajo en VVAA: El Tajo. Historia de un río ignorado* (pp. 35–88). Fundación Nueva Cultura del Agua.

Head, B. (2010). *Wicked problems in water governance: Paradigm changes to promote water sustainability and address planning uncertainty*. Urban Water Security Research Alliance Technical Report, No. 38.

Head, B. W. (2019). Forty years of wicked problems literature: Forging closer links to policy studies. *Policy and Society*, *38*(2), 180–197. https://doi.org/10.1080/14494035.2018.1488797

Head, B. W. (2022). *Wicked problems in public policy. Understanding and responding to complex challenges*. Palgrave Macmillan.

Hernández-Mora, N. (2019). *A vueltas con el trasvase Tajo-Segura*. Fundación Nueva Cultura del Agua. https://fnca.eu/73-boletin/titulos/567-a-vueltas-con-el-trasvase-tajo-segura

Morote Seguido, Á. F., Olcina Cantos, J., & Rico Amorós, A. M. (2018). Un trasvase cuestionado: El Tajo-Segura. Repercusiones socio-económicas en el sureste español e incertidumbre ante el cambio climático. *Revista de Estudios Regionales*, (113), 29–70.

National Water Council Meeting minutes 26/12/2013. Provided by The Basque Water Agency (URA).

Perez de los Cobos, E. (2021). *Litigios competenciales en materia de aguas* (1.a ed.). Tirant lo Blanch.

Peters, B. G. (2015). Policy capacity in public administration. *Policy and Society*, *34*(3–4), 219–228.

Rittel, H. W., & Webber, M. N. (1993). Dilemas de una teoría general de planeación. In L. I. Aguilar Villanueva & M. A. Porrua (Eds.), *Problemas públicos y agenda de gobierno*. English original, 1973: Dilemmas in a General Theory of Planning. Source: *Policy Sciences*, Vol. 4, No. 2, pp. 155–169. Published by: Springer. http://www.jstor.org/stable/4531523

Tajo Water Demarcation Council. Meeting minutes 15/06/2012 and 28/10/2014. *Minutes from the Water Council and from the Committee of Competent Authorities*. Provided by the Tajo River Basin Authority.

Wu, X., Ramesh, M., & Howlett, M. (2015). Policy capacity: A conceptual framework for understanding policy competences and capabilities. *Policy and Society*, *34*(3–4), 165–171.

Chapter 10

From Wicked Problems to the Wickedization of Solutions: The Case of the French Citizens Convention for Climate

Magdalena Potz, Solange Hernandez and Sarah Serval

Aix-Marseille Université, France

Abstract

This chapter analyzes the French Citizens Convention for Climate (CCC), a democratic experiment in public policy cocreation, responding to climate change and the democratic crisis. The CCC, involving 150 citizens, aimed to propose measures for reducing greenhouse gas emissions. Despite producing 149 proposals, the government's limited implementation led to widespread dissatisfaction, which highlights the complexities of policy cocreation. Through textual statistics analysis, the study reveals the "wicked" nature of cocreation, intensified by diverse values and interests among participants. It underscores the critical need for the government's political readiness and absorptive capacity in cocreation processes. While citizens showed commitment and capability, political-administrative elites displayed resistance, indicating a policy capacity gap. This resistance not only undermined the CCC's efforts but also exacerbated public distrust in political processes. The CCC's experience suggests that future cocreation initiatives in public policy must better integrate with political decision-making. The balance between standardization and contextual adaptation is key to effectively addressing complex societal issues. This chapter advocates for close monitoring of cocreation applications in public policy to assess their effectiveness in resolving societal challenges.

Keywords: Absorptive capacity; citizen participation; cocreation; policy capacity; wickedization

Policy Capacity, Design and the Sustainable Development Goals, 201–217

doi:10.1108/978-1-80455-686-320241017

1. Introduction

The alarm bells have not stopped ringing since the publication of the Intergovernmental Panel on Climate Change's (IPCC's) first report on the state of the art of scientific knowledge about climate change in 1990 and the 1992 Rio Earth Summit. For the past 30 years, the need for sustainable development has been clear, and the objective of reaching it is shared worldwide. While progress has been made since the beginning of the 1990s, it is neither fast nor broad enough. Given this observation, a possibility to accelerate and widen the scope of this movement is to consider the United Nations' Sustainable Development Goals (SDGs) as wicked problems that require joint and innovative public policy and public action. Indeed, while technical and scientific solutions exist, it is clear that the envisaged solutions are difficult to legitimize, and the change difficult to implement. The SDGs respond above all to an eminently political logic in the construction of responses that explain these difficulties and invite us to conceive of them as wicked problems. Moreover, the wicked dimension of the SDGs can be applied to both the nature of the problem posed and the responses provided. Even though these responses can be politically and managerially very innovative, as in the case of extensive citizen participation mechanisms, they seem to systematically fail in the face of the magnitude of the challenge. We suggest that the pitfall comes from solutions that are thought of in a technical and rational way, to problems that are certainly scientific in nature but embedded in their social environment, responding to a political and nontechnical logic. Consequently, well-crafted technical solutions can evolve into politically intricate challenges during their implementation, undergoing a process of "*wickedization*".

We propose to explore this assertion in the context of the French Citizens Convention for Climate (CCC). The CCC has been launched by the French government in 2019, asking a panel of citizens to think about policies through which France could drastically reduce its carbon emissions. This initiative was relatively unprecedented: apart from anecdotal and not always successful examples such as Iceland's (so far failed) participatory revision of its constitution in 2010 or Ireland's citizen assembly working on issues such as abortion or gay marriage, hardly any cases of extensive citizen participation on important policy questions can be found. In the fight against the climate crisis, several participatory initiatives such as the UK Climate Assembly[1] have recently emerged in European countries – among them, the French CCC as what might be the one of the most ambitious undertakings.

These innovative citizen participation projects are part of a new paradigm in public management: cocreation (Torfing et al., 2019). However, such practices are not yet standardized, and are deeply contingent; they are a managerial innovation with its share of surprises and challenges. Thus, we propose to explore the extent to which a cocreation process, initially intended as a means of providing responses to wicked problems, becomes itself the wicked problem. We assume that this "wickedization" process could be explained by an analysis of the political capacity

[1]https://www.climateassembly.uk/

of the government to innovate which is based on readiness and absorptive capacities of political decision-makers to seize the potential of cocreated responses.

This chapter is structured as follows: the first section provides elements to define and frame the problem in order to understand the major change cocreation constitutes in the field of public policy and more particularly in sustainable development. We develop here an analysis of the political capacity as the main determinant of cocreation success, but also failure when it is lacking. We assume that the political capacity of the government to innovate through cocreation is directly linked to the readiness and absorptive capacities of political decision-makers. Then, we present the case of the CCC and the methods based on statistical textual analysis from a corpus of secondary data. The findings demonstrate the wicked dimensions of the cocreation process. We show that cocreation, intended as a solution to a technical and scientific problem, is politically exploited to counter a democratic crisis. However, it ultimately reinforces the crisis because of the inability to connect scientific and technical proposals from civil society to political and governmental decision-making processes. It is not so much the problem that is wicked as the process that can lead to the wickedization of the same object.

2. From Wicked Problems to the Wickedization of Problems and Solutions

The first section highlights the institutionalization of the SDGs and the wickedization of the problems posed (1.1). Then prior literature serves to understand the outlines of cocreation as a new managerial response to address the SDGs. But, like the problems it is supposed to solve, cocreation seems in turn to be pernicious as the bureaucratic and political context is unfavorable (1.2). Then, we propose that the wickedness of cocreation could be explained through an analysis of the political capacity of government (1.3). To benefit from cocreation, the government must be able to seize solutions cocreated by a plurality of actors, including citizens and nonexperts. We thus establish the inextricable link between the absorptive capacity and political capacity of government when it comes to cocreation.

2.1 Back to the Institutionalization of SDGs: From Tame to Wicked Problems

The SDGs are the result of a construction over several decades. And it is only recently that they have been assimilated to wicked problems.

Indeed, from the 1970s onward, the environmental issue became part of scientific debates, with the publication of the Meadows report (The Limits to Growth, 1972). In the same year, the Organization for Economic Cooperation and Development (OECD) adopted the Polluter-Pays Principle, whereby the polluter has to bear all the costs of preventing and controlling any pollution that it originates. The observation of the biodiversity decline (disappearance of plant and animal species, depletion of natural resources) is reflected in international agreements, such as the Convention on International Trade in Endangered Species of Wild Fauna and Flora (1973, Washington) or the Convention on the Conservation of European Wildlife and Natural Habitats (1979, Bern). Nature, its preservation, and pollution, are at the heart of these discussions.

In the 1980s, new global challenges appeared, such as the phenomenon of acid rain or the deterioration of the ozone layer. International and national authorities reacted by promoting technical solutions: adoption of the catalytic converter in Europe, stricter emission standards for large combustion installations (factories, power stations, etc.), the Vienna Convention on the Protection of the Ozone Layer (1985), and the Montreal Protocol (1987).

However, the turning point came in the 1990s with the United Nations Conference on Environment and Development (1992, Rio de Janeiro). This first Earth Summit highlighted two challenges of a different nature than the previous ones: sustainable development and climate change. It is no longer a question of acting on the environment but of achieving balanced development based on the economy, society, and the environment, while at the same time making in-depth changes to the way our societies function to limit the (multiple and intertwined) greenhouse gas emissions. This multidimensionality of today's most urgent problems shows that the complexity of global challenges related to sustainable development does not cease to increase. Despite numerous summits (including the Conferences of the Parties to the United Nations Framework Convention on Climate Change – COP), as many conventions and protocols (for example, the 1997 Kyoto Protocol, or the 2015 Paris Agreement) and proven scientific knowledge (IPCC reports), progress is slow and narrow.

The expected energy, economic, and societal transitions … have yet to be achieved. Yet.

The causes are of course numerous, and it is not our purpose here to list them. However, let us simply consider the nature of the successive problems set out above. The first ones, although on a large scale, were largely resolved thanks to technical innovations, generalized by *ad hoc* regulations. This is no longer the case with sustainable development and the fight against climate change. These require profound changes in the way our societies function. Finally, it is as much the scale of the problem as the scale of the solutions to be implemented that has changed. To express it differently, we have gone from tame problems to wicked problems (Fig. 10.1).

While tame problems are solved through engineering processes with trial-and-error logic and technical rationality, wicked problems in contrast rely on political judgments of ill-defined problems and ex ante unverifiable solutions (Rittel & Webber, 1973). Wicked problems are "*complex, unpredictable, open ended, or intractable*" (Head & Alford, 2015). Thus, rather than an a priori categorization of tame or wicked problems, it seems essential to take into account both contextual elements and the evolutions of problems that can move from tame to wicked like the SDGs (Alford & Head, 2017). In doing so, it is appropriate to consider a spectrum of possibilities between tame and wicked problems corresponding to degrees of wickedness (Head & Alford, 2015; Ooms & Piepenbrink, 2021). Note

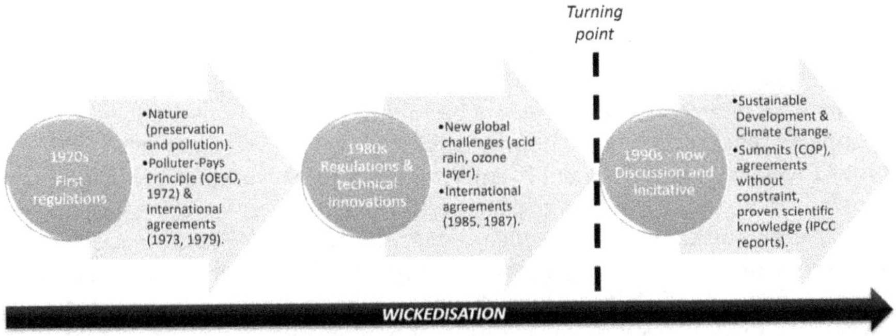

Fig. 10.1. The Wickedization of SDGs. *Source:* Authors.

that in the face of wicked problems, problems and solutions are unclear, requiring a large volume of knowledge, and are both problems and solutions, contested by those involved (Ooms & Piepenbrink, 2021). While an abundant literature has developed around the concept of wicked problems since the 2000s, ultimately, little work has focused on the solutions and particularly the managerial solutions to be deployed (Alford & Head, 2017; Head & Alford, 2015). In this respect, an innovative but highly complex managerial response to tackle the wicked problems of the SDGs is of particular interest to us here: cocreation.

2.2 Cocreation: A Managerial and Organizational Response to Tackle SDGs

As repeatedly highlighted within the SDGs, actors, levels, and countries must come together to address them. One of the goals is explicitly dedicated to the development of "Partnerships for the Goals" (SDG17). Multi-stakeholder partnerships are pointed out as crucial steppingstones toward the achievement of all other goals. On their own, not even the most power- and resourceful actor is able to reach the goals; the involvement of all relevant and affected actors and collaboration with them is what makes it possible to effectively tackle complex policy problems. While cocreation tends to be presented as a cure all in this regard (Voorberg et al., 2015), it does not come without its challenges itself. An important obstacle to overcome is related to the heterogeneity of actors and the potential conflicts this might produce. However, this diversity of actors involved in cocreation is also key for the development of innovative solutions which the SDGs, as wicked problems, require: these ever-evolving, uncertain, and multi-faceted problems cannot be resolved through traditional public action but need emergent responses.

The public sector is today ill-equipped to take on this challenge (Ansell et al., 2021). Its bureaucratic structure and long-established portfolio of responses do not allow for much creativity or adaptation to the complexity of these problems. Recently, a shift in the functioning of public sector organizations can be observed:

citizen participation is on the rise (Sørensen & Torfing, 2019; Torfing & Ansell, 2017) in a public sector that is increasingly marked by collaboration. Among the multiple forms this can take, cocreation, with its aim to develop innovative solutions to societal issues, is quickly becoming popular among public administrations searching for ways to address wicked problems (Hofstad et al., 2021). It brings together a variety of public and private actors around a shared problem, for which they aim to develop new and innovative solutions through an exchange of their different kinds of knowledge, ideas, and resources (Torfing et al., 2019). As a problem-driven and highly creative approach to policymaking, cocreation allows to design ideas that create value not only for participants but for society as a whole. In this perspective, citizens are not only included at an operational level during the implementation of a policy solution, or the delivery of a public service, but also at a more strategic one, as they take part in policy development (McMullin, 2022).

In this regard, cocreation can facilitate the identification and formulation of policy problems, as well as the development of shared understandings and interpretations of these problems as dispersed actors gather and debate. By including actors with diverging interests and motivations in the policymaking process, potential conflicts can be avoided before they arise, and compromise can be found. To do so and achieve the most valuable outcomes, ideally, cocreation would be continuous (Bentzen, 2022), allowing citizens to participate in all stages of the process, from the identification of problems to the design of solutions, their implementation, and evaluation (Nabatchi et al., 2017).

2.3 Cocreation and Political Capacity to Innovate: A Matter of Readiness and Absorptive Abilities?

Cocreation practices have the potential to provide an "additional capacity" that enhances the governing abilities to address wicked problems of sustainability. Indeed, we can assume that the ideas, resources, and work deployed by a plurality of internal and external actors bring an additional capacity that should ultimately improve the performance and effectiveness of the policymaker. Thus, in the case of cocreation, additional policy capacity depends directly on the appropriation of the cocreation work by policymakers who recognize both the reliability of the work undertaken and the relevance of the cocreated solutions. Indeed, the advantages of cocreation rely on the enrichment of knowledge by external sources from which policymakers benefit through the design of original solutions that are de facto legitimized by the democratic nature of the process. In the field of management sciences, this capacity to take possession of ideas and solutions developed by other actors, external to the traditional decision-making processes, refers to the absorptive capacity. Coined by Cohen and Levinthal (1990), the absorptive capacity is defined as the ability to recognize the value of new information from the environment, to assimilate it and to exploit it. This implies that a group of actors such as the political-administrative elites must tap into various sources of external knowledge and be able to integrate them. In this perspective, when government needs to design innovative policies, political capacity (Howlett & Ramesh, 2015) is determined by the absorptive capacity of policymakers. Thus, here we consider absorptive capacity as a determinant of political capacity when it comes to performing political functions in order to innovate. Analyzing the political capacity of the government and more precisely the absorptive capacity enables to better understand why cocreation is so little deployed whereas it is so attractive on paper.

Cocreation is far from being a taken-for-granted practice. It is a major challenge in the transformations underway to achieve the SDGs. While it encompasses a set of technically elaborate practices covering all stages of the public policy process, cocreation is hardly ever this extensive today. Citizens are most likely involved in later stages of the policy process – i.e., its implementation – and less so in the planning and design phases (Sørensen & Torfing, 2022) or the final decision-making that tend to happen in-house. Especially when citizens are not part of important decisions or the process lacks transparency, cocreation might entail negative consequences instead of the proclaimed benefits. In lieu of improving democracy, social cohesion, innovativeness, and legitimacy of decisions and joint ownership of them (Torfing et al., 2019), cocreation gone wrong might generate frustration, alienation, and disconnection, and reinforce inequality and power disparities (Steen et al., 2018). These negative aspects of cocreation arise from the lack of absorptive capacity, which in turn affects the political capacity of the government. Thus, we assume that, within a cocreation framework, the ability to exploit external knowledge – the absorptive capacity – is a critical component of political capacity to address SDGs.

For politicians, the main challenge in such contexts consists in avoiding the pathology of the "not-invented-here" (NIH) and the "All-Stored-Here" (ASH) syndromes (Ooms & Piepenbrink, 2021). NIH syndrome is symptomatic of people traditionally in charge of new proposals in an organization who negatively perceive and oppose ideas coming from outside. The ASH syndrome is a form of disregard for the potential input of external stakeholders. Essentially, these two syndromes go hand in hand and reflect the lack of absorptive capacity. The strategies of obstructing transparency, reducing spaces for cocreation, and predominantly anecdotal evidence of citizen practices are rather clear symptoms. If policymakers were more prepared and trained in cocreation, it would reduce their chances of developing NIH and ASH syndromes. They could then deploy their absorptive capacity to enhance the value of cocreated solutions. Their political capacity to innovate would thus be strengthened. As underlined by Lippi and Tsekos in the introduction of this book, the question of the readiness of political decision-makers is therefore crucial and especially when they must absorb the outputs of cocreation.

Thus, we assume that cocreation, as a response to the SDGs, can itself become a wicked problem. We propose to highlight this process of wickedization based on a lack of absorptive and political capacities through the case of the CCC in France.

3. Case Study: The French CCC, a Democratic Experiment for a More Sustainable Future

This section presents the case of the CCC (3.1), the methodology adopted (3.2), and the findings (3.3).

3.1 The French CCC: Context, Modalities, and Results

In 2019, the French government was not only dealing with the climate crisis and finding ways to comply with the 2015 Paris Agreement but confronted with a democratic crisis at the same time, sparked by the Yellow Vests. What began as a protest against the carbon tax quickly turned into a much larger movement, pointing out social inequalities and injustice in France. As a reaction to this upheaval, French president Emmanuel Macron first decided to launch the "Grand Debate," a nationwide consultation of the population on topics such as the environmental transition, democracy, or the organization of public service. To go one step further, he announced mid-2019 the creation of the CCC where a group of citizens would be asked to suggest measures to reduce greenhouse gas emissions by at least 40% by 2030 in a spirit of social justice. Promising to submit "without filter" this group's proposals to his government, the president instructed the Economic, Social and Environmental Council (CESE) to organize this citizen assembly for which a budget of 5.4 million Euros was provided.

3.1.1 150 Citizens, 7 Weekends, and 149 Propositions

To ensure descriptive representation of the French population, 3,000 telephone numbers were randomly selected based on multiple demographic criteria. Ultimately, 150 of them were chosen to represent the population in the CCC: aged between 16 and 80, with different levels of education, and coming from all over the Hexagon, this group of citizens was meant to depict the country's diversity. Over the course of nine months, they would gather on seven weekends at the CESE headquarters in Paris.

Divided into five predefined working groups (housing, food, work and production, transportation, consumption) and supported by facilitators, legal and economic experts, as well as scientists acting as fact-checkers, these citizens got to work in early October 2019. The first three-day weekend consisted of the installation of the CCC, the presentation of working methods, and a first look into the topics to be treated. The government was represented by the Prime Minister as well as the Minister of Ecology to formally launch the CCC. The second weekend started with keynotes to establish a common knowledge base before the working groups got together and began to establish first objectives for each topic. On the third weekend, further discussions with experts allowed to delve deeper, and first lists of ideas and proposals were produced. The fourth session was marked by the speech of president Macron, ensuring continuous involvement after the end of the CCC. Over the course of the fifth weekend, each working group pitched their ideas to the others, so that the final deliverable could be prepared. In early March 2020, this final report was discussed and validated by the CCC. Then, COVID-19 hit. After months of lockdown, the CCC got together again in June 2020 for a final debate, and to formally submit their 149 proposals to the French government. The 150 members of the CCC were invited to the Elysée Palace the following week, where the president declared that 146 of their measures would be examined, rejecting the three remaining ones using the "jokers" he had announced at the beginning of the CCC.

3.1.2 What Happened With the Proposals?

Over the following months, first decisions were taken: a handful of measures such as the ban of the heating of outdoor public spaces in winter were implemented. In the "France Relance" plan announced in September 2020 as a reaction to the pandemic, several proposals were included, as well as in the Climate and Resilience law of February 2021. The CCC convened for one final time in February 2021 to react to the governmental responses to their work: they declared that the actions taken by the government were not satisfactory given the ambition of their proposals. While in 2022, the government points out that of the 149 measures proposed by the CCC, 100 have been implemented entirely or partially, at a closer look, it quickly becomes obvious that only anecdotal measures have been implemented, while others have been largely modified and hardly resemble what the CCC had in mind.

3.2 Methodology

The following paragraphs describe the data collection process that led to the construction of the corpus, on which the textual statistics analyses were conducted.

The empirical analysis is based on secondary data corresponding to information, published between spring 2019 and September 2022, and all related to the work of the CCC.

In total, 210 documents, or 424,451 words (occurrences), were collected. According to our research objectives, we assigned four variables to each document: the document number, the timeline (before, during, and after the convention), the type of document (press, governmental report, convention report, press release, internal technical documents, and presidential speech), and the source (name of each journal, government, presidency, and CCC). All these documents form our corpus, which we have exploited through quantitative analysis of qualitative data (textual statistics) with the IRAMUTEQ software.

The main interest of textual statistics methods is to consider texts as they have been written, without interpretation or codification by a mediator (Lebart &

Salem, 1994). They are also recommended when the researcher is confronted with a large mass of data that they wish to condense, classify, and structure to make it more intelligible.

The main objective of cluster analysis (in this case, hierarchical top-down classification) is to group objects into homogeneous classes, so that those within a class are very similar and those in different classes are very dissimilar. Factor analysis simplifies the data by highlighting a few general factors or key dimensions. These methods are based on statistical frequency calculations.

3.3 Findings

We conducted a first cluster analysis, in which 97.57% of the initial corpus were classified. Three significant classes emerged. The first (46% of the classified corpus) focuses on the CCC, the second (35%) on the public policy instruments needed to implement the Convention's proposals, and the third (19%) on the problems identified and requiring intervention measures (e.g. greenhouse gas emissions, agriculture, imports, consumption, plastics, fishing, etc.).

We choose not to elaborate on the outcomes of this initial cluster analysis, as two categories fail to clarify how innovative citizen participation practices, initially a solution to wicked problems, have become a wicked problem themselves.

Therefore, we performed a second cluster analysis and a factor analysis on the sub-corpus of the CCC class (Fig. 10.2).

The factorial design summarizes the results of the second cluster analysis. The factors explain 100% of the variance. Factor 1 (*y*-axis) corresponds to the wickedization of problems. Its ends are Tame problems (bottom of the quadrant) and Wicked problems (top of the quadrant). This factor has greater explanatory power than the second, accounting for about two-thirds of the variance. The second factor is also significant (although to a lesser extent): this is the stakeholder axis (*x*-axis). This axis has two ends: on the left, Public Authorities, on the right, Citizens.

Let us now detail the three classes that appear on the factorial design.

Class 1, named "*Political decision*," includes different groups of public authorities. The most significant forms designate the *president*, the *government*, the *ministers* (exercise of executive power). They also refer to the legislative work (*law, review, proposal, regulation, moratorium, measure*) carried out by members of parliament (*Senate, National Assembly, Senator, MP*).

Beyond the political actors, this class highlights political strategies and tactics implemented during the process of the citizens convention: *filter, joker, ambition, unraveling, surprise, arbitration*, as they have been widely denounced by convention members, media, and a part of the civil society (NGO):

> *They* [the members of the convention] *point out that many of their measures have been completely distorted by taking up only part of them. They emphasised the coherence of their proposals and their*

> *objectives, taken as a whole, as well as the damage done by the government's unravelling.* (Statement of the Convention after the end of their work)

> *After the enthusiastic speeches, comes the time for the unravelling. Week after week, one by one, the strong measures of the convention are abandoned. It is a denial of both the substance and the method.* (Press article, La Correspondance Économique, October 2020). *The government is in an awkward situation with members of the citizens convention and environmental NGOs. The former denounces the unravelling of their proposals and the latter a law of renunciation.* (Press article, La Croix, July 2021)

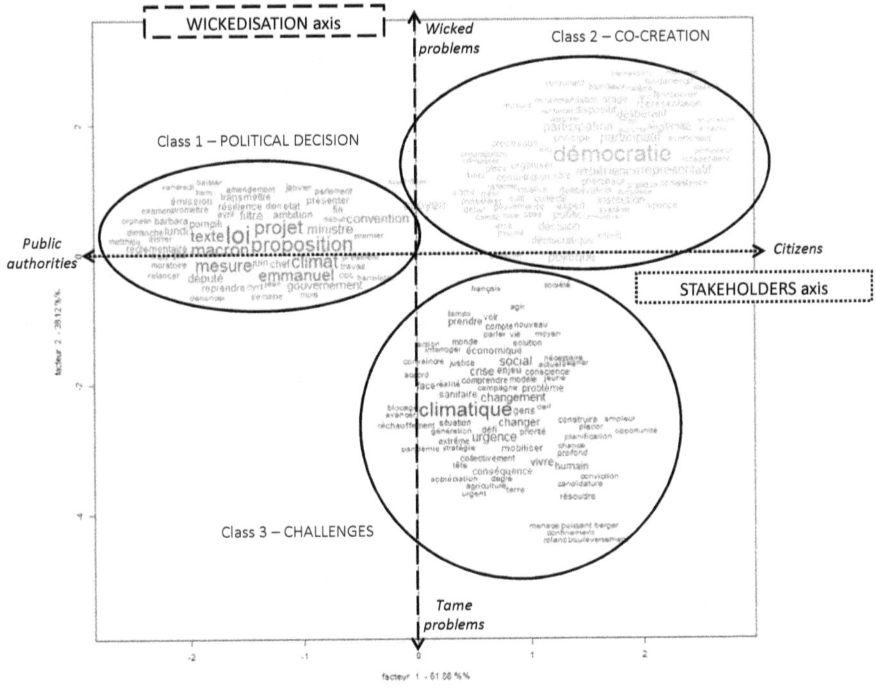

Fig. 10.2. Results of the Factor Analysis (Sub-Corpus). *Source:* Authors.

Then, Class 2 concerns *Cocreation*, from both the point of view of its engineering and its principles. On this first point, we find among the most significant forms associated with the class: *decision, elected, random selection, panel, expert, competence, training, plan, governance, initiative, method, tool, approach, facilitation*, etc. On the second point, the most significant elements relate to *democracy, participation*, the *collective* (group), the place of *debate*, *diversity*, the *representative, deliberative* and *civil* characters, the *transparency* of the processes, and the *legitimacy* that derives from them. This class also points out the limits of the cocreation process: "*For the environmental lawyer, if the recommendations of the convention are not followed by politicians, citizens will have no legal recourse. The consequences depend solely on the will of the President of the Republic*" (press article, Le Monde, published just after the end of the Convention).

Finally, Class 3 refers to the *Challenges* that the convention addresses from three perspectives: the challenges' extent, the challenges' purpose, and the duty to act in response.

The *extent* of the challenges is not only qualified by its intensity (*crisis*) and *urgency* (*threat*, *upheaval*, *blockage*, *risk*) but also by the *issues* at *stake* (the challenges themselves), such as *global warming, biodiversity, agriculture, social, economic, health, human, Earth, justice,* etc. In its work (April 2020), the convention underlines "*the contribution of the Citizens Climate Convention to the crisis recovery plan. We want a crisis recovery strategy to prepare for the future, i.e., a different economic and societal model, more humane and more resilient to future crises (…)*".

Faced with these elements, *action* is necessary: we must *question*, *understand* challenges, build *new responses*, find *solutions*, *solve* problems, *mobilize, convince*, and find *opportunities*.

> *We want to enshrine the green rule in the constitution, no longer taking more from nature than it is capable of replenishing. It is an immense human and technical challenge, but France has the assets to take it up and to be at the forefront of the global change that must take place.* (Press article, L'Humanité, April 2021)

Let us now turn to the discussion section to understand, from the empirical study, how and to what extent the cocreation process has become a wicked problem.

4. Discussion

To what extent does the cocreation process itself become a wicked problem? Based on the evidence in our findings of a wickedization of the CCC, we discuss in the following paragraphs the wicked dimensions of cocreation explained through a lack of political capacity and especially the lack of readiness and absorptive capacities from political decision-makers.

4.1 The French CCC Experience and the Wicked Dimension of a Cocreation Process

Considering differences in values and interests as the main characteristics of wickedness, it seems clear that a response through cocreation necessarily leads to an intensification of wickedness. Indeed, by integrating a plurality of actors, cocreation increases the range of possibilities in terms of divergent perceptions, conflicting interests, and diverse values. Then, considering wickedness as an analytical perspective and not a tool for problem classification (as pointed out in the introduction of this book), we propose here a new approach to cocreation, namely a "wicked" approach that applies not only to societal problems but also to the responses aimed at solving them.

Initially, the problems related to the practice of cocreation lay in its implementation and structuring, with, for example, the methods of selection and drawing of citizens. At the time of the launch of the process, the practice seemed to be taken for granted by the government, with the commitment of the French President to retain "without filter" the proposals made by the CCC. However, a gradual disengagement took place, and problems – particularly of political nature – emerged as the cocreation process unfolded. In the end, out of the 149 proposals formulated by the convention, only the anecdotal measures were the subject of a political decision without any filter. Finally, while the complexity of the problems seemed to be related to the content of the CCC at first as it had to work on solutions to the climate crisis, eventually, it was even more acute at the level of the very functioning of the CCC and its connection to effective political decisions. The complexity of the form thus took precedence over the complexity of the content. In the case of the French CCC, cocreation as a policymaking tool was meant to generate socially acceptable solutions to the wicked problem of climate change. However, what was initially thought of as a technical tool to be used to tackle other problems quickly became a problem itself – and a rather wicked one.

4.2 The Explanatory Factors of the CCC's Failure: A Lack of Readiness and Absorptive Capacities

In our case, it is political disagreement that leads to wickedness. Indeed, analytical capacity and operational capacity to design innovative policies to address the SDGs have been provided by the CCC. The CCC's output was based on training sessions for citizens and the intervention of numerous experts to both accompany the citizens' reflections and help them build relevant and feasible proposals. The identified solutions are based on technical and scientific logics. In this regard, it is worth noting that the CCC demonstrated their capacity to elaborate technical responses. While the use of simplified and persuasive narratives is a common strategy adopted by political and administrative elites who wish to convince their stakeholders whose understanding of the issues may be limited, in our case, the CCC has adopted the exact opposite strategy. The objective is precisely to demonstrate the technicality of the developed solutions, whose argumentation is based on a scientific narrative. The challenge here is to convince political and administrative elites of the validity and technical reliability of the solutions provided. These elites are perceived here as being a priori capable of understanding the complexity. The challenge for the CCC is also to ensure its technical legitimacy through elaborate discursive strategies and a lexical field linked to the expertise of the treated domain. Then, CCC's work demonstrates that it is possible to hybridize both technocratic and participatory responses. While the CCC fulfilled the analytical and operational expectations through the design of technical solutions in different sectors, the failure of the cocreation process relies on the political capacity. Although these solution proposals seem difficult to refute, the government and the President only retain anecdotal measures based on political and not technical rationality. The proposals resulting from the cocreation process are thus finally evaluated according to "good-or-bad" political criteria and not "true-or-false" scientific and technical criteria (Rittel & Webber, 1973). Indeed, in this cocreation process, the political capacity is in the hands of the politicians who still have the decision-making power and the responsibility to prioritize. Here, the main failure noted lies in the acceptability of politicians vis-à-vis the policy measures designed by the CCC. It is their political capacity that is lacking to ensure the success of such a cocreation process.

The wickedness of cocreation can be explained by the uncertainty generated by managerial innovation. Cocreation as an emerging approach is a managerial innovation that is also rooted in local and contingent realities. As a result, practices are constantly renewed and difficult to envisage in their entirety before being implemented. In this respect, it is pointed out that the CCC was supposed to be directly connected to the public decision-making process with an "unfiltered" commitment from the President. This methodological choice was finally abandoned, and cocreation was quickly disconnected from the decision-making processes. As a cocreation process, CCC is a new practice, and the political elites here show a strong path dependence and thus a strong attachment to more traditional public policy design practices. The political disagreement observed in our case could be understood as politicians' lack of ability to change: they demonstrate a strong resistance to adopt new arrangements that have not been designed by themselves. The ability to change refers to the readiness capacity of politicians mentioned above by Lippi and Tsekos. Politicians show a lack of readiness capacity that prevents them from dealing with urgency and resisting pressures from outside when it comes to assuming and supporting the work of the CCC through the passage of political decisions and legislation. Thus, in a cocreation framework, the readiness capacity of politicians is an antecedent of their absorptive capacity, which is itself a factor of their political capacity to innovate. When the readiness capacity fails, policymakers are closed to outside ideas and unable to acknowledge their value. In this regard, they developed the NIH and the ASH syndromes (Ooms & Piepenbrink, 2021) which in our case results in the rejection of most of the solutions proposed by CCC.

Furthermore, the lack of absorptive capacity, highlighted by the development of the NIH and SAT syndromes, can lead to highly counterproductive effects on the political capacity of the government through the loss of legitimacy. Let us remember that the CCC was originally initiated with the political will to fight against the crisis of representative democracy that France is experiencing. Particularly in response to the Yellow Vests crisis, this cocreation process was intended to rebuild trust and promote the legitimacy of the State by establishing a participatory and democratic body. Citizens' expectations were therefore particularly high. Also, given the political abandonment of most of the proposals, the disappointment was so great that this cocreation process finally reinforced citizens' distrust. Then, the CCC, the first experience of its kind in France, was not without consequences. Indeed, in the face of the failure of the mechanism that was supposed to rebuild trust and bridges with citizens, a few years later, the observation of a democratic fracture was confirmed in the last presidential elections of 2022 with a record rate of abstention and the rise in power of populist parties. Thus, the extent of the democratic crisis does not allow for any space for trial and error. Each attempt at cocreation, let alone each failure, has consequences and leaves its marks. Consequently, the readiness capacity of policymakers to implement their absorptive capacity to citizens' proposals can have a lasting and significant effect on the political capacity of the government, but also on institutional capacity in a broader sense when it is lacking.

5. Conclusion

The work of the CCC ended according to a predefined timetable, considering that it was "good enough," having done its job in the time available – it did not end because it had actually "resolved" the climate crisis in France. In this regard, it could even be considered a failure if one takes into account the actual national political decisions that resulted from the process: this number remains anecdotal.

Our study reveals that many barriers to the deployment of cocreation exist. While civil society seems ready to adopt such processes and practices, the government turns out to be more resistant. On the one hand, citizens proved their willingness to get involved and acquire new knowledge and competences, as well as their ability to develop highly technical and concrete policy solutions to complex problems, despite their lack of expertise. On the other hand, we also shed light on the significant role played by the absorptive capacity of policymakers. If cocreation practices can lead to additional political capacity to address the SDGs, their success depends directly on the absorptive capacity of the political-administrative elites, who need to be sensitized and trained. If cocreation practices can lead to additional political capacity to address the SDGs, their success depends directly on the absorptive capacity of the political-administrative elites. They need to be sensitized and trained even before developing any cocreation practices, however innovative they may be.

Their discovery of this resistance and lack of absorptive capacity was a harsh return to reality for the members of the CCC as they did not see the results they had hoped for. Citizens' expectations for this cocreation process had been high, and this disappointment had important repercussions on the already strained relationship between societal and political spheres. Expectations on the side of policymakers had been high as well: officially, the CCC was intended and expected to provide solutions for the climate crisis. More implicitly, there was also hope that it would help alleviate the democratic crisis and improve the overall political climate in France, which, following the Yellow Vests movement, was tense. Given these high expectations on both sides, every wrong move and slippage could have significant consequences.

Despite, or precisely because of their dissatisfaction with the results of the CCC, shortly after its end, its members have established an association in order to ensure independence and continuity. Now, the CCC's undertaking is to build the legitimacy of their solutions through territorial dissemination on the one hand and lobbying on the other. Local citizen convention initiatives have emerged, too, this time connected to local public policies. Moreover, while one might think that this new mechanism of cocreation would be dropped after this relatively unsuccessful first attempt, it has recently been revived through a new citizens' convention on the issue of end-of-life support. Thus, the practice of cocreation and its modalities are being re-examined in order to improve the process so that it is better connected to political decision-making processes, showing that "some additional investment of effort might increase the chances of finding a better solution" (Rittel & Webber, 1973, p. 162). This goes to show the evolving nature of cocreation, its dependence on the context in which it unfolds as well as on underlying perceptions and interpretations. The CCC represents a first attempt at national-level cocreation amidst a backdrop of particularly complex problems. To evaluate whether the cocreation approach is adapted for the resolution of wicked policy issues, it would be interesting to closely follow the evolutions and new applications of this mechanism, and study their results.

While cocreation corresponds to a new paradigm of public management, its implementation is eminently contextual and requires adaptation to local contingencies. As a new paradigm, it follows clearly identifiable principles such as the orientation toward innovation, the integration of citizens in the decision-making process, decompartmentalization, and collaborative work with diversified actors. Certain standards, best practices, or models can therefore be identified and applied in different cases and contexts. However, adapting cocreation mechanisms to local circumstances and requirements is necessary to effectively connect them with political decision-making processes. This balance between standardization and uniqueness is where cocreation reveals its complexity – and wickedness.

References

Alford, J., & Head, B. W. (2017). Wicked and less wicked problems: A typology and a contingency framework. *Policy and Society*, *36*(3), 397–413.

Ansell, C., Sørensen, E., & Torfing, J. (2021). The COVID-19 pandemic as a game changer for public administration and leadership? The need for robust governance responses to turbulent problems. *Public Management Review*, *23*(7), 949–960.

Bentzen, T. Ø. (2022). Continuous co-creation: How ongoing involvement impacts outcomes of co-creation. *Public Management Review*, *24*(1), 34–54.

Cohen, W. M., & Levinthal, D. A. (1990). Absorptive capacity: A new perspective on learning and innovation. *Administrative Science Quarterly*, 128–152.

Head, B. W., & Alford, J. (2015). Wicked problems: Implications for public policy and management. *Administration & Society*, *47*(6), 711–739.

Hofstad, H., Sørensen, E., Torfing, J., & Vedeld, T. (2021). Leading co-creation for the green shift. *Public Money & Management*, 1–10.

Howlett, M., & Ramesh, M. (2015). Achilles' heels of governance: Critical capacity deficits and their role in governance failures. *Regulation & Governance*, *10*(4), 301–313.

Lebart, L., & Salem, A. (1994). *Statistiques textuelles*. Dunod.

McMullin, C. (2022). *Non-profit organizations and co-production: The logics shaping professional and citizen collaboration*. Taylor & Francis.

Nabatchi, T., Sancino, A., & Sicilia, M. (2017). Varieties of participation in public services: The who, when, and what of coproduction. *Public Administration Review*, *77*(5), 766–776.

Ooms, W., & Piepenbrink, R. (2021). Open innovation for wicked problems: Using proximity to overcome barriers. *California Management Review*, *63*(2), 62–100.

Rittel, H. W., & Webber, M. M. (1973). Dilemmas in a general theory of planning. *Policy Sciences*, *4*(2), 155–169.

Sørensen, E., & Torfing, J. (2019). Designing institutional platforms and arenas for interactive political leadership. *Public Management Review*, *21*(10), 1443–1463.

Sørensen, E., & Torfing, J. (2022). Co-creating ambitious climate change mitigation goals: The Copenhagen experience. *Regulation & Governance*, *16*(2), 572–587.

Steen, T., Brandsen, T., & Verschuere, B. (2018). The dark side of co-creation and co-production. Seven evils. In T. Brandsen, T. Steen, & B. Verschuere (Éds.), *Co-production and co-creation: Engaging citizens in public services* (1re éd., p. 284). Routledge.

Torfing, J., & Ansell, C. (2017). Strengthening political leadership and policy innovation through the expansion of collaborative forms of governance. *Public Management Review*, *19*(1), 37–54.

Torfing, J., Sørensen, E., & Røiseland, A. (2019). Transforming the public sector into an arena for co-creation: Barriers, drivers, benefits, and ways forward. *Administration & Society*, *51*(5), 795–825.

Voorberg, W. H., Bekkers, V. J., & Tummers, L. G. (2015). A systematic review of co-creation and co-production: Embarking on the social innovation journey. *Public Management Review*, *17*(9), 1333–1357.

Chapter 11

The Wicked Future of Cities: Localizing Sustainable Development in the Case of the Metropolitan City of Florence

Edoardo Amato[a], *Daniela Bernaschi*[b] *and Maria Camilla Fraudatario*[c]

[a]University of Milan, Italy
[b]University of Florence, Italy
[c]IRPPS-CNR, Italy

Abstract

The UN 2030 Agenda defines sustainable development (SD) in a multidimensional approach that encompasses economic, social, and environmental aspects. The Sustainable Development Goals (SDGs) serve as conceptual ideals, specific targets, and standards that determine global and local priorities. SD falls into the realm of wicked problems due to its multilayered definitions, untamable nature, and possible solutions at an operational level. Addressing these complex problems and challenges requires the localization of the SDGs and the creation of a new governance model tailored to sustainability. These efforts aim to improve policy coherence for SD. This contribution focuses on the importance of localizing the SDGs, which aims to streamline the 2030 Agenda and tailor the SDGs to local needs. Therefore, the importance of multi-stakeholder participation in the formulation of local definitions of the SDGs, policymaking strategies, and consequently the measurement of the SDGs is emphasized. This chapter provides insights into the specific tools and strategies used by the Metropolitan Cities (MCs) in the implementation of coherent SDG policies, with Florence serving as a case study. Despite the challenges faced by MCs, including ambiguous leadership, conflicting objectives between municipalities, and challenges in coherent policy design, this institutional level shows interesting elements, such as functions of long-term planning and coordination, inclusive tools of

Policy Capacity, Design and the Sustainable Development Goals, 219–239

doi:10.1108/978-1-80455-686-320241019

participation, and the development of new capacities (political and administrative) that could be useful for strengthening governance for SD.

Keywords: Agenda 2030; SDGs localization; multilevel governance for sustainability; wicked problems; policy coherence

1. Introduction

Sustainable development (SD) is unequivocally a concept that holds both soft law and increasingly emerging hard law attributes (Bristol-Alagbariya, 2020). It serves as a guiding political norm ever since the publication of the report Our Common Future by the Brundtland Commission in 1987. This steering role gained prominence and intensity with the introduction of Agenda 21, one of the final documents of the *United Nations Conference on Environment and Development* in 1992 and particularly with the UN 2030 Agenda for Sustainable Development Goals (SDGs) adopted in 2015.

The 2030 Agenda represents a global call to action against poverty, the protection of the planet's natural resources, and the assurance of peace and prosperity for all individuals by 2030 (UNDP, 2020). Despite the adoption of the SDGs at the supranational level, their successful implementation relies on the active participation of local stakeholders, thereby necessitating a bottom-up approach. Indeed, it has been estimated that 62% of the targets cannot be fully accomplished without the involvement of local stakeholders (OECD, 2020). The growing interest in city-level actions has sparked international interest in the concept of *localizing* SDGs (Bardal et al., 2021; Kanuri et al., 2016), as well as in the territorial embeddedness of SD to ensure the adoption of coherent policies (Sianes, 2017). Territorialization enables the translation of global goals into local goals and actions, facilitated by urban governance (Pierre & Peters, 2005), thereby addressing the controversial, ambiguous, and intricate nature of SD (Giddings et al., 2002; Meadowcroft, 2007). This approach allows for the tackling of challenges, complexities, and conflicts specific to a particular context and its social actors. In accordance with the Leipzig Charter (2007–2020), which emphasized the significance of multilevel and multi-stakeholder governance in promoting SD at the urban level, the State assumes the role of a partner or facilitator for Metropolitan Cities (MCs), regions, and urban areas in formulating their own strategies.[1] This not only contributes to the ongoing discourse on the definition, measurement, and implementation of SD but also offers valuable insights and inspiration that can be replicated in other local contexts (Fox & Macleod, 2021).

This chapter seeks to examine the impact of localization on the governance of sustainability through an empirical case study conducted at the local level, specifically focusing on the Metropolitan City of Florence (MCF). In the Italian context, MCs represent newly established local authorities. In this context, MC

[1]The "Leipzig Charter on Sustainable European Cities" (2007) and its 2020 update, the New Leipzig Charter, are crucial in shaping European urban development policies.

refers to both its administrative boundaries and the collective sum of local municipalities. On one hand, the MC is responsible for planning and coordination, while on the other hand, the Italian municipality has played a crucial role since the 1970s in the management and provision of public and social services, particularly in the areas of environment and social welfare. The purpose of this study is to assess the extent to which the MC is effectively empowered to drive change.

2. Localizing SD

SD is the pursuit of equilibrium among the environmental, social, and economic dimensions (Crabtree & Gasper, 2020; Fitoussi & Malik, 2013; Sen & Anand, 1994). In the endeavor to attain this equilibrium and coherence among the three dimensions, the conflicts are becoming apparent. It is thus primarily a concept that lacks comfort; it is highly demanding and necessitates grappling with implicit and latent contradictions among the various dimensions.

Urban areas, as the tangible manifestations of human existence, are the locales where the viability or nonviability of SD and its most significant challenges emerge. Indeed, in an increasingly urbanized world, the destiny of cities and the destiny of SD are intertwined. Fundamental socio-environmental challenges (e.g., mounting urban population pressure, escalating inequalities, rising energy consumption, and carbon emissions) render cities an ideal domain for comprehending and evaluating the sustainability of development.

By the presence of Goal 11 in the UN 2030 Agenda, which is concerned with the achievement of *sustainable cities and communities*, the leading role played by cities in shaping and promoting sustainability is also confirmed and reinforced. Fig. 11.1 demonstrates the synergy between Goal 11 and the other SDGs, such as ending poverty, promoting equality, and ensuring that citizens live healthy lives.

Moreover, according to the Organization for Economic Cooperation and Development (OECD, 2020), a considerable number of the 169 targets of the 17 SDGs – precisely 105 – necessitate the active involvement and coordination of local and regional governments. This aspect highlights the strategic role that localization plays in the 2030 Agenda (Oosterhof, 2018; United Nations Habitat, 2020).

The concept of localization, defined as the process of adapting, implementing, and monitoring the SDGs at the local level (Global Taskforce of Local and Regional Governments, 2016, p. 6), serves to bolster the influence of local authorities and local social actors in the attainment of the SDGs. This approach aligns with the fundamental principle of *no one is left behind*.

The significance of localization is underscored by three key factors. Firstly, local authorities often bear responsibility for critical policy domains such as health care, transportation, waste management, urban and spatial planning, local economic development, social inclusion, and basic services (Oosterhof, 2018, p. 4). Secondly, due to their close proximity to the territory and citizens, local authorities possess a profound understanding of the pivotal areas, vulnerabilities, and capacities of their respective regions.

Furthermore, localizing SD may present itself as a viable strategy for addressing the challenges associated with sustainability. This pertains to both the definition and

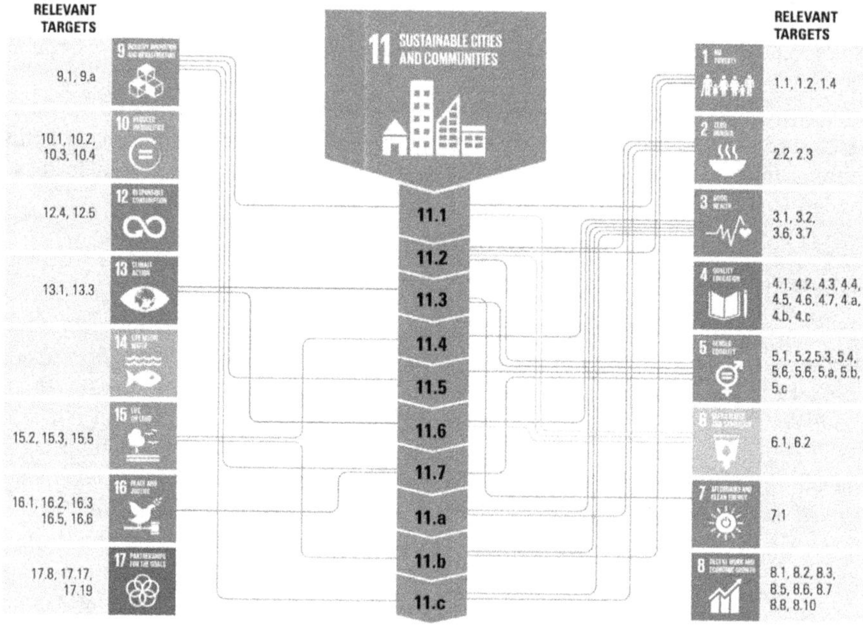

Fig. 11.1. Interlinkages Between SDG11 and the Other SDGs.
Source: UN Habitat (2018).

policy actions that have contributed to the complexity of the issue (Eden & Wagstaff, 2021; Head, 2019; Van Tulder, 2018). It is worth noting that while there is a general consensus on the significance of SD as a universally important principle, Pearce et al. (1989) liken it to "motherhood and apple pie." On the contrary, others argue that the lack of clarity and analytical rigor in its meaning renders the concept almost meaningless (Giddings et al., 2002, p. 188). Consequently, this hinders the search for effective solutions (Peters & Tarpey, 2019).

In terms of its definition, the literature suggests that the sustainability paradigm embodies elements of ambiguity, flexibility, and conflict (O'Connor, 1994). The broad scope of the concept allows for a wide consensus to be formed around the idea of SD. By localizing sustainability, it becomes possible to narrow down the broad and abstract definition, creating specific sustainability frameworks that align with local priorities derived from the SDGs (Krueger & Agyeman, 2005; MacGillivray & Franklin, 2015).

When it comes to policy actions, the territorialization of sustainable development not only involves its distinct definition based on local characteristics and *socioeconomic-environmental needs*, but also takes into account the *awareness plan* of these elements among local institutions and stakeholders responsible for its implementation. Consequently, SD becomes a matter of local governance (Sachs,

2015), organized through multiple institutional assets capable of ensuring the quality of their actions and functions and involving different stakeholders who represent diverse and potentially conflicting local needs.

As a result, the inclusion of multilevel governance (MLG) structures and mechanisms for stakeholder participation in the formulation and execution of shared priorities for local SD (Senatore & Bellabarba, 2021) may serve to mitigate potential conflicts.

In simpler terms, local governance of SD refers to a range of processes, strategies, and policy instruments implemented by various local actors that play a critical role in achieving the goals of the 2030 Agenda within each local context. In this regard, inter-municipal cooperation spaces can serve as a form of cross-cutting coordination, potentially valuable in reducing inconsistencies by aligning the planning efforts of local authorities across different decision-making levels or by connecting actors with conflicting local interests operating at multiple decision-making levels, thus establishing local governance networks (Danken et al., 2016).

3. Conflicts and Coherence: Local Solutions for SD?

The Agenda 2030 changes the model, shifting the SD from hierarchically ordered regulatory mechanisms to a *pattern* of goals and results adopted in terms of sustainability policy. This new perspective has increased the importance of territorial governance in achieving the SDGs through the process of localizing SD (Kanie et al., 2019). While constructing a shared Agenda may aim to reduce conflicts over SD's definition, this new model cannot entirely eliminate conflict. The SDGs are tools useful to circumscribe operatively the concept of sustainability, but even this model presents at least four kinds of conflict: (1) conflicts around the definitions of the goals, (2) conflicts between actors about goals, (3) conflicts among actors regarding the means useful to achieve goals, (4) conflicts that concern the allocation of *burdens and honors* of realizing SDGs (Dusseldorp, 2017). Therefore, conflict persists and can also be exacerbated by other phenomena such as the politicization of the problem structuring process (Hoppe & Turnbull, 2022).

Conflicts from the definitional plan also pass to the operative one. In terms of policy, these conflicts may generate incoherencies in the decision-making process, contributing to the increasing degree of complexity. *As many authors have stated, there has been no generally agreed upon definition for the concept of policy coherence* (Sianes, 2017, p. 135). The concept of *Policy Coherence for Development* (PCD) appeared for the first time in the 1990s (Ylönen & Salmivaara, 2020) and then it is even stated in goal 17.14 of the Agenda 2030 dedicated to the Policy Coherence of Sustainable Development (PCSD). Indeed, *the 2030 Agenda has expanded policy coherence in many ways and concerns all countries regardless of their development level* (Gregersen et al., 2016, p. 16).[2,3]

[2]The literature offers various categorizations of policy coherence development (Carbone, 2008; Forster & Stokke, 1999; Hoebink, 2004; Picciotto, 2005).

[3]The aim is to enhance policy coherence for SD.

Actually, policy coherence may be addressed from several diversified prospects, primarily, both from an output/outcome and a process perspective (Di Francesco, 2001). The complexity of policy coherence poses challenges for local authorities (Barry et al., 2010). Firstly, there's an issue with policy coherence related to the meanings and definitions of sustainability, which Agenda 2030 has not fully addressed. There is not complete consensus on the concept of SD, potentially causing a gap between definitions and actions aimed at achieving SDGs. The process of localizing SD may bring local authorities to link specific context-relevant declinations of the SDGs to actions that are grafted positively on the territory, so even containing the risk to produce not effective responses to the goals of Agenda 2030. This approach mitigates conflicts and reduces the risk of policy inconsistencies stemming from the use of loosely related and contextually unadapted definitions of SD and goals (Jiménez-Aceituno et al., 2019; Nilsson et al., 2018).

Secondly, on the one hand, there is a horizontal declination of Policy Coherence (PC) that *refers to the potential problems raised by the interaction between various policy areas* (Carbone, 2008, p. 326). The Agenda presents conflicting SDGs, and the actions adopted in a policy field may influence others policy areas. Hence, the local authorities often have to deal with problems of coherence between economic, social, and environmental policy goals. On the other hand, there is *internal coherence*, namely *the consistency between goals, objectives, and modalities of a development-related policy or program* (Ylönen & Salmivaara, 2020, p. 832). In addition to the interactions between policies, local authorities must manage the coherence between the solutions proposed and the means to achieve the goals, especially with a view to coordinating the different decision levels involved.

Policy coherence is also a concern related to the actions carried out by various actors. Local governance involves multiple actors with diverse goals and approaches. SDG is a multi-stakeholder arena marked by significant competition, potentially leading to conflicts in SDGs' attainment due to variations in actor interpretations and implementation approaches to sustainability (means and modalities). A place-based approach, leveraging shared cultural and social attributes among actors operating within the same decision context, can help mitigate this type of conflict (McCarter et al., 2018). Moreover, local governance should consider *representational* and *inclusive* coherence. Unequal access or participation by actors can impact sustainability strategies and actions, raising concerns about specific actors' influence and the social disparities that differential access may create. These aspects raise several concerns about the influence of specific actors on the decision-making process and the social differences that this diversified access could generate. Even this dynamic is more manageable in a local decision-making context.

The PCSD agenda includes other levels of policy coherence (Table 11.1). Domestic interests can disrupt coherence in several ways. Firstly, conflicts may arise between different national agendas. Secondly, global SDGs may clash with those at the national level. Additionally, PCSD introduces another facet of coherence, the vertical one, which concerns the alignment of policies across different decision-making levels in their collective effort to attain SD.

The OECD outlines three vital aspects for PCSD implementation: (1) institutional mechanisms, (2) political interactions, and (3) political effects (OECD, 2016).

Table 11.1. Policy Coherence and Wickedness the SD.

<table>
<tr><th>Policy coherence</th><th>Area</th><th colspan="2">Wicked-problem</th><th>SD</th></tr>
<tr><td>Problem Structuring</td><td>Meanings and definition</td><td colspan="2">No definitive formulation of wicked problem</td><td>Problems and goal complexity</td></tr>
<tr><td>Interpretation of stakeholders</td><td>Meanings and definition
Actors
Content</td><td colspan="2" rowspan="3">There is always more than one explanation for a wicked problem because the explanations vary greatly depending on the individual perspective</td><td>Presence of multi area stakeholders</td></tr>
<tr><td>Participation and inclusiveness of actors</td><td>Actors
Decision level</td><td rowspan="3">Partial solutions AND Intertwined problems and interactions among SDGs</td></tr>
<tr><td>Implementation of stakeholders</td><td>Actors</td></tr>
<tr><td>Interactions among policies</td><td>Content</td><td colspan="2" rowspan="2">Every wicked problem can be a symptom of another problem</td></tr>
<tr><td>Internal (aims modalities and tools)</td><td>Content</td><td>Richness of SDGs and goal-means conflict</td></tr>
<tr><td>Global coherence</td><td>Decision Level</td><td rowspan="3">Wicked problems do not have a set number of potential solutions</td><td></td><td>Several SD interpretations</td></tr>
<tr><td>MLG coherence</td><td>Decision Level</td><td rowspan="2">There is no immediate test of a solution to a wicked problem</td><td>Time-horizon of intervention</td></tr>
<tr><td>Local coherence</td><td>Decision Level</td><td>Nuanced nature of the authority</td></tr>
</table>

Focusing on the first element, eight pillars have been identified for enhancing policy coherence through structures, processes, and methodologies. Several of these are closely related to local decision-making levels. Alongside *subnational and local engagement*, these pillars encompass *adopting a long-term planning perspective* and recognize the role local authorities can perform in terms of both *coordination and participation.*

Governments should work together with the regional and local authorities in the implementation of SD policies. In dealing with incoherencies linked to SD policies, these pillars need the development of policy capacity understood *as the set of skills and resources – or competences and capabilities – necessary to perform policy functions* (Wu et al., 2018, p. 3).[4]

From the last decade of the 19th century, there was the empowerment of local authorities in institutional, procedural, and organizational profiles.[5] The improvement

[4]Available resources consist of various capacities: (1) analytical, essential for handling technically complex matters like sustainable development; (2) operational, aiding policy planning and implementation management; (3) political, for building consensus. These capacities operate at individual, organizational, and systemic levels.

[5]The adoption of the direct election of local government leaders in the 1990s played a significant role.

of local authorities' performances in policymaking and service delivery was especially relevant, as well as the process of devolving new competencies to regions promoted with the Constitutional Reform of 2001. The increasing need to manage complexity and new challenges have influenced the selection processes of the administrative team, providing for the recruitment of new managers with different backgrounds (Bonaretti & Tomassini, 2003) and the adoption of rules and tools typical of the private sector, thus strengthening the cultural change of the organization (Lippi, 2011).[6]

In terms of policy capacity, coordination between decision-making levels and among the actors involved falls into the category of *systemic operational capacity*. Indeed, *policy integration concerns the management of cross-cutting issues in policymaking that transcend the boundaries of established policy fields, and which do not correspond to the institutional responsibilities of individual departments* (Wu et al., 2018, p. 13). From an MLG perspective, MCs have a role in coordinating the efforts of municipalities and local governance actors to achieve SDGs coherently. Decision-making levels should collaborate to address SD as a process, involving stakeholders in formulation, implementation, and interpretation. Additionally, from a regulatory perspective, MCs can coordinate service provision (Furlan, 2016). This underlines other aspects that concern the operational policy capacity at the organizational level. On the one hand, the capacity of (and the need for) coordination of internal processes (Peters, 2018), while on the other hand the capacity to be a coordinator of the stakeholders.

The planning capacity is one of the declinations of the operational capacity, indeed *apparently conflicting interests may be more closely aligned if a sufficiently long-term perspective is taken* (Barry et al., 2010, p. 210). Furthermore, planning underscores the importance of the local decision level within metropolitan contexts. MCs often grapple with heterogeneous policy landscapes, requiring tools like planning to manage complexity. Municipalities within these areas may have conflicting objectives and positions on SDG-related topics, as well as discrepancies between various decision levels, necessitating alignment and decision arenas to achieve policy coherence. Long-term policy planning enables responsive management (needs and emergencies) and strategic goal realization, acknowledging complex interconnected objectives. It addresses conflicts, identifies trade-offs, and helps the harmonization of policy goals. Some policies require extended timelines due to feasibility and social change requirements. This approach leverages SDG synergies, involving local communities and enhancing sustainability awareness (UN-Habitat, 2016).

4. MCs in the Italian Local Government System

From a structural perspective, the Italian local government system is characterized by a three-level structure: municipalities, provinces, and MCs. The 20 regions hold legislative authority over all areas not specifically governed by national

[6]Profound organizational change occurred with the spread of the NPM approach in local administrations.

legislation, allowing them to choose which responsibilities to delegate to local levels (Citroni et al., 2018).

The institutional characteristics, the administrative tradition, and the legal culture made the Italian state of the 19th century fall within the *French Napoleonic model* (Kuhlmann & Wollmann, 2013). The role of local authorities in this system was strictly subordinate (functionally and organizationally) to a centralized government. This setup produced specifical effects like the fragmentation of the authority, the increasing ambiguity, in terms of competencies, among institutional roles, and the lack of both effectiveness and democratic accountability (Lippi, 2011). After the local institutional reform (at the end of the 1990s) and especially the 2001 Constitutional Reform, the system was so defined as *quasi federalist,* superseding the previous arrangement to a more decentralized asset (Bolgherini & Lippi, 2016; Brunazzo, 2010).

Metropolitan administrations were a new kind of local authority deriving from the merger of big municipalities and their neighboring townships (Lippi, 2011, p. 500), aimed even at containing the fragmentation thanks to their tasks of planning and coordination.[7] In 2014, the intervention of the legislator known as the DelRio Law (l. 56/214) outlined the characteristics of the MC even identifying the areas of intervention. This institutional reality had been discussed for several years before, and it has new and different functions, compared to the Province. From a structural perspective, the MC presents three organs, first of all, the (1) *Metropolitan Mayor.*[8] The Mayor of the capital municipality not only represents the body but also presides over the metropolitan council and conference. They hold the authority to initiate actions concerning the Metropolitan Strategic Plan (PSM) and oversee service operations.[9] (2) *Metropolitan Council* comprising the Mayor and varying councilors based on population; it holds authority to approve regulations, plans, and acts submitted by the Mayor, propose statute changes, and prepare budgets.[10] Indirect elections[11] impact leadership abilities (Torselli & Pira, 2016) and the management of imbalances and conflicts among local authorities due to municipal weight and integration issues (Mobilio, 2017). The (3) Metropolitan *Conference*, formed by the mayors of the municipalities belonging to the MC. The Conference has powers of proposal and consultation, for example, on the budget and not on control. It may also adopt or reject the statutes and amendments.[12]

[7]The MC's creation in 2014 aimed to replace the provinces.

[8]The Metropolitan Council (MC) was introduced by l.142/1990 and later enshrined in the Italian Constitution's Art. 114 in 2001. However, its concrete boundaries and implementation remained undefined.

[9]As a parallelism with prediction concerning municipalities (TUEL art.50.2) the Metropolitan Mayor exercises the other functions established by Statute.

[10]Ranging from a minimum of 14 to a maximum of 24.

[11]Paragraph 25 of l.56/2014 states that the metropolitan council is elected by the mayors and municipal councilors of the metropolitan city's municipalities. In the case of Florence, there are 18 councilors (mayors and councilors of the territory) in addition to the Mayor.

[12]It exercises the other functions established by Statute.

MCs play a vital role in achieving SDGs. They represent a new form of subregional governance that emerged from the increasing emphasis on the dynamics of political interaction and coordination exerted in the local authorities (Mayntz, 1999). This subregional governance emphasizes the principle of subsidiarity both vertically and horizontally. Vertically, they empower local decision-making within the MLG framework. Horizontally, they enhance coordination among municipalities and local authorities, fostering partnerships between public and private actors. This shift toward open decision-making processes involves various socioeconomic actors and citizens, influencing public policies by necessitating boundary adjustments and promoting interaction and negotiation between stakeholders. Additionally, MCs functionally coordinate and align actions at the municipal level, addressing fragmentation and ensuring consistent policy implementation and service delivery (Citroni et al., 2016).

Planning and coordination are two key functions. Particularly, the tasks of the MC are (a) strategic planning, (b) general spatial planning, (c) the structuring of coordinated public service management systems and the organization of public services of general interest in the metropolitan area, (d) mobility and viability, (e) the promotion and coordination of economic and social development, (f) the promotion and coordination of computerization and digitization systems in the metropolitan area. In addition to these, some functions are inherited by the corresponding provinces.[13]

However, from a socioeconomic point of view, *metropolitan areas* in Europe serve as focal points for national economies due to their higher-than-average gross domestic product (GDP), making them crucial for SD initiatives. The Florence metropolitan context, it is a vast area operating since 2015, encompasses 41 municipalities and 4 unions, spanning 3,500 square km, primarily hilly (68.7%) and mountainous (26.8%), with a smaller flat area (150 sq. km). Its population totals 998,431, with over a third residing in the provincial capital.[14] MCF is internationally renowned, boasting a diverse economic landscape encompassing culture, education, craftsmanship, and manufacturing, ranking among Italy's top urban economies. Tourism, thanks to its rich cultural heritage, is a significant contributor, housing 30% of UNESCO's renowned artworks. The region's sustained political stability enables a concentrated approach to sustainability and long-term planning. Moreover, the political continuity of the territories under analysis has also allowed both a particular attention to issues related to sustainability and a potentially effective stability in terms of long-term planning (Lah, 2017).

[13]As recalled by comma 46 of the law: State and regions can delegate tasks to metropolitan areas, respecting their competencies, for implementing subsidiarity, differentiation, and proportionality principles mentioned in Article 118(1) of the Constitution.

[14]Population density is 285.3 ab/kmq. Little more than ⅓ of the population (368,419) is concentrated in the area of the provincial capital. Data updated to 31/12/2020.

4.1 Tools for Planning and Coordination in MC

The achievement of the SDGs depends [...] on the ability of local and regional governments to promote integrated, inclusive, and sustainable territorial development (UN Habitat, 2016, p.7). Planning and coordination are fundamental in complex governance with elements of conflict such as that relating to sustainability. Some aspects of the role of the MC were generally outlined in the previous paragraph, but it could be useful to deepen the functions of these local authorities, especially observing the statute of the MC of Florence. So, it is possible to identify the areas of intervention in terms of the policy of this local intermediate authority more precisely. On the one hand, the MC plays a (1) strategic type of planning, aimed at the *territorial, economic, and social development shared with the municipalities and the socioeconomic realities of the territory* (PSM → *Strategic Metropolitan Plan*), a function of direction that encompasses long-term actions and visions of MC.[15] On the other hand, there are tools related to urban planning, (2) the *Territorial plan of the MC* (PTM), *a reference tool for the knowledge and interpretation of the territory, its transformation, redevelopment, conservation, and enhancement, for the settlement-infrastructural systems and for agricultural and environmental ones, according to the provisions of regional legislation*, and the (3) *Metropolitan structural plan* (PSM), a structural plan in agreement with the municipalities that are part of the urban area.[16,17] Especially from an urban point of view, the metropolitan territorial plan will perform strategic, coordinating, and prescriptive functions.

Moreover, the *urban sustainable mobility plan* (PUMS) is a planning document that is aimed at coordinating the local mobility strategies and implementation actions to improve the effectiveness of public transport and at coordinating the development of the mobility system with *urban and territorial developments, in a perspective of environmental, social and economic sustainability*.[18]

The strategic planning is integrated by those actions promoted by the MCF in terms of SD assigned by law.[19] The Metropolitan Council seeks to achieve social development equity across the *metropolitan area*, streamline services through district area redefinition, and ensure uniformity in social welfare service levels. The council also approves the *General Citizen Services Charter*, outlining minimum service standards, fosters economic development, supports businesses and infrastructure, integrates tourism promotion with territorial governance, manages corporate crises and disputes, preserves cultural and archival heritage, collaborates with universities and cultural institutions, protects the environment, and

---

[15]Based on the Art. Five Statute of MCF, the strategic plan constitutes the general reference framework for all forms of planning and programming of the MC.

[16]Art.6 Statute of MCF. The spatial plan of the Metropolitan City is the reference tool for the plans of competence of the municipalities and their regulatory instruments, as required by regional legislation.

[17]Art.7 Statute of MCF.

[18]*La città metropolitana di Firenze verso lo sviluppo sostenibile* (2022, p. 45).

[19]Art.8 Statute of MCF.

promotes integrated agricultural, park, and green area management while addressing pollution.[20]

The analysis of this function shows that planning and coordination may be considered tools to respond to both the fragmentation and the heterogeneity in the service delivery that often characterizes the Italian case (Citroni et al., 2016). MCs can be considered as part of a *new regime of governance of local utilities that emphasised vertical subsidiarity between municipalities and the upper levels of government* [...] (Citroni et al., 2018, p. 233). Smoke et al. (2016) explore the responsibilities of local authorities concerning the SDGs, that can be grouped in five kinds of actions: a) Monitoring (SDG 1,2,3,4,5); b) Integration of strategies (SDG 1,2,5,8,9,11,16); c) Implementation of services (SDG 1,3,4,10,11,16) (social protection programs & basic services, health services, education services, justice services); d) Infrastructure (SDG 9, 11); and e) Support (SDG 2,9,11).

The task of local governments is building the local definition of sustainability and consequently planning for their territory or aligning national or regional plans with the SDGs. Regarding localizing SD, two decision tools are presented here in chronological order, particularly concerning sustainability definition and local action implementation.

The elaboration of the *Metropolitan Renaissance* in 2017 was the first step in the Florentine context.[21] This strategic plan of the MC proposes a vision for 2030. In drafting this planning tool, the connections with the goals of the 2030 Agenda are visible. This general strategy has been divided into three specific visions: *universal accessibility,* an indispensable condition for participation in social life, and the use of spaces and services; *widespread opportunities* thanks to the activation of multiple and varied resources/opportunities present throughout the metropolitan area; a conception of the metropolitan territory that enhances the rural territory as an integrated set of *lands of well-being*, in terms of quality of life and ecosystemic balance. In Fig. 11.2, these visions are reported with their respective sub-strategies. In the column next to the sub-strategies, there are the related actions to be implemented, the necessary time horizon, and the related SDGs on which they can produce effects.

The MCF planning tool, called *Metropolitan Renaissance*, is divided into visions. Each vision proposes several strategies with relative policy actions as reported briefly in Fig. 11.2. The first vision, *Universal accessibility,* is composed of four strategies that aim to address various SDGs. The first focuses on multimodal mobility integration. The second emphasizes technological development for municipalities. The third seeks institutional coordination for administrative efficiency and SDGs 16 and 17. The fourth involves mapping solidarity institutions and fostering social policy synergies among local actors.

[20]MC inherits the long experience of the Province of Florence in the field of corporate crises.

[21]Plan updated in 2018.

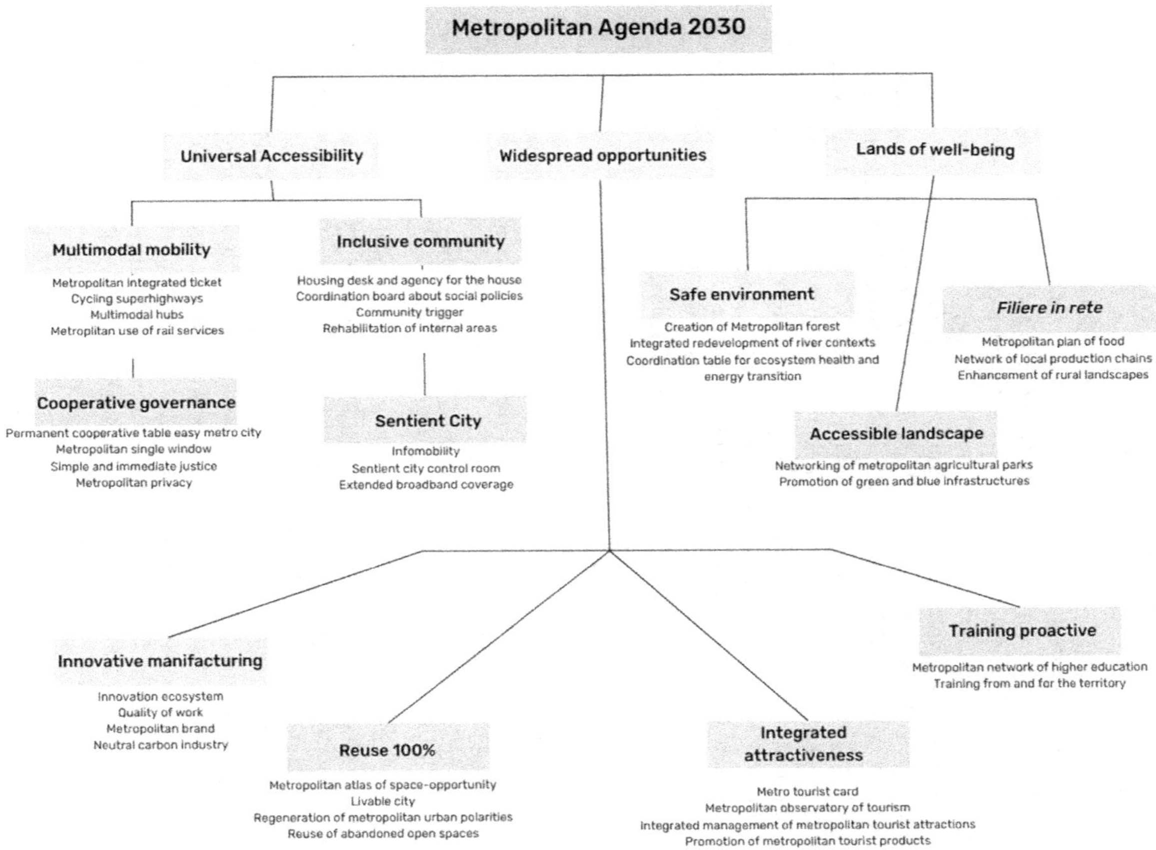

Fig. 11.2. The Interventions Area of Metropolitan Agenda 2030. *Source:* The authors.

The second vision, *widespread opportunities*, encompasses four strategies aligned with SDGs 8 and 9. These strategies include fostering a knowledge-based entrepreneurial community (first), enhancing knowledge resources for synergy with local socioeconomic realities (second), managing tourist resources (third), and planning urban policies to promote space reuse and holistic development in line with SDG11.

The third vision, *lands of well-being*, comprises three strategies. The first addresses accessibility, promoting rural development and ecological network protection. Coordination among actors is crucial. The second, *networked supply chains*, coordinates food policy, creating institutional tools and boosting local economies. Lastly, *safe environment* focuses on energy resource development, ecological heritage protection, and pollution containment.

Secondly, the MCF elaborated a 2030 *Metropolitan Agenda for Sustainable Development* in March 2022 with a building path composed of multiple steps. This process was a work on the local definition, and it is organized in several participatory phases involving experts, local authorities, stakeholders, and citizens in many appointments and with different methods of intervention (survey, focus group, roundtable). Together with the *metropolitan strategic plan*, this tool serves to insert and align the MC path with the various higher levels (regional, national, and global) of sustainability governance. In other words, from an MLG perspective, this strategy integrates the national and regional agendas of SD. The participatory process aimed at local stakeholders has represented another element of policy capacity that the MC has put in place to localize the goals of the 2030 Agenda. Both systemic and organizational, the involvement and knowledge of the positions of the local actors involved can be an important political competence of the MC. It is thus possible to better manage the conflict thanks to the support/knowledge gained and build consensus and legitimacy of both the organization and the policy actions identified. Moreover, an important aspect of the SD is the relationship with civil society also allows the increasing awareness of the need to adopt specific policy measures. In the realization of the project of drafting the Metropolitan Agenda, there was also strong involvement of external expertise (research and scientific support), an analytical tool useful to gather information and analyze the policy actions (Wu et al., 2018).

There are 10 *metropolitan goals* identified tied with the relative SDG.[22] The metropolitan agenda presents for each metropolitan goal both the subgoals and the relative policy proposals, so completing the metropolitan strategy to achieve the SDGs. This represents the output of the localizing path of the SDGs, which contextualization should favor a simpler achievement of individual targets. As can be deduced from the *breadth* of the 10 proposed objectives, the MC will need to manage both the strong synergies between goals and potential conflicts. This will involve developing coordination networks to ensure consistent policies across the territory, as well as updating and adapting the envisaged policy planning tools at an intermediate decision-making level. It can be noted that the visions and

[22]https://www.cittametropolitana.fi.it/wp-content/uploads/Agenda2030CmFIRENZE.pdf

strategies contained in the PSM were then linked to the 2030 Metropolitan Agenda. In terms of coordinated actions, it should be remembered that MCF, in addition to drafting the agenda, has devised a system of sustainability governance that may be useful even in order to increase the policy capacity of these local levels.[23]

- *Metropolitan coordination table for SD* will be established. It will include an Agenda 2030 representative for each MC department, a coordinator overseeing these representatives (a technical role with directive responsibilities), and a Councilor in charge of the Agenda 2030 (Metropolitan Council). This board, operating across sectors and disciplines, aims to coordinate and report on 2030 Agenda actions, ensuring stakeholder engagement.
- *Permanent table of municipalities for sustainability* with the task of providing a collective direction for the entire territory, to harmonize the actions that they decide to take to achieve the SDG and then to share good practices.

The MCF and intermediate local levels should establish a coherent framework for implementing Agenda 2030, addressing complex issues through concrete actions. Agenda 2030 addresses high-profile problems which, however, require simplification and concrete actions that many local governments have already started to implement. Municipalities' policy actions for SDG achievement are outlined in *mayors' guidelines* and the *Single Programming Document* (DUP), which guides local authorities strategically. DUP encompasses policies aligned with institutional goals, aiding in systematic management of environmental and organizational discontinuities, and it is *built* coherently with the subsequent financial statement documents. From an MLG perspective, this strategic framework must be coordinated and coherent with the guidelines of regional planning and take into account national and European constraints and competences. A shared development of these planning tools may act on the reduction of wickedness related to the decision levels involved.

Like budget documents, this planning document is structured around missions, which represent the functions and strategic objectives funded by public expenditure and could be associated with the corresponding SDGs. As the programs outlined suggest, the declination of SD adopted focuses heavily on the environmental dimension.[24] The part devoted to *social rights, social policies and the family* covers many of those areas where municipalities deal with the social services delivery and management and which therefore provide answers to the goals of the social dimension of SD. It is worth noting that municipalities are directly responsible for responding to emergencies, as demonstrated during the pandemic when they provided exceptional social services to citizens.

[23]Deliberation n. 87 of Metropolitan Council.

[24]Soil protection, environmental recovery, waste, water services, protected areas, water resource improvement, mountain areas, air quality, pollution reduction.

5. Measuring Coherence for SD

The 2030 Agenda identifies broad areas of need to be achieved in an integrated manner, but whose realization is further constrained by the timing factor for which there is less than a decade left. Measurement is a pivotal element in the new context of SD governance, in which all policies must rely on measurable indicators (Biermann et al., 2017; Bornemann & Christen, 2021). Data play a crucial role for local authorities in addressing socioeconomic and environmental issues coherently within the SDGs' interdependent framework. Therefore, monitoring sustainability and unsustainability helps prioritize interventions and track social-environmental changes. The Agenda 2030 offers a proper monitoring identifying 231 indicators (UN Habitat, 2016). However, most of the indicators currently suffer from a partial convergence between the measures identified at the global level and those available for countries (Fox & Macleod, 2021). Subnational levels often face data access and adequacy challenges, limiting effective sustainability governance.[25] Ultimately, localizing is also a measurement challenge, as it is unclear which integrated approach would best address the multidimensional and interconnected nature of the targets while promoting coherent policy actions. Hence, coherence is an inherent element of measurement. Distinctions can be made between coherence within the SDGs' relational system, mainly concerning the goals, and coherence in the decision-making process, known as policy coherence. Internal coherence focuses on the indicator alignment with SDGs. When indicators show synergy with an SDG, the goal is logically consistent and straightforward (Ritchie & Mispy, 2018). Conversely, unsuccessful SDG implementation risks grow as indicator compromises rise, causing negative impacts between areas. Such relational aspects introduce the fundamental principle of policy coherence, which entails integrating social, economic, and environmental sustainability at all stages of policymaking (Coscieme et al., 2021). Achieving policy coherence involves breaking down institutional and political silos and considering institutional factors, including the capacities and functions of governing bodies. In this sense, many local governments have adopted Voluntary Local Review (VLR), a reporting mechanism designed to depict the progress toward SD and then reviewed by the *High-level Political Forum on Sustainable Development*. Although the number of cities is growing in adopting such a tool, voluntary compliance risks leaving out those contexts with low vocationally and awareness of compelling issues such as sustainability. The VLR serves to "*establish a coherent transformation paradigm for the design and execution of development policies*" (Osman et al., 2021, p. 2). In constructing its metropolitan agenda, the MCF has included the development of the VLR, encompassing 108 indicators linked to provincial functions, effectively localizing the monitoring system. The VLR provides a snapshot of the metropolitan area, aiding in monitoring, issue identification, and identifying weaknesses. Furthermore, it enhances the organization's analytical policy capacity by influencing planning,

[25]In Italy, like elsewhere, ISTAT works on progress measures following Inter-Agency Expert Group indicators.

elevating policy priorities, and adjusting local interpretations of SDGs. The system mapping associated with the Metropolitan Agenda, on the other hand, analyses goal alignment, highlighting interconnections among metropolitan-level SDGs, revealing potential trade-offs, synergies, and mutually beneficial objectives. In conclusion, these tools evaluate coherence between the MC's planning documents in terms of goal definition and action implementation.

6. Conclusion

This chapter emphasizes the importance of localizing SD to simplify the 2030 Agenda, align SDGs with local needs, and strengthen institutional responsibilities. Failure to adapt the Agenda to local contexts and territories may hinder its implementation, so impeding an urgent societal change. The *local turn* offers a practical approach to expedite achieving these goals. Local communities serve as *drop points* of action for sustainability efforts, involving various stakeholders, institutions, and citizens. Effective coordination within these territories is crucial for successful implementation.

This chapter recognizes the significance of MCs in SD. MC is at the core of social and economic development, and the metropolitan area of Florence represents an area of robust implementation for SD policies. MCF establishes its local SD goals developing specific tools (*Metropolitan Renaissance and Metropolitan Sustainable Agenda*) and other documents aimed at planning the strategic, territorial, and urban sustainable actions. Furthermore, MCF is enhancing *institutional tables* to coordinate the policy actions implemented by the lower level decision-makers (*Permanent Table of Municipalities for Sustainability and Metropolitan Coordination Table for SD*). Indeed, the MC also plays a role in SD governance by managing intergovernmental relationships and promoting policy consistency across different decision-making levels. Positioned between local and regional levels, the MC serves as an ideal interlocutor for SD dialogs, promoting coherent SD policies across territorial and institutional scales. In other words, MC declines the higher sustainability strategies and aligns policies on the territories. Hence, MCs play a key function in managing conflicts inherent in sustainability challenges, fostering coordinated actions, and aligning stakeholders' positions and goals. Their proximity to constituent municipalities enables effective interventions planning and conflicts resolution among diverse stakeholders. Their status as second-level entities allows for the adoption of a broader time horizon, thereby also reducing potential conflicts with upper decision levels.

This chapter outlined even some challenges faced by MC, because the localizing of SDGs isn't enough to achieve sustainability. Firstly, MCs' development varies significantly based on context, leading to fragmentation. Secondly, MC hasn't fully replaced provinces, causing transformation issues. Thirdly, financial constraints hinder MC's role, still resembling provinces. Fourthly, municipalities gain prominence over MC in management and services. Lastly, the indirect election of MC councilors blurs leadership and responsibilities, impacting effectiveness. Still, there is a need for a greater provision of tools to support open and inclusive governance. In this regard, it remains necessary to delve into the use of sustainability data and indicators and their integration into the decision-making process, while adhering to the criteria of *relevance* (for policymakers), *credibility* (for scientific and technical validity), and *legitimacy* (in respect of stakeholders' divergent values and beliefs).

In conclusion, SD is the widest public policy demanding revisions in governance, varied expertise, and advanced management tools. It necessitates clear roles and responsibilities at all territorial levels, emphasizing the need to strengthen the MC's influence, awareness, and utilization of effective policy tools for successful implementation in local contexts.

References

Bardal, K. G., Reinar, M. B., Lundberg, A. K., & Bjørkan, M. (2021). Factors facilitating the implementation of the Sustainable Development Goals in regional and local planning—Experiences from Norway. *Sustainability*, *13*(8), 4282.

Barry, F., King, M., & Matthews, A. (2010). Policy coherence for development: Five challenges. *Irish Studies in International Affairs*, *21*(1), 207–223.

Biermann, F., Kanie, N., & Kim, R. E. (2017). Global governance by goal setting: The novel approach of the UN SD Goals. *Current Opinion in Environmental Sustainability*, *26*(27), 26–31.

Bolgherini, S., & Lippi, A. (2016). Italy: Remapping local government from reallocation and re-shaping to re-scaling. In U. Sadioglu & K. Dede (Eds.), *Theoretical foundations and discussions on the reformation process in local governments*. IGI Global.

Bonaretti, M., & Tomassini, P. (2003). Le comunità di pratica. In F. Battistelli (Ed.), *La Pubblica Amministrazione tra Retorica e Innovazione*. Milano.

Bornemann, B., & Christen, M. (2021). A new generation of sustainability governance: Potentials for 2030 Agenda implementation in Swiss Cantons. *Politics and Governance*, *9*(1), 187–199.

Bristol-Alagbariya, E. T. (2020). The UN Global Compact as a Soft Law Business Regulatory Mechanism Advancing Corporate Responsibility towards Business Sustainability and Sustainable Development Worldwide. *JL Pol'y & Globalization*, *94*, 27.

Brunazzo, M. (2010). Italian regionalism: A semi-federation is taking shape — Or is it? In H. Baldersheim & L. E. Rose (Eds.), *Territorial choice*. Palgrave Macmillan. https://doi.org/10.1057/9780230289826_10

Carbone, M. (2008). Mission impossible: The European Union and policy coherence for development. *European Integration*, *30*(3), 323–342.

Citroni, G., Di Giulio, M., Galanti, M. T., Lippi, A., & Profeti, S. (2018). Apprentice Sorcerers. Evaluating the programme theory of regulatory governance in Italian public utilities. In I. Koprić & H. Wollmann (Eds.), *Evaluating reforms of local public and social services in Europe, governance and public management*. Springer.

Citroni, G., Lippi, A., & Profeti, S. (2016). Local public services in Italy: Still fragmentation. In H. Wollmann, G. Marcou, & I. Koprić (Eds.), *Public and social services in European countries*. Palgrave Macmillan.

Coscieme, L., Mortensen, L. F., & Donohue, I. (2021). Enhance environmental policy coherence to meet the Sustainable Development Goals. *Journal of Cleaner Production, 296*, 126502.

Crabtree, A., & Gasper, D. (2020). Conclusion: The sustainable development goals and capability and human security analysis. In *Sustainability, capabilities, and human security*. Palgrave Macmillan.

Danken, T., Dribbisch, K., & Lange, A. (2016). Studying wicked problems forty years on: Towards a synthesis of a fragmented debate. *Der Moderne Staat—Dms: Zeitschrift für Public Policy, Recht und Management, 9*(1), 15–33.

Di Francesco, M. (2001). Process not outcomes in new public management? Policy coherence in Australia. *The Drawing Board: An Australian Review of Public Affairs, 1*(3), 103–116.

Dusseldorp, M. (2017). *Zielkonflikte der Nachhaltigkeit. Zur Methodologie wissenschaftlicher Nachhaltigkeitsbewertungen*. J.B Metzler.

Eden, L., & Wagstaff, M. F. (2021). Evidence-based policymaking and the wicked problem of SDG 5 Gender Equality. *Journal of International Business Policy, 4*(1), 28–57.

Fitoussi, J. P., & Malik, K. (2013). *Choices, capabilities, and sustainability*. Human Development Report Office Occasional Paper, New York, NY.

Forster, J., & Stokke, O. (1999). Coherence of policies towards developing countries: Approaching the problematique. In J. Forster & O. Stokke (Eds.), *Policy coherence in development cooperation*. Frank Cass.

Fox, S., & Macleod, A. (2021). Localizing the SDGs in cities: Reflections from an action research project in Bristol, UK. *Urban Geography*, 1–21.

Furlan, F. (2016). Le funzioni delle Città Metropolitane, tra Statuti e leggi regionali attrattive della riforma Delrio. In G. F. Ferrari (Ed.), *Nuove province e città metropolitane: Atti del Convegno dell'Associazione di diritto pubblico comparato ed europeo, Milano*. Dipartimento di Studi Giuridici dell'Università Bocconi, G. Giappichelli Editore.

Gregersen, C., Mackie, J., & Torres, C. (2016). Implementation of the 2030 Agenda in the European Union: Constructing an EU approach to policy coherence for sustainable development. European Centre for Development Policy Management Discussion Paper 197.

Giddings, B., Hopwood, B., & O'brien, G. (2002). Environment, economy, and society: Fitting them together into sustainable development. *Sustainable Development, 10*(4), 187–196.

Head, B. W. (2019). Forty years of wicked problems literature: Forging closer links to policy studies. *Policy and Society, 38*(2), 180–197.

Hoebink, P. (2004). Evaluating Maastricht's triple C: The "C" of coherence. In P. Hoebink (Ed.), *The Treaty of Maastricht and Europe's development co-operation*. Academic Publishers.

Hoppe, R., & Turnbull, N. (2022). *The politicality of problem structuring*. IWPP3 workshop paper. https://www.researchgate.net/publication/364946645_The_politicality_of_problem_structuring

Jiménez-Aceituno, A., Peterson, G. D., Norström, A. V., Wong, G. Y., & Downing, A. S. (2019). Local lens for SDG implementation: Lessons from bottom-up approaches in Africa. *Sustainability Science, 15*, 729–743.

Kanie, N., Griggs, D., Young, O., Waddell, S., Shrivastava, P., Haas, P. M., Broadgate, W., Gaffney, O., & Kőrösi, C. (2019). Rules to goals: Emergence of new governance strategies for sustainable development. *Sustainability Science, 14*, 1745–1749.

Kanuri, C., Revi, A., Espey, J., & Kuhle, H. (2016). *Getting started with the SDGs in Cities: A guide for stakeholders*. Sustainable Development Solutions Network.

Krueger, R., & Agyeman, J. (2005). Sustainability schizophrenia or "actually existing sustainabilities?" toward a broader understanding of the politics and promise of local sustainability in the US. *Geoforum*, *36*(4), 410–417.

Kuhlmann, S., & Wollmann, H. (2013). *Verwaltung und Verwaltungsreformen in Europa: Einführung in die vergleichende Verwaltungswissenschaft*. Springer VS.

Lah, O. (2017). Continuity and change: Dealing with political volatility to advance climate change mitigation strategies – Examples from the transport sector. *Sustainability*, *9*(6), 959.

Lippi, A. (2011). Evaluating the quasi-federalist programme of decentralisation in Italy since the 1990s: A side-effect approach. *Local Government Studies*, *37*(5), 495–516.

MacGillivray, B. H., & Franklin, A. (2015). Place as a boundary device for the sustainability sciences: Concepts of place, their value in characterising sustainability problems, and their role in fostering integrative research and action. *Environmental Science & Policy*, *53*, 1–7.

Mayntz, R. (1999). La teoria della "governance": sfide e prospettive. *Italian Political Science Review*, *1*, 3–22.

McCarter, J., Sterling, E. J., Jupiter, S. D., Cullman, G. D., Albert, S., Basi, M., Betley, E., Boseto, D., Bulehite, E. S., Harron, R., Holland, P. S., Horning, N., Hughes, A., Jino, N., Malone, C., Mauli, S., Pae, B., Papae, R., Rence, F., … Filardi, C. E. (2018). Biocultural approaches to developing well-being indicators in Solomon Islands. *Ecology and Society*, *23*, 32–44.

Meadowcroft, J. (2007). Who is in charge here? Governance for sustainable development in a complex world. *Journal of Environmental Policy & Planning*, *9*(3–4), 299–314.

Mobilio, G. (2017). *Le città metropolitane: dimensione costituzionale e attuazione statutaria* (Vol. 12). G Giappichelli Editore.

Nilsson, M., Chisholm, E., Griggs, D., Howden-Chapman, P., McCollum, D., Messerli, P., Neumann, B., Stevance, A. S., Visbeck, M., & Stafford-Smith, M. (2018). Mapping interactions between the sustainable development goals: Lessons learned and ways forward. *Sustainability Science*, *13*, 1489–1503.

O'Connor, J. (1994). Is sustainable capitalism possible? In M. O'Connor (Ed.), *Is capitalism sustainable?* Guilford.

OECD. (2016). *Better policies for sustainable development 2016: A new framework for policy coherence*. OECD Publishing.

OECD. (2020). *A territorial approach to the sustainable development goals: Synthesis report*. OECD Urban Policy Reviews. OECD Publishing.

Oosterhof, P. D. (2018). *Localizing the sustainable development goals to accelerate implementation of the 2030 agenda for sustainable development*. Governance Briefs, Asian Development Bank.

Osman, T., Kenawy, E., Abdrabo, K. I., Shaw, D., Alshamndy, A., Elsharif, M., & Elboshy, B. (2021). Voluntary local Review framework to monitor and evaluate the progress towards achieving Sustainable Development Goals at a city level: Buraidah City, KSA and SDG11 as A case study. *Sustainability*, *13*(17), 9555.

Pearce, D., Markandya, A., & Barbier, E. (1989). *Blueprint for a green economy*. Earthscan.

Peters, B. G. (2018). *The politics of bureaucracy*. Routledge.

Peters, B. G., & Tarpey, M. (2019). Are wicked problems really so wicked? Perceptions of policy problems. *Policy and Society*, *38*(2), 218–236.

Picciotto, R. (2005). The evaluation of policy coherence for development. *Evaluation*, *11*(3), 311–330.

Pierre, J., & Peters, B. (2005). *Governing complex societies: Trajectories and scenarios*. Springer.

Ritchie, R., & Mispy, O. (2018). *Measuring progress towards the Sustainable Development Goals*. SDG-Tracker.org.

Sachs, J. D. (2015). *The age of sustainable development*. Columbia University Press.

Sen, A., & Anand, S. (1994). *Human development index: Methodology and measurement*. Human Development Report Office Occasional Paper 12, New York, NY.

Senatore, G., & Bellabarba, S. (2021). Localizing the Agenda 2030: The ICLEI Network's five pathways as a driver for local governance. *Journal of International Cooperation and Development*, *4*(1), 1.

Sianes, A. (2017). Shedding light on policy coherence for development: A conceptual framework. *Journal of International Development*, *29*(1), 134–146.

Smoke, P., Wagner, R., & Nixon, H. (2016). *Sharing responsibilities and resources among levels of government: Localizing the sustainable development goals*. UN Department for Economic and Social Affairs, Division of Public Administration and Development Management, New York, NY.

Torselli, C., & Pira, C. (2016). Città metropolitana: Burocrazia, amministrazione e governo. In R. Danielis (Ed.), *La città metropolitana: sfide, rischi e opportunità*. Edizioni Università di Trieste.

UN Habitat. (2016). *Roadmap for localizing the SDGs: Implementation and monitoring at subnational level*. Global Taskforce of Local and Regional Governments.

UN Habitat. (2018). *Tracking progress towards inclusive, Safe, resilient and sustainable cities and human settlements*. SDG 11 Synthesis Report-High Level Political Forum 2018.

UNDP. (2020). *Sustainable Development Goals*. https://www.undp.org/sustainable-development-goals

Van Tulder, R. (2018). *Business & the sustainable development goals: A framework for effective corporate involvement*. Erasmus University.

Wu, X., Ramesh, M., & Howlett, M. (2018). Policy capacity: Conceptual framework and essential components. In X. Wu, M. Howlett, & M. Ramesh (Eds.), *Policy capacity and governance*. Studies in the political economy of public policy. Palgrave Macmillan.

Ylönen, M., & Salmivaara, A. (2021). Policy coherence across Agenda 2030 and the Sustainable Development Goals: Lessons from Finland. *Development Policy Review*, *39*, 829–847.

Chapter 12

Wicked Problems and Policy Coherence in Global Britain: Lessons Learned From the UK Context on Achieving the SDGs

Ileana Daniela Serban

Comillas Pontifical University, Spain

Abstract

Understanding the challenges and opportunities of policy coherence when dealing with wicked problems is a particularly relevant approach to policy analysis. Coherence and complexity condition each other in the context of the different policy domains, jointly offering an enabling debate angle to account for and unbox policy success and failure. A complexity perspective invites an analysis of the interdependencies between the different elements of a system (Argyris & Schön, 1996). This is very similar to the ambition of policy coherence of promoting synergies between policy domains in order to encourage policy success (Nilsson et al., 2012). The current chapter looks at the nexus between policy coherence and complexity, analyzing lessons learned from the UK context while aiming to fulfill policy commitments related to the policy goals of the Sustainable Development Framework. Looking at the United Kingdom's policy journey includes analyzing the ambitions of the United Kingdom as a European country with global presence, aiming for policy coherence and integrating, for example, its security, defense, development, and foreign policy strategies, through the Integrated Review, therefore creating the institutional arrangements for materializing ambitions across different policy domains.

The analysis developed here uses an outward perspective to understand how a complexity reading of the United Kingdom's efforts for achieving the SDGs can unveil an understanding of how and if its nature as a global governance actor within the Sustainable Development Framework has changed in significant ways and which are the potential related challenges.

Policy Capacity, Design and the Sustainable Development Goals, 241–257

doi:10.1108/978-1-80455-686-320241021

Keywords: Sustainable development; wicked problems; complexity; policy coherence; integrated review

1. Introduction

1.1 Governing Wicked Problems: The Nexus Between Complexity and Policy Coherence

In an increasingly complex global policy environment, a growing strand of the public policy literature has focused its efforts on analyzing how policy problems have become harder to deal with by the different governments around the world because of their complexity. Such policy issues can be regarded as wicked policy problems, which differently from tame problems are ambiguous and contested (Rittel & Webber, 1973; Termeer et al., 2015; Van Bueren et al., 2003). They are "subject to multi-layered interdependencies and complex social dimensions" (Candel et al., 2016, p. 789). Wicked problems require intense cooperation between a high number of policy actors and introduce novel governance challenges (Serban, 2021). One of the main governance challenges is related to policy coherence across policy domains. The high level of uncertainty involved by these policy problems together with the "fragmentation of policy systems fosters [...] disjointed policymaking" (May et al., 2006, p. 381). As Peters and Wright highlighted (2001, p. 158), governing wicked problems comes with the additional complexity of needing to manage "the problems of fragmentation, sectoralisation and policy interdependence". Wicked problems governance has been portrayed as in need to "find ways to incorporate potentially conflicting or incommensurable types of knowledge from diverse and often locally dispersed sources" (Daviter, 2017, p. 572), being thus in need of reinforcing organizational learning mechanisms (Serban, 2022).

Therefore, when aiming to cope with the complexity of wicked policy problems, policy actors have been asked to address the increased demand for policy knowledge. It is in this context that network and collaborative governance are presented in the wicked problems literature as governance approaches harnessing the use of broader sources of information helping to deal with complexity by encouraging policy actors to reach out to and incorporate views from a wide range of stakeholders (Roberts, 2000; Weber & Khademian, 2008). Collaborative arrangements are seen as ways "to gain access to fragmented and local knowledge, mobilise dispersed resources, and build up legitimacy through the construction of common purpose and communal problem-ownership" (Daviter, 2017, p. 574). Thus, collaborative settings appear as particularly enabling policy tools (Barr & Mintz, 2018; Feldman et al., 2006; 't Hart, 1998; Janis, 1972, 1982; Jordan & Schout, 2006). When emerging within specific institutional structures, such collaborative endeavors are presented as well equipped to "incorporate and institutionalise consideration of more, rather than fewer, dimensions of the issue" (Baumgartner & Jones, 2015, p. 49).

Closely related to network governance, a second widely debated governance response is the whole-of-government approach, aiming for policy coherence and joined work across government departments (Christensen & Lægreid, 2007, 2008). This is seen in the related literature as leading to the emergence of policy networks. Being labeled as cross-cutting policy issues, wicked problems are considered in this context as "primed for a joined-up solution" (O'Flynn et al., 2011, p. 246). Therefore, this governance approach to wicked policy problems wants to avoid departmentalism in order to allow effective cross-sectoral problem-solving (Kavanagh & Richards, 2001), accounting for a systemic perspective (Argyris & Schön, 1996; Jervis, 2012).

Looking at how policy actors can cope with policy complexity and aim for policy coherence across policy domains, the current chapter analyses how and if the United Kingdom has built suitable governance arrangements for dealing with the wickedness of the Sustainable Development Goals (SDGs). Sustainable development, in general, and the SDGs, in particular, have raised the need for governments across the world to look for coherent policy approaches when dealing with the most pressing issues of the 21st century (Alexander et al., 2022). In this context, the United Kingdom's renewed institutional arrangements and strategies such as the Integrated Review are analyzed as a pilot case study showing how building a nexus across policy domains (for example, a nexus between security, defense, international development, and foreign policy) can impact the ability of policy actors to deal with wicked policy problems. The United Kingdom is a relevant country case study given its governmental focus on incorporating complexity tools into policymaking. Recent publications such as the guidance on *An introductory systems thinking toolkit for civil servants* published in 2022 and republished in January 2023 show how the government conceives the connections between different policy domains and encourages the use of a complexity perspective by civil servants in different departments. In this context, the UK Integrated Review is one of the policy documents in which an attempt is made by the UK Government to connect policy domains that can enable the achievement of SDGs as wicked and therefore interconnected policy problems. This makes the document a relevant case study through its institutional implications and a policy laboratory for testing out and learning about the challenges of working across policy domains while advancing with the SDGs agenda.

The first part of this chapter proposes a conceptual approach that connects policy coherence concepts with the literature on wicked problems. The subsequent part looks at how the establishment of renewed institutional arrangements aimed to help steering the complexity of SDGs in the UK context. This includes examples such as the UK Integrated Review in the context of the SDGs as a case in point and an attempt to set up adequate institutional designs and policy tools to manage the wickedness of the related policies. The final part includes the concluding reflections and opens a space for discussing the implications of such institutional development for the United Kingdom as a global governance actor within the SDGs framework, looking at its capacity to manage decision-making and effective policy implementation in relation to the SDGs.

2. Conceptual Framework for Analyzing the United Kingdom's SDGs Context

This section builds on the conceptual approach proposed in the Introduction chapter by the editors of the current book (Lippi & Tsekos, 2024). The section narrows down the theoretical elements used for analyzing the UK case in the SDGs context. It builds on two main strands of the literature: policy coherence and wicked problems. Concerning policy coherence, scholars have analyzed it as a policy process that can arguably be deployed to reinforce the nexus between policy objectives and implementation modalities, encouraging policy synergy (Shawoo et al., 2022) and integration (Biermann et al., 2009; Nilsson & Weitz, 2019). Analytically, policy coherence can be understood as being conditioned by policy interactions that constitute the policy input, identifying "how different sectors or ministries relate to each other in terms of their respective [policy] objectives, and on what topics negotiations are required to manage trade-offs". This first policy stage is then connected to a process of policymaking integration accounting for "institutional procedures, structures and rules that enable integrated policymaking processes". The third policy stage looks at assessment and impact of policy measures as experienced by different policy audiences (Nilsson & Weitz, 2019, p. 254).

In connection to the ambitions of policy coherence, the literature on wicked problems offers insights on the policy capacities that need to be developed by policy actors to avoid siloed governance and transform institutional arrangements and policy tools (Nilsson & Persson, 2017). The analytical capacity relates to "the cognitive dimension of policymaking where actors accumulate data and evidence" (Denis et al., 2022, p. 2). This is well connected to the policy input stage of the policy coherence literature, involving the sources of knowledge to be used in the policy process. This stage might be limited by competing interests, institutional priorities, as well as limited technical capacity for collecting evidence, leading to changes across the subsequent policy capacities and limited governance readiness based on evidence.

The second policy capacity is the operational capacity that emerges as interlinked with the analytical capacity, involving the use of knowledge or evidence that was previously collected and aiming to develop concrete policy measures to achieve specific policy objectives. The operational capacity can also be connected to the policy integration process mentioned by the policy coherence literature and invites a reflection around the policy tools that could be deployed to achieve the established objectives through policy integration. While breaking down silos is important for policy coherence, in the context of wicked problems, the input stage is conditioned by the ability to account for the needed expertise. Therefore, a complexity approach is deployed at the institutional level, with policy tools such as systems thinking, foresight, and cross-departmental cooperation within governments being used as examples of specific policy tools within such a policy environment (Nilsson et al., 2012; Nilsson & Persson, 2017). This capacity is conditioned by policy actors and by the ways in which competing interests and/or limited technical ability to collect the needed evidence get to limit the analytical capacity and, through this, the operational capacity of dealing with complexity. Systems thinking or cross-departmental work might indeed have a limited contribution to the operational capacity when there are, for example, conflicting interests or limited evidence, thus conditioning governance readiness based on complexity.

The last capacity needed to deal with wicked problems is the political capacity, managing to reach out to and involve a wide range of stakeholders to support the acceptability and legitimacy of policy decisions (Denis et al., 2022). The political capacity appears as connected to both assessment processes as a policy stage of the policy coherence literature, and to network governance as a relevant policy tool for collecting the needed information (Roberts, 2000). Governance readiness based on deliberative governance is also conditioned by the previous capacities, including institutional contradictions or limited agency by some of the policy actors involved in the use of the related policy tool, that is, in this context, network governance.

These capacities for dealing with wicked problems together with the policy stages highlighted by the policy coherence literature can be placed together when adapting the drivers identified by Shawoo et al. (2022), looking at ideas, institutions, and interests as the core blocks for policy coherence needed in the context of sustainable development ambitions. Ideas "guide actors' behavior and influence their strategic approach to (in)coherence" while "institutions (such as coordination mechanisms between ministries) [and] the distribution of interests" (Shawoo et al., 2022, p. 4) condition the ways in which sustainability policies can be implemented. In this context, ideas and institutions are connected to interests which can relate to economic objectives or can have the objective of pursuing political power (Schirm, 2016). This connection also leads to what Lodge and Weigrich have coined as "governance readiness [involving] preparedness and the ability to solve problems", including the ability to develop coherent policy strategies (2014, p. 18).

Table 12.1. Ideas, Institutions, and Interests When Dealing With Picked Policy Problems.

	Ideas	**Institutions**	**Interests**
Policy stage	Policy interactions (*input*)	Policy integration (*process*)	Policy assessment (*output*)
Policy capacity	Analytical capacity	Operational capacity	Political capacity
Policy tools	Use of policy evidence	Foresight and systems thinking	Network governance
Governance readiness	*Governance readiness based on policy evidence*	*Governance readiness based on complexity*	*Governance readiness based on deliberative governance*

Source: Own synthesis.

The connections between these conceptual elements which are deployed in this chapter to perform a reading through complexity lenses of the United Kingdom's journey to achieving the SDGs are highlighted in Table 12.1.

Governance readiness is highlighted in Table 12.1 as having three different features: readiness based on policy evidence, complexity or systems thinking, and deliberative governance preparedness. These three dimensions of governance showcase instances of governance agency by different policy actors. While governance readiness is presented in relation to institutions, given the need for institutional tools to be used in order to cope with complexity, the deployment of such tools will be carried out by policy actors, whose presence might lead to additional complexity arising when, for example, veto players might influence the use of evidence and the operational capacity in the policy integration stage.

Finally, before moving into applying this conceptual framework to the United Kingdom's journey, pursuing the achievement of its commitments to the SDGs agenda, we need to acknowledge and briefly reflect on the nexus between policy coherence and the governance mechanisms needed for dealing with wicked problems. This nexus is not one without inherent tensions. Policy coherence might not always be seen as a desirable policy objective, given that whenever a dominant policy actor exists (for example, a ministry or governmental agency), that policy actor can overrule the content within the specific policy domain (May et al., 2006). Thus, other actors might face limitations when trying to propel their policy influence and consolidate coherent policy approaches through which their ideas can be accounted for. Moreover, while breaking down silos is "a slogan often invoked in the 2030 Agenda discourse, [it] is a likely dangerous strategy [given that] sectoral expertise is [still] necessary to build coherent policies" (Nilsson & Persson, 2017, p. 259).

Policy coherence might also be severely limited when "policies are formulated by different government ministries and departments that hold different values, worldviews, and areas of prioritisation" (Shawoo et al., 2022, p. 6). This means that policy silos might be hardly avoidable given the institutional and value-related differences between the various ministerial structures or governmental departments (Kingdon, 2002; Pickering et al., 2015).

Another dimension related to the link between policy coherence and the complexity of wicked problems is the one related to unintended consequences. Unintended consequences are seen in this context as "long-term or secondary effects of an action [that] differ from the intended effect" (Jervis, 2012, p. 393). They become a source of unpredictability given the complexity of wicked problems, leading in turn to questioning the impact of policy coherence. That is because, while potential negative unintended consequences are aimed to be avoided through a coherence approach, policy coherence ambitions might limit, for example, the number of actors considered under network governance. This means that, by limiting the number of interests that get to be represented when deploying governance readiness based on deliberative governance, potential negative unintended consequences and related experiences showcased by policy actors or stakeholders do not always get to be acknowledged under a coherent policy approach.

3. Policy Coherence and Complexity of the SDGs Agenda in the UK Context

Policy coherence has been presented in the context of the SDGs as one of the main institutional promises to ensure that the 17 sustainability objectives will be accomplished while avoiding that advancing on one of the objectives could lead to lagging on other policy ambitions of this same policy agenda. More concretely, SDG target 17.14 talks about the need to enhance policy coherence for sustainable development (PCSD) as an "approach and policy tool to systematically integrate the social, economic and environmental dimensions of sustainable development at all stages of domestic and international policymaking" (OECD, 2018, p. 83). This acknowledges the need to account for the interdependencies between the different policy domains considered under the SDGs agenda while also setting the stage for avoiding potential unintended negative consequences across policy domains. The framework was considered as "integrated and indivisible" and "the interlinkages and integrated nature of the Sustainable Development Goals [was seen of] crucial importance" to its implementation (UN, 2015, *online*).

In order to align their national agendas to the PCSD ambitions, governments from around the world have started to create or adapt existing institutional frameworks that could potentially enable the policy coherence needed "to navigate [the] trade-offs between goals in a transparent and equitable manner" (Shawoo et al., 2022, p. 1). However, such adaptation strategies have encountered a number of challenges that can be thought of as the main barriers to PCSD, including policy processes such as, for example, the coordination between ministries (Persson et al., 2018). When highlighting the importance of PCSD, scholars have stressed that if these strategic contradictions are not dealt with, they can lead to potential implementation gaps and contradictions (Nilsson et al., 2016; Rogge & Reichardt, 2016).

In this context, the current section applies the conceptual framework summarized in Table 12.1 to the UK journey while establishing renewed policy approaches better fitted for dealing with the SDGs and aiming to achieve the goals related to policy coherence. The sources used for conducting this analysis include several key policy documents published by the UK Government since 2015 when the SDGs agenda was formally adopted, such as the UK Integrated Review and its Call for Evidence, different UK Government documents detailing renewed policy tools such as the use of complexity tools and foresight and futures planning, as well as relevant UK Government documents on the UK progress toward achieving the SDGs, including the first voluntary national review. To refine the understanding of how these different strategic documents relate to each other and to the broader SDGs agenda in the UK context, the analysis was triangulated through participant observation to a series of events between 2021 and 2023 with UK policymakers and scholars working on topics related to the role of the United Kingdom as a global actor. Participant observation as a research method allows "access to the backstage [policy] culture; it allows for richly detailed description with the goal of describing behaviors, intentions, situations, and events" (Kawulich, 2005, *online*). The analysis below is based on the information gathered through these different sources of primary data and is structured around ideas, institutions, and interests, including under each one of these dimensions a discussion around the policy stage, policy capacity, and policy tools, and envisaging consequences for the United Kingdom's governance readiness in relation to SDGs as wicked policy problems in need for a policy coherence approach.

3.1 Ideas

Ideas as a source of guidance for governments to achieve the SDGs agenda and of "influence [over] their strategic approach to (in)coherence" (Shawoo et al., 2022, p. 4) were acknowledged by the UK Government in different forms. The United Kingdom's journey to accomplish the SDGs has included a renewed policy discourse around Global Britain, increasing *UK's impact as a force for good* (HMG, 2021a). In this context, efforts were made by the government to understand policy interactions between different relevant government departments for the implementation and success of the SDGs agenda. One of such examples has been the Integrated Review (HMG, 2021a), which offered an empirical context for looking into how foreign policy can be connected with international development and aid policies, bringing security and defense as additional policy domains with which a relevant nexus was identified. The Integrated Review was seen as "a policy-led, evidence-driven, whole-of-government process" (HMG, 2020, p. 1). Through its Call for Evidence, the UK Government aimed for the previous steps to the publication of the final Integrated Review document to build into the process "the cognitive dimension of policymaking where actors accumulate data and evidence" (Denis et al., 2022, p. 2). Subsequently, this can be argued to contribute to consolidating the analytical capacity of the government at the policy input stage. At the same time, the Call for Evidence could also be looked at as a policy tool used for collecting evidence, for example, around how the United Kingdom can "change its governance of international policy" and what would be the "key opportunities, challenges, threats and vulnerabilities facing the UK" (HMG, 2020, p. 1).

Once published, the Integrated Review was aimed to provide a first strategic answer toward:

> a more integrated approach [supporting] faster decision-making, more effective policymaking and more coherent implementation by bringing together defence, diplomacy, development, intelligence and security, trade and aspects of domestic policy in pursuit of cross-government, national objectives.
>
> (HMG, 2021a, p. 19)

Additionally, the Integrated Review was seen as based on a logic of policy integration, thus being able to:

> make more of finite resources within a more competitive world in which speed of adaptation can provide decisive advantage. It is a response to the fact that adversaries and competitors are already acting in a more integrated way – fusing military and civilian technology and increasingly blurring the boundaries between war and peace, prosperity and security, trade and development, and domestic and foreign policy. It also recognises the fact that the distinction between economic and national security is increasingly redundant.
>
> (HMG, 2021a, p. 19)

Concerning the way in which these renewed policy ideas should be used for achieving policy coherence when dealing with the SDGs agenda, the Integrated Review presents the UK Government as aiming to:

> remain a world-leading international development donor, committed to the global fight against poverty and to achieving the UN SDGs by 2030 [by] support[ing] others to become more self-sufficient through trade and economic growth and increase [ing] [UK's] ability to achieve long-term change through combining diplomatic and development expertise.
>
> (HMG, 2021a, p. 20)

The UK Government's policy efforts toward achieving policy coherence can be seen here as an attempt to break silos and establish governance readiness based on evidence and policy synergy that could provide better fitted responses to the wickedness of sustainability policy problems. The Integrated Review appears in this context as a strategic document providing the policy context justifying why and how new institutional arrangements and related processes of policy integration could translate promises of policy coherence into mergers across policy domains. In this particular case, policy coherence is aimed to connect the United Kingdom's ambitions in its global fight against poverty with both diplomatic and development expertise. This is presented as a commitment toward a better suited way of achieving SDG 1 concerning the fight against poverty, with implications across the subsequent SDGs and potentially a good connection with SDG 13 on the fight against climate change and SDG 16 on peaceful and inclusive societies (UN, 2015).

3.2 Institutions

Examples of renewed institutional arrangements and processes of policy integration happened mainly through the merger between the Department for International Development (DFID) as the UK Government Department in charge with International Development and Foreign Commonwealth Office (FCO) as the UK diplomatic service. This arguably required deploying the governmental operational capacity, creating renewed "institutional procedures, structures and rules that enable integrated policymaking processes" (Nilsson & Weitz, 2019, p. 254). In a report by the Foreign Affairs Committee in the House of Commons, policy coherence is envisaged when stating that:

> the aim of the merger is to harmonise UK foreign and development policy, [so] that the Government does not focus solely on the ODA spend of the FCDO [Foreign, Commonwealth and Development Office], but ensures that the new Department has responsibility for the coordination of ODA spending across Whitehall. [However,] the Government [is still] to set out the ways in which ODA spending by other Departments will support the delivery of the UK's international objectives.
>
> (House of Commons, 2021, p. 14)

A connection with the Integrated Review is established when highlighting that the institutional aims of the newly created Foreign, Commonwealth, and Development Office (FCDO) will depend on the final version of the Integrated Review document (House of Commons, 2021, p. 3). Moreover, these new institutional arrangements through the creation of FCDO are acknowledged as also bringing in specific challenges related to the merger between "two Departments with their own cultures" (House of Commons, 2021, p. 3), therefore holding "different values, worldviews, and areas of prioritisation" (Shawoo et al., 2022, p. 6). This could in turn limit the success of the newly created department when dealing with both international development and foreign policy issues, with international development potentially being the one losing importance when trade-offs are to be identified against foreign policy. Foreign policy can be seen in this context as the policy domain which could dominate the processes of establishing policy priorities within the newly created (merged) policy domain (May et al., 2006). It means also that policy silos might be hardly avoidable given the institutional and value-related differences between these two previously independent government departments (Kingdon, 2002; Pickering et al., 2015).

Civil society actors have highlighted that they:

> welcome the government's prioritisation of the climate crisis and biodiversity loss as their foremost international priority, as well as the explicitly mentioned links between climate change, poverty, instability and conflict. In [the] evidence to the Integrated Review, [...] climate change and environmental degradation [were highlighted] as one of the biggest risks facing the UK.
>
> (Abernethy, 2021; *online*)

However, critiques have referred to how the review will only be able to achieve its ambitions for policy coherence "if development is given equal attention alongside the diplomatic, defense, and trade aspects of the review. Otherwise, development and aid would be reduced to tools for achieving these other objectives" (Abernethy, 2021; *online*).

Moreover, the merger happened within a broader governmental context in which the use of policy tools was encouraged to account for the wickedness of policy issues, including those related to international development and, therefore, the SDGs. The use of foresight and futures planning is envisaged in the Integrated Review (HMG, 2021a, p. 97) as a policy tool that could build in governance readiness accounting for complexity. In addition to foresight techniques, systems thinking has been proposed by the Office of Science to be deployed by the departments across the UK Government:

> when dealing with a complex problem, such as achieving net zero. [That is because] there is no such thing as a correct solution or potentially even one best solution. Different interventions should be developed and compared and defining interventions as such are value judgements that will be evaluated differently by different groups.
>
> (Office of Science, 2022, p. 43)

The use of systems thinking for sustainability policy purposes was aimed to encourage a deeper understanding and mitigation of unintended consequences. This is closely related to policy coherence given the ambition to avoid negative consequences in relation to specific policy domains while advancing on achieving policy objectives in other domains. However, the link with policy coherence might also be perceived as a contradictory one when conflicting perspectives are acknowledged and need to be incorporated in the implementation steps, thus opening a space for rather limited policy coherence.

3.3 Interests

In relation to interests and impact or results of the United Kingdom's efforts toward achieving the SDGs, the national voluntary review conducted in 2019 provides an initial assessment and overview of both how network governance has been consolidated and how the different levels of governance, including devolved administrations, have contributed to the consolidation of the political capacity. Political capacity is understood here as the ability to reach out to and account for the policy input coming from a wide range of policy stakeholders in order to support the acceptability and legitimacy of policy decisions (Denis et al., 2022). The United Kingdom's implementation strategy of the SDGs is portrayed in this context as accounting for the devolution settlements in Scotland, Wales, and Northern Ireland, each of them being "responsible for implementing [their] own policies in areas of devolved competence, resulting in approaches that respond to national and local needs" (HMG, 2019, p. 5). Besides recognizing the interlinkages between the different goals included on the SDGs agenda, therefore the interdependencies between the different Government Departments beyond

FCDO as one of the externally faced departments, the report also highlights that the government recognizes that "delivering sustainable development depends on engagement beyond government, particularly by civil society and the private sector" (HMG, 2019, p. 5). This creates the potential of using network governance as a policy tool, fitted for supporting the accomplishment of the SDGs. In terms of next steps that would be needed to further consolidate the political capacity of the government, leading to governance readiness based on deliberative governance:

> the UK government will review and further strengthen the existing means and mechanisms to oversee its contribution to domestic delivery of the Goals, building on the Single Departmental Plan process. This review will take place as a matter of priority and will examine both official and ministerial level structures. Given the importance of partnership and cross-sector collaboration, an effective mechanism will also be established to enhance stakeholder engagement and cooperation with government in the domestic sphere.
>
> (HMG, 2019, p. 213)

However, these efforts have not remained without critique. Summarizing views coming from the civil society, key points that have been raised in relation to the effectiveness of the use of network governance have been that the mechanism for stakeholder engagement which was envisaged in the 2019 national voluntary review is yet to be established. This would ensure the success of network governance by incorporating evidence on how the policies designed to address the SDGs agenda have been experienced by citizens nationally and internationally, and if the efforts for policy coherence have achieved their potential, improving connections across policy domains.

Moreover, the link between international aid and trade or investment priorities is seen as affecting policy coherence between domestic and foreign policy. In this sense, the national planning framework (HMG, 2021b) "missed an opportunity to resolve this through critical analysis about how each government department's plans affect the other, or how domestic policies affect the UK's work internationally" (Whitehead, 2022, *online*). If this link is to be further strengthened, policy coherence can enhance its ability to affect the achievement of the different SDGs, with both a national and an international perspective. This policy approach would look at coherence as a key governance feature not only across policy domains but also across governance levels (from local to national and international).

4. Concluding Remarks

What are the consequences of how ideas, institutions, and interests have evolved in the UK context when aiming to fulfill the SDGs policy ambitions? How can a complexity reading of the United Kingdom's role as a global governance actor within the global landscape of sustainability policies unveil policy success and policy failure? This section will briefly conclude on these points while acknowledging and summarizing how the UK perspective has accounted for sustainability goals as being wicked problems and has ambitioned to deal with such wicked problems by reinforcing policy coherence across the different government departments through key documents such as the Integrated Review.

We should start by first stressing that within the different analytical angles that can be adopted when looking at the United Kingdom's strategy for addressing the SDGs, the current chapter has adopted an external focus through, for example, looking at policy changes in relation to international development and aid. While domestic dimensions have been briefly mentioned when looking at devolved administrations and how a plethora of actors have been considered for monitoring and evaluation purposes, the main discussion was unfolded in an external context looking at the connection between ideas, institutions, and interests and analyzing the policy stages needed for policy coherence (input/processes of policy integration/output), policy capacities needed to deal with wicked policy problems (analytical, operational, and political), and related policy tools (from evidence to foresight, systems thinking, and network governance). This, in turn, was argued as building governance readiness involving "preparedness and the ability to solve problems", including the ability to develop coherent policy strategies (Lodge & Weigrich, 2014, p. 18).

Through the analysis of the empirical evidence, the United Kingdom appears as having accomplished important progress in relation to ideas and institutions, mainly through a solid integration of policy tools needed to deal with the complexity of SDGs as wicked problems. In this sense, the Integrated Review has contributed toward acknowledging the different external policy domains that might need to be integrated if the United Kingdom is to consolidate its role as a global governance actor. However, the policy integration process between international development and aid, on one side, and foreign policy, on the other side, has proved a challenging policy task, testing the strength of the FCDO's operational capacity.

In relation to the analysis of interests and the involvement of stakeholders, important tasks remain to be fulfilled, such as, for example, the materialization of the mechanism for stakeholder engagement (promised in the most recent national voluntary review which was published in 2019). This mechanism could and should include both domestic and foreign audiences. If aiming to step up its ambitions around network governance, and therefore its governance readiness based on deliberative governance, the United Kingdom will need to find ways of involving foreign audiences in its institutional arrangements. This will need to appear in more direct ways through both the strategic planning documents and the assessment reports on how much the United Kingdom has progressed on its sustainability journey. Adding to this, the National Planning Policy Framework appears as an enabling policy framework to look for policy coherence between the domestic and foreign policy ambitions under the SDGs agenda. Moreover, the next national voluntary review is a document whose publication might shed light on the most recent successes and the remaining policy challenges.

An important implication of this analysis is related to the nature of the identified interests. Even though the study has shown how diverse interests have been faced by the UK Government while implementing policy solutions to achieve the SDGs, solutions identified encourage mostly policy learning between different actors and at different levels of governance. This means that divergence as a source of wickedness was shown here as having a primarily cognitive nature rather than arising from structural differences that generate incompatible solutions and conflicts. However, when accounting for institutional mergers, we can envisage potential unintended consequences that in the long run might lead to switching from competing to conflicting interests. Yet, the evidence collected in the current chapter does not suggest that such structural differences have emerged so far.

These concluding remarks stress that coherence and complexity can condition each other in the context of the UK efforts for achieving the SDGs. However, coherence between governance levels (from local to national and international) was identified as the next step that is needed to consolidate the efforts made with the ambition of building a nexus between policy domains. These two angles to policy coherence can jointly offer an enabling debate angle to account for and unbox policy success and failure, looking at how policy domains and policy actors connect as part of the broader efforts for policy coherence. The importance of coherence between the different governance levels was identified in relation to interests looking at how different policy actors or stakeholders have experienced policy implementation. Coherence at this level or the lack therefore can provide insights which can be used to understand the reasons for the so-called gap between the ambitious SDGs policy agenda and the limited evidence on the impact of its implementation by actors around the world.

References

Abernethy, P. (2021). *What the integrated review means for international development.* https://www.bond.org.uk/news/2021/03/what-the-integrated-review-means-for-international-development/. Accessed on February 20, 2023.

Alexander, A., Walker, H., & Delabre, I. A. (2022). Decision theory perspective on wicked problems, SDGs and stakeholders: The case of deforestation. *Journal of Business Ethics*, *180*, 975–995.

Argyris, C., & Schön, D. (1996). *Organisational learning II, theory, method and practice.* Addison Wesley OD Series.

Barr, K., & Mintz, A. (2018). Public policy perspective on group decision-making dynamics in foreign policy. *Policy Studies*, *46*, S69–S90.

Baumgartner, F. R., & Jones, B. D. (2015). *The colitics of information: Problem definition and the course of public policy in America.* University of Chicago Press.

Biermann, F., Davies, O., & van der Grijp, N. (2009). Environmental policy integration and the architecture of global environmental governance. *International Environmental Agreement*, *9*, 351–369.

Candel, J. J. L., Breeman, G. E., & Termeer, C. J. A. M. (2016). The European commission's ability to deal with wicked problems: An in-depth case study of the governance of food security. *Journal of European Public Policy*, *23*, 789–813.

Christensen, T., & Lægreid, P. (2007). The whole-of-government approach to public sector oeform. *Public Administration Review*, *67*, 1059–1066.

Christensen, T., & Lægreid, P. (2008). The challenge of coordination in central government organizations: The Norwegian case. *Public Organization Review*, *8*, 97–116.

Daviter, F. (2017). Coping, taming or solving: Alternative approaches to the governance of wicked problems. *Policy Studies*, *38*, 571–588.

Denis, J.-L., Usher, S., & Préval, J. (2022). Health reforms and policy capacity: The Canadian experience. *Policy and Society*. https://doi.org/10.1093/polsoc/puac010

Feldman, M. S., Khademian, A. M., Ingraham, H. M., & Schneider, A. S. (2006). Ways of knowing and inclusive management practices. *Public Administration Review*, *66*, 89–99.

HMG. (2019). *Voluntary national review of progress towards the sustainable development goals*. https://assets.publishing.service.gov.uk/government/uploads/system/uploads/attachment_data/file/816887/UK-Voluntary-National-Review-2019.pdf. Accessed on January 20, 2023.

HMG. (2020). *Integrated review: Call for evidence*. https://assets.publishing.service.gov.uk/government/uploads/system/uploads/attachment_data/file/909008/Integrated_Review_call_for_evidence.pdf. Accessed on January 15, 2023.

HMG. (2021a). *Global Britain in a competitive age. The integrated review of security, defence, development and foreign policy*. https://www.gov.uk/government/publications/global-britain-in-a-competitive-age-the-integrated-review-of-security-defence-development-and-foreign-policy. Accessed on January 15, 2023.

HMG. (2021b). *National planning policy framework*. https://www.gov.uk/government/publications/national-planning-policy-framework–2. Accessed on January 15, 2023.

House of Commons. (2021). *Merging success: Bringing together the FCO and DFID*. Second Report of Session 2019–21. https://committees.parliament.uk/publications/2058/documents/19632/default/. Accessed on January 15, 2023.

Janis, I. L. (1972). *Victims of froupthink: A psychological study of foreign-policy decisions and fiascos*. Houghton Mifflin.

Janis, I. L. (1982). *Groupthink: Psychological studies of policy decisions and Fiascos* (2nd ed.). Houghton Mifflin.

Jervis, R. (2012). System effects revisited. *Critical Review*, *24*, 393–415.

Jordan, A., & Schout, A. (2006). *The coordination of the European Union: Exploring the capacities of networked governance*. Oxford University Press.

Kavanagh, D., & Richards, D. (2001). Departmentalism and joined-up government: Back to the future? *Parliamentary Affairs*, *54*, 1–18.

Kawulich, B. B. (2005). Participant observation as a data collection method. *Forum for Qualitative Social Research*, *6*. http://nbn-resolving.de/urn:nbn:de:0114-fqs0502430

Kingdon, J. W. (2002). *Agendas, alternatives, and public policies* (2nd ed.). Pearson.

Lippi, A., & Tsekos, T. (2024). Introduction. In A. Lippi & T. Tsekos (Eds.), *Policy, design, capacity and the sustainable development goals: Uncertain environments and wicked problems*. Emerald.

Lodge, M., & Weigrich, K. (Eds.). (2014). *The problem-solving capacity of the modern state: Governance challenges and administrative capacities*. Oxford University Press.
May, P. J., Sapotichne, J., & Workman, S. (2006). Policy coherence and policy domains. *Policy Studies Journal*, *34*, 381–403.
Nilsson, M., Griggs, D., & Visbeck, M. (2016). Policy: Map the interactions between sustainable development goals. *Nature News*, *534*, 320–322.
Nilsson, M., & Persson, Å. (2017). Policy note: Lessons from environmental policy integration for the implementation of the 2030 agenda. *Environmental Science & Policy*, *78*, 36–39.
Nilsson, M., & Weitz, N. (2019). Governing trade-offs and building coherence in policy-making for the 2030 agenda. *Politics and Governance*, *7*, 254–263.
Nilsson, M., Zamparutti, T., Petersen, J. E., Nykvist, B., Rudberg, P., & McGuinn, J. (2012). Understanding policy coherence: Analytical framework and examples of sector–Environment policy interactions in the EU. *Environmental Policy and Governance*, *22*, 395–423.
OECD. (2018). *Policy coherence for sustainable development: Towards sustainable and resilient societies*. https://sdghelpdesk.unescap.org/sites/default/files/2018-07/OECD.pdf. Accessed on January 10, 2023.
Office for Science (UK Government). (2022). *Systems thinking: An introductory toolkit for civil servants*. https://assets.publishing.service.gov.uk/government/uploads/system/uploads/attachment_data/file/1079384/GO-Science_Systems_Thinking_Toolkit_2022_v1.0.pdf. Accessed on December 4, 2022.
O'Flynn, J. L., Buick, F., Blackman, D. A., & Halligan, J. (2011). You win some, you lose some: Experiments with joined-up government. *International Journal of Public Administration*, *34*, 244–254.
Persson, Å., Runhaar, H., Karlsson-Vinkhuyzen, S., Mullally, G., Russel, D., & Widmer, A. (2018). Editorial: Environmental policy integration: Taking stock of policy practice in different contexts. *Environmental Science & Policy*, *85*, 113–115.
Peters, B. G., & Wright, V. (2001). The national coordination of European policy making. In J. J. Richardson (Ed.), *European Union: Power and policy making* (pp. 158–178). Routledge.
Pickering, J., Jotzo, F., & Wood, P. J. (2015). Sharing the global climate finance effort fairly with limited coordination. *Global Environmental Politics*, *15*, 39–62.
Rittel, H. W. J., & Webber, M. M. (1973). Dilemmas in a general theory of planning. *Policy Sciences*, *4*, 155–169.
Roberts, N. (2000). Wicked problems and network approaches to resolution. *International Public Management Review*, *1*, 1–19.
Rogge, K. S., & Reichardt, K. (2016). Policy mixes for sustainability transitions: An extended concept and framework for analysis. *Research Policy*, *458*, 1620–1635.
Schirm, S. A. (2016). Domestic ideas, institutions or interests? Explaining governmental preferences towards global economic governance. *International Political Science Review*, *37*, 66–80.
Serban, I. D. (2021). The European Union: From a complex adaptive system to a policy interpreter. *Journal of Common Market Studies*, *59*, 388–403.
Serban, I. D. (2022). From organisational learning and knowledge acquisition to the learning organisation: The case of the European commission through DG DEVCO. *European Politics and Society*, *23*, 754–771.

Shawoo, Z., Maltais, A., Dzebo, A., & Pickering, J. (2022). Political drivers of policy coherence for sustainable development: An analytical framework. *Environmental Policy and Governance*, 1–12. https://doi.org/10.1002/eet.2039

Termeer, C. J. A. M., Dewulf, A. R. P. J., Breeman, G. E., & Stiller, S. J. (2015). Governance capabilities for dealing wisely with wicked problems. *Administration & Society*, *47*, 680–710.

't Hart, P. (1998). Preventing groupthink revisited: Evaluating and reforming groups in government. *Organizational Behavior and Human Decision Processes*, *73*, 306–326.

UN. (2015). *Transforming our world: The 2030 agenda for sustainable development (No. A/RES/70/1)*. United Nations. https://www.un.org/en/development/desa/population/migration/generalassembly/docs/globalcompact/A_RES_70_1_E.pdf. Accessed on January 10, 2023.

Van Bueren, E. M., Klijn, E. H., & Koppenjan, J. F. M. (2003). Dealing with wicked problems in networks: Analyzing an environmental debate from a network perspective. *Journal of Public Administration Research and Theory*, *13*, 193–212.

Weber, E., & Khademian, A. M. (2008). Managing collaborative processes: Common practices, uncommon circumstances. *Administration & Society*, *40*, 431–464.

Whitehead, A. 2022. *Four ways the UK is behind the curve on SDG implementation – And what to do about it*. https://sdg.iisd.org/commentary/guest-articles/four-ways-the-uk-is-behind-the-curve-on-sdg-implementation-and-what-to-do-about-it/. Accessed on December 2, 2022.

Chapter 13

Dealing With Policy Nexuses Through Policy Integration: Governance Strategies and the Policy Capacities Needed to Meet UN Sustainable Development Goals

Kidjie Saguin[a] *and Michael Howlett*[b]

[a]University of Amsterdam, Netherlands
[b]Simon Fraser University, Canada

Abstract

The UN Sustainable Development Goals (SDGs) use indicators in an attempt to foster policy integration and coherence in order to achieve transformative societal change. But the SDGs, like their predecessor Millennium Goals, have not been entirely successful in this effort. Many studies have identified continuing challenges to integrating multiple goals in this way, linked to the complex patterns of interaction between the goals and the nature of the policy systems and subsystems in which they operate. This chapter builds on the policy design literature to argue that the main aim of the SDGs is to reconcile what are otherwise incoherent policy goals and inconsistent policy instruments in a process of policy integration. This process is made more complex in the case of this kind of "super-wicked" problem in which multiple actors face time constraints across multiple policy levels, sectors and venues. It identifies four different techniques for policy integration in such policy nexuses – policy harmonization, mainstreaming, coordination, and institutionalization – and assesses their possibilities for success in the SDG case against what is possible given the nature of the nexus and the capacity of governments to deal with it. The paper contributes to the current literature on policy integration, wicked problems, and the SDGs by further conceptualizing how integrative strategies can be better designed and implemented through capacity-building efforts aimed at developing coordinative relationships within conflict-ridden, multi-actor and multilevel cross-sectoral policy domains.

Policy Capacity, Design and the Sustainable Development Goals, 259–279

doi:10.1108/978-1-80455-686-320241022

Keywords: Policy capacity; policy integration; policy nexus; sustainable development goals; policy coherence

1. Introduction: Sustainability and the Need for Integration in a Policy Nexus

The demand for transformative change toward environmental and socioeconomic sustainability has never been more urgent than now. Recent violent popular protests in Haiti, Sri Lanka, Syria, and Lebanon, for example, have been driven by the collapse of these countries' economic systems under demographic and environmental pressure, manifested in fuel shortages, severe inflation, widespread hunger, and political unrest which has stressed neighboring countries, regions, and the globe.

Unlike in the past when many problems such as hunger were uni-sectoral and affected mainly agro-food policy, many current problems like climate change, refugees, and migration are multi- or trans-sectoral and require efforts to better coordinate or integrate problem-solving across many policy domains. These cross-sectoral domains or "nexuses" (Boas et al., 2016; Liu et al., 2018; Stein & Jaspersen, 2019) are especially problematic as they require the coordination of many different actors and actions and pose additional difficulties in integrating policy responses compared to more traditional uni-sectoral problems. That is, policy "nexuses" or "regime complexes" (Biermann et al., 2009) require more than just coherent and consistent action in a single sector at one moment in time but sustained activity across multiple policy domains, exponentially increasing the complexity of successful problem resolution and policy-making.

In these regime complexes, however, the status quo is often that "nexus governance" seeking to better integrate cross-sectoral problems is fragmented in many different ways and to different degrees across the many constituent policy domains and requires careful and deliberate action and planning if it is to be at all successful (Biermann et al., 2009). These multi-sectoral and multilevel integrated solutions sometimes can include cross-sectoral institution-building but other times not (Leong et al., 2022; Shivakoti et al., 2021).

1.1 The Problems of Nexus Governance

Concern for better understanding the problems and barriers to this kind of multi-sectoral policy integration emerged as a concern in policy designs at the turn of the century largely in response to the growing incoherence of aggregated sectoral policy outcomes in the face of cascading and overlapping policy problems in areas such as climate change and land and resource use (Leong et al., 2022). As globalization proceeded apace in the 1980s and 1990s, specialization and single-solution mindsets which characterized previously existing notions of efficient policy solutions began to be seen as anachronistic in a time of more complexly interacting economic, social, and environmental problems or what has sometimes been referred to as "super-wicked" (Hogwood & Gunn, 1984; Levin et al., 2012) or "polycentric" (Morrison et al., 2023) problems.

The kinds of "nexus governance" required in such cases mandate collaborative problem solving among a wide sets of disparate policy actors including nongovernmental organizations and different levels of government, and often involves many different government agencies and private sector actors in multiple affected domains (Weber & Khademian, 2008). And such efforts may not be forthcoming or may fail. The EU Green Deal, for example, was ambitiously launched specifically to improve integration of climate policies across multiple sectors that allowed for "a stepwise layering of diverse economic, regulatory, procedural, and informational instruments, varying across different sectors" but has met only with mixed success (Oberthür & Von Homeyer, 2022, p. 2). Unlike domain-specific wicked problems like access to health care, super-wicked problems must be addressed urgently across multiple domains in order to prevent irreversible harm.

Many techniques exist which can potentially achieve this needed level of collaboration and cross-sectoral integration including *policy harmonization, mainstreaming, coordination, and institutionalization* (Howlett & Saguin, 2018; Saguin & Howlett, 2022). However some, like institutionalization, as discussed below, lend themselves more readily to single-domain problems than to multi-domain ones, while techniques such as harmonization and coordination require a level of collaboration that is also problematic in trans-sectoral domains.

This chapter examines an effort at nexus governance across many domains, that of the UN-inspired creation of the Sustainable Development Goals (SDGs), which was designed to promote the integration of policies expected to drive increased sustainability where both institutionalization and collaboration were problematic. It examines why this effort took the shape it did and why it has encountered difficulties in achieving the integrative outcomes expected of it. This discussion contributes to the current literature on policy integration and the SDGs by further conceptualizing how multi-sectoral integrative strategies can be better designed and implemented through capacity-building efforts aimed at developing the kinds of enhanced coordinating relationships needed in nexus policy domains in order to attain policy success.

2. The SDGs and the Need for Policy Coherence/Integration

The SDGs were adopted in 2015 to serve as universal developmental goals to be pursued by both developed and developing countries. The 2030 Agenda for Sustainable Development adopted at that time sought to achieve sustainable development in a "balanced and integrated manner" through the promotion and implementation of "integrated" and "coherent" solutions and approaches. It explicitly makes cross-sectoral goal integration and coherence a solution to the major sustainability development challenges of the world by arraying different indicators from multiple domains into a comprehensive network of interrelated goals (Le Blanc, 2015). The SDGs were meant to address the lack of policy coherence in solving problems related to sustainable development, an inherently multi-sectoral policy domain. Technically, this relates to the difficulty encountered by governments in attempting to link problems and solutions together in a manner which successfully resolves a problem, a hallmark both of single-domain "wicked problems" (Rittel & Webber, 1973) and multi-sectoral "super-wicked" ones (Levin et al., 2012).

However, integration and coherence represent two different concepts, and it is crucial to set these different concepts apart to fully understand how to best chart the relative success and failure of this effort at nexus governance (Tosun & Lang, 2017).

For Howlett and Rayner (2018), the components of a policy which need to match if a policy effort is to cohere are the policy's goals and the instruments used to achieve them and the consistency of instruments in the pursuit of goals is said to be a prerequisite in identifying strategies to promote policy coherence (Kern & Howlett, 2009).

Policy coherence in this sense has typically been defined as "coherence *within* a policy area" (emphasis added) (May et al., 2005, p. 39). But achieving coherence is more difficult in a multi-sectoral and/or multilevel context where policy mixes are more complex and difficult to coordinate (Howlett & Del Rio, 2015).

Governments have proved less capable of addressing these kinds of multi-domain "boundary spanning" problems, especially in situations in which conflicts are endemic and opportunities for authoritative or collaborative strategies are fewer.

This multi-domain effort can be termed *policy integration* to distinguish it somewhat from earlier concerns around domain-specific policy coherence. Cejudo and Trein (2022, p. 11) thus define policy integration: "as a political process that entails actors and agencies coordinating across different *policy subsystems*, the coherent combination of *instruments* from different policy sectors, as well as arrangements for their consistent implementation and evaluation to address different dimensions of a complex *problem*".

The integration process naturally involves an effort to bring together actors from different fields in order to coordinate their activity in a policymaking domain or regime (Howlett & Rayner, 2007). And a variety of integrative strategies exist which can inspire improved deliberation of the interrelated nature of problems and the articulation and execution of multi-domain solutions (Underdal, 1980).

These strategies generally focus on transcending the divisions and fragmentation caused by vertical levels of government and horizontal boundaries between departments (Meijers & Stead, 2004) and other similar aspects of multi-sectoral policymaking (Morrison et al., 2023). Integration thus often involves a movement away from the specialized, sector-specific bureaucratic decision-making that was effective in addressing "tame" problems in the past but which is problematic in the context of multi- and cross-sectoral ones.

This is true in areas such as national security and technology regulation that have always transcended sectoral boundaries (Lewallen, 2021; May et al., 2005) but also extends to many other areas such as migration and refugees or climate change. As it developed in the environmental policy sphere, this new level of integration was originally manifested in the creation of temporary institutional arrangements permissive of cross-sectoral policymaking in the face of specific short-term problems such as trans-boundary pollution or wildlife management. However, such *ad hoc* approaches have proved inadequate as trans-sectoral problems increased in both number and scale (Dmitrov, 2020), leading ultimately to the creation of the multi-sectoral SDGs and indicators.

3. The SDGs and Policy Nexus Governance

As effort at creating an integrated policy strategy, the SDGs cover a large-scale space between the already complex economic, social, and environmental spheres of activity. A kind of "meta-nexus", they unite already existing nexuses like food-energy-water and energy-poverty-climate policy with other areas of governance activities like finance, service provision, stakeholder participation, and the allocation of resources to name only a few (Liu et al., 2018). The expectation is that the indicators can be transformative when changes in all the dimensions reflected in the various goals and indicators occur and that these can be "lasting" and "institutionally sustained" (UNRISD, 2016).

The idea of such an SDG nexus implies that "different issue areas are intrinsically interconnected and must thus be governed as such" (Boas et al., 2016, p. 452) and that the complexity of these issues can be captured in many different indices and measures. These indicators and instruments are expected to promote improved cross-sectoral policy integration and drive transformative change in how sustainability is perceived, defined, and addressed. The situation of blending otherwise discrete goals into a larger integrated system of goals, in particular, was hoped to lead to a transformative process in the many specialized policy domains involved in sustainability efforts (Boas et al., 2016). Timko et al. (2018), for example, argued that looking at the nexuses between ecosystem services and livelihoods, green economy and rights, justice, equality, and inclusion can support improvements in a domain such as forest management under the SDGs.

The SDGs allowed for the emergence of interconnections that otherwise would be a "blind spot" in sectoral policymaking. Most UN governments committed to launch efforts to achieve all 17 goals and "contribute to the eradication of poverty in the world while ensuring the protection of the environment and promoting gender equality". While water, energy, and food are the starting point of many indicators, Bleischwitz et al. (2018) found a variety of interlinkages between different resources across the 17 goals (see Fig. 13.1). These measures are meant to capture possible synergistic effects across the SDGs while minimizing trade-offs and include already existing multi-domainal areas such as growth-water security and energy-poverty-climate (Liu et al., 2018).

In other words, the SDGs attempt to institutionalize the interconnection between different sectoral problems that were otherwise being separately or jointly addressed and are thus an archetypal tool for nexus governance. This approach to "global governance through goals" helped to legitimize other global development commitments because of its inclusive approach in defining the goals (Biermann et al., 2017).

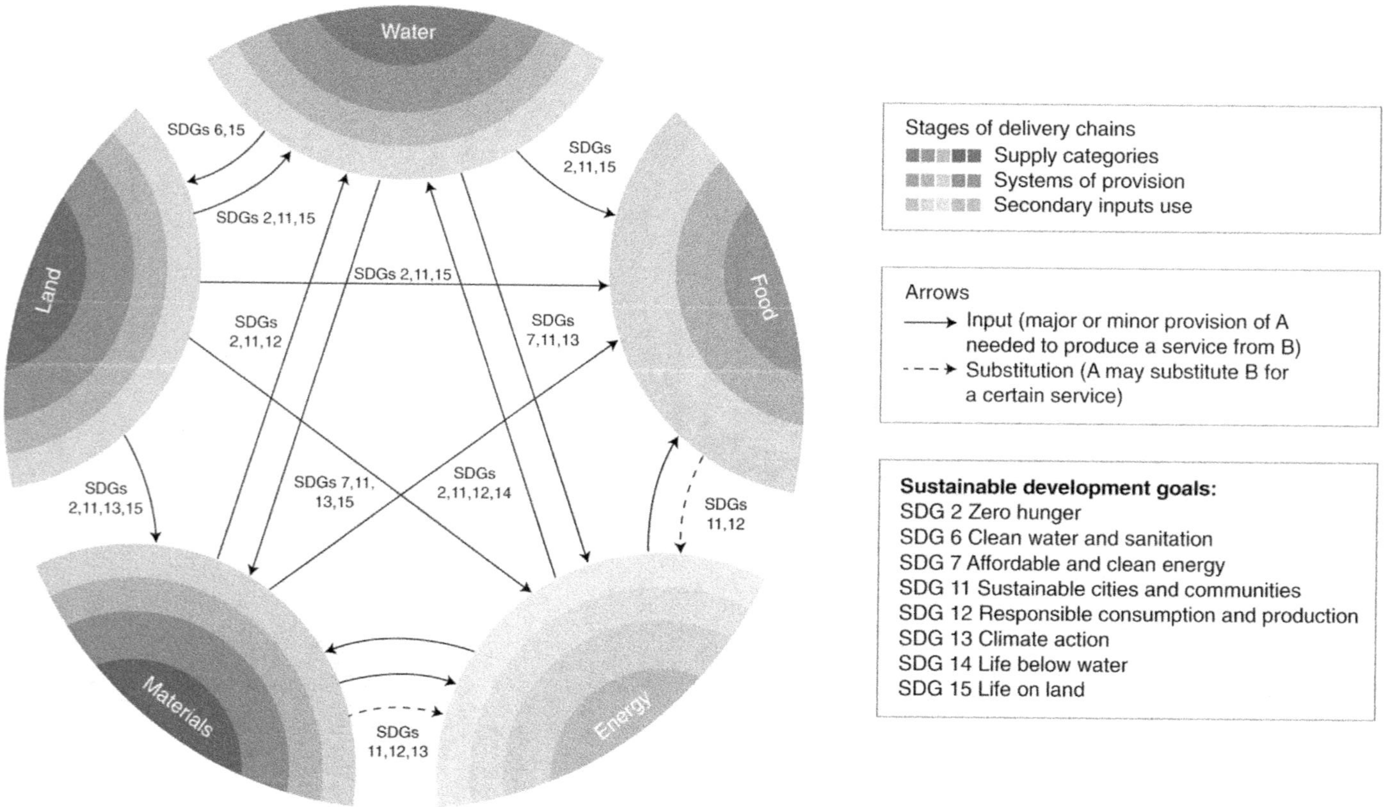

Fig. 13.1. Policy Nexuses Under the SDGs. *Source:* Bleischwitz et al. (2018).

This more legitimate, multi-sectoral approach was expected to guarantee the creation of impactful change through enhanced policy integration and constitutes a new type of strategy for dealing with integration in a conflicted multidimensional policy nexus.

4. Continuing Problems With the SDGs

Despite this initial promise, however, the SDGs have struggled to achieve the aim of fostering integration. Many studies have identified continuing challenges to integrating sustainability goals (Wong & van der Heijden, 2019) or to establishing the complex pattern of interaction between the goals required for such integration (Le Blanc, 2015).

There is no clear evidence, for example, that these processes have actually triggered meaningful reform (Jacob & Volkery, 2004, Jordan & Lenschow, 2010). In fact, as Tosun and Leininger (2017, p. 10) found, continual problems in integration remain pronounced. In an analysis of country-level policy sustainability strategies, for example, they found there is "no systematic relationship" between interlinkages in the goals and scale change governments adopted.

In particular, the SDGs have not delivered on their promised transformative (integrative) change. By looking at the discourses of international organizations, Bogers et al. (2022), for example, found increased attention to policy integration but also found the SDGs were not used as a guiding framework for efforts in that direction. More importantly, Biermann et al. (2022) established that while the SDGs may have fostered changes at the discursive level, this did not translate into legislative and allocative policy changes.

Thus, despite their salience, the SDGs have struggled, and their transformative potential remains to be seen. The limited impact of the SDGs can be seen in that, as Cejudo and Trein (2023, p. 11) note, they remain, "a mere acknowledgement that individual policies do not serve only their own purposes…without modifying the sector-specific logic of design and implementation". That is, the SDG indicator strategy should have overcome conflicts and prompted the creation of new "policy bundles" (Milkman et al., 2012) or more "complex multi-level policy mixes" (Del Rio & Howlett, 2013) that not only link the multiple instruments and goals from various policy domains but also manage the trade-offs involved in combining these otherwise discrete policies. It is for this reason that Moyer and Hedden (2020, p. 9) concluded that "the world is not on track to achieve human development related SDGs by 2030".

Rather, many of the same problems that preexisted the SDGs in the sustainable development area continue to exist. While the SDGs created knowledge effects in establishing relationships between different policy domains (Fukuda-Parr, 2014), the goals related to fostering zero hunger while limiting agricultural emissions, for example, remain conflicted, particularly in Sub-Saharan Africa (Okello et al., 2021). The achievement of one goal can still counteract the achievement of others.

Similarly, the fact that there is still no central authority in the implementation of the SDGs remains a significant problem. Norway, which is the only country that has achieved SDG 17, designated the Ministry of Local Governance and Modernisation as the lead agency in the coordination of SDG implementation. The lack of central authority in other countries goes against the prescription of Tosun and Leininger (2017) that institutional changes are also required to foster substantive policy changes to achieve the SDGs.

Partly as a result of its complexity, the SDGs have often led the government to cherry-pick SDG indicators in order to claim some success. SDGs 1 and 8 on poverty reduction and economic growth are often selected because these goals are aligned with "what their existing priorities were before the SDGs came about" (Forestier & Kim, 2020, p. 1275).

5. Going Beyond the Indicator Approach: Strategies to Promote Coherence and Integration

In nexus policy domains, policymaking manifests itself through a patchwork of different institutions (global, transnational, national, local) and subsystems of actors and policy publics. Although the creation of central authorities is a common way to sustain integrative action in a single domain, it is usually resisted in multilevel and multinational ones. Thus a nexus, like the water, energy, and food nexus, for example, could be held together by centralized international bodies as it occurs in areas like trade to finance, but is more likely to be organized as a loose confederation of ideas and agencies (Stein & Jaspersen, 2019) or on a transnational regional basis (Howlett & Shivakoti, 2018) making integration more difficult.

This is very true in the environmental domain, though by no means exclusively there, as the emergence of the COVID-19 pandemic in 2019–2020 clearly underscored in the health domain (Timko et al., 2018). However, the environmental area, given the interlocking and multidimensional nature of impacts and the global character of many, like global warming, serves as an exemplary case for evaluating the efficacy of the kinds of efforts made in recent years to deal with the super-wicked class of problems (Allen et al., 2023).

Efforts to create conceptual clarity about policy integration have suggested several strategies on how enhanced integration can be achieved or at least current efforts improved (Trein et al., 2023). Changes are needed in how goals are perceived, in the construction of means–ends relationship, and in the appraisal of what solutions are appropriate for particular problems (Nilsson, 2005). Understood as a "process of asynchronous and multidimensional policy and institutional change within an existing or newly formed governance system" (Candel & Biesbroek, 2016, p. 217), enhanced policy integration can be seen to require the promotion of joint-problem-solving by actors who may belong in different subsystems.

Not only does the policy frame need to change as a "nexus" develops, but it also should involve changes in the constitution of the policy subsystem and the actual instruments and goals of the policy. That is, integration inevitably involves considerations of changes in policy designs (Saguin & Howlett, 2022; Tosun & Lang, 2017), in order to better coordinate "cross-cutting policy programs that include transversal policy goals and policy instruments" (Trein et al., 2023).

In this effort, for example, integration requires some level of learning and the creation of activities that encourage learning and the more effective diffusion of the lessons learned. This can be achieved, for example, through the addition of procedural tools to existing policy mixes in order to provide a forum in which multidimensional problem-solving can take place (Bali et al., 2021, Howlett et al., 2015). And the creation of additional targets and indicators, very germane to the SDG case, can also serve to promote better policy coordination and outcomes (Candel, 2019; Kirschke & Kosow, 2022).

Roberts (2000) elaborated three kinds of strategies which can help overcome integration problems in such multilevel and multi-domain policy areas (see Table 13.1).

Authoritative strategies are appropriate when there is no dispersion of power. Such taming strategies resolve conflicts between problems and solutions by imposing understandings of problems and solutions on all parties. However, when power is dispersed, more *collaborative strategies* can work by bringing the actors together and allowing them opportunities for joint-problem-solving. And when power is contested, *competitive strategies* can also overcome wicked problems by triggering a search for new ideas in a "market" model (Daviter, 2017).

Authoritative strategies typically call for or rely upon *institutionalization*, a process of creating new policy subsystems to not only create substantive authority over a given wicked problem but also to bring *institutional* order and create substantive expertise (Massey & Huitema, 2013). This is the most difficult strategy to achieve in practice as it requires the construction of new routines and processes as well as, in a multilevel context, some reduction in individual actor autonomy or sovereignty which may not be achievable. Christensen et al. (2019) argued that wicked policy areas have weaker coordination compared to other policy areas, and May et al. (2005) identified the source of incoherence to be the organization of politics around the elements of the policy rather than the broader policy domain. Clear lines of authority must exist in a domain with one core institution and norms, and other institutions and norms are then largely integrated around it.

Table 13.1. Multilevel Nexus Governance and Integrative Policy Strategy.

Strategy for Nexus Governance	Integrative Policy Strategy
Authoritative/synergistic	Policy institutionalization
Collaborative/cooperative	Policy mainstreaming Policy harmonization
Competitive/conflictive	Policy coordination

Source: Roberts (2000), Biermann et al. (2009), and Saguin and Howlett (2022).

Domains that lack high levels of institutionalization, however, can sometimes be transformed by the construction of new institutions. Efforts at treaty construction or the creation of new supranational bodies such as the World Trade Organization are examples of such strategies, but the difficulties involved in their creation are well known (Howlett & Shivakoti, 2018), and few such multi-sectoral treaty regimes exist.

Collaborative strategies such as voluntary coordination are in fact the "most characteristics response of governments and policy makers" in areas of super-wicked problems, including multi-domain ones (Head & Alford, 2015, p. 718). In this context, complex policy mixes need to be built around largely complementary informal relationships. Cooperative policy domains allow for coordination-based nexus governance. Integration based on coordination emphasizes comprehensiveness in the identification of shared, uncontentious goals and aggregation of preferences between competing instruments (Peters, 1998). The lack of organization among different core institutions necessitates the "development of a clear, consistent and agreed set of policies, the determination of priorities and the formulation of strategies for putting these policies into practice" (Boston, 1992, p. 89). Coordination arrangements should advance both negative coordination to avoid and reduce the effects of negative consequences on other domains by discrete sector-specific decisions (Lindblom, 1965; Scharpf, 2000) and encourage positive coordination to jointly deliver services (Peters, 2005).

This collaboration often revolves around processes such as "harmonization" or "mainstreaming" which seek enhanced integration in the face of a lack of authoritative institutions. Several of the earliest *harmonization* strategies include voluntary standard setting (Scharpf, 1998). Thus, for instance, Streimikis and Baležentis (2020) suggest the adoption of an "agricultural sustainability assessment framework" as an effective means to harmonize the different agriculture-related goals with environmental and climate policies that requires a collaborative interaction between actors within a regime or nexus. This is because harmonization requires mandates to specify the appropriate form of interorganizational relationship, typically through a lead agency (O'Toole, 1988). This approach is particularly appropriate in regimes where there is one domain that dominates the process that leads to the identification of "principled priority" (Lafferty & Hovden, 2003), but this level of cooperation may not exist.

The strategy of *mainstreaming* similarly involves efforts to ensure at least a consideration of some key factors in policy deliberations such as gender equity or carbon reduction but without necessarily affecting outcomes (True, 2003). In cooperative scenarios, mainstreaming can become an important step in bringing a subordinate goal into a policy mix. Policy mainstreaming, mainly applied to issues such as gender equality, environment, and climate change, for example, involves greater recognition of an issue otherwise only dealt with at the margins. Thus Wamsler and Pauleit (2016) identified regulatory mainstreaming (modification of planning frameworks) and directed mainstreaming (transfer of resources) as complementary strategies in the integration of climate change adaptation. This convergence of domains will essentially be incremental and top-down and would sometimes involve a creation of a specialized unit responsible to driving the diffusion of responsibilities (Beveridge et al., 2000). But these too can be difficult to deploy in conflictual situations when no authoritative institutions exist to guide it or conflicts mean it is difficult to ensure compliance (Peters, 1998).

Conflictive regimes, in contrast, have multiple, largely unrelated institutions where norms are inherently contested by multiple actors. Here, the degree of inconsistency and incoherence is often the most apparent and requires the most significant work to be integrated *but without the kinds of institutions or collaborative arrangements allowing it to occur*. This means such regimes often use voluntary and nonbinding tools and techniques such as the construction of dashboards and the creation of key indicators and measures to encourage goal compliance.

5.1 The SDG Nexus as a Conflictive Regime

In the sustainability case, we are typically dealing with the third type of nexus, and the SDGs can be seen as an archetypal tool developed in the effort to improve integration within such a regime. The novel nature of the SDGs independence from existing international legal systems and involving weak institutional oversight came into being because "the lack of alternatives given the current state of global governance that is so far insufficiently responding to the challenges we face in the Anthropocene" (Biermann et al., 2017, p. 27). However, as is argued below, for the SDGs to engender integration in this area, they still require a level of cooperation, and since that does not yet exist, they continue to encounter difficulties.

That is, integration is particularly vexing for the SDGs because of the nature of sustainability and sustainable development in a complex and conflicted multidimensional policy space. The SDGs are an attempt to improve policy integration and coherence using voluntary *indicators* as a key instrument in order to achieve transformative societal change (Lehtonen, 2015). In doing so, they embrace a competitive strategy in a way which is markedly divergent from the previous thinking about sustainability which often promoted authoritative tools such as hard-law treaties or harmonization (Bornemann & Weiland, 2021; Howlett & Shivakoti, 2018) or mainstreaming (Kok & De Coninck, 2007) but with little effect or impact. They attempt to harness the desire of governments to score well on these measures in order to make up for the lack of institutions and cooperation needed for other techniques to work effectively.

The SDGs thus represent a complex multilevel policy effort to bring together many different subsystem actors at various levels of government with competing interests to enhance sustainability. But the SDGs, like their predecessor Millennium Goals, have not been entirely successful in this effort as the incentive they provide to governments is inadequate and easily ignored.

6. Improving Nexus Regimes in the Absence of Institutionalization: A Critical Capacity Perspective

Systematic thinking about why such indicator-based strategies have failed to be transformative and how they could be improved remains sparse. In general, however, the literature on nexuses shows that whatever integration strategy is followed in a nexus must be matched with the policy capacities required for its effective implementation, particularly when implementation remains at the national level (Biermann et al., 2009; Leong et al., 2022; Saguin & Howlett, 2021).

Conflictive policy domains such as sustainability *might* still be approached through efforts to better institutionalize the nexus at the transnational level. The strongest form of integration – institutionalization – thus could still sometimes be pursued if there is minimal conflict about the relative status of goals and there is some certainty about how the instruments interact with each other (Massey & Huitema, 2013). Institutionalization could entail the creation of "practical authority" or the "problem-solving capabilities and recognition from key decision makers that allow them to influence public or private behaviors" (Abers & Keck, 2013, p. 6). When institutionalized, sustainable development ideas could help coordinate policy action, organization of the bureaucracy, and close monitoring of its progress.

However, while institutionalization can be seen as the optimal solution to conflictive scenarios in dealing with policy nexuses, it remains a far-off goal.

The United Nations provides many good examples of the difficulties of such authoritative efforts to promote institutionalized integrative approaches to global governance. While the creation of the human rights regime governed through the UN High Commissioner for Refugees is an example of a successful statutory integrative approaches, many nexuses, including migration and natural resources management, are considered as an affront to national sovereignty, making the creation of statutory, institutional global arrangements extremely challenging (Howlett & Shivakoti, 2018, Shivakoti et al., 2021). Broadly, institutionalizing sustainable development involves demonstrating that the new policy can "solve problems that old institutions at once create and demand to be solved" (Moseley & Charnley, 2014, p. 92).

Without such institutions, as argued above, efforts at authoritative resolutions to nexus governance will fail, and more collaborative mainstreaming and harmonization efforts are also made more difficult. In this sense, the SDGs were on the right track in developing an alternate strategy, the construction of indicators, in the effort to deal with these problems in the absence of institutions for sustainable development at different levels.

For the SDGs to have their desired effect in the absence of institutionalization, however, it is necessary to enhance the capacity of the sustainability nexus to undertake effective action in a highly conflicted realm of autonomous or largely autonomous policy actors. Institutionalization of the nexus can be seen as the ultimate desired goal of integration, but in order to make the SDGs work at all, governments need to develop critical capacities to govern the sustainable development nexus in its absence.

In this regard, enhancing "integrative policy capacity" is crucial not only in enabling policy integration but also in sustaining it over time (Cejudo & Trein, 2022).[1] While the construction of dashboards and indicators of various kinds is an appropriate strategy in such fields (Fukuda-Parr & McNeill, 2019), as Christensen et al. (2019) have argued, there is still a need to build the right capacity for integration and to advance the coordination capacity of the sustainability nexus if an indicator-based scheme like the SDGs is to be effective.

Efforts to implement the SDGs at the national level, for example, have often failed not only because coordination remains poor (operational) but also because politicians do not often sustain support over integration efforts (political) and because individual competence of staff carrying out sustainability integration is often weak (analytical) (Heinrichs & Schuster, 2017). Preexisting poor levels of policy capacity tend to overwhelm the willingness and drive for transformative change (Moseley & Charnley, 2014).

Drawing on the experience of implementing the Millennium Development Goals (MDGs), it can be seen that several critical capacities need to be developed to support better SDG implementation at the national level (see Table 13.2).

There are three dimensions to this notion of integrative policy capacity: analytical, operational and political. These dimensions are similar to the dimensions identified by Jordan and Lenschow (2010) as factors critical for effective environmental protection integration, which are cognitive, institutional

Table 13.2. Critical Capacities Needed for Integration.

Dimension	Critical Capacities Needed
Analytical	• Evidence-based policymaking • Statistical capacity • Capacity to deal with new data demands • Measurement of inequalities and trade-offs
Operational	• Mainstreaming of SDGs • Recognition of alignment of SDGs with existing line agencies • Implementation and finance
Political	• Formal institutional reform • Prioritization • Champions

Source: Adapted from Report of the Capacity Building Workshop and Expert Group Meeting on Integrated Approaches to Sustainable Development Planning and Implementation (July 3, 2015).

[1]This broader definition is preferred over state capacity (Fukuyama, 2013, p. 352), public sector capacity (Polidano, 2000), or the narrower conception of policy capacity (Painter & Pierre, 2005), as the dealing with super-wicked problems goes beyond enforcement of rules, implementation authority, or simply marshalling resources.

(administrative), and political. These affect the kinds of activities that government and relevant nonstate actors must perform for policy integration to happen.

Enhanced analytical capacity, in this regard, is crucial in generating evidence to ensure that indicators are accurate and based on accurate and up-to-date data (Howlett, 2015). The possession of the necessary analytical capacity for this to occur allows organizations to measure the extent of consistency within and between the indicators and the domains that are to be integrated. For example, a suggested analytical precursor to establishing cross-sectoral arrangements is examining the broader legal and regulatory context of health to include policies related to food, housing, education, environment, and tax, all of which require extensive data collection and analysis (Bringezu, 2018; Schmidt et al., 2015).

Enhanced operational capacity is also required. This concerns the ability of a government or sets of agencies to get things done, roughly equivalent to administrative or implementation capacity (Holt & Manning, 2014; Polidano, 2000). It is the most critical because improving the organizations within and across a nexus requires mobilization of different forms of resources such as authority, treasure, and nodality (Hood, 1986, pp. 978–981) which a particular country or domain might not have but which can often be sourced, for example, from donor agencies and governments.

In most types of conflictual regimes, however, enhancing political capacity is the most critical because it is concerned with the ability to mobilize involvement of key stakeholders in the integration process and to resolve conflicts arising from their subsequent interaction. Reconciling potential conflicts in objectives in particular necessitates high political capacity, particularly in setting the agenda for jump-starting cross-domain efforts affecting domain-level actors such as businesses and industry. Champions need to be identified and sustained. Too often, studies on the effectiveness of integration strategies have identified lack of interest shown by politicians in (Steurer & Martinuzzi, 2005; Tils, 2007), or absence of support (or "political will") for, these integration strategies as an important determinant of their failure (and success) (Lafferty & Meadowcroft, 2000; Steurer, 2007). Political commitment tends to waver throughout the implementation of integration initiatives because interest from different policy actors emerges and only becomes known when integration is being carried out.

7. Conclusion: The SDGs, Super-Wicked Problems, and the Need for Greater Policy Capacity in a Conflicted Policy Nexus

As we have seen, the prescriptions for dealing with policy incoherence on a domain-specific level typically involves generating policy knowledge and refracting this knowledge through sociopolitical processes of policymaking like argumentation and collaboration (Head & Alford, 2015; Turnbull & Hoppe, 2019). But the knowledge and capacity to tackle more complex problems often is largely fragmented or missing, and this is the case both with wicked and super-wicked problems and in a policy nexus, rendering this strategy problematic even at the single domain level (Daviter, 2017, Millhorance et al., 2022).

By framing sustainable development as a "meta-nexus", we provide an explanation for why the SDGs look the way they do and for their failure to date to be transformative, as well as provide suggestions for how this situation can be improved.

As many critics have noted, the SDGs identified a comprehensive set of goals but left "scant guidance for prioritizing scarce resources" (Underdal & Kim, 2017, p. 234). The view of the SDGs as an indicator-driven strategy to govern a large-scale composite of multi-sectoral policy nexuses in a conflicted situation lacking institutions was expected to have witnessed an opening up a new way to overcome complex problems.

But while multilevel problems demand global or regional nexus governance structures (Biermann et al., 2009), nexus governance requires that vertical and horizontal coordination should take place both at governance settings and whole governance system (Pahl-Wostl et al., 2018), and this is what the SDGs intended. The SDGs' accountability system naturally puts national governments at the center of an institutional arrangement expected to meet goals and targets. What remains missing is clear guidance on how improved horizontal cross-sectoral collaboration can be accomplished.

As Easterly (2015) noted, with the SDGs: "nobody is ever individually accountable for any one action, but all the leaders, UN agencies, multilateral and bilateral aid agencies, and numerous other private sector, nongovernmental, and civil society actors are collectively responsible for all the outcomes".

That is, integrative failure in the SDGs occurred because the expected synergistic effects of the governments and domain actors striving to maximize indicators in the absence of authoritative or cooperative institutions did not materialize (Le Blanc, 2015).

The SDG indicators forced governments to draw the linkages between the different goals and not just within their own set of indicators and targets but did not provide for the enhanced analytical, operational, or political capacities required to do so (Tosun & Lang, 2017). Looking at the SDGs related to economic activities, the systematic review of van Zanten and van Tulder (2021) in fact finds negative associations between goals to be more widespread than positive ones. In other words, while the SDGs assume that the goals are increasing the likelihood of the achievement of other interconnected goals, it might end up counteracting them. Sachs et al. (2019) identified the need not only for the goal-based technology missions to explore and identify policy pathways to transformation but also the need to reorient private–public financing and public organizations to be aligned with these goals (Mazzucato, 2018).

As suggested above, efforts to enhance key or critical policy capacities in areas such as analytical and political capabilities and competences are required if this record to date is to be improved upon.

References

Abers, R. N., & Keck, M. E. (2013). *Practical authority: Agency and institutional change in Brazilian water politics*. Oxford University Press.

Allen, C., Malekpour, S., & Mintrom, M. (2023, January 9). Cross-scale, cross-level and multi-actor governance of transformations toward the sustainable development goals: A review of common challenges and solutions. *Sustainable Development*, *31*(3).

Bali, A. S., Howlett, M., Lewis, J. M., & Ramesh, M. (2021). Procedural policy tools in theory and practice. *Policy and Society*, *40*(3), 295–311.

Beveridge, F., Nott, S., & Stephen, K. (2000). Mainstreaming and the engendering of policy-making: A means to an end? *Journal of European Public Policy*, *7*(3), 385–405.

Biermann, F., Davies, O., & Van Der Grijp, N. (2009). Environmental policy integration and the architecture of global environmental governance. *International Environmental Agreements: Politics, Law and Economics*, *9*, 351–369.

Biermann, F., Hickmann, T., Sénit, C. A., Beisheim, M., Bernstein, S., Chasek, P., & Wicke, B. (2022). Scientific evidence on the political impact of the sustainable development goals. *Nature Sustainability*, *5*(9), 795–800.

Biermann, F., Kanie, N., & Kim, R. E. (2017). Global governance by goal-setting: The novel approach of the UN sustainable development goals. *Current Opinion in Environmental Sustainability*, *26*, 26–31.

Bleischwitz, R., Spataru, C., VanDeveer, S. D., Obersteiner, M., van der Voet, E., Johnson, C., Andrews-Speed, P., Boersma, T., Hoff, H., & Van Vuuren, D. P. (2018). Resource nexus perspectives towards the United Nations sustainable development goals. *Nature Sustainability*, *1*(12), 737–743.

Boas, I., Biermann, F., & Kanie, N. (2016). Cross-sectoral strategies in global sustainability governance: Towards a nexus approach. *International Environmental Agreements: Politics, Law and Economics*, *16*, 449–464.

Bogers, M., Biermann, F., Kalfagianni, A., Kim, R. E., Treep, J., & De Vos, M. G. (2022). The impact of the sustainable development goals on a network of 276 international organizations. *Global Environmental Change*, *76*, 102567.

Bornemann, B., & Weiland, S. (2021). The UN 2030 agenda and the quest for policy integration: A literature review. *Politics and Governance*, *9*(1), 96–107.

Boston, J. (1992). The problems of policy coordination: The New Zealand experience. *Governance*, *5*(1), 88–103.

Bringezu, S. (2018). Key strategies to achieve the SDGs and consequences for monitoring resource use. In *Managing water, soil and waste resources to achieve sustainable development goals: Monitoring and implementation of integrated resources management* (pp. 11–34).

Candel, J. J. (2019). The expediency of policy integration. *Policy Studies*, *38*(6).

Candel, J. J., & Biesbroek, R. (2016). Toward a processual understanding of policy integration. *Policy Sciences*, *49*, 211–231.

Cejudo, G. M., & Trein, P. (2022). Pathways to policy integration: A subsystem approach. *Policy Sciences*, 1–19.

Cejudo, G. M., & Trein, P. (2023). Policy integration as a political process. *Policy Sciences*, 1–6.

Christensen, T., Lægreid, O. M., & Lægreid, P. (2019). Administrative coordination capacity; does the wickedness of policy areas matter? *Policy and Society*, *38*(2), 237–254.

Daviter, F. (2017). Coping, taming or solving: Alternative approaches to the governance of wicked problems. *Policy Studies*, *38*(6), 571–588.

Del Rio, P., & Howlett, M. P. (2013). *Beyond the 'Tinbergen rule' in policy design: Matching tools and goals in policy portfolios (13-01)*. Lee Kuan Yew School of Public Policy Research Paper.

Dimitrov, R. S. (2020). Empty institutions in global environmental politics. *International Studies Review*, *22*(3), 626–650.

Easterly, W. (2015). The trouble with the sustainable development goals. *Current History*, *114*(775), 322.

Forestier, O., & Kim, R. E. (2020). Cherry-picking the sustainable development goals: Goal prioritization by national governments and implications for global governance. *Sustainable Development*, *28*(5), 1269–1278.

Fukuda-Parr, S., & McNeill, D. (2019). Knowledge and politics in setting and measuring the SDG S: Introduction to special issue. *Global Policy*, *10*, 5–15.

Fukuda-Parr, S. (2014). Global goals as a policy tool: Intended and unintended consequences. *Journal of Human Development and Capabilities*, *15*(2–3), 118–131.

Fukuyama, F. (2013). What is governance? *Governance*, *26*(3), 347–368.

Head, B. W., & Alford, J. (2015). Wicked problems: Implications for public policy and management. *Administration & Society*, *47*(6), 711–739.

Heinrichs, H., & Schuster, F. (2017). Still some way to go: Institutionalisation of sustainability in German local governments. *Local Environment*, *22*(5), 536–552.

Hogwood, B. W., & Gunn, L. A. (1984). *Policy analysis for the real world.* Oxford University Press.

Holt, J., & Manning, N. (2014). Fukuyama is right about measuring state quality: Now what? *Governance*, *27*(4), 717–728.

Hood, C. (1986). *The tools of government* (pp. 978–981). Chatham House.

Howlett, M. (2009). Governance modes, policy regimes and operational plans: A multi-level nested model of policy instrument choice and policy design. *Policy Sciences*, *42*, 73–89.

Howlett, M. (2015). Policy analytical capacity: The supply and demand for policy analysis in government. *Policy and Society*, *34*(3–4), 173–182.

Howlett, M., & Del Rio, P. (2015). The parameters of policy portfolios: Verticality and horizontality in design spaces and their consequences for policy mix formulation. *Environment and Planning C: Government and Policy*, *33*(5), 1233–1245.

Howlett, M., Mukherjee, I., & Woo, J. J. (2015). From tools to toolkits in policy design studies: The new design orientation towards policy formulation research. *Policy & Politics*, *43*(2), 291–311.

Howlett, M., & Rayner, J. (2007). Design principles for policy mixes: Cohesion and coherence in 'new governance arrangements'. *Policy and Society*, *26*(4), 1–18.

Howlett, M., & Rayner, J. (2018). Coherence, congruence and consistency in policy mixes. In *Routledge handbook of policy design* (pp. 389–403). Routledge.

Howlett, M., & Shivakoti, R. (2018). Improving international policy-making in the absence of treaty regimes: The international forestry, migration and water policy cases. *International Journal of Public Policy*, *14*(5–6), 303–319.

Howlett, M. P., & Saguin, K. (2018). *Policy capacity for policy integration: Implications for the sustainable development goals.* Lee Kuan Yew School of Public Policy Research Paper (18-06).

Jacob, K., & Volkery, A. (2004). Institutions and instruments for government self-regulation: Environmental policy integration in a cross-country perspective. *Journal of Comparative Policy Analysis: Research and Practice*, *6*(3), 291–309.

Jordan, A., & Lenschow, A. (2010). Environmental policy integration: A state of the art review. *Environmental Policy and Governance*, *20*(3), 147–158.

Kern, F., & Howlett, M. (2009). Implementing transition management as policy reforms: A case study of the Dutch energy sector. *Policy Sciences*, *42*, 391–408.

Kirschke, S., & Kosow, H. (2022). Designing policy mixes for emerging wicked problems. The case of pharmaceutical residues in freshwaters. *Journal of Environmental Policy and Planning*, *24*(5), 486–497.

Kok, M. T. J., & De Coninck, H. C. (2007). Widening the scope of policies to address climate change: Directions for mainstreaming. *Environmental Science & Policy*, *10*(7–8), 587–599.

Lafferty, W., & Hovden, E. (2003). Environmental policy integration: Towards an analytical framework. *Environmental Politics*, *12*(3), 1–22.

Lafferty, W. M., & Meadowcroft, J. (2000). *Implementing sustainable development: Strategies and initiatives in high consumption societies.* OUP.

Le Blanc, D. (2015). Towards integration at last? The sustainable development goals as a network of targets. *Sustainable Development*, *23*(3), 176–187.

Lehtonen, M. (2015). Indicators: Tools for informing, monitoring or controlling? In *The tools of policy formulation* (pp. 76–99). Edward Elgar Publishing.

Leong, C., Howlett, M., & Lai, T. (2022). Governing complex environmental policy mixes through institutional bricolage: Lessons from the water-forestry-energy-climate nexus. *Journal of Environmental Policy & Planning*, *24*(5), 540–552.

Levin, K., Cashore, B., Bernstein, S., & Auld, G. (2012). Overcoming the tragedy of super wicked problems: Constraining our future selves to ameliorate global climate change. *Policy Sciences*, *45*, 123–152.

Lewallen, J. (2021). Emerging technologies and problem definition uncertainty: The case of cybersecurity. *Regulation & Governance*, *15*(4), 1035–1052.

Lindblom, C. E. (1965). Economics and the administration of national planning. *Public Administration Review*, 274–283.

Liu, J., Hull, V., Godfray, H. C. J., Tilman, D., Gleick, P., Hoff, H., Pahl-Wostl, C., Xu, Z., Chung, M. G., Sun, J., & Li, S. (2018). Nexus approaches to global sustainable development. *Nature Sustainability*, *1*(9), 466–476.

Massey, E., & Huitema, D. (2013). The emergence of climate change adaptation as a policy field: The case of England. *Regional Environmental Change*, *13*, 341–352.

May, P. J., Jones, B. D., Beem, B. E., Neff-Sharum, E. A., & Poague, M. K. (2005). Policy coherence and component-driven policymaking: Arctic policy in Canada and the United States. *Policy Studies Journal*, *33*(1), 37–63.

Mazzucato, M. (2018). Mission-oriented innovation policies: Challenges and opportunities. *Industrial and Corporate Change*, *27*(5), 803–815.

Meijers, E., & Stead, D. (2004, December). Policy integration: What does it mean and how can it be achieved? A multi-disciplinary review. In *Berlin conference on the human dimensions of global environmental change: Greening of policies-interlinkages and policy integration.*

Milhorance, C., Bursztyn, M., & Sabourin, E. (2022). Analysing complex policy problems: A critical review of the literature. *International Journal of Public Policy*, *16*(2–4), 126–150.

Milkman, K. L., Mazza, M. C., Shu, L. L., Tsay, C. J., & Bazerman, M. H. (2012). Policy bundling to overcome loss aversion: A method for improving legislative outcomes. *Organizational Behavior and Human Decision Processes*, *117*(1), 158–167.

Morrison, T. H., Bodin, Ö., Cumming, G. S., Lubell, M., Seppelt, R., Seppelt, T., & Weible, C. M. (2023, January 23). Building blocks of polycentric governance. *Policy Studies Journal*, *51*(3).

Moseley, C., & Charnley, S. (2014). Understanding micro-processes of institutionalization: Stewardship contracting and national forest management. *Policy Sciences*, *47*, 69–98.

Moyer, J. D., & Hedden, S. (2020). Are we on the right path to achieve the sustainable development goals? *World Development*, *127*, 104749.

Nilsson, M. (2005). Learning, frames, and environmental policy integration: The case of Swedish energy policy. *Environment and Planning C: Government and Policy*, *23*(2), 207–226.

O'Toole, L. J., Jr. (1988). Strategies for intergovernmental management: Implementing programs in interorganizational networks. *International Journal of Public Administration*, *11*(4), 417–441.

Oberthür, S., & Von Homeyer, I. (2022). From emissions trading to the European green deal: The evolution of the climate policy mix and climate policy integration in the EU. *Journal of European Public Policy*, 1–24.

Okello, M., Lamo, J., Ochwo-Ssemakula, M., & Onyilo, F. (2021). Challenges and innovations in achieving zero hunger and environmental sustainability through the lens of sub-Saharan Africa. *Outlook on Agriculture*, *50*(2), 141–147.

Pahl-Wostl, C., Bhaduri, A., & Bruns, A. (2018). Editorial special issue: The nexus of water, energy and food–An environmental governance perspective. *Environmental Science & Policy*, *90*, 161–163.

Painter, M., & Pierre, J. (2005). Unpacking policy capacity: Issues and themes. In *Challenges to state policy capacity: Global trends and comparative perspectives* (pp. 1–18). Palgrave Macmillan.

Peters, B. G. (1998). Managing horizontal government. *Public Administration*, *76*(2), 295–311.

Peters, B. G. (2005). *The search for coordination and coherence in public policy: Return to the center*. Unpublished paper. Department of Political Science. University of Pittsburgh.

Polidano, C. (2000). Measuring public sector capacity. *World Development*, *28*(5), 805–822.

Rittel, H. W., & Webber, M. M. (1973). Dilemmas in a general theory of planning. *Policy Sciences*, *4*(2), 155–169.

Roberts, N. (2000). Wicked problems and network approaches to resolution. *International Public Management Review*, *1*(1), 1–19.

Sachs, J. D., Schmidt-Traub, G., Mazzucato, M., Messner, D., Nakicenovic, N., & Rockström, J. (2019). Six transformations to achieve the sustainable development goals. *Nature Sustainability*, *2*(9), 805–814.

Saguin, K., & Howlett, M. (2021). Transnational policy networks and development. *Handbook of development policy* (pp. 333–344). Edward Elgar Publishing.

Saguin, K., & Howlett, M. (2022). Enhancing policy capacity for better policy integration: Achieving the sustainable development goals in a post COVID-19 world. *Sustainability*, *14*(18), 11600.

Scharpf, F. (1998). *Negative and positive integration in the political economy of European welfare states* (pp. 157–177). Palgrave Macmillan UK.

Scharpf, F. W. (2000). Institutions in comparative policy research. *Comparative Political Studies*, *33*(6–7), 762–790.

Schmidt, H., Gostin, L. O., & Emanuel, E. J. (2015). Public health, universal health coverage, and Sustainable Development Goals: Can they coexist? *The Lancet*, *386*(9996), 928–930.

Shivakoti, R., Howlett, M., Fernandez, V., & Nair, S. (2021). Governing international regime complexes through multi-level governance mechanisms: Lessons from water, forestry and migration policy. *International Journal of Water Resources Development*, *37*(4), 658–675.

Stein, C., & Jaspersen, L. J. (2019). A relational framework for investigating nexus governance. *The Geographical Journal*, *185*(4), 377–390.

Steurer, R. (2007). From government strategies to strategic public management: An exploratory outlook on the pursuit of cross-sectoral policy integration. *European Environment*, *17*(3), 201–214.

Steurer, R., & Martinuzzi, A. (2005). Towards a new pattern of strategy formation in the public sector: First experiences with national strategies for sustainable development in Europe. *Environment and Planning C: Government and Policy*, *23*(3), 455–472.

Streimikis, J., & Baležentis, T. (2020). Agricultural sustainability assessment framework integrating sustainable development goals and interlinked priorities of environmental, climate and agriculture policies. *Sustainable Development*, *28*(6), 1702–1712.

Tils, R. (2007). The German sustainable development strategy: Facing policy, management and political strategy assessments. *European Environment*, *17*(3), 164–176.

Timko, J., Le Billon, P., Zerriffi, H., Honey-Rosés, J., de la Roche, I., Gaston, C., & Kozak, R. A. (2018). A policy nexus approach to forests and the SDGs: Tradeoffs and synergies. *Current Opinion in Environmental Sustainability*, *34*, 7–12.

Tosun, J., & Lang, A. (2017). Policy integration: Mapping the different concepts. *Policy Studies*, *38*(6), 553–570.

Tosun, J., & Leininger, J. (2017). Governing the interlinkages between the sustainable development goals: Approaches to attain policy integration. *Global Challenges*, *1*(9), 1700036.

Trein, P., Fischer, M., Maggetti, M., & Sarti, F. (2023). Empirical research on policy integration: A review and new directions. *Policy Sciences*, *56*(1), 29–48.

True, J. (2003). Mainstreaming gender in global public policy. *International Feminist Journal of Politics*, *5*(3), 368–396.

Turnbull, N., & Hoppe, R. (2019). Problematizing 'wickedness': A critique of the wicked problems concept, from philosophy to practice. *Policy and Society*, *38*(2), 315–337.

Underdal, A. (1980). Integrated marine policy: What? why? how? *Marine Policy*, *4*(3), 159–169.

Underdal, A., & Kim, R. E. (2017). The sustainable development goals and multilateral agreements. In *Governing through goals: Sustainable Development Goals as governance innovation* (pp. 241–258). The MIT Press.

United Nations Research Institute for Social Development (UNRISD). (2016). *Policy innovations for transformative change–UNRISD flagship report 2016.*

United Nations (UN). (2015). *Transforming our world: The 2030 agenda for sustainable development.* United Nations.

Wamsler, C., & Pauleit, S. (2016). Making headway in climate policy mainstreaming and ecosystem-based adaptation: Two pioneering countries, different pathways, one goal. *Climatic Change*, *137*, 71–87.

van Zanten, J. A., & van Tulder, R. (2021). Towards nexus-based governance: Defining interactions between economic activities and sustainable development goals (SDGs). *The International Journal of Sustainable Development and World Ecology*, *28*(3), 210–226.

Weber, E. P., & Khademian, A. M. (2008). Wicked problems, knowledge challenges, and collaborative capacity builders in network settings. *Public Administration Review*, *68*(2), 334–349.

Wong, R., & van der Heijden, J. (2019). Avoidance of conflicts and trade-offs: A challenge for the policy integration of the United Nations sustainable development goals. *Sustainable Development*, *27*(5), 838–845.

Chapter 14

Conclusions: Taking Seriously Complexity, Wickedness, and Capacity for Sustainable Development Policymaking

Andrea Lippi[a] *and Theodore N. Tsekos*[b]

[a]University of Florence, Italy
[b]University of the Peloponnese, Greece

Abstract

The conclusions summarize the main empirical evidence that emerged in the book and put forward final reflections and some recommendations for scholars and policymakers. First, the reader is reminded that the book focuses on how a desirable and ambitious agenda that contemplates a progress-oriented policy system is feasible when confronted with the challenges of its implementation and the related problem of coordination between the goals it postulates. The purpose of the concluding chapter is to extrapolate the findings from the individual analyses and synthesize them into a single interpretative proposal centered on two analytical pillars. The first is the analysis and management of the complexity generated by wickedness, through the reconstruction of types of complexity and consequences that the policymaker must acquire in terms of problem setting. The second is the analysis of the skills needed to manage said complexity, distinguishing between linear and nonlinear skills. These are the skills that the policymaker must acquire in terms of problem-solving. Both problem setting and problem solving are summarized in some final recommendations on what to do to improve the feasibility and effectiveness of sustainable development policies: the pragmatic culture of government and some supporting institutional tools, the importance of training as a lever of change, and the building of knowledge infrastructures in terms of evidence-based policymaking.

Keywords: Complexity; zero-sum-games; conflicting values and interests; structural conflict; linear and nonlinear capacities; UN 2030 agenda

Policy Capacity, Design and the Sustainable Development Goals, 281–315

doi:10.1108/978-1-80455-686-320241024

1. Introduction

This book has focused on how a desirable and ambitious agenda that contemplates a progress-oriented policy system is feasible when confronted with the challenges of its implementation and the related problem of coordination between the goals it postulates.

The UN 2030 Agenda is a commendable and embraceable global political project, so attractive and desirable that it is impossible not to be in favor of it. At the same time, however, it is also a project that is overdetermined in terms of value and emotional charge and expectations of realization on the part of public opinion concerning the possible capacities that states, and policymakers in general, can and must have.

This can generate, and has generated, disappointment and further democratic overload on representative institutions, both supranational and national, as well as on local authorities that in turn are called upon to implement goals with second or third-order degrees of policy change and with a correlated degree of complexity due to the coordination between potentially divergent objectives and actors with conflicting interests.

The risk is that such a political operation may become an enormous collective frustration in the face of a project that could be assessed by the public and stakeholders as too idealistic or overly abstract, thus being abandoned by throwing out the "baby with the bathwater", i.e., confusing the problems of implementation with the desired change.

Sustainable development policies are not "unfeasible", they are simply very complex and require a pragmatic culture of their implementation alongside a necessary degree of idealism. This culture of achievability lies in the method, not in the moral ends, as the 17 Sustainable Development Goals (SDGs) alone are not capable of self-generating change.

The 17 SDGs are simply an extremely general plan of action that has to be translated into practice through local and contingent strategies that underlie even wicked, tensions, contradictions, and potential conflicts. The capacity, and quality, of a sustainable development policy, in essence, does not lie in the quality of ideas and values, which we take for granted, but in the method through which these are translated through negotiation processes between numerous stakeholders and where policymakers are called upon to exercise "specific virtues" and perhaps even special ones.

2. An Analytic Framework for Governing Sustainable Development

Sustainable development policies are not implemented in a stable and self-restrained environment such as we see in documents because these are acts, i.e., outputs of negotiated decision-making processes between states, and in acts, conflicts remain latent or smoothed.

Instead, sustainable development policies are implemented in the turbulent environments of specific national and subnational contingencies, where the ideal momentum of objectives clashes with local realities, the structure of interests, and the tensions between expected outputs and undesirable outcomes, the difficulty of making public administrations and levels of government that consider themselves independent of each other or traditionally divergent, if not conflicting, policy sectors cooperate in terms of the type of objectives, actors, ideas, interests, and strategies involved that are not harmonious "by decree", but require a delicate and constant work of harmonization and adaptation, without losing sight of the goal.

Once the ideal scenario of good intentions has been abandoned, the implementation of sustainable development policies therefore comes up against the ordinary, everyday hard work of the policymaker, this time, however, overloaded with the aforementioned elements of complexity and thus with an even greater degree of challenge.

Since we consider the UN 2030 Agenda to be a unique document and probably an unrepeatable opportunity for coordinated action toward moderate progress in development *among* and *within* nation-states, in this volume we wanted to focus attention not on the aspects traditionally given attention, i.e., the regulatory framework, international relations, the value system, and the individual policy instruments that can be adopted as effective in the various fields, but on the way through which such complexity can be managed.

This approach has the understanding that the complexity of reality, even without the UN 2030 agenda, is already very high by itself and that such a project alone does not add further complexity because policymaking is ordinarily already complex in itself. The UN 2030 agenda is just one type of complexity that fits into the complexity of reality by adding a strong interdependence, an element that by itself is a very critical factor and needs to be managed and not as a given or simplistically surmountable with a bit of rhetoric.

This book aims to address this issue by providing the reader with an analysis of experiences of sustainable development policies where formulation, decision-making and implementation of single, or pairs, or triads or clusters of SDGs has seriously challenged policymakers, both when dealing with specifically local and seemingly easy-to-handle issues, and when dealing with international or perceived as already challenging issues.

In this volume, almost all of the SDGs on the agenda have been addressed by the individual analyses in each chapter. The reader will have been able to see that there are no goals that are more intractable than others: environmental issues are no more complex or difficult to achieve than social, economic, or urban issues. All of them can be extremely complicated when it comes to creating consensus and harmony behind a strategy that seeks to translate a very general objective and extremely challenging targets into concrete projects where the perception of ends and means is confused, solutions are considered from divergent points of view, and there is no agreement either on their duration, effectiveness or potential, or on what the problem itself, its definition, and the policy instruments to be adopted are.

In order to deal with this type of object of study and offer the reader an analytical representation of its dimensions, the book has in fact been divided into two parts.

In the first part, we have gathered cases of wicked sustainable development policies where the formulation, decision-making, and implementation of SDGs in national contingencies generated situations where policymakers failed, or only partly succeeded, in managing with the tools at their disposal, taking it for granted that everyone possessed a convinced motivation to achieve those goals.

Some cases are of self-evident complexity: the case of gas flaring in Iran or the disposal of nuclear waste in Germany, France, and Italy are policies that alone generate in the reader a perception of complexity and challenge to governability that requires no further explanation. The wicked nature of sustainability and the consequent disorientation of policymakers in the face of very strong interests and spontaneous social and political tensions is all too evident.

However, alongside these clearly problematic cases, the first part of the book also presents cases of seemingly "easy" public policies in the eyes of public opinion, such as the child poverty examined in the Finnish case, or the agenda-setting of environmental versus agricultural policies in the case of Brazil. These are policies from the point of view of the value system a naïve observer might think of as all in all easy to implement and which instead turn out to be difficult and surprisingly arduous.

In these cases, the road to sustainability is uphill and requires additional efforts, different resources, and favorable circumstances. Even the case of the railway infrastructure between Italy and France seemed at first to policymakers to be a "good, fair, and simple" public work, yet in the end, it turned out to be an extremely complicated case, requiring efforts and a mix of resources, regulations, and skills that had not been foreseen. Analogously, the coexistence of the objectives of a national agenda of a small state like Latvia, where it became clear in a linear fashion that going from theory to practice is anything but elementary.

In the second part, we have grouped the contributions of scholars who focus their attention on the tools available to policymakers to resolve the complexity arising from the implementation of the UN 2030 agenda.

These tools concern from time-to-time specific devices that national states have put in place to support policymakers in dealing with this complexity, proving themselves to be a source of complexity, as in the case study on participatory decision-making and coproduction tools in France or the case of national approaches to sustainable development policies implemented by the British Government.

Alongside these innovative instruments is the inadequacy of "old" institutional instruments, such as the hydrographic resource management systems in Spain, the Jurisdictional Approaches to Amazonian Forest management in Ecuador, and the inadequacy of institutional instruments with excessive planning responsibilities, as in the case of metropolitan cities in Italy.

The problem of legislative instruments and institutional frameworks is what Saguin and Howlett define in their chapter as the absence of sufficient and effective policy nexus to overcome regulatory and institutional fragmentation and toward an integrated management of problems, processes, and solutions.

Therefore, the way out of the difficulties inherent in the agenda, and which depends partly on the complexity of the agenda, and much on the natural complexity of things and the ambitious mission of any policymaking aimed at generating second or third-order changes, is that the success, even partial success, or failure of sustainable development strategies is inexorably linked to *how actors construct their setting*: how they analyze and interpret problems, contribute to redefining them in a more or less conscious and expert manner, build coalitions between actors, exploit the institutional framework or interpret norms, utilize available resources and generate coordinated action that is sufficiently stable to allow the production of an output as close as possible to the desired one.

To do this, which is the challenge of all policymaking, we realize in this book that two additional competencies are needed when it comes to sustainable development.

The first competence concerns the *awareness of the inherent wickedness included in any sustainable development approach*. This awareness means that policymakers need to know what kind of change awaits them, what kind of tensions underlie their project, and what kind of complexity, with varying degrees and types, characterizes those processes.

The second competence concerns the *kind of capacities they must acquire*, taking it for granted that ideas alone do not produce outputs, but neither do budgetary resources, norms, or institutional structures. It is not enough to have an agency or a good law managing or regulating sustainable development to produce such outputs because specific skills are needed.

In the next few paragraphs, therefore, we try to reconstruct what we have understood from reading the case studies in this volume concerning the two skills that bind and hold together sustainable development and complexity: the wickedness skill and the capacity one.

3. The Wicked Nature of Sustainable Development Policymaking

There is already quite extensive literature linking public policies to achieve the SDGs with the concept of wickedness (Eden & Wagstaff, 2021; Kopnina, 2020; Monkelbaan, 2019; Sempiga & Van Liedekerke, 2023; Shinagawa, 2021). However, as we have argued in the introduction to this book, this concept has become too comprehensive to function as a framework for classification and analysis. Many types of public problems that are, ordinarily, difficult to address for varying reasons are often grouped, without differentiation, under this term.

Guy Peters, asking whether we refer to "wicked, complex or just difficult problems" (Peters, 2018, p. 72), distinguishes between wicked problems, which are characterized primarily by difficulty in "naming and framing", and complex problems, whose difficulty in understanding and dealing with is due to the nonlinear relationships among their variables.

For this analysis, we will use complexity as a broader concept involving wickedness as a specific category, i.e., as a special form of complexity, due primarily to differences in values and clashes of interest. We will also distinguish between differences and contradictions of values and interests that present a structural incompatibility and lead to conflicts that are difficult to resolve and contradictions of a nonstructural nature that, under appropriate conditions and with the proper handling of policymakers, can be bridged.

Continuing our analysis, we will delve into the different forms of complexity and types of conflicts that serve as determinants of wickedness. Then, we will proceed to a taxonomic differentiation of this concept.

The main idea around which the analysis of wickedness is developed is the one proposed by Rittel and Weber: these are problems that cannot be dealt with by classical Newtonian logic.

If we define the concept of complexity as the basis of determining the difficulty of solving a public problem (the more complex a problem is, the more difficult it is to deal with), we should distinguish between types of complexity because complexity does not always equate to an inability to use Newtonian logic. A problem can become complex because, e.g., there are not enough data to allow its description or because the prevailing scientific theory at the time is not able to classify and interpret a situation, a phenomenon, or an event. But all the above: description, documentation, interpretation, and classification, are elements of the classical rational process of policy analysis and correspond to what Rittel and Weber refer to as the Newtonian approach. Therefore, they constitute complexities that are dealt with better data, more careful analysis, and innovative approaches, i.e., with tools of classical rationality, without departing from the framework of Newtonian logic. In this sense, they are complex problems that cannot be easily dealt with, but one cannot characterize them as wicked.

3.1 The Theoretical Framework on Complexity

Different types of complexity can be identified by examining their general characteristics.

According to Mitchell (2009, pp. 12–13), complex systems can be defined as large networks consisting of numerous individual components, each of which typically follows simple rules. There is no central control, yet the collective actions of these components give rise to complex, hard-to-predict, nontrivial emergent patterns of behavior that are self-organizing and constantly changing. Complex systems have nested subsystems with continuous interaction (Byrne, 1998, p. 10).

Gilpin and Murphy (2008, pp. 24–27) add that all these numerous subsystems interact with each other through multiple, nonlinear, and recursive feedback loops. Nonlinearity is a term used to describe processes that are erratic, which means that they exhibit unpredictable behavior.

Complexity in each public policy domain resists standardization and classification, making predictability limited.

According to Sanger and Giddings (2012), complex systems are:

- Intertwined and mingled, referring to systems whose parts are connected through multiple, recursive, nonlinear feedback loops. Intertwingularity is a term coined by Ted Nelson to describe the complexity of interrelations in human knowledge. According to Nelson (1987), "everything is deeply intertwingled. In other words, there are no clear-cut "subjects" in the world; rather, all knowledge is interconnected and interdependent. The cross-connections among the myriad topics of this world simply cannot be divided up neatly.... Hierarchical and sequential structures, especially popular since Gutenberg, are usually forced and artificial. Intertwingularity is not generally acknowledged people keep pretending they can make things hierarchical, categorizable, and sequential when they can't."
- Often unpredictable due to their sensitivity to changes in initial conditions. This means that it is impossible to predict the outcome of a specific intervention with certainty. Given knowledge of initial conditions, one cannot anticipate the future state of a system, making it difficult to make accurate predictions (Mihata, 1997, p. 33).

Simple and complex systems exhibit significant differences due to the factors mentioned above, and therefore, methods of rationality useful in simple systems may not suffice for complex systems. Social reality – including its economic dimensions – is by its own nature complex. Simplicity is a quality of analytical taxonomies, of ideal types according to Weber, but not of the real world.

According to Teisman et al. (2009), "Complexity is the most important explanation for why public officials and organizations have difficulty getting things done" (p. 14). If the world were static, decisions and policies would always be carried out according to plan. Of course, the world is not static, and decision-makers often face unexpected situations. It's important to recognize that even the best decisions can have negative outcomes in a constantly evolving world.

For a public administration to be effective and efficient, it needs to understand the intricate relationships between complex systems and the nonlinear evolution of governance structures and processes over time. This is especially important as these structures and processes must adapt to and cope with ongoing changes in their environment. By definition, governance systems are complex. A reductionist approach that only focuses on its parts fails to generate an understanding of the whole. A systemic approach is required to achieve this. It is essential to analyze the self-organizing components of complex systems and the resulting emergent patterns from their coevolution. From a complexity perspective, policymaking must be structured around three fundamental elements: nonlinear dynamics, relevant autonomy ("self-organization") of systemic subparts, and coevolution of complex social and governance systems. Self-organization refers to the autonomous development and the emergence of order from disorder. This concept explains how processes come about, evolve, and transform. Processes arise from events, actions, and interactions and create a structure that can later be defined by its inertia, stability, dynamics, and vaporization (Teisman op.cit, pp. 5–8).

Based on the above, it becomes clear that complexity is analytically the opposite of stability and predictability. Forming a "kaleidoscopic" environment requires increased efforts to standardize and classify the phenomena and situations it includes. Very often, this can only be achieved by approximating techniques of an ideotypical character, according to Weber's definition.

Social complexity is an emergent property that arises naturally and continuously generates efforts by individuals to direct policies toward their desired outcome. Yet, various actors and factors, including technology and the environment, also influence the process of change, often leading to outcomes that are different from what the actors intended.

However, in order to tackle the challenges posed by various forms of complexity, more exact, thorough, and adaptable tools are needed. Rittel and Weber position these tools within the framework of classical logic and Newtonian mechanics.

Therefore, in order to distinguish those special forms of complexity that are not dealt with by the tools of classical rationality/Newtonian logic, we should proceed, in section D below, to a typology of complexity that will allow us to differentiate its various forms and to determine their etiology as well as the way dealing with them.

3.2 The Theoretical Framework for Social, Political, and Administrative Conflict

According to Matland (1995), the rational model assumes that decision-making involves finding the best way to achieve agreed-upon goals to maximize individual or social welfare functions. On the contrary, according to the bureaucratic politics model, conflict is inevitable due to the lack of an agreed-upon set of goals. In this model, actors focus on resolving conflicts through bargaining mechanisms such as side payments, log rolling, and oversight to form and maintain coalitions. In some cases, coercive tactics may be employed to ensure adherence. During the bargaining process, the parties involved usually do not agree on goals but rather concentrate solely on agreeing on actions or methods. In many instances, the process results in no action, as the involved actors are unable to reach a consensus.

Maire Dugan (1996) presented a "Nested Model of Conflict" classifying the following conflict types:

- Issues-specific conflicts.
- Relational conflicts. These issues may be institutionalized within the social system, and it is important to differentiate between structural conflict at the broad system level and structural conflict that originates at the subsystem level.

Conflict can often lead to complexity. Dugan's model provides potential conflict categories but also highlights the interconnectivity between these categories.

Goal divergence may cause conflict among parties involved in social or economic activity. When individuals have different desired outcomes for the future and behave as rational actors who aim to maximize their interests and objectives, it can result in incompatible goals (Byrne & Senehi, 2009, p. 5).

Conflict can also occur from value divergence. Galtung (2009) states that "Conflict is said to exist in an action system if two or more values are pursued and they are perceived as incompatible or mutually exclusive."

Conflict, in its essence, represents a clash of fundamentally incompatible perspectives, leading to a state of mutual exclusion. To better capture the diverse range of factors involved, goals can be introduced, allowing for the inclusion of interests alongside the values defined by collective or individual cultures. Furthermore, the concept of "parties" can be used besides the notion of "actors", enabling the incorporation of positions within structures, irrespective of any explicit pursuit or avoidance of values.

Communication can become in some cases a key to resolving conflicts. Firstly, conflicts often arise due to scarcity and uncertainty, which makes clear and open communication essential in finding viable solutions. Secondly, the subjective nature of scientific knowledge poses communication challenges, emphasizing the importance of consensus on reliable information. Thirdly, public decisions inherently involve procedural components, providing opportunities to reward ethical behavior that aligns with widely shared norms. Lastly, the division of labor between analysts and decision-makers can lead to costly distortions in communication, especially when experts interact across disciplinary boundaries or engage with the general public. Therefore, placing a high priority on communicative action can prevent unintended misunderstandings and unnecessary conflicts. It is crucial for all public decisions to strive for a certain level of communicative rationality (Andrews, 2007, p. 169).

Policy analysis thus emerged to inform a "rational model" of decision-making, where rational decision-makers are seen to follow steps that closely parallel the requirements of scientific research. Basic to the approach has been an effort to sidestep the partisan goal and value conflicts generally associated with policy issues. Policy analysis, in this model, seeks to translate political and social issues into technically defined ends to be pursued through administrative ends. Difficult economic and social problems are treated as issues in need of improvement management and better program design; their solutions are to be found in better collection of data and the application of technical decision approaches. Much of policy analysis has thus been a matter of applying empirically based technical methodologies, such as cost–benefit analysis and risk assessment, to the technical aspects of all policy problems. .... The "postpositivist" argumentative turn recognizes that knowledge is the product of interaction – even conflict – among competing interpretations of a policy problem and that multiple perspectives are involved in the interpretation and understanding of social and political reality and the competing definitions of policy problems to which they give rise. This is done in part by emphasizing citizen participation, including the examination of how citizens' interests are discursively constructed, as well as how they come to hold specific interests. By getting more deeply involved in the discursive and symbolic sides of politics, policy analysis helps decision-makers and citizens develop alternatives that speak to their own needs and interests rather than those defined and shaped for them by others (Fischer, 2007, pp. 224–225).

Finally, there is a potential for collaborative resolution when it comes to specific policy conflicts that can be viewed as bargaining situations. This presents an opportunity for cooperation among opposing factions, resulting in a policy conflict that is not a zero-sum game (Quirk, 1989).

Subsystems characterized by low or intermediate levels of policy conflict intensity are arguably more conducive to collaboration. Policy conflicts arise when policy actors have slight divergences in positions, with a focus on means rather than ends. In such situations, people tend to perceive their opponents' policy positions as presenting only small to moderate risks, thus fostering a greater willingness to find common ground and compromise on their own policy positions (Weible et al., 2018).

3.3 A Typology of Complexity, Conflict, and Wickedness

Based on the above analysis, the following forms of complexity are roughly recorded:

(1) Complexity due to technicalities.

- Multidimensional problems that fall into different fields of human action or are handled by different scientific disciplines, e.g., the recent pandemic that had epidemiological, economic, and social dimensions and consequences.
- Failure to gather sufficient quantitative and qualitative data.
- Inadequacy of existing theoretical models that are unable to explain new phenomena or situations.
- Institutional inadequacy overlaps and ambiguity of responsibilities, etc., which create delays and inability to make decisions and act.

(2) Complexity due to confrontations and conflicts.

- Different systems of values and ideas that lead to a different perception and framing of the problem.
- Different social/economic interests which define the problem in different ways, give it different priorities (e.g., they characterize it as nonurgent, possibly sometimes they don't even perceive it as a problem), and/or propose different ways of dealing with it.
- Different institutional/intra-administrative strategies (coming from different public agencies) that also lead to mutually exclusive divergent definitions, prioritizations, and proposals for handling specific problems.

In general, we can accept that complexities linked to technicalities, in their essence, can be dealt with by upgrading, renewing, and improving the existing scientific, cognitive, methodological, and institutional tools. In other words, by enhancing the effectiveness of the Newtonian approach. In this sense, they cannot be characterized as wicked problems.

Complexities associated with conflicting values and interests and with conflicting strategies can be divided into two subsets:

First, oppositions and conflicts of a nonstructural nature that do not take the form of a zero-sum game. In this case, there is a possibility of mutual common approaches and convergences through:

- Cognitive solutions that allow opposing parties to build a common understanding of the problem.
- Compromise solutions at the implementation level, e.g., institutional rebalancing.
- Enhanced dialog processes that allow for mutual adjustments and the adoption of common positions.

Second, oppositions and conflicts, of values, ideas, and interests, of a structural nature that fall into the category of zero-sum games. In this case, the solution is not possible with cognitive and institutional tools and dialog.

4. Complexity and Wickedness in This Book

The findings recorded in the various chapters of this book provide a complicated picture of almost all the cases studied. What is common in all cases is complexity and uncertainty – as to the nature of the problems and the correct way to proceed – which arises precisely because of the complexity. However, the causes of complexity are varied. There is each time a mixture of causes spread across a spectrum from structural/systemic and procedural complexity at one end to complexity generated by divergent values, ideas, and interests at the other.

The above analytical scheme provides the framework that fits the findings and conclusions on the wickedness of the various chapters as follows:

4.1 Complexity Due to Technical Reasons

The complexity of a public problem which makes it difficult to solve could in principle be due to technicalities in the broad sense of the term. Such may be the procedural complexity and/or inadequacy that hamper communication, cooperation, and the implementation of actions designed and executed by sectoral public policies. It may also arise from structural issues linked to the institutional levels and their organizational subdivisions involved in each public policy as well as the quality of the interactions between them. In a different formulation, it may result from the complexity and quality of interactions between systems and their subsystems. The complexity and resulting inappropriateness can come from two levels of technicality: (a) at a narrower level from the procedures adopted for the design and implementation of a particular public policy and (b) at a broader level, which we can characterize as systemic, from the structural complexity of the field, such as the involvement of different institutional tiers.

4.1.1 Procedural Complexity and Inadequacy

Paúl Cisneros, Kate Macdonald, and Cristhian Parrado discussing the contribution of the "PROAmazonía" program to tackle deforestation in Ecuador note that, "The greatest drawbacks have been maintaining coordination mechanisms at national and local levels." For example, the instability of the governing body in charge of coordinating the process, the instability of appointed officials that affects the timing of the program's implementation, and the disconnection between the different levels of government. Likewise, the delay in formalizing inter-institutional collaborations is the main challenge to achieving progress.

Path dependency and poor analysis of real social needs and conflicting interests are part of procedural complexity and inadequacy. However, path dependency could be just the technical facade and behind it, perhaps, there are political positions and collective interests. Technical path dependency could be related to bureaucratic delays and slow change of legal framework, while political path dependency is linked with the persistence of interests guiding specific technical solutions.

Giovanni Esposito and Andrea Terlizzi in their study of the Lyon-Turin, cross-border high-speed railway megaproject remark that "the complex, uncertain and conflictual nature of the LT is given by its multilevel, transnational and pluralistic nature: (1) multi-level because decision making is dispersed from the national to the supra-national level; (2) trans-national because, at the national level, and it is implemented within two countries having different domestic institutions; (3) pluralistic because of the co-existence of divergent actor groups, each with its own legitimate set of beliefs and objectives."

Alberto de la Peña and Jaione Mondragón studying the Water Planning in Spanish inter-regional Basins as a Wicked Problem note that interests would appear to be determined by the position of the regional actors on the river course, while the project was undertaken based on calculations on rainfall, internal basin demands, urban pressure on the basin, and the surplus upon which the very idea of a transfer is based. So here are observed complexity and conflict generated by technicalities affecting interests.

Giulio Citroni in his study of the siting of repositories for high-level nuclear waste remarks that evidence about nuclear energy is complex and difficult to classify within a taxonomy. Considering excessive uncertainties in the calculation of risk and damage to the environment a Technical Expert Group that was set up by the Commission took the very controversial decision to exclude nuclear waste disposal from its calculation of environmental impact. In a similar approach, a report by the Joint Research Center of the European Commission concluded that "impacts of nuclear energy on the human health and the environment are mostly comparable to hydropower and the renewables *if non-radiological effects are considered*" (emphasis ours). In this case, the procedural inability of policymakers to comprehend a technical complexity leads them to ignore it.

C.J. Smith, P. Virtanen, A. Hiilamo, and T. Ristikari analyzing child poverty in Finland state that *scientific uncertainty* relates to different types of poverty measurement metrics, while problems remain in terms of measurement, particularly around indicator choice generating "wickedness" in terms of scientific uncertainty. Therefore, technical complexity due to measurement ambiguity generates scientific uncertainty that in its turn is translated at an administrative level to procedural complexity regarding the methods of measuring poverty.

Daniela Serban studying the United Kingdom as a global player, aiming for policy coherence through policy tools such as the Integrated Review, shows "how building a nexus across policy domains can impact the ability of policy actors to deal with wicked policy problems." This case study analyses the effort to harness wickedness, understood mostly as institutional and procedural complexity, through enhanced political capacity, especially of a communicative, coordinative, and learning nature.

Edoardo Amato, Daniela Bernaschi, and Maria Camilla Fraudatario approaching the Metropolitan City of Florence as a wicked case of Sustainable Development point out that "like a matryoshka, Sustainable Development encloses areas of differentiated need at every level of territorial scale for which and in turn, the definition of advocacy and responsibility roles is necessary." Lack of coherence is generated by institutional and political silos and mostly by the absence of "vertical coherence between local, sub-national, national, and international levels as a form of distributed responsibility for planning and implementing sustainable development policies". Therefore, this case highlights systemic complexity that can be dealt with through procedural concretization and rationalization.

Maria Alejandra Costa and Eric Montpetit examining the relations between media framing and the legislative agenda on agri-environmental issues in Brazil underline that addressing:

> complex wicked problems such as the environmental impact of agriculture requires careful analysis of contradictory information from multiple sources. Policymakers have scarce resources and limited time and therefore struggle to obtain all the information from the wide range of experts and stakeholders needed to make the best possible decisions.

Javad Keypour in his study of gas flaring reduction in Iran points out how informal procedures interfering with formal ones can increase complexity: "Managers are surrounded by their own designated like-minded and trusted individuals for decision-making…Although expertise departments and think tanks may submit reports, their outputs must pass through this surrounding ring – consisting of individuals who may lack expertise – to reach the center [of decision-making]. Consequently, these reports may fail to reach the top manager, leaving the final decision at the discretion of the central individuals. As a result, cultural – national, political, and organizational – factors increase procedural complexity".

Iveta Reinholde, Inese Āboliņa, and Ilze Auliciema researching sustainability problems in Latvia remark that assessment tools are not fully utilized and cannot provide a systemic impact. Latvia is not conducting enough policy assessments and there is also:

> a severe implementation gap.... The climate change policy is facing a lack of horizontal and vertical coordination...it is a complex mix of policy tools and approaches that fuels institutional uncertainty as bureaucratic practices differ from case to case....while from the procedural perspective, it is about dealing with many stakeholders and shared authorities.

This study showcases that procedural complexity is paired with procedural inadequacy, meaning procedures that are designed and, maybe, implemented but cannot adequately deal with policy field complexity and, therefore, generate incapacity to resolve a given problem.

4.1.2 Structural/Systemic Complexity

Paúl Cisneros, Kate Macdonald, and Cristhian Parrado in their discussion of the "PROAmazonía" program detect an inadequate interconnection of the political with the administrative level, so that the change of political leadership leads to inertia in the administrative services and delays the implementation of the policies pursued. This is a parameter of a structural-systemic nature. Such parameters can feed into the wicked character of a problem to the extent that they are rooted in the political-administrative culture of a country, which is a dimension that is difficult to change. Conversely, if institutional arrangements, that are easier to change, are the cause, then they can be included in the "complexity mix" as "tame complicated problems."

Esposito and Terlizzi in their study of the Lyon-Turin, railway megaproject remark that it involves a great variety of governmental and nongovernmental actors holding different interests, preferences, attitudes, visions, imaginaries, cultures, and logics of collective action. Sources of complexity can be technical (e.g., megaproject scale), political and administrative (e.g., involvement of multiple governments and administrations), social and cultural (e.g., stakeholders' multiple interests, visions, interpretations about the megaproject), and legal and regulatory (e.g., changing legislation and regulations). All these diverse dimensions create a structural complexity.

In cases of systemic complexity, such as the one in this study, we observe that, potentially, the goals' concretization and specification at a subsystem level can help in dealing with them, overcoming divergences occurring at the hyper-system.

De la Peña and Mondragón underline that since problems

> spread through different levels – local, regional, national and global – and pay no heed to existing political and administrative borders. .... they develop their own geography and create a complex map of 'scale overflow' that vexes public administrations, accustomed as they are to operate from a territorial standpoint.

Complexity derives not only from embedded subsystems – national, regional, and local – but also from the multidimensional nature of each of them: institutional (competencies, powers, jurisdictions) and political (nationalistic local powers).

Citroni detects systemic complexity by discussing the problem of High-Level Radioactive Waste (HLW) disposal, by observing that it occurs over time from several sources, technical obviously but also legal and political, relating to international as well as national and local politics.

Smith, Virtanen, Hiilamo, and Ristikari show that in the Finnish case, institutional complexity equals administrative "uncertainty" of action and results, generating coordination problems. On the other hand, social problems can also be systemic: while the encompassing system works well – e.g., poverty goals are already attained, and more generally, Finland has a globally positive profile on social inclusion incorporating child poverty, but some subsystems, such as low income, immigrant, and single parents' families child poverty, are failing. The two dimensions are interconnected as far as technical/institutional/procedural complexity is negatively affecting policy focus on subsystems of the broader policy area hindering the elaboration of focused and targeted solutions to more specific problems.

Amato, Bernaschi, and Fraudatario identify structural complexity in the very nature of sustainable development that seeks to achieve a balance between environmental, social, and economic dimensions. Coherence between these three dimensions is difficult because of their particular characteristics and the potential contradictions among them and often leads to conflicts. In the specific case of the metropolitan city, the municipalities composing the metropolitan area can have conflicting goals or approaches concerning some specific SDG topics, while conflicting approaches arise between different policymaking and decision levels. Localization, therefore, appears as a remedy against structural/systemic complexity.

Keypour concludes that the causes and origins of problems indicate that Iran's APG flaring problem "is a symptom of problems at a higher level; sanctions, corruption, regulatory system, structural problems (rentier system), the role of interest groups, and even development policies and approaches which are all decided at the highest governmental level". Similarly, the APG flaring problem,

> is a symptom of flaws in higher policymaking levels which are highly resistant to reform. Hence, until other major bad governance problems have been dealt with, we may alleviate the APG flaring issue within the current organizational structure instead of solving it.

Reinholde, Āboliņa, and Auliciema point out that complexity is generated by the fact that the encompassing system (international and European policy ecosystems/environments) affects the national subsystem even if the latter is restrained about the given policy issue. Systemic complexity also occurs from contradictions between subsystems. One such example is the incompatibility, at the national level, between the objectives of environmental sustainability and economic development under conditions of limited financial resources. If we consider these two areas of policymaking as distinct subsystems of the broader system of governance, we observe that, in the Latvian case, the increased priority of issues related to development, income, and social protection generates social pressure (social subsystem) on governance (policymaking subsystem) and affects policy focus. Social pressure in a broader sense can include both extensive social strata – public opinion – or specific powerful groups.

It should therefore be noted that structural complexity occurs when numerous subsystems interact. Even if commonly acceptable options could be found within potential alternative sets of choices (non-zero-sum game, nonstructural conflict), such a structural/procedural complexity will not permit building easily common grounds and transforms non-zero to zero-sum games generating hence structural – difficult to resolve-conflict. On the other hand, complexity that arises in the supersystem may be more difficult to solve and has a wider effect. Conversely, subsystem complexities may be solved, under conditions, more easily and quickly, but the impact of such solutions is more limited.

4.2 Complexity Due to Conflict

A different form of complexity, potentially much closer to wickedness as defined by Rittel and Weber, is that which arises from the divergence of values, interests, aspirations, and priorities among actors in a given policy field. In this case, we can also distinguish two subsets:

(1) Firstly, the case of differentiations and contradictions leading to "structural conflict", i.e., zero-sum games and conflicts.
(2) Secondly, the case of divergences that lead to conflicts that are not insurmountable and could be resolved through win-win strategies and tactics using the tools of dialog, negotiation, expanded institutional participation, and mutual learning.

4.2.1 Divergence of Interests and Values

4.2.1.1 Zero-Sum Conflicts. This category classifies insurmountable differences of interests and/or values between collective actors involved in a given policy field.

Cisneros, Macdonald, and Parrado draw attention to the fact that Amazon development debate "has been torn between attempts to reconcile two somewhat opposing views: on the one hand, a vision of setting aside large tracts of the

Amazon forests for conservation purposes and, on the other hand, seeking a 'sustainable' resource-intensive development, mainly through agriculture/livestock, energy, and mining". However, reality shows that a "convergent reconciliation" is not happening. In this case, lack of political capacity equals a refusal to promote the specific interests of small producers.

According to Esposito and Terlizzi, the Lyon-Torino case can be described as "an organizational field where the competing institutional logics of contradicting groups (proponents VS opponents of LT) generate controversies. Differences in the evolution of these controversies may be explained because of differences in national proponents' capacity to make agreements with opponents". "Low capacity" can be a by-product of cultural (divergent values and ideas) or structural ("zero-sum" conflicting interests) developments.

De la Peña and Mondragón while examining the two Spanish inter-regional water basins – the Ebro and Tajo – note that hydrographic demarcations bring together a complex array of interests and actors. "The question of environmental flows does not appear to be approaching a consensus among the regional actors affected, despite significant environmental damage occurring... It is difficult to see a path toward bilateral negotiation". This situation showcases a structural divergence, leading to a "zero-sum-conflict", as far as it is based on "a basic dichotomy between water as an economic resource and the fluvial ecosystem as habitat and natural heritage".

Citroni notes that evidence itself becomes a conflict field as far as the collection and analysis of data cannot transform complex techno-social problems into pure mathematical equations, eliminating all conflictual and political aspects. Evidence complexity and controversy function as a mechanism for pretextual dialog and generate "conflict over data" hampering the broader public and, sometimes even some members of the relevant policy community to understand evidence and the stakes. A "pretextual dialog" is an instrument for the legitimization of a given position supported by the power-holders and/or other powerful actors. In other words, it is a communicative instrument for the demonstration of the pretextual spirit of conciliation and in fact of unilateral imposition of a point of view, that counteracts any meaningful dialog that potentially could allow conflict to be managed through mutual concessions and compromises.

Magdalena Potz, Solange Hernandez, and Sarah Serval reach relevant conclusions by studying the "cocreation" procedure in the case of the French Citizens Convention for Climate (CCC). Their findings demonstrate that "co-creation, intended as a solution to a technical and scientific problem, is politically exploited to counter a democratic crisis ...[but] ultimately reinforces the crisis because of the inability to connect scientific and technical proposals from civil society to political and governmental decision-making processes. It is not so much the problem that is wicked as the process". The French Citizens Convention for Climate seems therefore to be a frame for pretextual dialog delivering proposals that are not implemented – not fully or even not at all.

Smith, Virtanen, Hiilamo, and Ristikari state that political pluralism, in Finland, reflects disagreement over the causes of poverty and the best way to alleviate it. Such dissimilarities are illustrative of a core political philosophy divide leading to significantly different policy responses. The authors conclude that while in the Finnish child poverty case "the locus of 'wickedness' is clearly identifiable in the realm of technical and institutional problematics" nevertheless "value differences do exist", affecting thus the overall policy framework and contributing to the wickedness mix.

Costa and Monpetit emphasize that in Brazil, the debate about the wickedness of the agri-environmental topic

> has been structured around the opposition between agribusiness who advocate for economic growth and affordable food and the environmental groups which defend the preservation of the environment and the implementation of sustainable practices. Hence, policymakers are often aligned with powerful agricultural interests. Therefore, the overrepresentation of the agribusiness sector in Congress makes it difficult for pro-environmental legislators to shift the balance of power and the dynamic of the agenda.

Such minor policy adjustments equal unidimensional and insufficient incrementalism which, according to the authors, favor "stronger policy fields against weaker policy fields", where policy fields correspond to relevant interest groups or coalitions. Consequently, this is also a case of structural conflict.

According to Keypour ... "The intensification of conflict between interest groups has added complexity.... In the highly politicized Iranian oil industry finding a transparent evaluation system for assessing the decisions is challenging..". The polarized perception was not an ordinary opinion gap, but it stems from different value judgments in accord with the group or personal interests, values, and ideological preferences. In such structural conflict settings, the absence of dialog and the discredit and exclusion of the antagonistic opinions serve as a method to avoid or reduce conflict or even as a weapon to resolve conflict in a positive manner for given interests, generating, in both cases, consequently, zero-sum games instead of a non-zero game setup that requires mutual adjustments.

4.2.1.2 Non-Zero-Sum Conflicts. Examples in this category relate to conflicts of interest and perceptions or values that can, nevertheless, be bridged through dialog and other win-win solutions techniques toward mutually beneficial policy mixes.

De la Peña and Mondragón observe that,

> Spain at a more complicated than ever political conjuncture, marked by the need to meet the old interests represented by socio-economic actors with other ones coming from competing definitions like the environmentalist and the obligation of integrating the sub-national level in the decision-making...Furthermore, the challenge of creating new shared strategies and processes will require organizational learning and a degree of cultural change.

The potential for a non-zero game is conditioned, however, by several factors beyond the control of the policy designers such as the intensity of divergences, the possibility to balance dynamics belonging to different subsystems, such as the institutional framework, the technical methods, the values and ideological principles of the diverse actors involved, etc.

Citroni comments that through stakeholder and citizen engagement and participation, participatory research, or network management, different proposals can converge in identifying a number of common issues, which participation, deliberation, and network governance are meant to tackle: the interaction between citizens, politics, and experts, whereby participatory research especially is meant to bridge the communication and legitimacy issues raised by processes which are one-sidedly technocratic or political. What we can learn from this case study is that in some instances, disagreement occurs and remains at a technical level regarding specific technical solutions while on the general policy concept and theoretical framework convergences are possible and reconciliation ability appears, while some critical events can reframe the discussion and reduce conflict potential.

Smith, Virtanen, Hiilamo, and Ristikari point out that while political pluralism permits a core political divide leading to significantly different policy responses, within the broadly consensus-based Finnish social policy context during the period covered by the analysis political consensus emerged around NPM-inspired approaches, "driven by the need for efficiency measures and cost containment in the public sector". The common features of public policy pursued by several successive governments with different political orientations indicate the existence of a non-zero frame where, despite ideological differences and their impact on concrete policy measures of a short-term nature, some long-term policy characteristics remain unaltered within the broader consensual framework generated by the Finnish political culture and tradition. On the other hand, the programmatic convergence toward the principles of the New Public Management reveals a reframing of the ideological and political perception of the problem transcending different political assessments of poverty by limiting all policy alternatives to efficiency and cost reduction rather than policy impact.

4.2.2 Divergence of Administrative Agencies' Strategies

4.2.2.1 Zero-Sum Conflicts. This category includes cases where co-competent public agencies with radically different objectives and dissimilar administrative cultures adopt distinct perceptions of the problems and the appropriateness of the available solutions. These different, even contradictory, approaches do not allow convergences through dialog and cooperation.

De la Peña and Mondragón report that the hydrographic demarcations "caused a multitude of conflicts between different territorial administrations… all of whom are involved in a game involving different languages and no hope of understanding." They conclude that finally "shared planning by all actors … is a zero-sum game in which it is difficult to find a middle ground". This case study illustrates structural conflict emanating from antagonisms around competencies and processes, and not merely from policy content. One can also discern here institutional conflict fueled by political and cultural disagreements.

Citroni gives in his chapter an account of intra-institutional conflict over problem definition where a European agency and the competent body of a member state are at odds over the definition of the problem. Similar controversies are taking place between co-competent EU bodies. Such divergence of actors in the early stages of the agenda-setting around the perception, definition, and structuring of the problem makes convergences difficult in later stages and largely generates zero-sum games.

Reinholde, Āboliņa, and Auliciema, finally, comment that policy problems related to sustainable development are multidimensional and, thus, fall into different bureaucratic territories where they generate segregated bureaucratic images of the same challenging situations leading to implementation gaps and failures. Despite attempts to bridge the disparities between the different approaches of diverse institutions and agencies to common problems, with communication and learning tools, administrative complexity itself reproduces wickedness.

4.2.2.2 Non-Zero-Sum Conflicts. It is important to note that while there may be strategic contradictions and differing aspirations among administrative services, they are not necessarily structural. With the right conditions in place, these differences can be overcome using traditional consensus-building techniques such as participation, dialog, agreed documentation, and mutual learning.

Cisneros, Macdonald, and Parado state that the inclusion of a diversity of actors in a network established within the overall "PROAmazonia" policy framework to develop analytical capacity through the creation of various fora for discussion and decision-making has increased the capacity of the entire network to surpass pre-existing conflicts related to the inclusion of indigenous peoples. Outstanding results have been achieved on collective knowledge and rights and local participation. Such mechanisms have generated a positive response from local populations. In this case, aspects of a nonstructural conflict are observed where "democratic technicalities" seem capable of reducing nonstructural divergence and conflict.

De la Peña and Mondragón report that in the regions where the respective governments held, at that time, an absolute parliamentary majority in their respective assemblies, the central government was able to tackle legislative change from a position of strength and with fewer incentives to seek consensus among conflicting interests. In this case, as bargaining takes place in a multi-subsystem environment (political, institutional, technical), political dominance and institutional control can reduce possible negative correlations and balances at the technical level.

Citroni states that in Germany, in some stages of the policy case, he studies, a "fair, transparent, and science-based process" took place under the control of the Ministry of Environment within which a Committee composed of Members of

Parliament, representatives of Land governments, scientists, and members of civic organizations was set up to develop strategies and criteria. Some years later, a Monitoring Committee is also set up as a neutral, pluralistic board representing citizens, associations, and institutions, entrusted with the monitoring and consultation on the nuclear waste siting process. We see here an attempt of objectivization and neutralization of a policymaking procedure through transparency, evidence, and participation.

Smith, Virtanen, Hiilamo, and Ristikari point out that Finland's response to the child poverty issue is "weakly coordinated and is reliant, ... to inter-institutional level disputes or 'turf wars' within the domestic social policy setup... [and that] this reflects problems with 'trust' between government departments and/or implementation levels." However, as Finland has a "stable and highly consensual governance system" multistakeholder partnerships could strengthen the capacity of the state and society, in partnership, to design and implement strategies that minimize the negative impacts of social, economic, and environmental crises "through the creation of public-private partnerships and the adoption of whole of government thinking."

Serban, finally, mentions the case of the merger of "two Departments with their own cultures holding different values, worldviews, and areas of prioritization". This would in turn limit the success of the newly created department as far as "policy silos might be hardly avoidable" given the institutional and value dissimilarities between the two formerly independent Departments. A solution to such type of problems could be sought in the use of tools that promote common understanding such as foresight techniques and systems thinking that have been proposed by the UK Office of Science to be deployed by the Departments across the Government.

The awareness and acceptance of the existing diverse approaches and the search for syntheses, within the specific framework of contradictions that are not structural, may allow common understanding and reduce procedural, technical, and institutional complexity, avoiding thus, the "wickedization" of the problems.

4.2.3 Concluding on Wickedness

The findings on wickedness suggest that while there are many forms of complexity, only some of them fit within Rittel and Weber's definition. The ones that do are those that arise from intense conflicts of interest and values between actors in a given policy field. In cases where policy failures are a result of technical, procedural, and institutional complexities that can be addressed through improved interventions at scientific, institutional, and procedural levels, it is important to avoid labeling them as wicked to prevent conceptual confusion.

Another important conclusion is that failure in public policy is rarely due to a single cause. In all case studies, a "mixture of complexity" is detected, which includes both technical and institutional causes, as well as political, value-based, and interest-based contradictions. Examples show that multidimensional complexity can arise from technical, procedural, or institutional factors as well as conflicting values, perceptions, and interests. In other words, complexity can be generated by a combination of all these factors.

The methods to solve complex problems depend on their origin. Technical solutions, institutional redesigns, more accurate data, and improved analytical and explanatory schemes can address institutional, procedural, and scientific complexity. When it comes to the divergence of perceptions and interests, dialog, negotiation, mutual concessions, and learning in a win-win framework can potentially bridge the gap. However, deep-rooted differences in values and core interests usually create a zero-sum situation that cannot be resolved through communication and learning tools. When ideological and value differences dominate the discussion, they result in zero-sum games and transform even non-zero-sum problems into structural conflict issues generating wickedness.

5. A Framework of Capacities When Looking at Sustainable Development Policymaking

The dilemma for governments when facing complex problems due to technicalities (procedural or structural-systemic) or conflicts (divergences between institutional strategies or values) is whether expected policies are at least sufficiently adequate to respond to the nature of the problem itself. The measure of capacity is the problem of responding adequately to the problem itself.

5.1 Many Types of Capacity for Managing Wickedness

Capacity, as anticipated in the Introduction, is a polysemic quality, but it is not simply a virtue, because it expresses several meanings at the same time. First and foremost, it is a potential, living up to expected performance, competence, and knowledge, but also a material (e.g. technological, human, spatial, financial, etc.) equipment.

In the etymological history of the concept, however, there are also even more subtle semantic nuances that refer to the meanings of (a) intelligence, in the sense of knowing how to solve problems, (b) aptitude, in the sense of being able to express a thought or an opinion, and (c) intellectual ability, but also (d) knowing how to understand, intend, and intuit.

Finally, at the root of the concept of capability, there is also the idea of (e) power, in the sense of being able to hold together and coordinate, but also (f) the idea of possibility, freedom, and limitation at the same time, and even, for the ancient Romans, (g) the right to inherit property or goods.

All these nuances refer to a common idea, that of a potential ability to meet needs, expectations, and desires in the face of a common problem to be solved. All those meanings have been scrutinized in this book: the idea of expected performance is well documented in many chapters, but especially in the chapter by Daniela Serban on the UK sustainable development framework and in that by De la Pena and Mondragon about the interregional rivers' basins and water management seen as a problem of ineffective policymaking.

Again, the perspective on capacity as knowledge and intelligence is well described in the work by Magdalena Potz, Solange Hernandez, and Sarah Serval, while the idea of intelligent reshaping has been argued by Kidjie Saguin and Mike Howlett, but also in other chapters.

The problem of capacity as a matter of equipment is creeping into all the chapters, but particularly argued by Smith, Virtaanen, Hiilamo, and Ristikari, where the lack of data and need for better systematic knowledge is seen as depressing the capacity of the policymaking against children poverty.

Equally, the chapter by Amato, Bernaschi, and Fraudatario shows the limits of an institutional equipment, the metropolitan city, excessively charged by responsibilities for planning and implementing sustainable development, as well as the limits of jurisdiction in managing PROAmazonia project well described by Paul Cisneros, Kate Macdonald, and Cristhian Parrado. In those cases, capacity means a lack of resources: cognitive, institutional, political, etc.

A further insight on different meanings of capacity is described by Alejandra Costa and Eric Montpetit who debate the capacity to express opinion and to create a good narrative for policymaking. This is also the case of the megaprojects in cross-border transport illustrated by Giovanni Esposito and Andrea Terlizzi. They discuss the specific capacity for building up narratives that can enhance the people to create coalitions and the following need for reinforcing capacity building in conflicting policies through the involvement of citizens and stakeholders through collective intelligence.

Lastly, the idea of capacity as a matter of power is included in this book, since Javad Keypour, on the one side, shows the problem of (in)capacity of policymakers facing strong interests, and Giulio Citroni, on the other one, argues the resistances in the policy system and incapability to overpass them grounding on the stakeholders and their interests who play a role in the arena of nuclear waste. In both cases, capacity is seen as (im)possibility to manage the wickedness due to the scarcity of power.

All in all, capacity remains a multifaceted word with different uses but a common playground: it highlights what the policymaker must achieve to be up to the task. Indeed, capacity is the property the policymakers are expected to have when faced with the kind of problem that defines that capacity. If the problem is complex, it could be argued that relative capability must also at least be of the same degree of complexity, or perhaps, even more.

5.2 Capacity as Democratic Aim to Solve Sustainable Development Problems

In democratic regimes, capability is an assumption of authority. The policymaker is expected to answer questions whether they may be simple or complex.

The questions in democratic regimes, however, are often more difficult than those in nondemocratic regimes because democracy stimulates the intelligence of citizens, their demands, and needs. As Norberto Bobbio wrote many years ago (1984), democracy is the regime that tries to provide complex responses to complex problems, while nondemocratic regimes are used to provide simple (populist) answers to complex problems.

Probably, a nondemocratic regime has not elaborated any type of demand about sustainability, and if so, presumably, it does it on paper only. More specifically, it is presumed that nondemocratic regimes are not called to manage the problem of the SDGs' implementation. As a result, the capacity to manage wickedness is a dilemma for democratic regimes. The case of gas flaring in Iran is also a case of a weak local commitment to solving global problems.

As stated by many scholars, democratic regimes are ambitious: they mobilize their institutions to go beyond what is already established and try to master problems that were initially remote, dominate their nature, and propose solutions.

This happens because democracy has a representation of itself as a dynamic system: it is always progressing, and it assumes evolution. Once basic needs have been satisfied, it then seeks to go further. It does not limit itself to solving simple problems and providing sectoral answers but transcends these boundaries toward the possibility of exploring new possibilities concerning new needs and ever-greater complexities and interconnections. Sustainable development programs are a case in point.

Consequently, democratic institutions are called upon to be responsive and accountable for results that are often very difficult to achieve. To deny this, or to attempt to play down its importance, is tantamount to concealing the problem.

This dilemma does not only concern the value of democratic authority as such but above all invests policymakers' effectiveness and the capacity to meet the demands by acquiring competence, intelligence, knowledge, equipment, performance, power, and whatever can be useful to respond to its citizens' needs (Lippi, 2024).

The democratic regime, as formulated in the definition by Robert Dahl (1989), is the regime with the capacity to respond to the citizens' needs. Therefore, an authority may be considered fully democratic, valid, and socially and politically acceptable in virtue of its capacity to respond to the demands in terms of both input and output: the capacity to collect sound and promising (and ambitious) input and to transform them into output. This means to be able to guarantee institutional accountability since it raises the idea of justice lying under any policy and that ties together the definition of a problem, its formulation, and the related idea of equity.

All these three dimensions not only demand a certain level of performance but also identify the core idea of wickedness. Often, wicked problems are those policy problems that more than any others relate to the idea of the capacity of being democratic since they face ambitious and seemingly unsolvable problems. Wickedness implies the idea of progress and the ambition to go beyond the limits to meet more democratically needs, expectations, and desires.

Consequently, unaccountable, or unresponsive authorities that are not able to solve new problems and accomplish a challenging task can be deemed as incapable and probably unjust.

6. Linear and Nonlinear Capacities

What we are arguing is that sustainability development is a matter of democratic life, and it can't be achieved if we are not able to become "more capable" of understanding the game of democratic policymaking taking into account the features and the limits of wicked games, where problems are not immediately solvable, interests are naturally diverging, the consensus is automatically driven by norms or power, and the solutions can be repeatedly considered as failing by the stakeholder and the public opinion.

Capacity building results as a needed step for treating sustainability development in democratic regimes, but what type of capacity is relevant and suitable for managing wicked formulations, decisions, and implementations?

Beyond the specific semantic uses adopted by individual authors in studying how sustainable development policies are formulated, decided, and implemented, through the individual chapters we can see that the concept of capacity is handled in two different meanings.

The first meaning concerns the idea of a *linear capacity*: here capacity is the potential to perform. For this reason, capability can be understood both as endowment, equipment, and resources (human, material, cognitive, technological, etc.) that are understood as preconditions for subsequent action, and as the action itself.

This logic refers overall to capability as strategic planning. It could be called, following what has already been stated in the introduction, a Newtonian capacity. This means that it assumes a linear mechanism of capacity building: one reinforces certain properties to generate virtuous circles. One reinforces causes to generate better effects.

A Newtonian approach to capacity is consistent with the rationalism of policymaking: public policies are the convergence of a design, often bounded, sometimes incremental, in some cases even random, but still the product of an intention to generate linear change from a political will. Sustainable development policies are no exception, and a large part of these capacities employed by policymakers and described in the individual chapters are linear capacities.

Linear capabilities can be traced to Wu et al.'s (2015, 2018) typology where they emphasize the need for three linear causal capabilities: analytic, operational, and political. Policymakers need to work on all three fronts and accumulate a mix of different capabilities that will then be useful during the process. Each of these capabilities can be understood as a resource for action.

Even some of the capabilities extracted from the thick and messy literature on administrative capacity that we discussed in the introduction (see Lippi & Tsekos in this book) can be traced back to linear capabilities.

The main reference is to performance capacity and, even earlier, to stock capacity, which refers to endowments, material resources, and regulatory provisions.

These administrative capacities, together with the idea of institutional, political, or state capacity, always assume the importance of context and framework (institutional, economic, political, regulatory, etc.). In all these cases, the virtue of the initial capacity, the potential inherent in the premises, is undoubtedly the factor that then explains the final outcome.

They do not automatically lead to success nor indeed to failure. In the sustainable development policies, we have observed, they act virtuously, but they do not allow the achievement of the desired goals, but this does not mean that these capacities were useless or detrimental.

Rather, linear capacities are premises without which it would hardly have been possible to even begin such a process. Finally, linear capabilities belong to all types of regimes, as causality is a generative assumption of change of any policymaker. Sometimes, the rationalism inherent in linear capabilities is even more present where leadership disregards pluralism because it focuses more on the possibility of achieving the output, fair or unfair, success or failure.

What is important, however, is that in the observed cases, linear capabilities are described as widely present, whether they lead to partial results or fail to mobilize successful action.

Other capabilities are also identified in the book, which we will describe as empirical, since they almost all arise from observation, sometimes by derivation from branches of literature that had previously isolated such capabilities, and sometimes directly from the bottom up through field research.

These are additional skills that have been identified concerning wickedness and its zero-sum and non-zero-sum games: these skills relate to the problematic dimensions of wickedness. They emphasize contingency, incrementalism, seeing the views of others, feeding processes through knowledge, co-participation, coproduction, etc. They are second-level capacities. We cannot simply call them analytical, operational, or political because they go beyond that. Nor can we simply treat them as stock or performance variables.

In some ways, they are the intersection of all three of these simultaneously, which characterize nonlinearity because they overlap and influence each other. They are not independent of each other, but interdependent; they are not only found ex ante, but also ongoing, during the process; they do not constitute a premise for action but are identified, exploited, developed, and abandoned during the process.

Of the capabilities examined in the introduction, the one that comes closest is undoubtedly that of governance readiness raised by Lodge and Weigrich (2014) or coordination (Nelissen, 2002) or innovation (Caiden, 1973).

These latter meanings blur toward skills that are not strictly causal and not necessarily linear. These are capacities that lie above and involve, so to speak, "capacity building capacities", i.e., capacities that can foster, by standing above, the development of linear capacities.

Of course, the contributions in this volume continually refer to nonlinear capacities as a possible solution to linear (in)capacity when this clashes with wickedness due to divergent visions and conflicts.

6.1 Linear Capacities

Linear capacities are analyzed in the chapters as the basis for sustainable development policies. The input is that of the competence, resource, and power base needed to be able to formulate, decide, and implement an intervention. We can define these linear capabilities as the rational potential of a public policy, which represents a starting platform without which no chance is even given.

We distinguish on the one hand references to capacities of a general type and on the other hand the typology of Wu et al. (2018).

6.1.1 Institutional, Governmental, Technical, and Planning Capacities

As regards the preliminary rational capacities investigated in the individual chapters, the references are to a group of differentiated properties ranging from an extreme of institutional capacity to one of technical and planning capacity.

Firstly, Costa and Montepetit introduce a general reading of capacity through a qualitative indicator of state capacity, understood as a set of (power) factors that make the potential of a policy area characterized by a mobilization of resources, knowledge, and stakeholders such as to completely control that context. A strong or weak state capacity consequently coincides with a stock of power that is capable of mechanically, i.e., linearly, generating a process and thus, probably, an output. In the case of Brazil, they outline how the strong state capacity in the field of agricultural policies, which compares with the similarly weak ownership in environmental policies, was precisely counterbalanced by the role of the media, which allowed the circulation of information and knowledge capable of surrogating the more fragile endowment of the environmental sector, thus allowing a balance between SDGs.

Institutional capacity, on the other hand, is interpreted as the necessary institutional frame that can contextualize action and thus shape it by laying the groundwork for adequate performance. The variant labeled government capacity, on the other hand, refers to the more specifically political potential that the government policymaker possesses.

It refers to both the strength of the political mandate and parliamentary majorities, public attention on the part of citizens and the support of interest groups and institutions in general, as well as the quality and intensity of the coalitions that the initiator can mobilize.

Government capacity is also used as a reference to the soundness, reliability, and technical resource endowment of agencies, administrative apparatuses, technologies, and personnel, understanding it as a synonym for organizational potential.

Both institutional and government capacity denote the static potential of an action to be undertaken, but this does not mean that their influence should be considered less significant.

For example, in their chapter, Reinholde, Abolina, and Auliciema emphasize the limited institutional capacity of the Latvian government by pointing out how "the institutional ability to design, implement, and monitor climate change policies and actions is still limited as politicians or citizens do not recognize climate change as a priority".

There is also a specific institutional capacity to use specific institutional tools such as planning. As Amato, Bernaschi, and Fraudatario write in their chapter on the metropolitan city of Florence, this resource resides in the institutional mission of the local authority which they study and which rests above all on planning tools. The planning capacity makes it possible to combine on paper apparently conflicting interests that may be more closely aligned if a sufficiently long-term perspective is taken.

Following this path, the three authors highlight the limits and potential of the institutional capacity of metropolitan cities by highlighting, on the one hand, the role of intermediation in intergovernmental relations and mediation of the conflict between local and regional dimensions, and on the other, the rigidity of regulatory instruments, without sufficient other cognitive resources. The conclusion is that the institutional capacity perspective allows the potential of the institutional profile in the promotion of sustainable development to be tested. Their assessment reveals criticalities and possible improvements alongside an undoubted role.

6.1.2 Analytical, Operational, and Political Capacity

A second group of empirical elements emerging from the chapters concerns the tripartition between analytical, organizational, and political capacity which is employed by the authors to test the potential with which the policymaker is approaching the policy process.

The prevailing references are to the strategic nature of analytical capacity, which is interpreted as one of the most critical factors by most of the contributions. The absence, or at least the weak presence, of analytical capacity within the policy arena – and in particular in policymakers – is interpreted as the main symptom of weakness.

Smith et al., on the other hand, point out that the governance system dealing with Goal 1 in Finland must certainly and above all strengthen cognitive factors through actions: that enhance evidence-based policymaking both in terms of (1) proper problem definition grounded on trustworthy evidence able to bring to policy narrative needs to be consistent with the societal problem definition; the absence of properly used and systematically interpreted data and evidence is an element of weakness when dealing with wicked problems.

Also, Cisneros, Macdonald, and Parrado in their chapter emphasize the important improvement that the system of action would gain from the possibility of emancipating the analytical capacity through certain and homogeneous data: "When analytical capacity is effectively deployed to identify different perspectives, needs, cultures, issue definitions, and potential frictions, organizational capacity can be activated to process these differences to reduce uncertainty and divergence".

For their part, Costa and Montepetit in their chapter emphasize the distorting role that information conveyed by the media can play in issue-making and, in particular, for policy fields, such as agriculture, where there is already a high state capacity: "We have found that in policy fields with limited state capacity, the media can play a significant role in raising awareness of key issues and shaping the legislative agenda".

Operational capacity, which refers to resources and know-how used to act upon policy intentions and achieve policy goals, is also emphasized as relevant and closely connected to analytical capacity. For example, again Cisneros, Macdonald, and Parrado conclude their analysis with a diagnosis by calling for an increase in organizational potential to deliver technical assistance and strengthen local organizations and networks within the value chains, as well as to implement security measures.

Finally, political capability is analyzed as strategic, but the topic opens up a broader view that we will discuss in more detail. Political capacity is emphasized as decisive to enable, as Serban points out in his chapter on the United Kingdom, in his definition "to reach out to and involve a wide range of stakeholders to support the acceptability and legitimacy of policy decisions". In short, it is the prerequisite that provides a general framework for legitimacy.

Saguin and Howlett in their chapter use political capacity by exploiting more its dynamic potential in the possibility of building networks and alliances. They argue that,

> political capacity is the most critical because it is concerned with the ability to mobilise involvement of key stakeholders in the integration process and to resolve conflicts arising from their subsequent interaction. Reconciling potential conflicts in objectives in particular necessitates high political capacity.

6.2 Nonlinear Capacities

Nonlinear capacities are those properties that emerged from the chapters as specific qualities that enabled, or could have enabled, successful policy action with respect to wickedness.

As Cisneros, Macdonald and Parrado write, "what can be achieved through linear capacities is important but leaves open a question as to whether these capacities are sufficient to respond to the emerging properties that affect the capacity of forests and ecosystems to provide services".

Nonlinear capacities do not presuppose a cause-effect mechanism; they are not prerequisites or preconditions for action. They are skills that policymakers show they have developed and that demonstrate their sensitivity in dealing with situations where the problem definition is unclear, stakeholders are not cooperative, solutions are scarce, and action cannot be coordinated sequentially so that the possession of the aforementioned linear capacities can no longer be an asset to achieve the objective, as something else is needed.

In this direction, the contributions are divided between the recovery of some concepts already present in the literature and some novelties.

6.2.1 Governance Capacity and Readiness

The first group certainly includes references to governance capacity and readiness, understood as the capacity to react, activate, and adapt to external stimuli. The reference to readiness, in particular, advanced by Potz et al. and Serban, is identified as a necessary property to manage wickedness, when one can no longer rely on linear capacities and then the only resource is readiness in being able to react and reorganize with respect to exogenous stimuli.

Similarly, both Esposito and Terlizzi, on the one hand, and Smith et al., on the other, highlight governance capacity as the only way to overcome wicked policies by improving the ability to take a systemic view and reorganize variables. Both chapters emphasize the importance of building not half-baked sequences but flexible and adaptable governance systems that can lead to results even without imposing linear mechanisms from the outset but relying on existing resources and intelligence in restructuring and adapting them to situations, a kind of situational capacity.

6.2.2 Innovative Capacities

In the second group, there are neologisms along with other concepts already found in the literature but relaunched in the light of empirical observation. The chapters identify several distinctive capacities that represent one of the main innovative pieces of evidence. Let us try to summarize the four different types of capabilities that have been observed in the field studies and then develop a reflection.

The first type is the so-called *absorptive capacity* treated comprehensively by Potz, Hernandez, and Serval. Absorptive capacity "is defined as the ability to recognize the value of new information from the environment, to assimilate it and to exploit it".

It distinguishes a property that intersects all the previous ones and takes on a dynamic characteristic. This capacity of policymakers and the policy arena coincides with the maximum receptivity that allows cocreation processes without generating vicious circles resulting from the fact that institutions and citizens each remain in their own positions.

The absence of absorptive capacity, write Potz, Hernandez, and Serval, "can lead to highly counterproductive effects on the policy capacity of the government through the loss of legitimacy". Obviously, this is not a discrete capacity that can be quantified and translated into norms or budgets, but the skill that, more than any other, fosters empathy and knowledge transfer among stakeholders.

As the three contributors point out about the French case on the failure of cocreation tools, absorptive capacity is not acquired by mechanical transmission because it is a sensibility that policymakers must develop through training before starting such a process.

A second type of capacity is highlighted in a very analytical way by Esposito and Terlizzi who explicitly refer again to participatory processes through the so-called *capacity for organizing*. This is the ability to manage wickedness in the specifics of megaprojects thanks to three socioeconomic properties that make it possible to create adequate governance: (1) open decision-making systems, (2) bottom-up performance management, and (3) active dialog between proponents and opponents.

Esposito and Terlizzi go further in explaining how through capacity-building for organizing: "Capacity-building in megaprojects should instead embrace a comprehensive socio-economic logic-as opposed to a techno-economic one-to deal with the complex, uncertain, and conflictual nature of a wider set of policy processes and subsystems that all organizational players have to confront with".

In short, it is possible to overcome the limits of wickedness if and only if one abandons linear logic: when the policy problem is nonlinear, one needs a nonlinear ability to organize the capabilities one has.

Along these lines, Citroni isolates four specific properties that make it possible to overcome wickedness and which we now label *participatory capacity*:

(1) The capacity to define the engagement of citizens, expert audiences, and scientists and how the community is recruited into the decision-making process.
(2) The ability to build consensus from the outset on problem definition among actors.
(3) The coordination between actors and between levels of government, between public and private and different types of institutions through a specific mediation capacity.
(4) The ability to manage time and build controlled processes that are adequate to achieve the objective.

Similarly, to what is advanced by Citroni, a specific capacity for coordination as a specific and qualifying skill to manage wickedness is reiterated by other authors with different accents and different nuances.

These range from the emphasis on policy harmonization, mainstreaming, coordination, and institutionalization advanced by Saguin and Howlett, to the coordination capacity that goes beyond mere political capacity and rises to a true independent capacity pointed out by Amato et al., to the specific skill highlighted by Potz et al. in terms of coordination capacity, as organizational expertise to activate multi-level governance networks.

Finally, Saguin and Howlett employ a neologism that expresses well the attempt to express the need for superior skills that are synthesizing and belong to the cognitive, relational, and strategic competencies of policymakers in the concept of *integrative capacity*. The capacity for integration allows the advancement of the coordination capacity of the sustainability nexus. Integrative capacity is the ability to hold together the whole system.

All in all, nonlinear capacities concern a broader ability to read the context, to listen to the actors, and to be part of the system. In other words, it means the capability to exploit the variables to solve the problems. It also concerns personal not quantifiable skills, like sensitivity, empathy, and intuition, as well as the ability to create good relationships and to change during the process ends, means, and to adjust them to the environment without losing the goals.

7. Lessons Learned and Main Findings

The purpose of this book was to deliver to scholars and policymakers some learning traces on which directions sustainable development policies in the world can be improved through a collection of heterogeneous case studies but sharing the same characteristic: the intractability of the problem generated by the degree of generalization and interdependence of policies induced by the 17 SDGs of the UN 2030 agenda.

The common concern of all the chapters in this book has been to deliver tools to the readers to analyze the problems that any well-intentioned policymaker may encounter when starting to translate the goals from the general to the particular, from documents to practice.

With this in mind, each chapter has developed case studies separated by (1) subject matter, i.e., the type of SDGs investigated, (2) national, individual, or comparative cases, (3) levels of government involved, but all of them had a common ground for analysis: the policymaking processes through which the complexity of sustainable development policy design and the relationships between interdependent and not necessarily cooperative actors gathered around problems whose definition was elusive to all of them, where there were no clear and unambiguous scientific, normative, political references, and where there were no precedents of already tested, shared, socially accepted, and technically or politically evaluated solutions positively and adequately.

This condition probably constitutes the starting point for a large part of contemporary policymaking, but it certainly represents most sustainable development policymaking situations.

For this reason, we try to deliver to the reader the emerging trends and lessons learned from this reading.

First, the nature of the wickedness of sustainable development is a permanent and widespread condition in all the observed case studies. Wickedness is neither a curse nor a condition of infeasibility but an acknowledgment of the inherent nonlinearity associated with such ambitious and interdependent goals in turbulent environments.

As described in these pages, there is a competence in being able to recognize, distinguish, and cope with the different types of complexity that arise from wicked problems in the field of sustainable development, and the 11 case studies – plus the chapter written by Saguin and Howlett – have shown this in analytical detail. Complexity competence is the first step toward effective policymaking in the field of sustainable development.

The second step is the development of specific capacities aimed at learning how to read contexts, identify strategies and actors, reshape processes, and know how to carry them out, thanks on the one hand to traditional administrative capacities, which we will call linear, and others, which we will call nonlinear which are more consistent with complexity and which require the development of specific skills ranging from empathy to the ability to read and learn from contexts, to select and manage participants during the processes themselves, to organize and reorganize actors, resources, constraints, and objectives in a reactive manner (capacity for organizing, readiness, governance capacity), to the ability to deal with governance systems through systemic competence.

8. Conclusions and Recommendations

All these elements allow us to isolate some recommendations for policymakers that can be extrapolated to an even more general level and which can be summarized in three.

The first recommendation is the increase of a pragmatic culture of sustainable development policies by abandoning a technocratic top-down perspective. The success of the SDGs will never depend on sophisticated regulatory devices nor on specific guidelines that are not generalizable for all situations, but only by helping policymakers to adapt the principles and inspirational logic of the UN 2030 agenda to specific situations.

Wicked problems require, first of all, a cultural capacity for vision and management that can only be nurtured by favoring more bottom-up approaches, i.e., by supporting territorial actors and institutions, in addition to states, by involving subnational authorities, and by favoring localization processes more than anything else. This means fostering the construction and dissemination of narratives that support local actors to implement the SDGs creatively.

Throughout the individual chapters, the role of legitimation that national and subnational stakeholders and authorities need beyond rhetoric also emerged.

An institutional culture of sustainable development oriented toward localization through adaptation and accepting a moderate degree of redesign will certainly be more effective and successful than rigid prescriptions to be implemented top-down. Rather than reinforcing the rhetoric of values and documents, it is therefore appropriate to legitimize the actors by giving them credibility, authority, and trust.

In this direction, the works in this book also testify how mechanistic institutional frameworks and rigid administrative cultures that delegate planning tools and management tasks to specialized bodies by institutionalizing functions have not been successful, as in the case of Spain's interregional basins or Italy's metropolitan cities.

The enactment of flexible instruments that enhance the negotiation, participation, and cocreation of public policies with stakeholders in a flexible, yet effective manner beyond abstract formulas and norms unaccompanied by a culture that adheres to them is, from this point of view, strongly recommended.

A second recommendation concerns the instrument of training as a lever for change. As has emerged somewhat from all the chapters, but in particular from some that focus more on the soft skills that policymakers must learn to succeed in developing the expected capacities of coordination, reinvention, and absorption from contexts, there is a clear and explicit direction that is that of training, which indiscriminately invests stakeholders of different types: representatives from political bodies, administrative staffs (in particular), groups of interests, citizens, experts, etc. All these actors need incremental learning and gradual involvement that favors solid and progressive assimilation.

Finally, a third recommendation that emerges overwhelmingly from the individual studies is the great attention to be paid to the role of knowledge and evidence-based policymaking.

It is practically impossible today to implement effective sustainable development policies without adequate infrastructures and knowledge that feed the policy arenas with targeted information and expert knowledge to broaden the limited rationality of stakeholders on topics on which the degree of expertise on the part of the actors is certainly low.

The provision of adequate datasets, monitoring tools, impact assessments, expert panels, and similar mechanisms of advice and cognitive support to decision-makers should be the main institutional response in order not to leave policymaking to the fate that often befalls many innovations made up of rhetoric and too many abstract rules, which is that of recipe books and improvisation.

All these elements are suggested not as prescriptive solutions but as evidence-based recommendations that in turn policymakers will be able to adapt to the contexts and objectives of each national case, helping to localize sustainable development and make it a real practice.

References

Andrews, C. J. (2007). Rationality in policy decision making in Fischer Frank. In G. J. Miller & M. S. Sidney (Eds.), *Handbook of public policy analysis: Theory, politics, and methods* (pp. 161–172). CRC Press Taylor & Francis Group.

Bobbio, N. (1984). *Il futuro della democrazia*. Einaudi.

Byrne, D. (1998). *Complexity theory and the social sciences: An introduction*. Routledge.

Byrne, S., & Senehi, J. (2009). Conflict analysis and resolution as a multidiscipline. A work in progress. In D. J. D. Sandole, S. Byrne, I. Sandole-Staroste, & J. Senehi (Eds.), *Handbook of conflict analysis and resolution* (pp. 1–16). Routledge.

Caiden, G. (1973). Development, administrative capacity and administrative reform. *International Review of Administrative Sciences*, *39*(4), 327–344.

Dahl, R. A. (1989). *Democracy and its critics*. Yale University Press.

Dugan, M. (1996). A nested theory of conflict. *A Leadership Journal: Women in Leadership Sharing the Vision*, *1*, 9–20.

Eden, L., & Wagstaff, M. F. (2021). Evidence-based policymaking and the wicked problem of SDG 5 gender equality. *Journal of International Business Policy*, *4*, 28–57.

Fischer, F. (2007). Deliberative policy analysis as practical reason: Integrating empirical, and normative arguments. In F. Fischer, G. J. Miller, & M. S. Sidney (Eds.), *Handbook of public policy analysis: Theory, politics, and methods* (pp. 223–236). CRC Press Taylor & Francis Group.

Galtung, J. (2009). Toward a conflictology: The quest for transdisciplinarity. In D. J. D. Sandole, S. Byrne, I. Sandole-Staroste, & J. Senehi (Eds.), *Handbook of conflict analysis and resolution* (pp. 511–524). Routledge.

Gilpin, D. R., & Murphy, P. J. (2008). *Crisis management in a complex world.* Oxford University Press.

Kopnina, H. (2020). Education for the future? Critical evaluation of education for sustainable development goals. *The Journal of Environmental Education, 51*(4), 280–291.

Lippi, A. (2024). *Legitimacy and legitimation of political authorities. Credibility and trust in public institutions.* Edward Elgar Press.

Lodge, M., & Weigrich, K. (Eds.). (2014). *The problem-solving capacity of the modern state: Governance challenges and administrative capacities.* Oxford University Press.

Matland, R. E. (1995). Synthesizing the implementation literature: The ambiguity-conflict model of policy implementation. *Journal of Public Administration Research and Theory, 5*(2), 145–174.

Mihata, K. (1997). The persistence of "emergence". In R. A. Eve, S. Horsfall, & M. E. Lee (Eds.), *Chaos, complexity, and sociology: Myths, models, and theories* (pp. 30–38). SAGE.

Mitchell, M. (2009). *Complexity: A guided tour.* Oxford University Press.

Monkelbaan, J. (2019). *Governance for the sustainable development goals. Exploring an integrative framework of theories, tools, and competencies.* Springer.

Nelissen, N. (2002). The administrative capacity of new types of governance. *Public Organization Review: A Global Journal, 2*, 5–22.

Nelson, T. H. (1987). *Computer lib: Dream machines.* Tempus Books of Microsoft Press. 1974, 1987.

Peters, B. G. (2018). *Policy problems and policy design.* Edward Elgar Publishing.

Quirk, P. J. (1989). The cooperative resolution of policy conflict. *American Political Science Review, 83*(3), 905–921.

Sanger, M., & Giddings, M. M. (2012). A simple approach to complexity theory. *Journal of Social Work Education, 48*(2), 369–376.

Sempiga, O., & Van Liedekerke, L. (2023). Investing in sustainable development goals: Opportunities for private and public institutions to solve wicked problems that characterize a VUCA world. In *Investment strategies: New advances and challenges intechopen* (pp. 1–21). http://doi.org/10.5772/intechopen.110580

Shinagawa, K. (2021). Are the SDGs challenges to tame problems? In *ISPIM conference proceedings* (pp. 1–9). The International Society for Professional Innovation Management (ISPIM).

Teisman, G. R., Gerrits, L., & van Buuren, A. (2009). An introduction to understanding and managing complex process systems. In G. R. Teisman, A. van Buuren, & L. Gerrits, *Managing complex governance systems: Dynamics, self-organization and coevolution in public investments* (pp. 1–16). Routledge.

Weible, C., Heikkila, T., & Pierce, J. (2018). Understanding rationales for collaboration in high-intensity policy conflicts. *Journal of Public Policy, 38*(1), 1–25.

Wu, X., Ramesh, M., & Howlett, M. (2015). Policy capacity: A conceptual framework for understanding policy competences and capabilities. *Policy and Society, 34*(3–4), 165–171.

Wu, X., Ramesh, M., & Howlett, M. (2018). *Policy capacity and governance: Assessing governmental competences and capabilities in theory and practice.* Palgrave, Macmillan.

Index

www.ingramcontent.com/pod-product-compliance
Lightning Source LLC
Chambersburg PA
CBHW072309180325
23617CB00002BA/4
9781804556870